MARKETING ON THE INTERNET

Fifth Edition

Other Titles of Interest From Maximum Press

MARKETING ON THE INTERNET

Fifth Edition

Seven Steps to Building the
Internet Into Your Business

Jan Zimmerman

MAXIMUM PRESS
605 Silverthorn Road
Gulf Breeze, FL 32561
(850) 934-0819
www.maxpress.com

Publisher: Jim Hoskins

Manager of Finance/Administration: Donna Tryon

Production Manager: ReNae Grant

Cover Design: Lauren Smith Designs

Compositor: PageCrafters Inc.

Copyeditor: Andrew Potter

Proofreader: Kim Stefansson

Indexer: Susan Olason

Printer: P.A. Hutchison

This publication is designed to provide accurate and authoritative information in regard to the subject matter covered. It is sold with the understanding that the publisher is not engaged in rendering professional services. If legal, accounting, medical, psychological, or any other expert assistance is required, the services of a competent professional person should be sought. ADAPTED FROM A DECLARATION OF PRINCIPLES OF A JOINT COMMITTEE OF THE AMERICAN BAR ASSOCIATION AND PUBLISHERS.

Recognizing the importance of preserving what has been written, it is a policy of Maximum Press to have books of enduring value published in the United States printed on acid-free paper, and we exert our best efforts to that end.

Library of Congress Cataloging-in-Publication Data

Zimmerman, Jan.
Marketing on the Internet : a 7-step plan for selling your products, services, and image to millions over the information superhighway / Jan Zimmerman.— 5th ed.
p. cm.
Includes index.
ISBN 1-885068-49-2
1. Internet advertising. 2. Internet marketing. 3. Internet. I. Title.
HF6146.I58 M38 2001
658.8'4—dc21
00-011743

For Karen & Lawrence

Acknowledgments

This book would not have happened without months of extraordinary assistance from Alex Knox, whose Web research talents are without peer. Not only did he handle all the fact checking and updating for this edition, he also searched for art and assembled both the Resource Appendix and Companion Web Site. I don't know how I could function without him. I enjoyed the additional assistance of Aries Light, Elizabeth Cofell, and Tenley Zumwalt for copyright clearance. Ms. Light spent hours on the phone locating appropriate companies and conducting interviews for Chapter 11, while Ms. Zumwalt provided ongoing administrative support. I am enormously grateful to them all for their skills, their commitment, and their patience. There is no thank-you big enough.

I want to thank my clients, from whom I learn every day about innovative ways to market on the Internet. They provide me with a reason to search the Web perpetually for new discoveries.

My thanks also go to all the vendors and organizations that answered endless questions and gave copyright permission. The companies discussed in Chapter 11 were especially generous with their time and information.

With the Internet changing so rapidly, I can only hope that all my errors and omissions will be overtaken by a new reality before they are noticed.

Disclaimer

The purchase of computer software or hardware is an important and costly business decision. Although the author and publisher of this book have made reasonable efforts to ensure the accuracy and timeliness of the information contained herein, the author and publisher assume no liability with respect to loss or damage caused or alleged to be caused by reliance on any information contained herein and disclaim any and all warranties, expressed or implied, as to the accuracy or reliability of said information.

This book is not intended to replace the manufacturer's product documentation or personnel in determining the specifications and capabilities of the products mentioned in this book. The manufacturer's product documentation should always be consulted, because the specifications and capabilities of computer hardware and software products are subject to frequent modification. The reader is solely responsible for the choice of computer hardware and software. All configurations and applications of computer hardware and software should be reviewed with manufacturer's representatives prior to choosing or using any computer hardware and software.

Trademarks

The words contained in this text that are believed to be trademarked, service marked, or otherwise to hold proprietary rights have been designated as such by use of initial capitalization. No attempt has been made to designate as trademarked or service marked any personal computer words or terms in which proprietary rights might exist. Inclusion, exclusion, or definition of a word or term is not intended to affect, or to express judgment upon, the validity of legal status of any proprietary right that may be claimed for a specific word or term.

Foreword

The World Wide Web has emerged in the last decade as the preferred mass medium, one that uniquely combines interactivity, content, and commerce. The Internet is unique in that it is an information network that is ubiquitous, global, and decentralized. It is quickly becoming not only a "commercial" medium, but also a mass medium that rivals TV, radio, and other vehicles for information dissemination and exchange. The Net is the only medium in which users can both receive information as they can in the broadcast medium (by going to Web sites like Yahoo!) and communicate with others individually through e-mail.

Several trends are pushing the Internet toward a bigger and brighter future. The first trend is that there is a very healthy and competitive Internet access provider market. With the telecommunications market in the United States being deregulated, it is expected that the access-providing business will be even more competitive, as local and long distance phone companies, as well as cable providers, are expected to jump into the game. The net result will be a faster, cheaper, and more user-friendly service for the average consumer.

The second trend is that the transmission speeds available to businesses and homes will rapidly be increasing. This means that delivery of more demanding content such as full-motion video and other forms of multimedia content will be a better experience for users. Another trend is the development of more sophisticated software and technology, such as future generations of browser software (Java, VRML, etc.).

Last, because of the development of inexpensive standardized tools for publishing on the Web, more and more people will be putting content on the Web. Content will be increasingly more compelling and of higher quality, as models for content being funded get established.

The big promise is for the Internet to become the premier medium for information, entertainment, and business transactions. The intranet is the current rush, as businesses are quickly adopting the Internet as the platform for conducting communication and document management. This, combined with the mass media aspect, makes the Internet a truly ubiquitous and standard information medium. Given these factors, the future of the Net is indeed bright. However, this is still a rapidly developing medium. Pricing models for supporting quality content development are still lacking, although some form of advertising, transactions, or subscription is developing. Furthermore, regulations imposed on the still nascent industry could seriously affect the potential growth of this medium.

The Net will continue to draw millions of new users every year. The powerful thing about the Net is that it is a very organic, user-driven medium. The users can shape what the Net looks like through their interaction and feedback. What will sustain the Net and its businesses will be the creativity and participation of its users. The users and businesses of this new-found medium and community must not take the growth and freedom for granted. Without responsible actions, this medium can go away as quickly as it came. The future of the Net depends on the people as much as it depends on technology.

Jerry Yang
Yahoo! Cofounder

Table of Contents

Chapter 4:
Setting Up Your Web Site   107

Chapter 5:
Designing an Effective Web Site   163

Chapter 6:
Maintaining and Monitoring Your Site   222

Chapter 7:
Marketing Your Internet Presence   247

Chapter 8:
Marketing with Search Engines and Online Ads   293

Chapter 9:
Business Sense   335

Chapter 10:
Model Web Sites for Internet Marketing   369

Chapter 11:
Conclusion   **399**

About This Book

Whether your business is small, large, or merely a glimmer of a dot-com dream, *Marketing on the Internet* is *the* book to read for every aspect of doing business online. It covers every step from integrating Web efforts into your overall business plan to building a Web site that works for you. Whether you are already on the Web or are trying to make the online decision, the fifth edition of *Marketing on the Internet* will provide you with invaluable advice, worksheets and hot tips to ensure success.

This edition has been updated to keep business owners, CEOs, and marketing managers current on the status of online sales and marketing. It has proved equally useful as a resource for Web developers, graphic designers, and Web promotion companies looking for new ideas to assist their clients. It's an unbeatable one-stop reference book on all aspects of Internet marketing, from how to select vendors to how to accept payment online. The book is organized to work equally well whether read straight through or consulted on specific points of research.

The popular first edition, published in 1995, sold over 10,000 copies in the first two months and went on to become the publisher's best-selling title. The third edition, with its expanded focus on the Web and emphasis on business-based decision making, sold out its printing in one year. The fourth edition, which went through three printings, helped readers make the best possible choices for online marketing. The fifth edition has been expanded to include the needs of an increasingly sophisticated audience of Web businesses, many of which are launching the second, third, or even tenth generation of their Web site, by including

- The latest statistics to give you a solid base of information on Internet demographics, user buying habits, and business transactions.

- Many new Web sites to stimulate your imagination and serve as models for Web development.

- Lessons in looking at sites to understand their effectiveness from design, navigational, marketing, and promotional points of view.

- In response to popular demand, an expanded section on international e-commerce.

- A brand-new section about writing for the Web.

- More information about online advertising, bought and sold.

- A complete section on creating a transaction site, from shopping cart and checkstand software to accepting payment.

- Increased emphasis on paid advertising options and spotting trends to prepare you for the fast-changing world of electronic commerce.

- A complete index of all URLs in the book.

Here is what's inside:

- Chapter 1 reviews the growth of commercial activity on the Internet and the World Wide Web, with emphasis on its potential value for sales and marketing.

- Chapter 2 outlines seven basic steps for online marketing success, starting online research, and a business plan.

- Chapter 3 describes low-cost, non-Web electronic tools to initiate Internet marketing efforts, including opt-in e-mail, listservers, and news groups.

- Chapter 4 details the preliminary steps for developing a Web site, from selecting various Web service providers to estimating costs, accepting payment, and putting back office operations into place.

- Chapter 5 explores the process of Web design, including analyzing site effectiveness, writing for the Web, building storefronts, hints for a successful site, and the popular lists of sources for free Web resources.

- Chapter 6 explains the importance of maintaining and updating a Web site, and monitoring the traffic it receives.

- Chapter 7 tells how to promote a Web site using the site itself, other Web resources, non-Web Internet tools, online public relations, and offline activities.

- Chapter 8 focuses specifically on Web promotion using search engines, including tips to improve ranking, and paid or free advertising.

- Chapter 9 discusses privacy, security, and the legal considerations of marketing online, as well as global e-commerce.

- Chapter 10 looks at 13 model Web sites that successfully apply specific online marketing techniques.

- Chapter 11 considers long-range trends in government, financing, and rich media that may affect web commerce and reiterates the importance of integrating online marketing with other business operations.

- Appendix A is a list of helpful Internet resources organized by topic.

- Appendix B provides a glossary of acronyms and technical terms boldfaced on first use in this book.

- Appendix C provides a page index for all the URLs that appear.

Your "Members Only" Web Site

The online business world changes almost every day. That's why a companion Web site is associated with this book. On this site you will find the latest Internet commerce news, book updates, expanded information, and other Internet marketing–related resources. However, you have to be a member of the Marketing on the Internet Club to gain access to this site.

When you purchased this book, you automatically became a member (in fact, that's the only way to join). To access the companion Web site, go to the Maximum Press Web site located at *http://www.max press.com* and follow the links to the Marketing on the Internet companion Web site area. When you try to enter the companion web site, you will be prompted for a user ID and a password. Type in the following:

- For User ID: *mktint5e*

- For Password: *carbon*

You will then be granted full access to the "Members Only" area. Once you arrive, bookmark the page in your browser and you will never have to enter the user ID and password again. Visit the site often and enjoy the Internet marketing news and information with our compliments—and thanks for buying the book. We ask that you not share the user ID and password for this site with anyone else.

If you would like to suggest topics or Web sites for the next edition, or if you have questions about this edition, you can e-mail the author from the companion Web site.

Introduction

Outer space may be "the final frontier" for "Star Trek," but cyberspace is the latest frontier for marketing. Since its expansion as a visual medium in 1993, the Internet has opened a whole new dimension for promoting, browsing, buying, and selling both products and services.

Multinational companies such as Ford and J.P. Morgan, traditional retailers like Wal-Mart and J.C. Penney, and millions of specialty businesses have expanded onto the Web, along with Prince Andrew, the rock star Prince, travel agencies, breweries, movie studios, Girl Scout Cookies, and pizzerias. Commercial companies now operate about 80% of the more than 3.6 million active Web sites—up from only 50,000 commercial sites five years ago.

The Internet audience has grown apace. By March 2000 the Internet reached more than 200 million people in over 240 countries and territories. This growth far outruns that of any other telecommunications technology in history. It took less than 5 years to get the first 50 million people online; it took radio 38 years, television 13 years, and cable 10 years to reach an audience of equal size!

The Internet has unleashed creativity, business opportunities, and phenomenal growth in software, hardware, and services to support its expansion. One recent study showed that the contribution of the Internet to the U.S. economy, including infrastructure and advertising, exceeded $500 billion by the end of 1999. That statistic helps explain many trends in our economy: the well-publicized flow of venture capital into Internet-related companies; the furious rate of merger activity among telephone, cable, and Internet firms seeking to control broadband Internet access; and the aggressive acquisition of all the top 15 Internet content companies by large corporate interests.

Businesses selling everything from socks to socket wrenches see the information superhighway as a route to profits. What's most often ignored, however, is that most of those socks and socket wrenches, soups and space station parts, are sold to another business, not to the end user. Business-to-business (B2B) online sales projected at $185 billion in 2000 will far outdistance business-to-consumer (B2C) sales of only $40 billion. By 2004, online sales are forecast at $1.4 trillion, with B2B accounting for 90% of that.

You needn't think of the Web as only a venue for selling. Although some find it a great way to generate revenue, many more businesses use it to:

- Increase brand or product awareness.

- Enhance corporate image.

- Provide information or display samples of goods or services.

- Generate lists of prospects.

- Build relationships with customers.

- Improve customer service.

- Gather information about customer needs and preferences for future product development.

- Better understand customer demographics.

- Test consumer response to discounts or special offers.

- Find business partners, dealers, franchisees, or vendors.

- Recruit talent, members, employees, or subscribers.

- Save money by lowering the cost of customer communication and support, reducing the cost of order fulfillment, shortening the time frame for acquiring inventory, reducing stock on hand, and simplifying distribution channels.

Several themes echo throughout this book. First, you need a good business plan before investing marketing dollars online. There is no point in establishing an e-commerce Web site if you don't have the back office infrastructure and the financial resources to support it. A good business plan confirms that you've covered all these bases.

Further, with competition on the Web driving down profit margins, it's critical to make sure that the cost of new customer acquisition will not exceed the money you can make. Many dot-coms (and their investors) have been shocked to realize that the more sales they make, the more money they lose. The Web may continually spawn new technology, but the basics of business are old. In the words of a French proverb, "The more things change, the more they stay the same."

Second, you must commit to constant online research and continual site updates. It's become a truism to describe Internet time in dog years, with one year online now representing the business changes that used to occur over a seven-year period. Monitoring technology and the activities of your competitors, suppliers, and customers is essential to successful online marketing.

Third, Internet marketing is just another part of your overall marketing effort. Many businesses have built a Web site only to discover that the visitors did not come. Without actively marketing their sites online and offline, too many companies have found that only their Web developers are making any money from their investment. The Web has spawned its own forms of advertising, but traditional methods of getting out the word should not be ignored.

Finally, staying customer focused is just as important online as it is offline. Remnants of Web companies litter the cyberscape. They were unable to manage their inventory, ship product, respond to e-mail, or answer customer requests in a timely fashion. Ultimately, the companies that succeed online make it easy to do business from start to finish.

This book will help you decide whether the Internet and the Web can make your business more successful and more profitable. If the answer is yes, it will help you implement your electronic vision. Use this book as a reference, dipping into chapters as needed for "how-to" directions and online resources. Review it with your own marketing plan in mind and your own marketing staff involved. By all means read this book with one eye on the screen and the other on your business, one hand on a mouse and the other on your financial statement. Click on live links on the companion Web site at *www.maxpress.com* to check out many of the sites called out in the text.

Take advantage of the ideas in here to turn your Web site into a profit center. The Internet is a great place to have fun—but it's even more fun when it grows your bottom line.

1

The Internet: A Technology Means to a Marketing End

The lifetime of the Internet is a brief 31 years, yet it has profoundly changed how we search for knowledge in an age when knowledge is power. The **World Wide Web** (also known as **W3**, **WWW**, or the **Web**)— that graphical, easily accessible portion of the Internet—has energized its growth over the past seven years.

In this chapter we'll look at how the Internet, especially the Web, is redefining business communications, modifying consumer behavior, and mediating the relationships not only between a business and its customers, but between businesses as well.

Overwhelming all expectations, Internet revenues of all types, including infrastructure and advertising, exceeded half a trillion dollars by the end of 1999. Online retail sales in the United States, called **B2C** for business to consumer, swelled from $4.5 billion in 1998 to $16.2 billion in 1999, and are expected to reach $40 billion just one year later. U.S. business-to-business (**B2B**) electronic commerce growth rates are even greater, projected to balloon from $7.8 billion in 1997 to $185 billion in 2000 and $403 billion in 2003. By 2003, projected global e-commerce revenues are over $1.4 trillion, with B2B accounting for nearly 90% of that.

Should part of these revenues be yours? Should you invest your time, energy, money, and other resources to market and/or sell over the Internet? Or should you expend those scarce resources on offline marketing techniques that you know will work?

To help you make a good decision, this chapter provides basic background information about the Internet. We'll cover a little history, a few statistics, and some technology. Armed with this information and the review of your business and customers in Chapter 2, you can determine whether the Internet is a place for you. Specifically, we'll discuss

- The technology and history of the Internet and World Wide Web

- The range of activities available online

- Business opportunities and support online, including market research, advertising, and sales

- How new technologies may affect Internet use in the future

- An overview of efforts to measure the Internet audience and the effectiveness of advertising online.

What Is the Internet?

Computer networks link two or more computers to allow their users to share information, programs, and equipment, and to communicate with one another. Networks come in two flavors: **LANs** (**Local Area Networks**) link computers in the same building or area, and **WANs** (**Wide Area Networks**) tie together distant computer systems.

The Internet is simply the worldwide interconnection of many different networks. By hooking together **servers**, the large computers that manage individual networks, the infrastructure of the Internet allows over 200 million people to access information stored on hundreds of thousands of computers around the world. The Internet transmits messages between servers much the way the telephone system does, using satellites, microwaves, and dedicated cables such as Ethernet lines, fiber optic cables, cable television lines, or even the simple phone lines in your home.

There is one absolutely critical difference. The Internet turns every individual or business into a broadcaster, able to communicate from one person to many people, a privilege previously reserved for television, radio, and publishing companies.

Originally, computers on the Internet could exchange only text messages. Now the Web portion of the Internet allows users to exchange graphics, still photos, animation, voice, and even full-motion video. Think of the Web as a virtual publishing company through which anyone can distribute the electronic equivalent of glossy magazines or short films.

The Web is the fastest-growing, most user-friendly, and most commercially popular segment of the Internet. Any computer on the Internet equipped with a **browser** (software designed to look at Internet resources) and small pieces of specialized software called **plug-ins** can access different kinds of text, images, and sound. A **page** (part of a site) on the Web can be connected to another page with related information using a **link**, even if the computer hosting the other page is halfway around the earth, orbiting in the space shuttle, or sitting on Mars. How did all this come to be?

History of the Internet

The Internet owes its existence to the Pentagon and the Cold War. To solve the problem of a centralized computer system vulnerable to a single well-placed bomb, scientists at the Rand Corporation developed the concept of a **centerless network** in 1964. They envisioned thousands of computers connected with communication redundancy, much the way the human brain is wired, so that the loss of a few "neurons" or connecting cables would not result in a total loss of function.

In 1969, two **nodes** (computers connected to a network) were linked for the first time on the ARPAnet, the precursor to today's Internet. (ARPAnet was named after the Defense Department's Advanced Research Projects Agency, which sponsored its development.)

As the ARPAnet grew, researchers at UCLA, MIT, Stanford Research International, Bolt Baranek & Newman, and the British National Physical Laboratory defined a way to bundle information into structures called **packets**, which were labeled with the **network address** of the recipient's electronic mailbox. Like a message in a bottle, a packet of information is cast adrift in the sea of computers on the network. Each computer forwards the packet closer to the address on the bottle. Once the packet reaches its destination, the packet structure (i.e., the bottle) dissolves, leaving the message intact. All computer networks now use this packet scheme to package and deliver messages reliably. The **protocol** that moves these packets of information along Internet pathways is called **TCP/IP** or **Transmission Control Protocol/Internet Protocol.**

When the ARPAnet was decommissioned in 1989, NSFnet supplanted it as the main high-speed transmission line, or **backbone**, with support from the National Science Foundation. The Internet is now self-sustained by a network of interested parties, both public and private. Perhaps because its original government funding mandated public ownership of the enabling technology, or perhaps because of an open development process through public Requests for Comments (**RFCs**), the Internet grew of its own accord to meet the needs of its users.

Without a doubt, the rapid spread of sophisticated desktop computers in the 1980s and 1990s enabled the Internet to take off. ARPAnet was founded in the days of large mainframes located at universities and major corporations; NSFnet was originally funded to connect five supercomputer centers. Without PCs there never would have been so many computers to connect!

The 1993 release of Mosaic, the first browser capable of reading graphical information, provided the mechanism for user-friendly access and gave birth to the Web. Suddenly, Internet usage parameters that had been doubling each year began doubling in three months. Even with the enormous base now in place, the rate of doubling has not yet begun to slow. It will have to ebb eventually—at this rate, facetious forecasts predict that everyone in the world would be connected by July 31, 2003!

Curious? For more information on the history of the Internet, try *http://info.isoc.org/internet/history* or *http://www.pbs.org/internet/ timeline.*

Spectacular Growth

In its first 15 years, the Internet barely topped 1,000 **hosts** (computer systems connected to the Internet, whether full-time or part-time, by direct or dial-up connection). In its second 15 years, it exploded like a supernova. As seen in Figure 1.1, by January 2000, the Internet comprised over 72 million hosts. These hosts represent over 150,000 interconnected networks and over 300 million users in 240 countries and

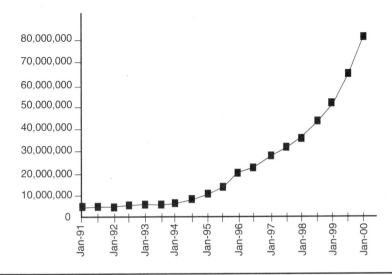

Figure 1.1. Internet domain survey host count, *http://www.isc.org/ds/www-200001/report.html.* Source: Internet Software Consortium (*http://www.isc.org*).

territories around the world; by 2001 an additional 150 million people plan to be online.

Internet access, particularly since the development of the World Wide Web, has grown faster than any other communications technology in history. Consider this: It took 38 years for 30% of U.S. households to have a telephone; 17 years to have a television; 13 years to have a computer. The World Wide Web has taken less than 7 years to reach the same 30%! This is one of the truly remarkable stories of the 20th century and shows every sign of continuing through the 21st.

As of June 2000 the total number of **domain names** (registered Web site names) registered by InterNIC (the company that maintains the primary domain name database) topped 18 million. However, over half of those lack an active site and another one third are either unfinished or temporary. Over 300,000 new names are now registered every week; more than 3 million names were registered in the first quarter of 2000 alone. (We'll discuss domain registration in Chapter 4.) Figure 1.2 shows the growth of domain name registration in graphic terms.

The number of Web sites in the commercial (*.com*) domain far outpaces that of network servers (*.net*) and educational institutions (*.edu*), as seen in Figure 1.3. Military, government, and not-for-profit organizations (*.org*) represent a negligible fraction of names. The number of do-

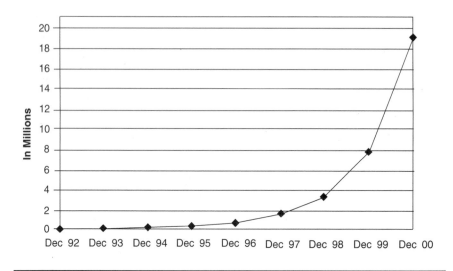

Figure 1.2. Registered domain names, *http://www.networksolutions.com.* Network Solutions domain name registration data is used with permission of Network Solutions, Inc. © Newtowk Solutions, Inc.

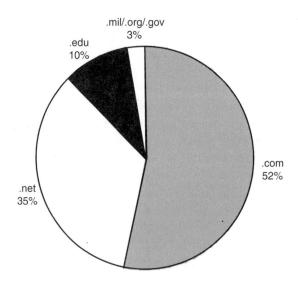

Figure 1.3. Distribution of top-level domain names by host count, July 2000, *http://www.isc.org/ds/www-200007/dist-bynum.html.* Source: Internet Software Consortium (*http://www.isc.org*).

main names registered in countries outside the United States is growing quickly. Commercial domains represented over 52% of all active domains in July 2000. If one counts registered, but inactive domains, the percent of *.com* URLs rises to 60% worldwide and nearly 80% in the U.S.

As of early 2000, about 60% of all U.S. businesses and 37% of small ones had Web sites. Another 20% of all businesses and 40% of small businesses plan to go online in the future. Altogether, there are an estimated 1.5 billion(!) pages on 3.6 million active Web sites, an 88% increase since 1998, with 1.9 million new pages going up daily worldwide. For marketing purposes, the implications are staggering.

For current statistical information, check out

- *http://www.domainstats.com/internic.cfm*

- *http://www.thestandard.com*

- *http://www.isc.org/ds/www-200001/report.html*

- *http://www.internetstats.com/*

Before Going Further: Get Access

Whether it's the past, present, or future of the Internet and the World Wide Web, the best way to learn is to get online. If you already have access, great. If not, here's what you'll need:

- A *computer:* the faster the machine and the larger its hard drive, the better it can handle graphics, sound, and video.

- A *modem:* hardware that enables computers to communicate with each other over telephone lines. The faster the speed, the more rapidly information can be downloaded from the Web. Modem speed is measured in thousands (kilo or K) of **bits per second (bps)**. Sometimes bps is called the **Baud** rate. A 28.8 Kbps modem is considered minimal for receiving graphics from the Web in a reasonable amount of time. Today's graphic-laden Web

sites can benefit from faster access. Modems usually come pack-
aged with communications software.

- *Browser* software, usually either Netscape Navigator or Internet Explorer.

- An *Internet connection,* either directly through one of more than
  7,000 **Internet Service Providers (ISPs),** through a commercial
  online service, such as America Online (AOL), CompuServe, or
  Prodigy; or through one of the free ISPs like Juno. In addition to
  acting as ISPs with full Web access, these services offer a private
  network of information services, shopping malls, advertising
  channels, and entertainment.

If you're uncomfortable selecting an ISP, you can easily start with
one of the major online services summarized in Figure 1.4, all of
which also offer access to the Web. Almost always, you can obtain
500 hours of free use for exploration. Or check a site like *http://
www.cnet.com/Reports/Special/ISP/index.html* to obtain rankings of
ISPs in your service area. (If you need Internet access for this type of
research, try your local public library; most now offer free Internet
time.)

Getting an account with an ISP or online service is very simple: You
can use any installed modem and browser to "dial-in" to one of the free
services. Or you can sign up online or telephone any ISP for an account.
You will receive communication and browser software, along with an
account number, and will be asked to supply a user name and password

Service	Subscribers	Phone Number	Monthly Rate	1st month trial
AOL (America Online)	19 million	(800) 827-6364	$21.95/mo	500 free hours
Compuserve	2 million	(800) 292-3900	$19.95/mo	500 free hours
Prodigy	1.5 million	1-800-776-3449	$19.95/mo	500 free hours
Freei.net	1.5 million	1-253-796-6505	FREE	N/A
Juno	9.4 million	(800) 654-JUNO	FREE	N/A
Juno Premium	NA	(800) 654-JUNO	$9.95/mo	150 free hours

Figure 1.4. Online service subscription rates.

to get online. Although some services offer lower monthly rates for limited time online, there is no point for most businesses to sign up for anything but unlimited use. Once you're set up, read this book with your browser on and mark favorite sites for future use.

How Do People Travel to Cyberspace?

How your customers obtain Internet access and the kinds of information they are able to receive affects your ability to reach your desired audience. It matters that in the year 2000 the installed base of computers was already over 164 million in the United States and 579 million worldwide. It matters that more than 10 million new PCs are now sold each year in the United States and over 100 million worldwide, many replacing outdated equipment.

It matters that more than 50% of U.S. homes (50 million) now have a PC, up from 15 million in 1995 and 23 million in 1997. That number may rise to 90% of households by 2005. Already almost 90% of those homes with PCs are online. It matters to you as a marketing person that 5 million Americans jumped into the Web surf in the first quarter of 2000, up 11% since the end of 1999 and 62% since the end of 1998. It matters that Internet traffic is increasing 1000% per year.

Prices on computers have fallen so low that multiple computer/Web-access homes may become commonplace, with PCs sometimes connected to each other with a phone-based, mini-networking card or external connection. In other cases, the second unit will be an Internet appliance or hand-held device. These new technologies—such as personal digital assistants like the Palm Pilot, cell phones with special built-in Internet browsers, WebTV, or Intel's new Dot.Station Web appliance, which integrates home organization with Web access and e-mail—have already gained ground as alternate forms of Internet access.

Figure 1.5 shows that home users are connecting to the Internet at faster and faster speeds, but there are significant differences between home and business users. Home users are still overwhelmingly modem based, with only 6% enjoying any form of high-speed access, while up to 40% of total users access the Web at more than 56 Kbps. Since *actual* modem connection speed averages 38% slower than modem or ISP capability, home users may be easily frustrated by graphics-intensive, feature-laden sites.

Although the high-speed access marketplace is growing rapidly, in subscriber numbers the most popular Internet access method remains

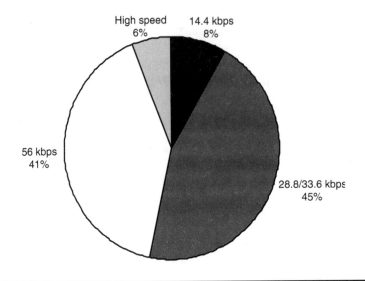

Figure 1.5.   Internet connection speeds at home, *http://cyberatlas. internet.com/big_picture/hardware/article/0,1323,5921-277191,00.html#table.* Reprinted with permission © 2000 Internet.com, LLC. All rights reserved.

dial-up ISP, with 46.7 million subscribers, compared to an aggregate of 3.5 million subscribers for high-speed methods such as cable modem, DSL, or other dedicated lines.

Faster access has been shown to increase dramatically the frequency with which viewers go to the Web (83% more often for viewers with 56 Kbps access or higher) and the number of pages they view (130% more). With download speed therefore still the number one design issue, you may need to adjust your Web site based on whether your target audience is more likely to log on from home or work.

It even matters to you which hardware platforms, browsers, and browser versions viewers use, since Web sites don't look equally good in all environments. Typical platform and browser distributions are shown in Figures 1.6 and 1.7. The most popular browsers, Netscape's Navigator and Microsoft's Internet Explorer, have long since supplanted Mosaic. These browsers allow access to e-mail, news groups, and mailing lists, as well as the Web, as long as an ISP handles them.

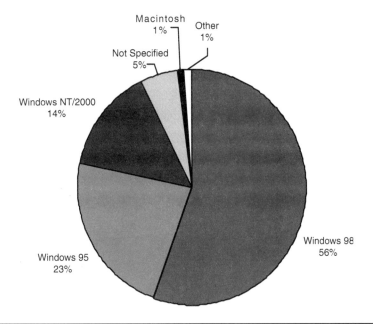

Figure 1.6. Platform distribution, *http://websnapshot.mycomputer.com/ systemos.html.* Courtesy Mycomputer.com.

What Happens in Cyberspace?

What's going on that has more than 57 million Americans logging on every day, many of them multiple times? (See Figure 1.8 for frequency of access.) A survey by Odyssey, L.P. in October 1999 concluded that e-mail, research, and education were the most popular reasons for being online, as seen in Figure 1.9.

Electronic Mail

Electronic mail, or **e-mail,** is one of the original and still essential uses of the Internet and online services. With e-mail, one person sends a message to the computer mailbox of another. E-mail also allows someone to broadcast a message to many people simultaneously. Most e-mail

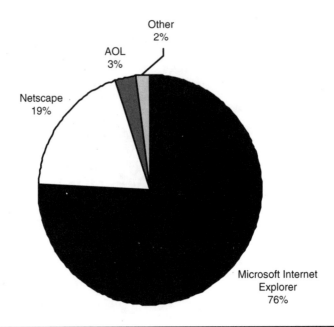

Figure 1.7. Browser distribution, *http://websnapshot.mycomputer.com/ browsers.html.* Courtesy Mycomputer.com.

programs permit users to attach a computer file containing any type of information, from spreadsheets to software programs. Over 100 million people now use e-mail, sending or receiving an average of 3.5 personal messages per day. Total worldwide e-mail traffic in 1999 was estimated at 350 million messages. This does not count over 100 billion commercial messages per day, a large percentage of which are unwanted.

Mailing Lists

An Internet **mailing list** stores the names and associated e-mail addresses of users with a common interest in a particular topic. Once an **opt-in** mailing list is started, Internet users can add their names and e-mail addresses to the list (called **subscribing**). They can exchange e-mail messages simultaneously with everyone else on the list, regardless of the e-mail program being used. About 21% of e-mail users are

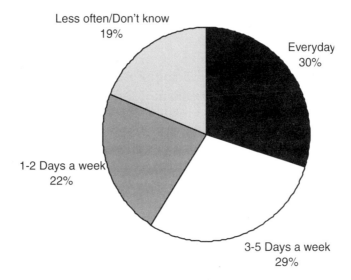

Figure 1.8. How often Americans go online, *http://cyberatlas.internet.com/ big_picture/traffic_patterns/article/0,1323,5931_152061,00.html. Reprinted with permission.* © 2000 Internet.com, LLC. All rights reserved.

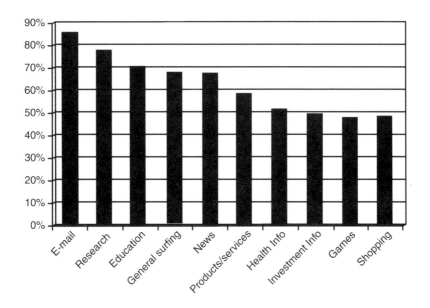

Figure 1.9. What the virtual audience does online, *http://cyberatlas.internet. com/big_picture/traffic_patterns/article/0,1323,5931_211381,00.html. Reprinted with permission.* © 2000 Internet.com, LLC. All rights reserved.

on mailing lists, which can range from a few hundred to tens of thousands of subscribers.

Over 90,000 mailing lists cover every subject imaginable. Scientists use mailing lists for peer discussion of theories and experiments. Philosophers use them. Priests use them. Techies and Dead Heads use them. Even marketers use them. On the Internet all kinds of people use mailing lists to stay informed of important events, exchanging data on everything from the flight path of killer bees to changes in concert schedules.

News Groups

Mailing lists are accessed via e-mail, but **news groups**, a worldwide system of about 30,000 discussion groups on a portion of the Internet called USEnet, require full Internet accounts and news group reader software provided by an ISP. News groups function like mailing lists in some ways, but they offer several different methods of sending messages. A user can **post** a message for everyone in the group or respond to someone else's comments on a particular topic. In the latter case, only those who read the original comments see the response.

A few of the more popular news groups have as many as 300,000 users at a particular time. More commonly, subscribers range from 200 to 10,000. A 1998 survey by the Graphics, Visualization and Usability (GVU) Center at Georgia Institute of Technology showed decreasing use of news groups, with 20.8% of all Internet users accessing at least one per week. However, 21% of Internet users seldom access them, with women and 19- to 25-year-olds the least likely users. Whether a news group will be a valuable marketing tool for you depends on your business and your target market. We'll discuss this more in Chapter 3.

The World Wide Web

The World Wide Web consists of those servers on the Internet programmed to handle specific information requests from browser software. To locate any resource on the Internet that is part of the Web, you enter an address into your browser in a standard format called a **URL** (Uniform Resource Locator). Typical Web addresses look like this: *http://www.maxpress.com*. The **http** (**HyperText Transport Protocol**) indicates a special method of moving **HyperText** files, which contain links to other Web pages, across the Internet. It is one of the most important methods used on the Web. The **www** after the double slash (*//*) means that the information is located on a dedicated Web server. Browsers allow users to **bookmark** any sites (by saving the URL address) they want to recall in the future.

By the Numbers: Business on the Internet

About 40% of Web users—120 million people—reported purchasing something online in 1999, up from 26% in 1998 and 15% in 1996. (See Figure 1.10.) Some of these buyers are "regulars": About 2.5 million people shop online at least once a week. Even if they don't actually buy on the Web, about half of online consumers obtain product information or research future purchases, especially for cars, books, and computers. Figure 1.11 compares the millions of consumers (by number of users)

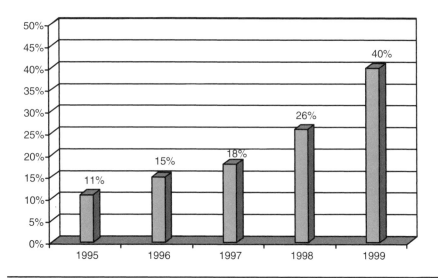

Figure 1.10. Percent of Web households purchasing online, *http://www. emarketer.com/estats-41300_angusreid.html* and *http://www.gvu.gatech.edu/ user_surveys*. Source 1999: Courtesy eMarketer, Inc.; source 1994-1998: GVU's WWW User Survey at *http://www.gvu.gatech.edu/user_surveys*. ©1994-1998 Georgia Tech Research Corporation. All rights reserved.

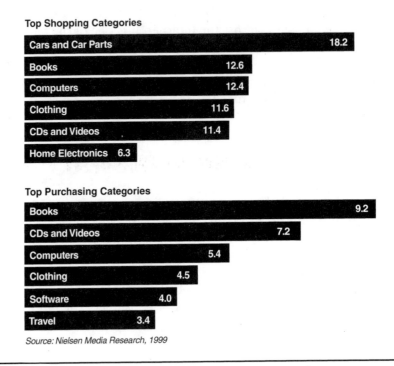

Top Shopping Categories

Cars and Car Parts	18.2
Books	12.6
Computers	12.4
Clothing	11.6
CDs and Videos	11.4
Home Electronics	6.3

Top Purchasing Categories

Books	9.2
CDs and Videos	7.2
Computers	5.4
Clothing	4.5
Software	4.0
Travel	3.4

Source: Nielsen Media Research, 1999

Figure 1.11. Comparison of online shoppers vs. buyers, *http://www. emarketer.com/images/062899naecom.gif. Courtesy, eMarketers, Inc.*

who research (the shoppers) to those who purchase by category. These numbers are a persuasive argument for going online even if you choose not to sell there. Certainly U.S. businesses are listening: More than 56% are expected to engage in some form of B2B electronic commerce by the end of the year 2000, more than double the 24% in 1998.

Perhaps the most interesting statistic about commerce on the Web, however, is that most of it is not retail, but business-to-business. Worldwide B2B numbers are staggering, with some projections for 2000 as high as $403 billion, growing to $7.35 trillion in 2004, more than 10 times worldwide B2C sales (see Figure 1.12). One caveat: as large as this number is, it will still represent only 7% of projected total global transactions of $105 trillion. These heady forecasts are fueled by recent announcements of plans for industry-wide, online buying sites for corporate giants in the automotive, airline, and computer industries.

To stay abreast of Internet statistics, watch sites such as the Internet Index at *http://www.openmarket.com/intindex.cfm, http://*

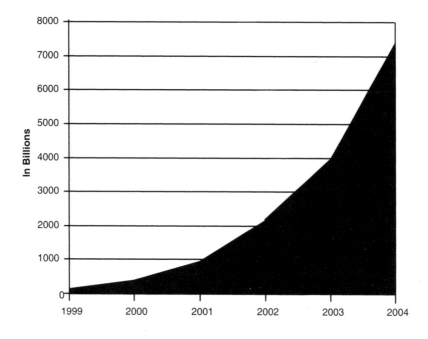

Figure 1.12.   Projected B2B sales worldwide, *http://cyberatlas.internet.com/ markets/professional/article/0,1323,5971_295831,00.html. Reprinted with permission.* © 2000 Internet.com, LLC. All rights reserved.

www.internetindicators.com, http://www.bizrate.com, and *http:// www.emarketer.com/estats.*

Who's Selling What?

Some products sell better on the Web than others. Brokerage houses and sites selling computer hardware and software, travel, and collectibles (often found on auction sites) are among the most lucrative, as seen in Figure 1.13, which ranks online purchases by dollars. Music/video, books, tickets, and flowers all do well on the Web; their dollar volume is lower because the price of the products is relatively low. For instance, PC Flowers & Gifts at *http://www.pcflowers.com/pcf/default.asp* now receives over 40% of its annual revenues from online sales.

Travel is another growth story. By the year 2000, online commerce related to travel is estimated at $12.4 billion, or 33.4% of total online

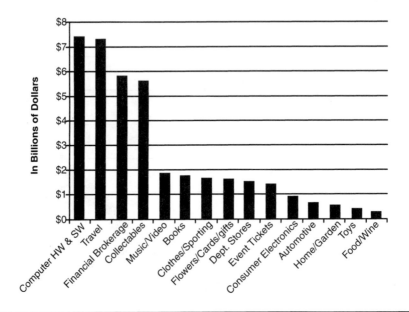

Figure 1.13. US online transactions 1999, *http://www.emarketer.com/images/ 062899naecom.gif.* Courtesy eMarketer, Inc.

retail sales in 2000 with visitors attracted by such sites as centralamerica.com (see Figure 1.14) at *http://www.centralamerica.com/ cr/parks/index.htm.* Close to 70% of online consumers use the Web to find out about their travel destinations, and about one third of those will book online. In fact, online reservations accounted for 5% of total bookings in 1999 and are anticipated to rise to 14% by 2005.

The number of real estate sites has also grown, from huge sites like *http://www.realtor.com* to individual agents' sites. It is difficult to quantify the dollar value of real estate sold because sales are initiated online but closed offline. However, with real estate sites attracting more than 40% of all potential home buyers, getting a property featured online has become the fourth most effective residential selling technique, after signage, multiple listing services, and referrals.

How People Find Sites

It's important to understand how people find the Web sites they visit, because this will affect your Web promotion strategy. Already newspa-

Figure 1.14. Travel site, *http://www.centralamerica.com/parks/index.htm*. Courtesy centralamerica.com.

pers and TV shows review Web sites and announce Web happenings, from scheduled chats with stars, athletes, and political personalities to live Webcasts of entertainment events. News programs, movies, and all forms of advertising now include URLs in their promotional matter—just watch an evening of television or tabulate the print ads with URLs in your favorite magazine.

A survey posted in June 2000 on Business Week Online *(http://www.businessweek.com)* ranked users' common strategies for finding new Web sites in the following order. The four most common were

- Search engines, 45.8%

- Word-of-mouth, 20.3%

- Random surfing 19.9%

- Magazines 4.4%

If you sell B2C online, potential customers may locate you through price-and-feature comparison sites like *http://www.mysimon.com* or *http://www.DealPilot.com*. Bid sites like *http://www.priceline.com* allow consumers to set a target price to try to obtain the best bargain on their desired products. Other consumer-oriented sites like *http://www.accompany.com* aggregate buyers to leverage group purchasing power for better prices.

Other sites offer shopping-specific search engines devoted exclusively to retail sales, like *http://shopping.yahoo.com* or *http://shopping.excite.com*. After the user enters a desired product, the engine returns information about locations and prices. Shown in Figure 1.15, Excite adds source sites when site owners click on "Add URL" at the bottom of the page.

Advertising on the Web

Viewers, including other businesses, are often enticed to sites by Web advertisements, which 42% of online businesses use to promote their URLs. According to the Internet Advertising Bureau's (IAB) Internet Ad

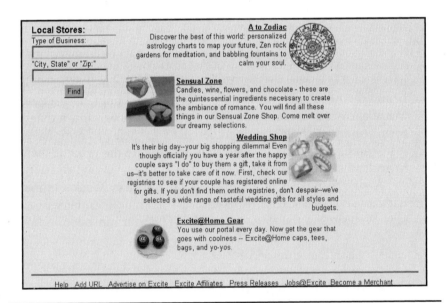

Figure 1.15. Shopping search engine, *http://shopping.excite.com/mini_shops*
© 2000 At Home Corporation. All rights reserved. Excite, Excite Shopping and Classifieds 2000 are service marks or registered service marks of At Home Corporation in the United States and other countries.

Revenue Report, total 1999 revenue exceeded $4.6 billion worldwide, more than twice that for 1998 and four times the ad revenue for 1997.

For the United States only, Internet advertising totaled $2.6 billion in 1999, with growth forecast to reach $4.82 billion in 2000 and 13.3 billion by 2003. For comparison, look at the distribution of $216.6 billion in total U.S. annual advertising expenditures for 1999 shown in Figure 1.16. In spite of its rapid growth, you can see that Internet advertising still accounts for only a small percentage of advertising dollars.

Although more and more sites are seeking advertising, only about 20% attract ad revenue, with a little over half of online advertising the money going for standardized **banner ads** (short, wide display ads). These are particularly popular on large gateway sites like Netscape's NetCenter or Yahoo! at *http://www.yahoo.com*, since recent research shows them to be as effective as television in building brand awareness.

Banner ads are now responsible for only 56% of Web ad revenue, down from 80% in 1997. Sponsorships at 27% and interstitials (larger display ads between Web pages) at 4% are responsible for most of the remaining ad dollars. As their novelty has worn off, banner ads have lost their destination appeal, with click-through rates now below 1% for static ads.

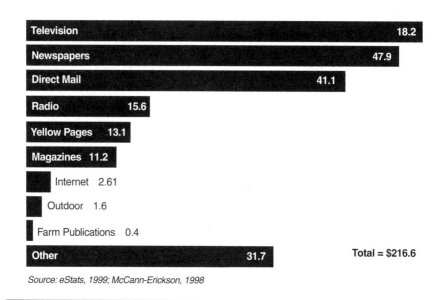

Source: eStats, 1999; McCann-Erickson, 1998

Figure 1.16. 1999 advertising spending by media type in billions, *http://www.emarketer.com/estats/041299_adspend.html*. Courtesy eMarketer, Inc.

Even so, the cost of banner advertising may be out of the ballpark for small to medium-size businesses except on small sites. Banner ads on portal sites have become part of the imaging game for large companies, who rely less on actual click-throughs to their site and more on the subconscious recognition of brand names. We'll discuss affordable, niche-market placements for banner ads and how to exchange free links and banner ads with complementary businesses in Chapter 8. Sites like *http:// www.emarketer.com*, shown in Figure 1.17, *http://www.adres. internet.com*, or *http://cyberatlas.Internet.com/segments/advertising/ ad_index.html* are good sources for up-to-date information about online advertising.

Mass vs. Target Marketing

A perennial advertising debate rages over Web promotion: Is the Web 90% brand imaging? Or is it 90% niche marketing? Should you aim for mass markets, maximizing your total exposure and the total number of viewers who see your name? Or should you aim at narrow demographic prospects who are more likely to turn into customers?

As a rule of thumb, unless you are a major corporation already managing brand imaging in national newspapers, network TV, radio and glossy magazines, you will be better off with a target marketing approach. Spend your precious dollars where they will reach the most likely buyers. The cost of exposure-driven marketing is likely to empty all but the deepest pockets.

Advertisers use the term **CPM** to represent the cost per thousand possible viewers or listeners (M is the Roman numeral for 1,000). Generally, the higher the CPM, the smaller but more targeted the audience in terms of geography or demographics. The table in Figure 1.18 compares typical CPMs for various media. The key, as always, is whether the viewers you reach are the right targets for the product or service you sell.

Even though its CPM may be low, the actual costs or minimum rates for an ad may not be. A 30-second Super Bowl 2000 ad, with a CPM of $16, sold for an average of $2 million to reach 125 million viewers. Some 38 different companies thought it was worth this price to include their URLs in the 2000 Super Bowl broadcast; 17 of those were "dot.com" (Internet-based) enterprises.

By comparison, the average CPM for a Web banner ad in Q4 1999 was $33.75, down for the third year in a row, partly due to the rapid

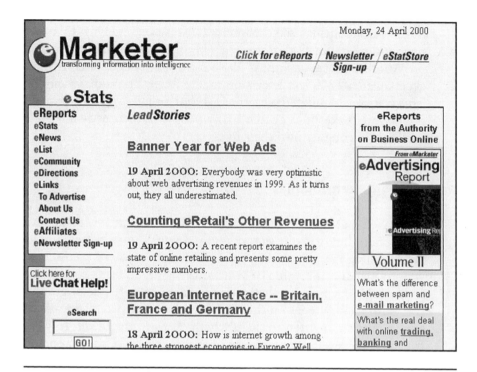

Figure 1.17.   Source for Internet advertising statistics, *http://www. emarketer.com/estats/welcome.html.* Courtesy eMarketer, Inc.

Form of Media	Typical Range CPM
Web Site	$18-$70
National Newspaper/Magazine	$30
Primetime Network TV, e.g. The Oscars	$27
Super Bowl	$16-$17
Typical Network TV Show	$7

Figure 1.18.   CPMs by media.

growth in the supply of online advertising space. Actual costs range from a few hundred dollars per year to tens of thousands of dollars per week. You'll need to balance your budget against your desired audience size and demographics.

Advertisers apportioning their budgets must think hard about a 1997 Price Waterhouse Consumer Technology survey that showed that over one third of respondents used the Internet instead of watching TV and nearly one third used it instead of reading a book, newspaper, or magazine.

Another survey in July 1999 showed that households with Internet access watch 13% less television, or 32 fewer hours of TV per month! This statistic, combined with the fact that e-mail is now used as often as the phone, makes it clear that many people have already integrated the Internet thoroughly into their lives.

Push vs. Pull Technologies

Most Web marketing is based on **pull**. Your Web site or banner ad waits for users to link to your site, download your information, subscribe to your mailing list, or otherwise pull the information to themselves. One way to increase the value of your advertising dollar is to look at **push** technologies, which may help you reach your desired demographic profile. Push technologies on the Web are more like broadcast ads. People have to watch or listen to them whether or not they want to.

Recently developed push technologies incorporate advertisements with automatic downloads of information that a user has requested. An ad for golf clubs, for instance, might reach only those who requested sports news about golf. Such narrowcasting technology allows you to send ads to the specific demographic groups—segregated by categories, such as interest, income, age, and gender—that best fit your target market. This turns Web advertising into very familiar territory. You can implement this technology on your own Web site, allowing those who register to decide what kind of products interest them. You can then send them information on a regular basis, without waiting for a specific inquiry.

Push techniques are just one of many technologies that may affect how you design and implement your Internet marketing strategy.

A Glimpse of the Future

The Internet couples a new broadcast medium with the allure of interactivity. It demands that viewers constantly make choices, whether jumping to a new page or selecting something from the page they are on. From a marketing perspective, there is nothing like the opportunity to communicate with potential customers at the very moment when they are looking for information or making a purchasing decision.

High-end computing capabilities teamed with high-speed Web access create a tantalizing Internet feast that more and more viewers are able to consume. A certain fraction of potential customers will get so annoyed waiting for an image to download that they will click away from a site or log off the Internet. You've probably done it yourself. Sites may lose customers who do not have adequate equipment to view a video-laden Web site or anger those who lack the know-how to install a plug-in needed to enjoy an expensive, animated Web site.

Let's look at some near-term technologies that make the Web feast more accessible, more enjoyable, but not necessarily more affordable for users. We'll discuss the technologies involved and what they imply for your company. Improvements are coming in three main areas:

1. Faster access to information from the Internet

2. Hand-held, wireless devices

3. Ease of use: Web appliances

First, you can assume that the enabling technologies of faster microprocessors, larger memory, and fast-access, economical storage will continue to offer better computer performance at the same or lower cost—multimedia PCs are already sold on specials for as little as $500.

Remember that the overall system can run only as fast as the slowest piece in it. Think of a stream of digital data as if it were a stream of water. The only way more water can flow through a pipe in a fixed length of time is to make the pipe bigger or the water smaller. Making water smaller is not an option in the physical world, but in the digital world, both options are available. You can make the pipe—**bandwidth**—bigger, or you can make information smaller through **data compression** technologies. Whichever way it is accomplished, running more information through a "pipe" translates to more connections, overcoming the well-known sluggishness of the Internet at busy times of the day. It also means that more information can be delivered to the same number of connections. For instance, video with audio can be transmitted in the same time it used to take to send only text. Let's look at some ways of obtaining bigger data pipes, which is referred to as **broadband** (wide bandwidth) in the telecom world.

Pipe Dreams: Faster Broadband Access

The first three technologies for increasing access speed over the "last mile"—ISDN, T1/T3 leased lines, and DSL—come from the telephone world; the fourth option, cable modem, derives from the perennial battle between phone companies and cable TV. Direct broadcast satellite and wireless broadband completely revamp methods of reaching the Internet. Although they are only a minute share of usage now, they may be required to wire rural areas of the nation in the future. On the far horizon, alternative broadband networks are under development for the next generation Internet.

All these options allow more data to flow more quickly between multiple individual computers and the Internet. Collectively, these technologies were used by only 1.9 million U.S. households in 1999 (3.8% of online households). This is forecast, perhaps optimistically, to grow to 31.7 million households (32% of online households) by the year 2003. Broadband access for business is more common, especially for large companies.

The table in Figure 1.19 compares the costs, features, benefits, and drawbacks of these technologies with that of standard dial-up phone modems over **POTS** (Plain Old Telephone Service).

ISDN

ISDN (**Integrated Services Digital Network**) has been available for a long time as a dial-up service in metropolitan areas. ISDN, which requires a separate line and an ISDN modem (I-modem) costing several hundred dollars, remains primarily a small business option.

T1/T3 Leased Lines

T1/T3 leased lines require rewiring an office building, which can be logistically and financially difficult. T1 lines, roughly equivalent to 6 ISDN lines, are often used to connect networks to the Internet, but it takes a T3 line to carry full-motion, full-screen video. Additional equipment is needed to divide the resources among different servers.

DSL

DSL (Digital Subscriber **Line**) is poised for big-time expansion to small businesses and residences as an updated version of ISDN. DSL takes advan-

Type of Access	Bandwidth	Typical User	Monthly Rates	Installation/ Equipment	Positives/Negatives
POTS (Plain Old Telephone Service)	Up to 56k	Home	$14-$40 + ISP charges	phone installation; 56K modem $50	+ some free Internet services available affordable, easysetup - no guarantee of speed, uploads slower than downloads
ISDN	56 to 64 Kbps	Small-Medium Business multiple users	$20-$50 fixed hours + $1.50 each additional hour	line installation; ISDN modem $200	+ guaranteed speed, can talk and browse simultaneously - can't support a server; limited availability
DSL	up to 6–8 Mbps	Residential or Small Business	$40 for 256 Kbps $65 for 512 Kbps $125 for 1 Mbps and up	$100-$500 may not include required ($200) DSL modem; often resold by ISPs	+ always on, works well with LAN/server, very fast - increased security risk and complexity; availability limited to locations close to central office; problems with reliability in residential areas

Figure 1.19. Comparison of Internet access methods. *(Continued on next page.)*

Type of Access	Bandwidth	Typical User	Monthly Rates	Installation/ Equipment	Positives/Negatives
T1/T3 Lines	T1: 1.5 Mbps T3: 44.7 Mbps	Large Business	T1: $300 T3: call phone company, fractional installations available	$1,500 installation, plus additional support equipment like routers to deliver service to different users	+ T1 excellent Internet connection; T3 needed for full-motion, full-screen video - cost, limited availability
Cable Modem	experience 128-256 Kbps subscriber bandwidth: 1.5-3.0 Mbps download; 33.6-1 Mbps upload	Home users	$50-$200	$50-$350 for 128-256K modem plus cost of installation	+ always on, good value - shared service can cause slowdowns, limited availability, no choice of ISPs
Satellite	400 Kbps		$30 and up	$300-$700 for dish, box and PC card; $200 installation	+ very fast, great for remote locations, always on, speed constant - expensive, requires outside dish, broadband inbound, but requires 56K modem outbound for e-mail and attachments

Figure 1.19. Comparison of Internet access methods. (*Continued from previous page.*)

tage of advances in compression and other technologies to cram more information into a standard telephone line. Some DSL lines are asymmetric, with slower uploads than downloads. These high-speed access lines, and sometimes even adequate copper phone lines, often are not available in rural counties or in all urban neighborhoods, leading to yet another form of digital divide. Even large metropolitan areas may not have enough lines available or the lines may be too old to be reliable. For more information on ISDN, T1/T3 and DSL, check out these sites:

- *http://www.PacBell.com/Products/business/fastrak/networking/ ISDN/*

- *http://www.specialty.com/hiband*

Cable Modems

Cable companies joust with phone companies over who will provide broadband digital connections into the home. Cable companies and ISPs battle over whether consumers must use a cablecompany's bundled Internet service, or whether they enjoy open access to other ISPs. A June 2000 court decision thrust the issue into the lap of the Federal Telecommunications Commission, which should rule within the year.

As a result, the corporate structure of the digital communication industry is in constant flux. AT&T has added cable operators Media One and TeleCommunications, Inc. (TCI) to its holdings, thus becoming the largest cable company in the United States, with the potential to reach 60% of U.S. households. TCI, in turn, has allied with the independent cable-based ISP access service Cox@Home, which claims over 1 million subscribers *(http://home.excite.com)*. Microsoft invested in cable operator Comcast Corp., and AOL is waiting for government approval to acquire Time Warner cable.

Users of ordinary dial-up modems outnumbered users of broadband devices by over 16 to 1 in November 1999. As seen in Figure 1.20, it will be several years before broadband Internet access in any form becomes ubiquitous: The various technologies will be available in only 60% of the country by 2003, and even then only about a quarter of the population will use them. For more information on cable modems and other options, try the following Web sites:

- *http://www.multichannel.com/bband.shtml*

	Dial-up	% Total	DSL	% Total	Cable Modem	% Total
1999	34.38	94.5%	0.54	1.5%	1.47	4.0%
2000	40.78	89.5%	1.84	4.0%	2.94	6.5%
2001	46.72	83.7%	4.08	7.3%	4.99	8.9%
2002	51.19	78.7%	6.62%	10.2%	7.27%	11.2%
2003	55.40	72.8%	10.95	14.4%	9.78	12.8%

Figure 1-20.   Dial-up/DSL/cable modem market share, *http://www. emarketer.com/enews/052200_dialup.html.* Courtesy eMarketer, Inc.

- *http://www.iconocast.com/whatis/whatis.html*

- *http://cyberatlas.internet.com/big_picture/hardware/hardware_index.html*

Wireless Broadband

Generally, satellite-based Internet service, such as that from DirecPC *(http://www.DirecPC.com),* offers great download speed (400 Kbps), but constrains uploads to a 56 Kbps phone modem. Because of the upload problem, satellites cannot yet resolve the problem of Internet access for rural areas. For those who already have a satellite dish, the monthly cost of adding an ISP service may be competitive, but combined monthly service charges may really add up. For instance, DISH Network adds monthly fees for WebTV charges and personal video recorder service to its own monthly programming charges *(http://www.dishtelevision.com).*

Alternate High-Speed, Broadband Networks

Frustrated by the increasing commercialization of the Web, the explosion of sites and users, and subsequent slow transmission speeds, the military long ago created MILNET, a network independent of the Internet. In addition, some 60 corporations and academic institutions turned on the Abilene Project in February 1999.

In case you're thinking of joining this exclusive club, expect to pony up $100,000 for membership, a $20,000 annual participation fee, and another $25,000 for maintenance and overhead. For more about the future, check out

- The Abilene Project at *http://www.time.com/time/index.html*

- The internet2 Initiative at *http://www.internet2.edu*

- The Next Generation Internet Initiative (NGI) at *http://smithsonian.yahoo.com/nextgeneration.html*

Broadband Implications: Telephones, Teleconferencing, and Multimedia, Oh My!

High-speed, broadband connections increase expectations. Today's Web sites will be supplanted by multimedia messages with video, animation, and high-quality sound. The nature of computing could change, with users accessing software on the Web instead of installing applications on hard drives.

Internet phone calls and teleconferencing are beginning to reduce the cost of voice communication, as well as the need for business travel. Large companies such as Microsoft are already experimenting with extended teleconferences, offering **Webcasts** that include real-time video, prerecorded graphics and slides, and real-time text chat lines. From a marketing perspective, the changes in technology translate into

- The potential to attract new customers with sophisticated, value-added sites.

- New forms of product and service delivery with value-added features such as voice and video teleconferencing and live performances.

- New products and markets in the form of pay-per-use software applications, such as word processing and spreadsheets.

- More satisfied online customers, which implies more online sales.

Hand-Held, Wireless Devices

One of the most rapid changes in Internet access is narrowband transmission for hand-held devices containing a MiniBrowser that sees only sites written in **HDML** (handheld device mark-up language) or **WML** (wireless markup language). Wireless connections display minimal, but essential, information on the small screens of cell phones, two-way pagers, or Personal Digital Assistants, like the Palm Pilot, Pocket PC or Franklin Organizer. According to a study by IDC, more than 7 million users with some form of wireless device logged on in 1999; this could grow to over 60 million by 2005.

Internet providers are busy reformatting their content for time-dependent, location-dependent, mobile applications such as changing plane reservations, booking theater tickets, or sending an order to buy stock. Web sites must, of course, be redesigned and reformatted for these text-only applications, since there is neither the time nor the screen space to download graphics. Major Web sites seeking to position themselves at the top of the wireless click-list include Ticketmaster.com, Travelocity.com, and E-Trade. Amazon Anywhere and B&N.com's On the Go services aim at impulse shoppers, while Starbucks gratifies customers' cravings for a mocha cappuccino by pointing them to the closest outlet with a "store locator" service. Such sites are expected to generate additional revenue streams for wireless providers from advertising and transaction fees.

Naturally, partnerships and alliances have proliferated. Yahoo! has allied with Online Anywhere, whose products help deliver content to wireless devices, while a number of telecommunications carriers and hardware manufacturers are entering the fray. Microsoft's finger is in this pie, too: It has launched the Microsoft.NET initiative to transform the company's products into Internet-based services that can be accessed from any type of machine.

Ease of Use: Web Appliances

At the low end of the market, companies are competing to test whether a marriage of the Web and the tube can be made in cyberheaven. If the fusion advocates have their way, using the Internet will be as easy as sitting on your sofa, clicking your remote control to channel surf for a classic flick.

Internet TV products use a regular television set, a special Web terminal that sits on top of the TV, a standard phone jack, a remote control unit with a "Web" button, a subscription to an Internet TV service, and an optional wireless keyboard and/or printer adapter. Earlier forecasts for the year 2000 indicated that about 12 million households were expected to use Internet TV to reach the Web, although that number may be unrealistic given that 1999 saw a decline in users. There's a lot of revenue at stake: Digitrends *(http://www.digitrends.net)* projects that Internet TV revenues from subscriptions, e-commerce, and advertising could rise from $665 million in 2000 to $32.1 billion in 2006.

Some see Internet TV as an opportunity to create a new form of interactive entertainment; others see an endless version of the Home Shopping Show. But almost all Internet TV options envision direct tie-ins between television shows, their sponsors, and related Web sites, such as clicking on a TV guidebook, reading reviews, or checking out the Web site of a hit show. Internet TV users can surf the Web like a pro, join entertainment chat groups, read fan magazines online, send e-mail to their favorite star, and order any product advertised on TV that's available on the Web.

Made by Sony, Philips, Curtis-Mathes, and Mitsubishi, set-top terminals for Web browsing run $80 to $200, with $30 to $50 additional for the keyboard. The units contain a 1.1 GB (gigabyte) hard drive and modems to download special Web content during available intervals in television transmission. Subscriptions to one of the Internet TV services run $12 to $25 a month.

An alternative approach from Worldgate *(http://www.wgate.com)* blends the Internet and television by offering Internet service through a standard cable converter box and television remote. Faster to set up and less complicated than the options just discussed, Worldgate expects to be cheaper—$12 a month—without any additional equipment required. Of course, unless there are significant improvements in psychic technology, you'll still need a keyboard to type e-mail. Stay tuned.

Large companies are trying to cover all bases. In 1998 Microsoft bought WebTV, a service that has garnered 800,000 subscribers since its launch in 1996. About the same time, Internet rival America Online bought NetChannel, a competing Internet TV service. Just two years later Microsoft has joint ventured with Compaq to launch the iPaq Home Internet Appliance, a small unit with a built-in screen, to focus only on Web browsing, instant messaging and e-mail functions. Other Internet appliances priced below $300 that promise "plug-and-play" ease of use include

- Dedicated units for e-mail only, such as the MailStation from CIDCO and Vtech's e-mail Express and e-mail PostBox. These portable devices, which attach to a standard phone jack, sell for about $150, with $10/month for e-mail service.

- The new kitchen-focused Dot.Station from Intel, which integrates home organizing software with e-mail and Internet access.

- Advanced game boxes, such as Sega's Internet device that transforms its game players into Web TV.

For the Internet marketer, these Web appliances, which counted 1.1 million combined users in 1999, open the possibility of reaching a market somewhat different from those currently on the Web. When the price drops from a $600 computer to under $200, when the computer is as familiar as the TV, when the interface is simplified, advertisers take note.

First, these viewers will have absolutely no problem receiving multimedia content. In fact, they will expect it, once again ratcheting up the cost of Web presence and promotion. Second, the demographics of Internet users will change, bringing an audience to the Internet that is more diverse in income, age, education, and employment, an audience more reflective of the overall population than the current audience skew to high-end demographics. Third, forecasters predict a lifestyle in which households have multiple devices for multiple applications, essentially operating online all the time in many different rooms. For up-to-date news about what's happening with Internet TV, see such Internet information sites as *http://www.ruel.net/settop_news.html,* shown in Figure 1.21.

The Bottom Line

The array of online data in this chapter should convince you of several things: The Internet is here to stay, usage is growing, and the rate of change in the business world will only increase. Using data to enhance your marketing efforts may seem daunting, but it can help you achieve

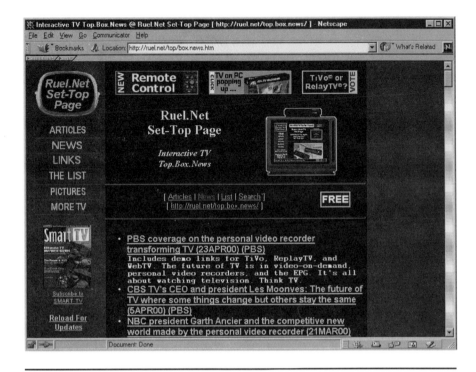

Figure 1.21. Internet TV information site, *http://www.ruel.net/top/box. news.htm.* © 1999-2000 Ruel T. Hernandez, *http://ruel.net* or *http://ruel.com.*

your business goals. As always, the most complex problems are really not technology based, but business based: finding your target market, turning prospects into customers, and keeping those customers as repeat buyers of your product or service. The Internet is just another method for solving those problems.

In the following chapters, you'll find more detail about how to evaluate and implement your Internet marketing options, from developing an Internet marketing plan (Chapter 2) to non-Web electronic marketing (Chapter 3) and designing an effective Web site (Chapter 4).

2

The ABCs of Internet Marketing

The Internet is at once an advertising medium, a form of sales literature, a distribution channel, a sales channel, a supplier chain, a method of customer service, and a source of operational cost savings. You should avoid the temptation to go online simply because everyone else is, but you also want to evaluate the potential benefits of the Web in the broadest possible way. To do that, you must have a clear understanding of your business goals.

Be creative and free-thinking in terms of what makes sense for your business. Molly's Manicures, with a clientele drawn from a single high-rise office building, might take advantage of the Web: Clients could schedule appointments online, saving Molly time on the telephone. A client could request a specialty nail polish so it will be in stock for her appointment, leading to greater customer satisfaction. The site could accept orders for glue-on nails with rhinestone studs and Molly could deliver in the building. By developing alliances with other shops in the same skyscraper, Molly may be able to extend her delivery service (and thus her revenues and profits) to include everything from dry cleaning or breakfast muffins to neck massages or birthday gifts that her busy clients don't have time to buy.

Of course, that kind of ambition means that you must think not only about a Web site, but about all the implications a site will have for your business, from personnel to inventory to strategic partnerships.

Then you can decide whether you want to join the 600,000 e-commerce small businesses already online. By the end of this chapter you will be familiar with

- The use of a business plan to help analyze your options.

- The importance of good business practices to online success.

- The seven steps to Internet success.

Your Business Plan: Internet and Otherwise

You do have a plan, don't you? A **business plan** is a written description of your business goals and how you will achieve them. If you don't have one, write at least a short draft before you go online. If your plan is sitting on a shelf, dust it off and update it. If you plan to start a new enterprise that exists only on the Internet or intend to seek investors for your dot-com start-up, it's absolutely critical to have a business plan.

For help with business plans, check out a Small Business Development Center (SBDC), generally located at a local community college. For the one nearest you, call the Small Business Administration (SBA) Answer Desk at 1-800-827-5722 or check out the SBA Web site *(http://www.sbaonline.sba.gov)* for this and other useful information for small businesses.

Obviously, the business plan for a Web-based purveyor of "cookie bouquets" will differ from the plan for a minority executive search firm. A producer of products for children of divorce needs to resolve different business issues than a factory-direct seller of hot tub covers, but they can all use the Internet to enhance their marketing. Look at their Web sites in Figures 2.1 through 2.4 to see how these businesses have taken advantage of the Internet's potential.

Many businesses write a plan only when they go to a bank to borrow money, but wise business owners write one annually as an internal gyroscope. They use the plan to set milestones for the coming year, to introduce a new product, or before entering another geographic (or virtual) territory.

If you are already in business, use the opportunity of revising your plan to evaluate critically what is currently working and what is not.

Figure 2.1.   Sample business Web site, *http://www.cookiebouquets.com.*
Courtesy Cookie Bouquets.

For instance, if you've been getting complaints about the slow shipment
of products, you need to find out whether the problem is order processing, the lack of goods in stock, a poor supplier, or a backlog in the
shipping department. Taking orders electronically might only compound
these problems.

Do you do any advertising or other marketing? If not, you have lots of
company: A recent survey found that 91% of small businesses rely solely
on word of mouth and referrals for customers. If you start advertising online,
will be you able to handle additional business? Would you need to expand
a manufacturing facility or contract with a fulfillment house?

Are you currently facing a competitor with deep pockets who can
afford to undersell you? Profit margins are under enormous pressure on
the Web. In the crowded and competitive cyber-marketplace, small businesses are particularly vulnerable as larger, more traditional companies
get online with the financial resources to produce sophisticated Web

Figure 2.2. Sample business Web site, *http://www.minorityexecsearch.com*. Courtesy Minority Executive Search, Inc.

sites and to advertise heavily for online customers. You just have to be a smarter guerrilla marketer and be savvy when selecting cyber-niches. Work the numbers to ensure that you will be able to make a profit online. This old-fashioned concept applies even in the new economy!

Understanding the problems you already face is essential before deciding whether the Internet would help overcome them or would merely magnify them. The Internet is not a panacea for other business difficulties, nor is it a get-rich-quick scheme. For that, stick to late-night infomercials. However, if you stick to the basics below, you can overcome all obstacles:

- Plan carefully.

- Pay attention to how this new medium can help you meet your business goals.

Figure 2.3. Sample business Web site, *http://www.mytwohomes.com*. Courtesy LadyBug Press.

- Understand how an online presence will affect your overall business operations.

For additional small business assistance, try these Web sites:

- *http://www.SmallBizPlanet.com*

- *http://www.onvia.com*

- *http://www.wilsonweb.com*

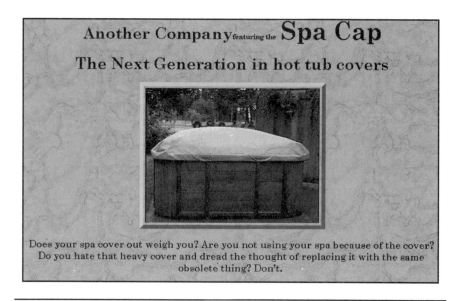

Figure 2.4. Sample business Web site, *http://www.spacap.com.* Courtesy Another Company.

Elements of a Business Plan

The content of a business plan may vary with the type of business, but it generally includes the following sections, which should be preceded by a brief Executive Summary:

1. Mission/type of business (e.g., manufacturing, wholesale, retail, catalog, service) and goals

2. Description of product or service

3. Competition

4. Marketing

   a. Target market (customer description or demographics)

    b. Why there's a market for your product or service and market size in customers and dollars

    c. Your objectives in terms of market penetration and revenue

    d. Marketing strategy and methods, including positioning vis-à-vis the competition and your competitive edge

    e. Promotion and advertising strategy (online and offline)

5. Sales plan

    a. Pricing

    b. Distribution channels, including any issues raised by selling online

    c. Sales methods (e.g., sales force, agents, reps, telemarketing, Web)

    d. Order fulfillment process

6. Operations

    a. Facilities (e.g., location, size, equipment) including status of space, access, hours

    b. Manufacturing methods (if applicable)

    c. Raw materials or inventory needed and suppliers

    d. Customer service and support

    e. Staff, including numbers and types of employees and hiring plans

7. Management and Financial

    a. Resumes of key management and time available, including board members or other advisers if applicable

b. Any legal, licensing, zoning, code requirements, insurance issues, etc.

c. Sources of funding and how funds will be spent

d. Financial statements (current, if any)

e. Projected revenues and expenses (one to five years) and break-even analysis

The Internet itself can help you write your business plan. For instance, through online research you might find new suppliers who could give you a better price, just-in-time delivery, or higher-quality goods. You could check whether the Internet has created new competition. With manufacturers, wholesalers, and retailers all selling on the Web, distribution channels—and price points—are shifting rapidly. You may need to adjust sales projections accordingly. You can use the Web to conduct a cyber-focus group to explore the opinions of your customers with a moderated online chat session. One company *http://www.cyberdialogue.com*) even specializes in recruiting participants and moderating such sessions.

Is the Internet Right for Your Business?

What kinds of businesses work on the Web? All kinds: genealogy search services (*http://www.itw.ie/roots*), career and outplacement (*http://careerlab.com/letters/default.htm*), private investigators , reference support (*http://www.surfchina.com*), coupon services (*http://www.ecentives.com*), crafts (*http://www.origamido.com*), gifts (*http://www.candlelightgifts.com*).

If you're thinking of starting a computer-based, virtual company but not sure what you want to do, try browsing through such lists as Work-at-Home Ideas on the news group biz.general. (See Chapter 3 for more information on news groups.)

You Can Do Much More Than Sell Online

Selling electronically instead of through a print catalog is usually the first thought that comes to mind with the Internet, but you can do much more. The marketing section of your Internet business plan may reflect many other goals:

- Increasing brand or product awareness

- Enhancing corporate image

- Achieving market leadership

- Providing information and/or displaying samples of goods or services

- Generating a list of prospective customers

- Building loyal relationships with customers

- Improving customer service

- Gathering information about customer needs and preferences to guide future product development

- Improving knowledge of customer demographics

- Testing consumer response to discounts or other special offers

- Finding strategic business partners, dealers, franchisees, or suppliers

- Recruiting employees, members, subscribers, or investors

- Saving money through automation, simplified distribution channels, reduced cost of order fulfillment, or smaller inventories.

The goals you select determine which methods you will use, Internet or otherwise. As seen in the survey in Figure 2.5, companies view their sites as multipurpose in nature. Only 30% originally saw selling products or services directly as one of the reasons for building their Web site. However, nearly twice that number ended up with increased sales (even if offline). Although only 10% project decreased costs, more than half the companies experience that.

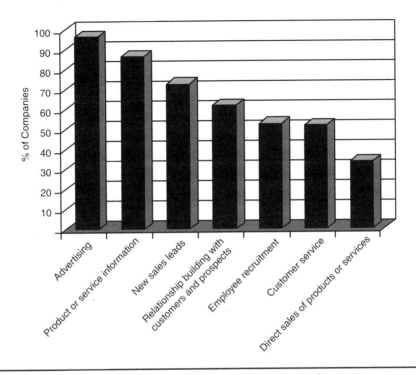

Figure 2.5. Purposes of corporate Web sites, *http://www.barometer surveys.com*. Courtesy Pricewaterhouse Coopers' "Trendsetter Barometer."

Your plan should determine what will constitute successful completion of your goals, at least in broad terms. Whenever possible, quantify those successes—for example, $25,000 in sales over the first year, 600 people a day learning about your business on the Web, speeding order fulfillment by two days, obtaining six new bookings as a wedding photographer, or hiring three new employees.

Essential Questions

Still uncertain whether the Web is right for your company? Ask yourself these questions:

1. Worried that your business is local in nature? That's not necessarily a deterrent; local sites now draw Web audiences for information and customer support.

2. Does your business depend on face-to-face contact with customers? Can you rethink it to add new services like The Shoe Guy.com (*http://www.shoeguy.com*, shown in Figure 2.6)?

3. Could you benefit from a national or global reach?

4. Do you have an unusual product or service that's difficult for customers to find?

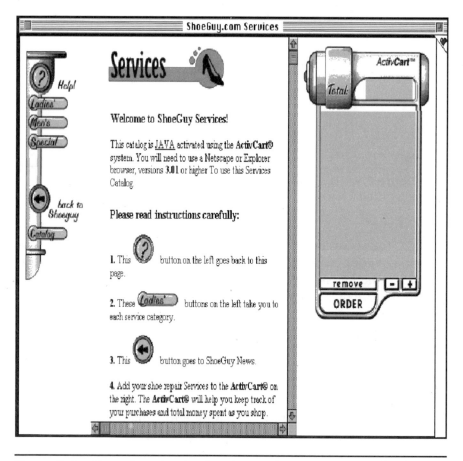

Figure 2.6. Unusual service site, *http://www.shoeguy.com/topserv.html.* Courtesy Shoeguy.com.

5. Can your product ship by mail or courier service? Can you provide some aspect of your service online?

6. Are your customers able and willing to use the Internet to obtain support or information?

Here's the ultimate question: Will an investment in Internet marketing pay off by increasing the value of your company? If the answer to that question is still no, then satisfy your Web cravings as a buyer, not a seller.

The Importance of Good Business Practices

Stories of easy dollars flowing in Internet commerce may leave you fantasizing about the cyberwealth of Bill Gates, or at least of Midas. The media may glorify Web winners, but business online is not all a bed of virtual roses.

For instance, if you can't fulfill customer orders promptly, you may easily go through cyber-crisis, as too many businesses found out with the $7 billion crush of online orders in Christmas 1999. Amazon.com, Barnes & Noble, and Toys R Us all had well-publicized problems processing orders online and making timely delivery. Surveys show the season took a toll. According to e-BuyersGuide.com, only 78% of Web shoppers were satisfied, compared to 97% of mall shoppers.

In our time-deprived society, customers shop online for convenience not price, as you can see in Figure 2.7 from a Department of Commerce survey conducted in 1998 (*http://www.ecommerce.gov/emerging.htm*). Consequently, poor performance that interferes with convenience is a sure way to lose a customer. Sites that make their products hard to find, forcing people to go through page after page on the Web, are just as discouraging as stores with similar products scattered across several departments on different floors.

If purchasing data and credit card information gathered online is not kept private and secure, customers will lose confidence about shopping in cyberspace, just as they would if their credit card numbers were stolen after charging dinner at a local restaurant.

Perhaps worst of all, Jupiter Communications found that 46% of sites surveyed didn't provide adequate customer response to e-mail,

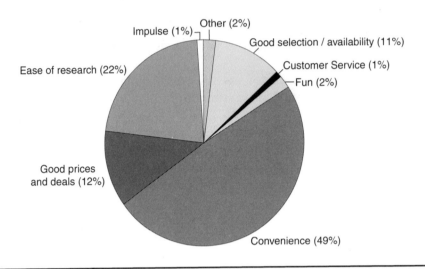

Figure 2.7.   Best thing about online shopping, *http://www.ecommerce.gov/danc5.htm.*

taking five or more days to answer, blowing off e-mail inquiries alto-gether, or neglecting to post an e-mail address. What a waste! Seventy percent of all incoming calls to small business are about price, avail-ability, and order status. Setting up a Web site and handling e-mail could actually cut customer service costs instead of increasing cus-tomer frustration.

The implications are clear: If you plan to sell online, you need to focus on service to attract and keep customers. There's nothing new about that. Figure 2.8 describes the top 10 problems people experience with online shopping; make sure your business plan shows how you can resolve them!

If you are selling, consider in advance how you will fulfill increased orders promptly. In addition to personnel issues, do you have access to the needed inventory or the space to store it? Can you arrange just-in-time contracts or drop-shipping with your suppliers? Can you process orders more efficiently? Can you meet price pressure on the Web? Will you be able to renegotiate pricing with your suppliers? Cut costs else-where? Do your forecasts show that you can increase volume to coun-teract a smaller profit margin?

As you experiment online, don't stop marketing your products and services in ways that currently gain sales. If you succeed online, you may

Problem	% of Internet Buyers
Gift wanted to purchase was out of stock	64%
Product was not delivered on time	40%
Paid too much for delivery	38%
Connection or download trouble	36%
Didn't receive confirmation or status report on purchase	28%
Selections were limited	27%
Web site difficult to navigate	26%
Web site didn't provide information needed to make purchase	25%
Prices not competitive	22%
Site didn't offer enough gift ideas	16%

Figure 2.8. Top 10 problems experienced by Internet shoppers, *http://cyberatlas.internet.com/markets/retailing/article/0,1323,6061_278991,00.html. Reprinted with permission.* © 2000 Internet.com, LLC. All rights reserved.

decide to shift your marketing mix or to open an all-online division, but wait for proof. In the meantime, keep doing what works. As you'll see throughout this book, a well-conceived Internet marketing strategy will complement your traditional marketing efforts and vice versa.

The Seven Steps to Internet Success

With your business goals in writing, you can start building a detailed online marketing plan that will increase your chances for success. As with any other form of marketing, the old maxim holds: Plan your work, work your plan.

There are seven important steps to success:

1. Get online and observe.

2. Evaluate your current situation.

3. Define online objectives, products, and markets.

4. Create and distribute info-tools.

5. Create or upgrade your Web site.

6. Measure your results.

7. Market your Internet presence.

We'll discuss the first three steps in this chapter, with a brief over-view of the remaining four.

Step 1: Get Online and Observe

It's time for research that won't ever go to waste. By obtaining feedback from your electronic marketing experiments, you'll learn for yourself the best way to reach your target audience. Once you have customer information, including e-mail addresses, you can develop extremely per-sonalized, targeted marketing campaigns to inform potential customers of products they might find appealing or of discounts available. You can solicit customers' input on future product design or enlist them in test marketing special promotions.

Let's get a feel for the way information, advertising, and sales move across the Internet. This may confirm your instincts, or it may lead you to change your plans.

First check out the online services, such as AOL or CompuServe, with one of those ubiquitous offers of free service. Evaluate how com-panies advertise and how they place their ads. Are they catching users with a special offer when they first sign on? Does a display ad pop up on the viewing screen? What types of ads appear on a news page? On a search page? Can you figure out whom these advertisers are trying to reach?

See how companies provide customer support through online ser-vices. What would you need to do to provide support this way? Look at the electronic shopping malls like the one in Figure 2.9. What would you have to do to showcase your product?

Now go to an online forum in your area of interest, whether it is computer hardware or travel. Observe the chat groups. Sign up with several mailing lists and see what kind of mail you receive.

Know Thy Business Universe

You need to gauge the electronic savvy of your business universe in every direction. Start by surfing the Web to review good sites. Analyze

Figure 2.9. AOL shopping mall, *http://shopping.aol.com/office/ communications.adp*. AOL screenshot © 2000 America Online, Inc. Used with permission.

sites that appear on the Cool Links or HotSite lists at such locations as *http://www.coolcentral.com*. Your goal is to educate yourself about the variety of Web sites, to develop an eye for the designs you find appealing. As you explore, bookmark the sites you like and the sites you don't like; it will save you a great deal of time downstream.

Target your competitors' Web sites to analyze the methods they use to communicate with customers. Just because they are online, doesn't mean they are turning a profit! One of the most famous business stories on the Web, Amazon.com (*http://www.amazon.com*) doesn't project profits until 2002 and has just laid off 150 employees.

Third, research your suppliers to see how many of them are on the Internet. You may find a potential for comarketing or other business opportunities. You might find potential links to and from your site, or identify other Web sites that would refer potential customers to you in exchange for a small commission.

Finally, compare the target audience described in your business plan to the profile of online users described later. If you sell to other businesses, see if those customers have an electronic presence. Remember, the really big story in Internet commerce is business-to-business selling, which accounts for triple the revenue of retail sales.

If your customers aren't using the Internet, should you be there? This isn't an automatic no, but it should make you pause. Consider whether online marketing is important to other target audiences, such as suppliers, potential employees, or possible business partners.

Is your target audience more likely to use the Internet at work or at home? Currently, about 46% of American users access the Internet from home and 54% access it from work. Typically, at-work users have faster Internet connections than home users, who rely on dial-up services.

If you don't know how your audience accesses the Internet, ask them! A simple process like randomly calling some existing customers can give you critical information. What Internet services besides the Web do your customers use: E-mail? News groups? Do they subscribe to mailing lists? Use AOL or CompuServe? If you don't have customers yet, you can still make simple research calls to define your target audience. If you need more information, include some enticement for customer response and/or completion of a short survey. Consider a giveaway or a discount coupon that can be used online or off.

Know Thy Target Audience

There were over 78 million Internet users over the age of 18 in the United States in 1999, representing 39% of all adults. Worldwide, there are over 200 million users, with some projections reaching 375 million by the end of the year, over 6% of the planet's inhabitants. The amount of time spent online is shown in Figure 2.10, with about 60% of users spending more than 10 hours per week. One-fifth to one-quarter of users go online daily.

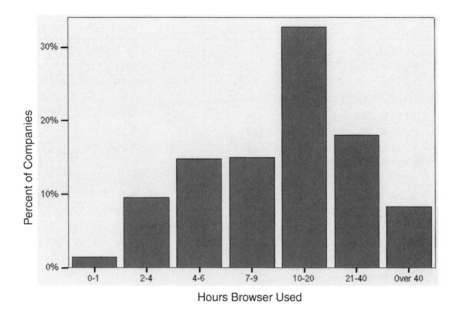

Figure 2.10. Time spent online, *http://www.gvu.gatech.edu/user_surveys/ survey-1998-04/graphs/user/q20.jpg.* © 1994-1998 Georgia Tech Research Corporation. All rights reserved. Source: GVU's WWW User Survey at *www. gvu.gatech.edu/user_surveys.*

No Internet demographic study is 100% reliable because everything changes so rapidly. With that caveat, consider the statistics seen in the table in Figure 2.11, which compares Web users with the general U.S. adult population. While educational and income statistics for Internet/ Web users still exceed those of the population as a whole, these statistics have shifted over time as the online community comes to more closely mirror the overall population.

Only 23% of the overall population had a household income over $75,000 in 1999; 40% of long-term Internet users did. Importantly, 50% more households earning below $25,000 a year are online than a year ago. Those online outdistanced the percent of the population with some college attendance by 75% to 48%.

Figure 2.12 shows the distribution of the U.S. online population by age. You can count on one thing: The participation of every age group

	All U.S. Adults	Web Users*	Index**
TOTAL	198.4 MILLION	78.2 MILLION	100
Male	%48	%51	106
Female	%52	%49	95
HOUSEHOLD INCOME			
$150,000 or more	%4	%7	195
$100,000-$149,999	%8	%15	184
$75,000-$99,999	%11	%18	164
$50-000-$74,999	%21	%26	128
$30,000-$49,999	%23	%20	84
$20,000-$29,999	%13	%7	50
Less than $20,000	%20	%7	34
Median	$44,038	$65,778	
EDUCATION			
Postgraduate	%7	%14	193
Bachelor's degree	%15	%26	171
Attend college	%26	%35	134
High school grad	%34	%21	62
Did not graduate H.S.	%18	%4	22
OCCUPATION			
Professional, manager	%20	%37	184
Technical, clerical, sales	%19	%26	140
Craft, precision production	%7	%6	85
Other	%19	%13	68
Not employed, retired	%35	%18	50
MARITAL STATUS			
Single	%24	%27	117
Married	%57	%62	108
Divorced, other	%19	%11	56

*Accessed the Web in the past 30 hours.
**e.g., An index of 106 means Web surfers are 6% more likely to be male, compared with U.S. adults overall.

Figure 2.11. Demographics of Internet users, Fall 1999. Mediamark Research, Inc. at *www.mediamark.com*.

is increasing. Some numbers may surprise you. Users 55 and over are the fastest growing segment on the Internet; they comprise about 12% of U.S. Web users. About 43% of this age group, which includes the

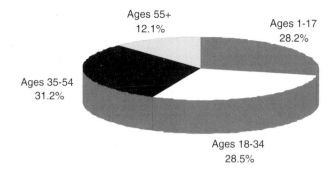

Figure 2.12. 1999 U.S. Internet user population by age, *http://www. emarketer.com/estats?sell_euu.html*. Courtesy eMarketer, Inc.

baby boomers, will be online by 2003. For sites devoted to seniors, you might want to target

- Elder Web: *http://www.elderweb.com* (information resources)

- Elderhostel: *http://www.elderhostel.org* (educational programs)

- Generation A: *http://www.generationA.com* (sophisticated content)

- MatureMart: *http://www.maturemart.com* (senior shopping site)

- Next 50: *http://www.next50.com* (information and news)

- Senior Net: *http://www.seniornet.com* (computer training site)

- Senior Sites: *http://www.seniorsites.com* (nonprofit services)

- Senior.com: *http://www.senior.com* (information resources)

- SeniorMart: *http://www.seniormart.com* (senior shopping site)

- Seniors.com: *http://www.seniors.com* (variety of topics)

If there are seniors online, there are kids and teens galore! The number of 1- to 17-year-olds online—now 25 million—has tripled since 1997 and is expected to double again by 2005. With teenage girls the fastest growing age group online, girls are now logging on as much as or more often than boys, although they visit different sites once online. A number of sites are taking aim at the increasing online presence of preteen and teenage females:

- *http://www.Cosmogirl.com*

- *http://www.Blink182.com*

- *http://www.dELiAs.com*

- *http://www.gurlmail.com*

- *http://www.seventeen.com*

- *http://www.smartgirl.com*

- *http://www.teenpople.com*

- *http://www.spacegirl.org*

Most significantly, the adult gender gap has closed: Slightly over half of Internet users are female, up from 38% in 1996 and from 5% only six years ago, although men go online more often and for more hours. Furthermore, women have become the driving force in Internet buying, comprising 63% of consumers who shop online more than once a week. Women are more utilitarian than men, returning to sites that save them time and money, rather than surfing many different sites.

The increasing number of women signifies one of the most important trends for Internet marketers, since women traditionally control household budgets. They are responsible for 70% of all retail sales and 80% of sales of personal and household goods. Undoubtedly, these statistics were in the minds of those who created three of the major Web sites aimed at women:

- *http://www.ivillage.com*

- *http://www.oxygen.com/*

- *http://www.women.com*

iVillage, which went public in March 1999, counts NBC among its investors. Oxygen Media (as seen in Figure 2.13), the umbrella name for several sites (Moms Online, Breakup Girl, Thrive, ka-Ching) with a direct tie-in to a cable channel of the same name, has funding from AOL, Disney/ABC TV, and Oprah Winfrey's media machine. Hearst Corporation (Redbook and Cosmopolitan magazines) backs Women.com.

These sites are not slouches, but they joined other venture-funded dot-coms in the Spring 2000 stock downturn. Although nearly 4 million women log onto these sites each month (over 10% of all women online), women seem to use these sites for information and a sense of

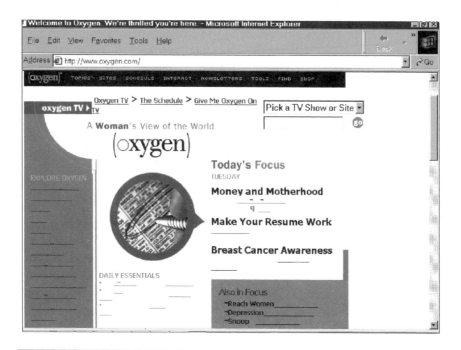

Figure 2.13. Web site aimed at women, *http://www.oxygen.com*. Courtesy Oxygen Media, Inc.

community, not for buying. That's bad news for sites that earn most of their revenue from advertising, but not surprising: It's rare to find a profitable ad-driven site. Some smaller women-oriented sites are doing better financially:

- *http://www.womenswire.com*

- *http://www.chickclick.com* (a Web ring that includes the "grrls" sites that follow)

- *http://www.webgrrls.com*

- *http://www.cybergrrl.com*

- *http://www.feminista.com*

- *http://www.hissyfit.com*

- *http://www.femina.cybergrrl.com* (a search engine for women)

Keep in mind that women and men tend to look for different things online. Women seek health and religious information or research jobs online, while men prefer news, sports, and financial information.

One word of dismay: The Internet does not look like the world when it comes to race. Web users are overwhelmingly white, as seen in Figure 2.14. The "World White Web," as one AP writer called it, is a serious problem.

Whites in America are twice as likely to own a computer and more than three times as likely to have Internet access as African-Americans or Hispanics. According to a 1999 report from the U.S. Department of Commerce, "Falling Through the Net: Defining the Digital Divide," this racial disparity is not just a matter of income. To deal with these discrepancies, the federal government has adopted several initiatives to make low-cost Internet access available in rural, low-income, and minority communities. A number of large corporations, including Ford Motor Company and Delta Air Lines, have started to give all their employees—including blue collar workers—free home PCs with Internet access to encourage their participation in the new economy (and make them more productive workers at the same time).

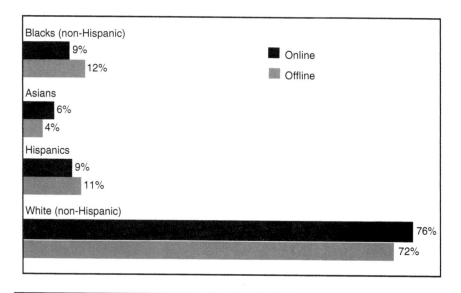

Figure 2.14. Distribution of ethnic groups within online population. Data from U.S. Census Bureau, 2000. Courtesy: eMarketer, Inc.

To reach an African-American audience, you might want to search out such sites as

- African American Internetwork (*http://www.africanamerican.com*), the first publicly traded African-American content site

- Africana (*http://www.africana.com*)

- AfroNet (*http://www.afronet.com*)

- BlackEntertainment Television (*http://www.BET.com*), which has funding from Microsoft, three major media companies, and two major black organizations. It offers content similar to its companion cable channel, with black celebrities, health, food, and finances, and sells products like books and music by black artists.

- Black Planet (*http://www.blackplanet.com*)

- Blackvoices (*http://www.blackvoices.com*)

- Melinin (*http://www.melinin.com*)

- NetNoir (*http://www.netnoir.com*)

If your audience is Hispanic, you might want to focus your commercial online service efforts on Prodigy, which offers a Spanish-language Internet access service ($19.95 per month), or AOL's newly launched AOL Mexico. Both hope to bridge the language barriers that have the kept the number of Hispanics online low (see Figure 2.14).

New Hispanic-oriented portals and sites have started to spring up. Check out

- Advancing Women: *http://www.advancingwomen.com/hispbiz.html*

- Hispanic Business: *http://www.hispanicbiz.com*

- Hispanic Business Magazine: *http://www.hispanstar.com/hb/default.asp*

- HispanicDotCom: *http://www.hispanic.com* (B2B links and experts)

- Hispano: *http://www.hispano.com* (professional job market

- Latin World: *http://www.latinworld.com* (Hispanic search engine, including kids' sites)

- Latino Link: *http://www.latinolink.com* (news, email, entertainment)

- Latino.com: *http://www.latino.com*

- Latino World Market: *http://www.latinoworldmarket.com*

- Que Pasa: *http://www.quepasa.com* (portal)

- Saludos Hispanos: *http://www.saludos.com* (employment service)

- Star Media: *http://www.starmedia.com* (worldwide Spanish and Portuguese site)

- U.S. Hispanic Chamber: *http://www.ushcc.com*

Other companies with Spanish services generally focus on Latin America, although the content, being virtual, is available in the United States. Star Media, out of New York and AOL's joint venture with a Venezuelan company both serve that market. AOL also has launched in Argentina and Brazil.

Although Asian Americans participate actively online, they have relatively few ethnic portals like Asian Avenue. Native Americans lag farthest behind in Internet use, particularly rural tribes with limited telephone access. Only 56% of households on Indian reservations have a phone, compared to 94% of households nationwide; on sparsely populated reservations like the Navajo, phone usage ranges around 22%. A government initiative to provide basic telephone service to reservations will be supplemented by money, training, and equipment from the high-tech industry.

Step 2: Evaluate Your Current Situation

With online research animating your brain, evaluate your current situation. Do you fully understand where your customers congregate on the Internet, the best way to reach them, the best way to deliver to them, and how to support the sale? If your research shows that it makes sense to start marketing online, look closely at the various methods available to you for achieving the marketing goals and objectives in your business plan. Which methods will work best for each goal? Make a list of both electronic and nonelectronic means. If you want, organize this material in a chart, with your goals along the side. Check off the appropriate methods for achieving each one, as seen in Figure 2.15.

Remember that marketing on the Internet may be faster and cheaper in absolute dollars than traditional bulk mail, but it is not always as cost-effective. Evaluate whether online niche marketing fits your business plan, as it does for the Red Hen Turf seen in Figure 2.16 (*http://www.redhenturf.com*). Test promotion costs offline versus online by

Possible Marketing Goal	Online Mailing Lists	News Groups	Direct E-mail	Online Services	Web
Build Customer List					
Display Sample of Goods or Services					
Enhance Corporate Image					
Find Business Partners, Dealers, or Franchisees					
Gather Customer Preferences					
Improve Customer Service					
Improve Supplier Relations/Performance					
Increase Brand/Name Awareness					
Obtain Better Demographic Information					
Product Development and Testing					
Recruit Employees, Members, or Subscribers					
Research Competitors, Marketplace, Suppliers					
Sell Goods or Services					
Test Consumer Responses to Marketing Offers					
Understand Customer Needs					

Figure 2.15. Online marketing worksheet.

trying a similar promotion using both methods. You may find that not enough of your customers use the Internet or that your true clientele is local, not international. It is tempting to avoid dealing with printers, mailing houses, bulk mail regulations, and the post office, but coping with a poor ISP, bugs in Web page programming, and slow Internet access can be just as aggravating.

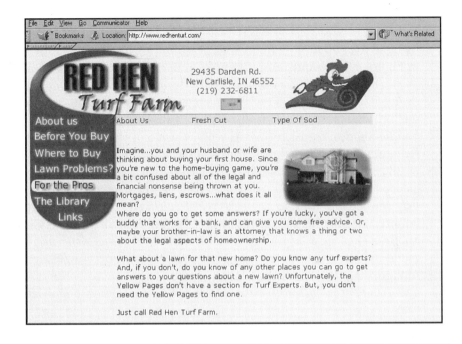

Figure 2.16. An unlikely business to find on the Web, *http://www.redhen turf.com*. Courtesy Stand Out Solutions.

There is a simple alternative to running your own site: online auctions. You can work either side of the auction equation, buying goods or selling your products through an existing retail auction site. This has proved to be an excellent way for small businesses to test pricing on a new product or to liquidate discontinued stock.

Some predictions for auction dollar volume go as high as $129 billion in 2002—about one third of all Internet commerce—with 70% of that in the business-to-business auction markets. These optimistic estimates are based on the Web's unique ability to link a critical mass of buyers and sellers in real time to establish market-driven prices on a dynamic basis. Many small businesses find that auctions are a good first step online: Some 670,000 small businesses either buy or sell this way already, with 1 million expected to participate by 2000.

To see if becoming an "auction-preneur" is for you, head for one of the big sites, such as *http://auctions.yahoo.com*, its recently launched competition on Amazon.com, or the pioneering auction site eBay, Inc.

at *http://www.ebay.com*. eBay is now worth more than $7 billion, and has sold over 60 million items since its founding in 1995. The site, shown in Figure 2.17, counts more than 7.7 million registered auction addicts. Typically, eBay collects a listing fee of 25 cents to $2 and a commission of 1.25% to 5% on every completed transaction. In a later chapter, we'll discuss software that allows you to set up your own Web site to handle auction transactions, as well as some of the problems that arise from unscreened matches between buyers and sellers.

B2B auction sites like Surplus Direct (formerly Egghead Software as seen in Figure 2.18) at *http://www.surplusdirect.com,* BidCom at *http://www.bid.com*, and OnSale at *http://www.onsale.com* offer discounted or surplus computer and office equipment. Industry-specific auction sites now abound, such as *http://www.metalsite.net* for the metal industry or *http://www.gofish.com* for seafood wholesalers (seen in Figure 2.19). Traditional surplus auctioneers, such as Norman Levy and Associates (*http://www.nlainc.com*) or the Defense Department's

Figure 2.17. eBay auction site, *http://www.ebay.com*. Courtesy eBay, Inc.

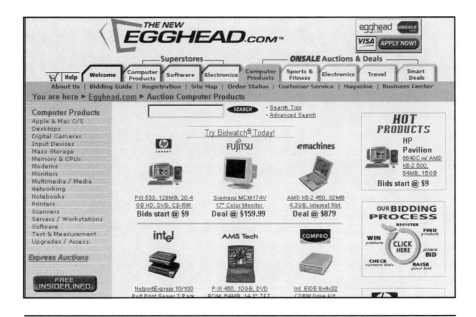

Figure 2.18. Sample business-to-business discount site, *http://www.surplus direct.com.* Courtesy Egghead.com, Inc.

surplus disposal site at *http://www.drms.dla.mil,* also post auction opportunities online.

Step 3: Define Online Objectives, Products, and Markets

Conservatively assess what quantitative objectives you want to achieve and in what order, given what you have learned. Be very specific in defining each of these categories. As with almost any new project, it makes sense to start in a small way and then expand your efforts as you learn what works. For instance, you may decide to establish an online presence for six months before selling your product.

If you are going to sell, select one or two items from your product line to start. If possible, pick a product with a successful and reliable sales history through direct response marketing, thus removing one of the variables in your online marketing experiment. Later, you can expand to hundreds of products or put your entire catalog on line.

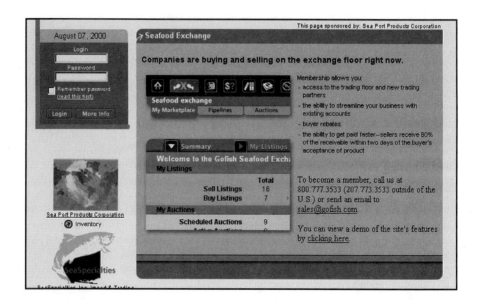

Figure 2.19. Sample commodity auction site, *http://www.gofish.com/cgi-bin/ WebObjects/Gofish.woa.* Courtesy Gofish.com.

By the same token, if you want to expand your corporate presence, think what aspect of your company is best portrayed through the Web. With multimedia capabilities, it's possible to showcase everything from musical talent to video histories. Consider the geographic area in which you want to provide your service. Decide whether you can or should create an auxiliary product, such as an audio CD for customers located too far away to hire your jazz trio to play at their next Christmas party.

If you don't receive at least minimal interest after three months, whether measured in terms of unique visitors to your Web site or online sales, you may need to rethink your approach. Perhaps your Web design isn't drawing the audience you expect. Perhaps people have not found your site and you need to expand your online and offline promotion efforts. If you're getting hits but not making sales online, perhaps your retail prices are too high for this electronic location. Alternately, perhaps others too easily match your product or you haven't asked for the sale effectively.

Step 4: Create and Distribute Info-Tools

To succeed online, you will need to restructure existing promotional material or create new materials to meet the Internet's insatiable demand for information. In many cases, the marketing value of a site comes from perceiving your company as a source of useful information, completely independent of point-of-sale activity.

In addition, you will need to publicize your site to ensure that large numbers of Web surfers continually learn about you, whether through search engines, What's Hot lists, news groups, mailing lists, or direct e-mail. As you'll see in Chapter 3, info-tools can be short messages, reports, books, newsletters, or excerpts from longer works.

Whether you have a new way of making peanut butter or sell an old-fashioned item like paper clips, tell people about your product with an interesting, informative angle. Describe how to make the world's longest paper clip chain, or list 1001 things that can be made from recycled peanut shells. Find a way to make your business sound fresh to the world, or at least new to the Internet universe. Graphic versions of text-based info-tools can later be placed on your Web site.

One company that successfully uses such tools is Wine.com (*http:// www.wine.com*), which provides ever-changing information from trivia to serious discussions of oenology as shown in the right-hand column of their site in Figure 2.20.

Step 5: Create or Upgrade Your Web Site

How do you develop a site that will work well for you? Do you do it yourself or get help? In most cases, unless you have preexisting technical sophistication or can utilize a prepackaged template, you're better off contracting with a Web designer to create your site and a Web hosting service to maintain it. To manage more than a simple home page in-house, you may need a local area network, server hardware and software, a high-speed connection to the Internet, and access to technical support, including a Web programmer, a graphic artist, and an MIS (management information system) specialist to oversee the project.

As you'll see, there is plenty for you to do on the business side, even when you hire an outside Web designer and Web hosting service provider.

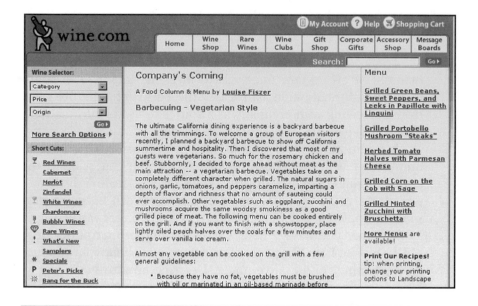

Figure 2.20.   Site using info tools, *http://www.wine.com/company/companys_coming.shtml.* Courtesy Wine.com, Inc.

Often, one facility will offer both: More than 85% of Web hosts currently provide some type of site design as a value-added service.

Anything truly valuable takes time or money to develop—often both. As a guideline, the average cost for building an introductory static Web site in 1999 was about $5,000. (There are less-expensive alternatives; many Web hosts offer free, template-based Web site development when you sign up to use them as your host.) Typical retail and B2B sites started in the mid-$20,000s. Straightforward e-commerce Web sites averaged $37,000, with B2C sites selling exclusively online averaging $68,000. Media and portal sites ran $10,000 more. These numbers are exclusive of ongoing costs, such as Web hosting, which start at $16 to $45 per month plus setup fees for a simple, small site. And of course, the costs of maintaining, monitoring, and promoting a site, and handling additional customer demands are additional.

Interactivity is one of the most intriguing possibilities in Web site development. You can move your viewer through your site towards a "buy" decision by having them take specific actions. Consider the interactive materials calculator at *http://www.todayshomeowner.com/calcu-*

lators/index.html, the Kitchen Arranger on the Better Homes and Gardens site (*http://www.bhg.com/kpg*) or the Room Planner at the Herman Miller office furniture site seen in Figure 2.21 (*http://www. hmstore.com/planner/index.html*).

In Chapters 4 and 5 we'll talk about these and other ways to develop a Web site that keeps viewers on your site and brings them back for return visits.

Step 6: Monitoring Your Results

There is no way to discover whether you have met the goals of your plan unless you build in measurement methods. In Chapter 6 you'll learn about specific services that are available through your Web host or other companies to measure precisely how well your Web site is working.

Everyone thinks about counting simple **hits** (total number of times any file on a site is accessed), but it may be more valuable to know how many unique visitors reached your site. You might also want to track how long people stay on your site, the path they follow through it, and whether they return. You will certainly want to know how they reach you (referral links) and which specific pages interest them.

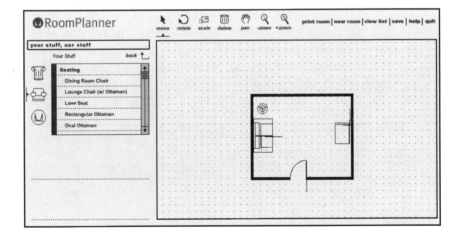

Figure 2.21. Interactive online tool (room planner), *http://www.hmstore.com/ planner/index.html*. Courtesy Herman Miller, Inc. Herman Miller for the Home.

Sites that accept advertising should be able to track both the number of visitors who see each ad and those who actually link to your site from the ad. All major services and **portals** (large Web sites used as a launching pad for other sites) offer sophisticated demographic analysis of their users. (A list of portals is found in Figure 2.22.)

Automated statistical tools are available only for the Web. For e-mail and mailing lists, you have to maintain your own records of responses to posted or e-mailed information.

If you are selling online, be sure to track the source, amount, and item number(s) of each sale. This enables you to compute your cost of sales more accurately and to compare the value of selling online with the value of selling through other methods, such as traditional mail catalogs.

Step 7: Market Your Internet Presence

No matter how successful a Web site you create, you must attract people to it. It does you no good to have the best site on the Web if no one knows how or why to find you. One of the most important parts of successful marketing on the Internet is achieving exposure amid overwhelming amounts of information. The Web is such a busy intersection on the Information Superhighway that you have to tell potential visitors which way to turn.

To get the maximum effect from your online marketing, all other advertising in print media, TV, or radio should mention your Web address. This offline supplement to your Web presence lets the world know you are an electronic player, thus making a statement about your company's involvement in contemporary technology.

Web addresses now appear everywhere in all kinds of advertising. You might expect Mitsubishi to advertise its URL in Newsweek, but did

http://www.yahoo.com	http://www.go.com
http://www.northernlight.com	http://www.AOL.com
http://magellan.excite.com	http://www.netcenter.com
http://www.hotbot.com	http://www.altavista.com
http://www.galaxy.com	http://www.infoseek.com
http://www.webcrawler.com	http://www.excite.com
http://www.net-find.com	http://www.lycos.com
http://www.snap.com	

Figure 2.22. Major portals on the Internet.

you realize that over 70% of the ads in American's top 50 magazines use URLs or e-mail to drive traffic to the Web? Just look at the statistics in Figure 2.23. Be sure to place your Internet address on your letterhead, mailers, flyers, business cards, and promotional items as well.

As you get more sophisticated, you can coordinate Web site activities with traditional advertising and promotional activities, such as an event, special sale, contest, customer feedback line, or PR campaign. Using standard target-marketing techniques, you could write a press release about the unique contents of your Web site to drive additional visibility in print. Chapters 7 and 8 are devoted to techniques for marketing your Internet presence.

A More Level Marketing Field?

Any business can appear significant and powerful online. By following the design concepts discussed later in the book, you can have a Web site as effective as Ragu's at *http://www.eat.com*, shown in Figure 2.24. The look and feel of your site can have all the flash of the big guys—for a price.

You can market online at all levels: very cheap, the equivalent of a photocopied handbill (black ink on colored stock); moderately inexpensive, like a used car commercial on cable TV; moderately expensive, the Web equivalent of a four-color, glossy brochure with lots of photos; and the all-out extravaganza, the electronic equivalent of a one-minute spot broadcast in prime time on the three major networks. The amount you spend will depend on your available budget, the nature of your company and its products or services, the kind of audience you are trying to reach, and the extent to which you need to use interactive multimedia on your site.

National Geographic	88%
Car and Driver	77%
Martha Stewart Living	74%
Seventeen	69%
Parents	68%
Prevention	64%
National Enquirer (tabloid)	55%

Figure 2.23. Percent of ads using URLs in major magazines, *http://www. npd.com/corp/press/press_000508.htm*. Courtesy The NPD Group, Inc.

Figure 2.24. Sample large site, *www.eat.com/dining.html.* Courtesy Lipton Investments, Inc. and Unilever USA, Inc.

How many people will use your site? One of the most popular sites in Internet history, NASA's Pathfinder photographs from the 1997 mission to Mars (*http://mpf.www.jpl.nasa/gov*), received more than 100 million hits from all its mirror sites combined in just one day, and 500 million during the month of July.

Dell Computer (*http://www.dell.com*) sells $3 million a day online, receiving some 25 million site visits per quarter. Even a moderate-size site like Cantour.com at *http://www.cantour.com*, the site of the Canadian Professional Golf Tour, received more than 3 million hits in its first five months of operation.

However, few sites attract these numbers. The Internet viewing population for most businesses is closer to the number of viewers that an infomercial receives on late-night television. Even if your Internet marketing is solely designed to provide corporate presence, set a goal for the number of viewers you want to attract.

Customer Service Is the Name of the Game

The Internet doesn't free you from doing what every business must do to get and keep customers: Provide good service. Whatever you promise—quick shipment, high quality, cheap price, individual attention—do it. Promises can be explicit (free monogramming) or implicit (write us). Don't risk customer goodwill by falling down on the job. Think not about how Internet marketing differs from what you are already doing, but about how your successful business practices can be incorporated online. You know the basic rules quite well. Certainly you know that it is easier to make a repeat customer from a satisfied current customer than to attract a new one.

Now it's time to turn your plan into reality. We'll look at the four remaining steps to Internet marketing success in the following chapters: non-Web info-tools; creating an effective Web site; monitoring site performance and promoting a Web site successfully. This is a good time to create folders on your hard drive to bookmark sites for various service providers, model sites, and potential advertising or link sites. You might also want to start a large three-ring binder to track your Internet marketing efforts. Make ten dividers for

1. Info-Tools

2. ISP and Web Hosting Service Providers

3. Web Designer/Subcontractor Selection

4. Site Development

5. Site Statistics and Maintenance

6. Site Feedback and Bug Reports

7. Web Site Promotion

8. Web Site Advertising

9. Schedules

10. Budget

3

Creating and Distributing Info-Tools

In this chapter we'll discuss the next step to Internet success: creating and distributing info-tools. These specific messages provide an ever-changing stream of information to generate interest and attention. You give away information while you tie in related products or services. Handled properly, the information you cast upon Internet waters will come back as customers.

Although establishing a Web site gets the most commercial attention, there are many other ways to take advantage of the Internet for marketing besides distributing info-tools via e-mail, listservers, and news groups. You can participate in message boards, libraries, and real-time conferences on online services, or advertise in online classified sections or on wireless devices.

Since these low-cost, easy-to-implement strategies all have proved effective, they are enough for some small businesses. Other firms test their audiences with these less-risky alternatives before inaugurating a full-scale marketing effort or use them to amplify their Web presence. The largest companies integrate them into a full spectrum program of online activities to build an online "buzz" about their business as part of their **site launch** and to maintain customer relationships.

To provide concrete examples, you'll look over the shoulder of a fictional business, The Perfect Kernel Popcorn Company. The Perfect

Kernel, a maker of organically grown gourmet popcorn, has annual sales of $2.5 million and employs 25 people. Marketing Manager Jane Ogilvie has been assigned the task of developing and executing an on-line marketing plan for The Perfect Kernel's new line of flavored popcorn. By the end of this chapter, you'll know how to

- Create info-tools, from signature files to FAQ files.

- Distribute these tools via e-mail, listservers, and news groups.

- Take advantage of message boards, conferences, and libraries available on major online services.

- Use classified ads and display ads on classified pages or on wireless services to expand the audience for your message.

Creating Info-Tools

Before you wade into the whitecapped marketing waters of cyberspace, you should create six electronic info-tools related to your product or service:

1. Signature files

2. Blurbs

3. Reports and white papers

4. Newsletters and e-zines

5. Press releases

6. Lists of frequently asked questions (FAQs)

These simple tools, which can be kept in the Info-Tools section of your notebook, will be valuable regardless of the distribution methods you select. You can create them with your word processor as simple text files, without any special formatting. There are ways to add graphics and other features to these tools, or you can modify them with art for inclusion on your Web site.

Signature Files

The electronic equivalent of your business card, a three- to six-line, text-only, **signature file** should be appended to the end of every e-mail message, blurb, report, or other posting. Not only does it include all critical information about how to reach you, it also incorporates a brief marketing phrase that positions your business (**tag line**). Like your business card, your signature file is left as often as possible. This little self-promotional file is not considered advertising, so you can use it everywhere you go on the Internet.

Be sure to include all feasible ways to contact you. If you have a toll-free number, show it. If you want users to visit your Web site, provide the URL. If you can be reached by carrier pigeon, give directions a bird can follow. The make-believe signature file that Jane Ogilvie creates for The Perfect Kernel is shown in Figure 3.1. She may change the addressee line to direct responses to appropriate individuals or to track the source of the inquiry. Or she may change the tag line ("Discover our latest flavors...") according to the target audience or the content of the message.

```
Jane Ogilvie
The Perfect Kernel
Specializing in Naturally Grown Popcorn
1234 Main Street, Waterloo, Iowa 50701
T: 800-555-POPS   F: 319-555-6666
E: Ogilvie@theperfectkernel.com

After The Perfect Kernel has a Website, she'll add:
Discover our latest flavors at http://www.theperfectkernel.com

(If The Perfect Kernel has a separate listserver address, she'll show that, too.)
```

Figure 3.1. Signature file for The Perfect Kernel.

Most e-mail programs have a simple procedure for creating a signature file. (Check "Help" to find instructions.) Once you have created a signature file, it can be attached automatically to every message you send. On older versions of some browsers, you may need to create a text file and paste it into messages manually.

Blurbs

Blurbs are short electronic messages about your business, products, services, or a related topic. The text can be lifted from an existing news release, newsletter, or brochure, or created from scratch. Be sure to tell readers how to contact you to place orders or get more information.

Your blurb will eventually enjoy wide distribution online—a kind of electronic word of mouth—so check it for spelling and typographical errors, and edit it for readability. Follow basic principles for "revving" your copy with energy:

- Use the first person (I, we) or second (you), not the third.

- Use positive phrasing, such as "buy now" instead of "don't hesitate to buy."

- Use short, commonly used words.

- Use active verbs; try to avoid forms of the verb *to be*.

- Use numbers and details, such as "ultramarine, mint green, and mango," instead of "many colors."

- Spark your text with vivid, emotive words (e.g., munchies, sun-dried, guilt, money).

- View your blurb both on screen and in print to ensure there are no problems.

Jane at The Perfect Kernel created the blurb in Figure 3.2 for use in electronic marketing. She will append her signature file, coding the addressee line to track the source of resulting inquiries.

Gourmet popcorn, a low-fat alternative to other munchies, is great for your entire family. With only 5% of calories from fat and almost no cholesterol, popcorn is a healthy way to snack without guilt. Our "savory" flavors—cheddar, sun-dried tomato and green chili—tease the taste buds with grown-up flavor. The Perfect Kernel's Gourmet Popcorn places good health and good taste at the top of our priorities.

For a free sample of The Perfect Kernel's organically-grown flavored popcorn, just hit REPLY. Type ONLY your name and address in the message field. (Follow with signature file)

Figure 3.2. Sample blurb for The Perfect Kernel.

Reports and White Papers

Longer than blurbs, reports or **white papers** are information-intensive files for the interested reader. They help establish your credibility as a resource or expert, but they don't contain much more marketing content than a signature file. You will upload these report files to strategically placed areas on the Internet that attract your target audience.

These reports should not be particularly time critical, or you will have to update them continually. They might be short feature stories that could appear in a trade journal or product fact sheets that are appropriate in a few news groups. You could create such items as a trivia question game about your industry, questionnaires with a free gift for completion, or industry-related crossword puzzles. Or you could write an informative background article on your subject. Be creative, but soft-pedal marketing appeals in these reports. Since they may appear in places that restrict advertising, keep the content factor high. People can always go to your Web site or contact you by phone or e-mail for more information.

For example, if you manufacture any kind of product, write a report about the process. Chronicle the history of your industry. How about a report on the inventor of the product? If you sell cars, create reports about Teflon coatings or racing or tune-ups. If you sell houseboats, create reports about hull design, outboard engines, or how to go through locks on the St. Lawrence Seaway.

For The Perfect Kernel, Jane creates several reports from her own knowledge or with input from others in the company. One deals with cultivation of corn by Native Americans; another describes different corn species used for popcorn, animal feed, and corn on the cob eaten on the Fourth of July. A third covers how popcorn is made, and yet another talks about the wide variety of flavored popcorns now available. As always, Jane appends her signature file.

Newsletters and E-Zines

Like their print counterparts, electronic newsletters may appear either regularly or irregularly, but change their content. Organizations from Symantec *(http://smallbiz.symantec.com)* to the U.S. Social Security Administration *(http://www.ssa.gov/enews)* use targeted electronic newsletters to communicate with specific audiences. Soft marketing also applies to newsletters. Don't oversell your product or service in a newsletter, but let readers know subtly what you have available. As before, include your signature file. Figure 3.3 shows excerpts of an online newsletter distributed via e-mail by Bidcast *(http://www.bidcast.com)*, a company that notifies small businesses and contractors of Federal government procurement opportunities.

To develop a successful newsletter, create a basic template for html e-mail. Keep the newsletter less than three pages, load it with color and design a layout that is easy to read. Some other basic design tips to consider:

- Try to keep the design consistent with your Web site

- Limit file size to 25K

- Provide obvious links to forward the newsletter to a colleague, to "unsubscribe," to provide feedback, and to print a text version.

As always, be sure to test the newsletter thoroughly to ensure the process will work. Select a few recipients to check delivery with all the major e-mail services. Let recipients know ahead of time that the newsletter is coming, both to encourage more of them to open the newsletter when it arrives and to provide an early opportunity to "opt out." Of course, publicize your newsletter as much as possible on your Web site, with online PR, and on your stationery. For additional assistance with newsletters, check out *http://www.wilsonweb.com* or *www.ezine-tips.com*.

```
BIDCAST BRIEFING
**************************************************
News on Government and Business-to-Business Contracting
**************************************************
December 1998. Vol 1 No. 1 News and resources for Contractors & Small
Businesses.

Because you are an active Government Bidder, BidCast is sending you two
months of our free BidCast Briefing Newsletter.

To permanently SUBSCRIBE to our free newsletter, please send mail to:
Newsletter-request@bidcast.com with SUBSCRIBE in the subject line.

BidCast matches, then e-mails you bids, awards and subcontracts from the
Federal Government and Prime Contractors. To get your Free Trial Month, visit:
http://www.bidcast.com
**************************************************
BIDCAST BRIEFING INDEX

1. FEATURE ARTICLE: Y2K ISSUES AND THE SMALL BUSINESS CONTRAC-
TOR.
2. SBA REQUIRES REGISTRATION FOR DISADVANTAGED CONTRACTORS.
3. NEW SMALL BUSINESS GUIDES.
4. COURTS MOVING AGAINST QUOTAS BASED ON DIVERSITY ARGUMENT.
5. BIDCAST TIP: WINNING PROPOSALS.


*********************
FEATURE ARTICLE
```

Figure 3.3. E-mailed newsletter from Bidcast, *http://www.bidcast.com.*
© 1999 Bidcast, the powerful Internet bid service.

If you are an electronic publisher, a newsletter might be your
end product. You could send extracts or sample newsletters over
the Internet to get people interested and ask for a subscription to
future issues, whether free or paid. **E-zines,** longer online publications that generally contain several stories or articles from multiple
authors, involve a much more ambitious publication effort, but can
also be effective marketing tools. If reports, newsletters, or e-zines
are unique, add a copyright notice at the bottom, indicating whether
others need permission to redistribute the newsletter or can do so
as long as you are credited. (For more information about copyright, see Chapter 9.)

Press Releases

One of the most-used forms of self-promotion, the press release is as effective online as off. Update old press releases for electronic placement. Create new ones as you go along, covering everything from product announcements to news about changes in your Web site and notices of promotions or awards. You'll post these releases, along with reports, in appropriate areas of the Internet. Be sure to include your signature file, designating a different contact person if appropriate for your organization. (Figure 3.4 displays one of Jane Ogilvie's fictional press releases.) See Chapter 7 for more information on conducting an online PR campaign.

FAQs

Files of answers to **frequently asked questions (FAQs)** can be extremely useful with Internet news groups and some mailing lists. Create several of these files in question-and-answer format. FAQ files

FOR IMMEDIATE RELEASE
CONTACT: JANE OGILVIE
DATE: MARCH 23, 2000
   ogilvie@theperfectkernel.com

Lip-smacking, finger licking, caramel apple popcorn. Fragrant memories of amusement parks, dunking for apples, and Thanksgiving pies burst from freshly-popped kernels of The Perfect Kernel's latest popcorn flavor.

Caramel Crunch joins The Perfect Kernel's product line-up on Monday, March 29, 1999. It initiates a "Sweet String" of flavors to come. The Perfect Kernel's current "Savories" line includes white cheddar, sun-dried tomato, and green chili.

Katherine Gadsden, president of The Perfect Kernel, says, "This new line will satisfy the sweet tooth of baby boomers, without adding fat, cholesterol, or high calorie count. Our studies show this population worries more about salt than sugar."

The Perfect Kernel (www.theperfectkernel.com) is the premier supplier of gourmet popcorn to upscale movie theaters, restaurants, gift shops, and specialty food distributors.

For more information, call Marketing Manager Jane Ogilvie at 800-555-POPS, or go to our Web site at *http://www.theperfectkernel.com.*
###

Figure 3.4. Sample press release for The Perfect Kernel.

usually contain little about your company except "Provided by" and your signature file. Users often read FAQ files to become familiar with a news group, so create FAQs that provide valuable information about your industry or innovative ways to use your product. Also create several product-specific FAQs to be used in locations other than news groups or to respond to e-mail.

FAQ files for news groups must conform to a specific format. To obtain this information, read the FAQs for the news group you want to join. Like all postings to moderated news groups, your FAQ file will be reviewed and either approved or disapproved. Files that smack of blatant advertising or promotion generally are not acceptable. Once FAQ files are posted, you can update them whenever you want. (Later in this chapter, you'll learn more about news groups.)

For instance, point your browser to a listing of news groups and browse for likely ones, such as biz.general. Select the desired group(s) and read their FAQs. With most systems, you just click an icon to post your message. If it's useful and interesting, your own FAQ or report might be copied to thousands of Internet sites. That could generate many new customers indeed!

E-Mail Marketing

Now that you have a portfolio of info-tools ready, the question is how to distribute them. E-mail is a good way to start. If you haven't already, you need to join the estimated 100 million people worldwide who exchanged some 350 million messages per day in 1999! E-mail can reach everyone on the Internet, even the several million customers with free e-mail accounts from Juno, Hotmail, or other Web sites. (To subscribe to one of the first two, write webmaster@juno.com, go to *http:// www.juno.com/index.html*, or call 1-888-829-5866. For Hotmail, go to *http://www.hotmail.com* or call 1-650-964-7200.)

Practice sending messages using your online service, your browser, or a freestanding e-mail program. Be sure you know how to attach your signature file. Set up an organized method of folders and files to categorize your saved e-mail correspondence.

To simplify your e-mail tasks and reduce the time it takes you to respond to inquiries, create a standard greeting that you can personalize quickly as a preface. This can be as simple as

> *Dear ____,*
>
> *Thank you for your interest in ____. You will find the answer to your question in the report that follows. Let me know if I can be of further assistance.*

Then select or create a series of text files for the most common replies or use any of your FAQ files, reports, or blurbs to speed up response time. With such tools you reduce your time spent responding to e-mail to minutes instead of hours. Try to include a **call to action:** Invite readers to join your mailing list or ask them to visit your Web site (include your URL with a hypertext link, if at all possible). As always, end with your signature file, using a customized tag line, and/or reply address if appropriate.

Try to keep your e-mail responses short. Your goal is just to get the message opened, with a pitch to take an action: Link to your site, e-mail a contact in your company, or subscribe to a mailing lists. Again, check the spelling and grammar of your messages. Avoid attachments because many people either can't open them or won't open them due to a legitimate fear of viruses. Most of all, do not send unsolicited e-mail (**spam**), whether it's a short blurb, a newsletter, or a brief notice. Spam can generate ill will that no business can afford. The safest bet is to mail only to people who have requested information directly from you or by subscribing to a mailing list.

Figure 3.5 provides excerpts from a marketing e-mail sent by AOL in response to a request for information. Large companies frequently take advantage of this low-cost method of communicating with their customers. As noted in the last chapter, your company could be perceived as nonresponsive if you don't handle e-mail response well.

Managing e-mail can become a daunting task when the number of messages reaches 45,000 a month, as it does for Dell Computers. The task has become so complex that firms like MessageMedia (*http://www.messagemedia.com*, seen in Figure 3.6), have grabbed this opportunity to manage e-mail for large companies. LiveContact (*http://www.balisoft.com*), and Right Now Web 2.0 (*http://www.rightnowtech.com*) are among the many companies that offer software ($6,000–$15,000)

Subj: AOL Advertising

Thank you for your interest in America Online (AOL). I have outlined some of AOL's advertising opportunities below. You have several options, however I recommend you look at the "search term" area of NetFind as one of the most cost effective forms of advertising on AOL. Please review the information and feel free to call or e-mail me with any questions.

You can find more advertising information online at AOL keyword <u>MediaSpace</u> , or on the web at *http://media.aol.com* (also fax on demand 800-832-8220). AOL offers special packages for any investment to help you harness the power of this medium. AOL can either drive traffic to your existing web site with banners located in highly targeted content areas or give you opportunities for content sponsorship.

Please feel free to contact me soon, if possible, as our most popular Search Terms are selling out rapidly. I have a number of success stories about businesses like yours who have used AOL very profitably. Please call me and tell me about your business so that I can help craft an online strategy with you. Thank you for your interest in advertising with AOL.

Best Regards,

Exxxx Tyyyyyyyy

AOL Interactive Marketing

415-XXX-XXXX, ETyyyyyyyy@aol.com

Figure 3.5. Responsive e-mailed blurb from AOL. © 1997-2000 America Online, Inc. All rights reserved. Used with permission.

to sort inquiries and generate automated responses in-house. They also offer hosting options with a fee based on monthly volume or per customer service agent. For more general information about e-mail marketing, check out *http://www.everythingemail.net*, *http://www.wilsonweb. com*, or *http://www.ezine-tips.com*.

Mailbots

There is another option for responding to a high volume of e-mail. Some ISPs can help you respond automatically to routine messages by using a program

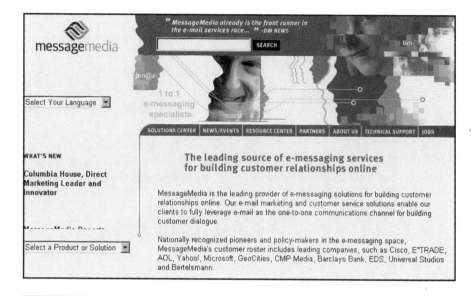

Figure 3.6. E-mail management service, *http://www.messagemedia.com.* *Courtesy Message Media.*

called a **mailbot** (a cross between mail and robot) or **autoresponder.** As seen in Figure 3.7, a mailbot automatically sends an appropriate message to anyone who sends an e-mail. Mailbots are often used to confirm receipt of an order placed at a Web site or to acknowledge a support inquiry.

The easiest way to set up a mailbot is to designate a separate e-mail address under your master account or create an alternate one. When a mailbot is active, you can't receive regular e-mail messages, so put only the alternate address into **vacation mode.** (Vacation mode is usually used to respond to tell senders you are away and direct them elsewhere for immediate assistance.)

Instead of a vacation message, write a blurb about a product or service. If you want to get more specific, create different mailbots at different addresses, each used for a particular purpose. Jane Ogilvie's fictional mailbot is shown in Figure 3.8. You can see why this powerful and inexpensive Internet tool may be worth your time.

To set up mailbots, coordinate with your ISP. (Not all have this service.) Most charge a modest setup and/or a monthly fee and offer their users 25–30K of free storage space for each incoming message. You can usually find information about vacation mode or mailbots in your ISP's own FAQ file.

Hello. (This is an automated response. There is no need to reply.)

Your message regarding:
[NMT Web Help #514] /TBD/stats
has been received and assigned a request number of 514.
We will respond to this problem as quickly as possible.

In order to help us track the progress of this request, we ask that you include
the string [NMT Web Help #514] in the subject line of any further mail about
this particular request.

For example:
Subject: [NMT Web Help #514] /TBD/stats

You may do this simply by replying to this email.

Figure 3.7. Service mailbot from New Mexico Technet, *http://www.technet. nm.org.* Courtesy New Mexico Technet.

Your free sample of The Perfect Kernel's Flavored Popcorn is on the way! For a full list of products, check out our Web site, The Perfect Kernel (*http://www.theperfect kernel.com*). You may place your order online or by fax. In a hurry? Call 800-555-POPS. Thank you for your interest in The Perfect Kernel's Popcorn.

(Follow with signature file).

Figure 3.8. Sample mailbot for The Perfect Kernel.

Listservers

A sophisticated mailbot called a **listbot** or **listserver,** a program that automatically processes requests, is even more useful. The advantage of a listserver over a regular mailbot is that a listserver can be **concatenated.** That is, prospects and customers who mail to it are asked to do something that will result in another document being mailed to them without further intervention. A listserver acts as an automated sales clerk or fax-back service, responding to requests for more information by sending the appropriate document. You can have hundreds of different files sent to different classes of customers, all automatically.

A newsletter or e-zine is a perfect way to utilize a listserver. Place announcements around the Internet giving the listserver address, which will be something like info-newsletter@theperfectkernel.com. When a person requests something from this address, the listbot will send out a sample newsletter. At the bottom of the newsletter, you tell people how to subscribe. When customers have confirmed (and paid, if required), their e-mail addresses will be added to another mailing list that automatically sends out monthly issues of the newsletter.

Price sheets, catalogs, and current inventory records are also excellent uses for listservers. You can change listserver files daily, weekly, or whatever it takes to keep users up-to-date. Be sure to include your signature file and your URL. Because people have specifically found your address and are requesting information, you can provide all the marketing materials you want with as hard or soft a sell as you find appropriate. This approach, where people must actively **opt-in**, is considered more ethical than requiring users to "opt-out." And, of course, you always provide information about how users can remove their names (**unsubscribe**) from the list.

Subscribing to Mailing Lists

An online public mailing list consists of people who have subscribed by sending their e-mail addresses to a listserver. There are over 90,000 mailing lists on the Internet packed with prequalified prospects whose enrollment establishes an interest in a subject area related to your business. As such, mailing lists can be an effective channel for promoting your company.

As seen at *http://www.liszt.com* in Figure 3.9, sites have facilities for searching lists in various ways. To see more of these lists, go to your browser and type one of these addresses:

- *http://www.neosoft.com/internet.paml*

- *http://www.tile.net/lists.*

- *http://www.l-soft.com/catalist.html*

- *http://www.copywriter.com/lists/*

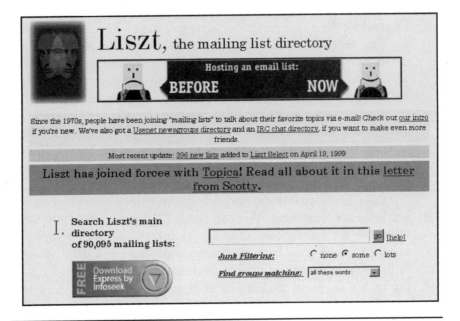

Figure 3.9. Mailing list source site, *http://www.liszt.com.* Courtesy Scott Southwick.

- *http://www.yahoo.com/business_and_economy/companies/mar keting/direct_marketing/direct_mail/mailing_list*

- *http://nsns.com/MouseTracks/tloml.html*

From one of these sites, you can either subscribe to a list or e-mail desired text to the listserver. Once you have subscribed, you will receive an updated list of the most recent messages. From then on, you will get a copy via e-mail of anything posted by any other subscriber and you can send a single e-mail message that will be distributed to everyone else.

As an exercise, subscribe to the RITIM-L list, which deals with telecommunications and information marketing. Send an e-mail to

- listserv@uriacc.uri.edu

In the body of the message, type

- subscribe RITIM-L

That's it!

Before you start posting e-mail to a list, always study incoming messages to understand the nature of the list and acceptable communications. A few lists, such as the Internet Advertising Discussion List with its 11,000 names, allow specific advertising or promotions (e.g., a discount for readers who buy from your site). Others strongly resist such messages.

Although you can usually find the e-mail addresses of others who are on the list, never, never, send them unsolicited, private e-mail. However, you can scan that information to confirm that you are participating in a list with appropriate potential customers for your company.

Back at The Perfect Kernel, Jane Ogilvie decides that a mailing list should be the next step in her strategy. After subscribing to her own list, Jane sends her first message to list members.

Creating Your Own Mailing Lists

To build a "snail mail" list, you purchase multiple direct mailing lists, mail a flyer, and get a response from one or two percent of the recipients. You may buy many mailing lists to have a significant number of "real" prospects for your products and services. Considering the expense of designing, printing, and mailing your literature, old-fashioned direct mail can cost anywhere from several dollars to several hundred dollars per lead. For much less money, you can create a mailing list on the Internet. When properly used, you'll find that electronic mailing lists can be a very effective marketing tool.

First tell your ISP that you want to establish a mailing list (listserver) regarding swimwear, space aliens, wok cooking, Elvis Presley—whatever is related to your product or service. Typical prices range from $20 to $30 for setup plus a monthly fee of $5 to $25. Some ISPs offer an annual rate or charge a transaction fee instead of a monthly one. LinkExchange, seen in Figure 3.10, offers a free listbot at *http://www.listbot.com*, complete with sign-up direct from your Web site, as long as you're willing to let people see ads. For $99 per year, you can sign up for ListBot Gold without ads.

You'll be asked to choose among options like those that follow so that the ISP can put together the appropriate listserver for you. It may take an administrator several days to set up your mailing list.

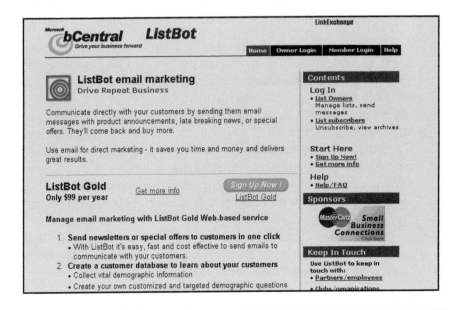

Figure 3.10. Listbot service, *http://www.listbot.com*. Screenshot reprinted with permission from Microsoft Corporation.

- **Auto:** The listserver performs all subscription requests without your prior approval.

- **Open:** Users can add or drop themselves, but not someone else, without prior approval.

- **Closed:** You, as owner, approve all subscriptions. This is often used for a paid subscription list.

- **Private:** Only people who are on the list can see who else is on the list.

- **Fully moderated:** You approve any incoming message before it can be mailed to the list. Potential participants view moderated lists as an indication of stronger content.

- **Externally moderated:** You approve only messages from outside the mailing list.

- **Maximum message length:** You must approve any e-mail larger than the preset length you've established.

As the list owner, you receive e-mail notification of all "subscribe" and "unsubscribe" requests. Like bulk mail at the post office, mail to lists is usually given a lower priority than regular e-mail and will take longer to be sent from a server. Most list software allows you to send an automatic "probe" message to confirm the e-mail addresses of subscribers and remove any faulty addresses.

You can use your own mailing list to advertise your product or services as aggressively as you want, whereas you can't advertise on somebody else's mailing list unless they specifically allow it. Be sure that recipients understand they can elect not to receive your e-mail. Above all, remember to subscribe to your own list!

Alternately, you can rent lists of e-mail addresses from "opt- in" list brokers. Most of them, like PostMasterDirect.com (*http:// www.postmasterdirect.com*) or Colonize (*http://www.colonize.com*), send your e-mail for you, without actually providing you the addresses. If you rent a list, direct recipients to your own mailing list database, rather than to your Web site. Rented names may not be as well qualified as names on a list you build yourself; many recipients may not know how their names got on a list for what they consider junk e-mail. Other e-mail resources include NetCreations at *http://www.netcreations.com* and The Direct E-mail List Source at *http://www.copywriter.com/lists*.

Posting to a List of Lists

Once your mailing list is running, add it to a List of Mailing Lists. Your mailing list address will be copied to hundreds of thousands of nodes where major network users reside. This distribution enables you to build a large list. Some services ask you to send an e-mail message with your announcement to the mail master. Others have you fill out the questionnaire, such as at *http://www.liszt.com*, where you add your list by selecting "Liszt Link" or "Web Link," and filling in the blanks. Another way to announce your list is by filling out a form at *http://www.mail-list.com*. A similar method is used to announce your mailing list on the online services.

You should soon receive dozens of messages telling you that someone has joined or dropped off your list. Neither requires any more attention on your part. To find out how your list is doing at any given time, simply send the message Who to your own list. The e-mail addresses of all subscribers should bounce back to you. Unless you have restricted access, any subscriber on your list can do the same thing.

You will need to nurture your list. Set up a regular schedule to monitor the traffic. This is a good time to create a chronological **infolog**, like the one in Figure 3.11, to include under the Info-Tools heading in the binder you created in Chapter 2. Note each scheduled task, collect copies of each info-tool, and log when tools are created, when they are posted, and the volume of response each one generates.

If responses to your mailing list start to lag, it's up to you to keep the postings hot and encourage others to do the same. If the messages get boring, your subscription list might start to shrink. Invite important and interesting people to subscribe, or take several aliases and stir up discussion yourself.

This is your list, so you can end each of your messages with a call to action. Invite recipients to ask for your sales literature through private e-mail, to visit your Web site, or to request ordering information. Of course, include your signature file.

Reaping What You've Sown

You can use the power of e-mail to follow up on hundreds of leads by responding with another, already created info-tool. When you see from a message that someone is ready to become a customer, you may want to individualize the response or close the sale offline. At this point, basic business practices come into play. Use your sales force to "farm and feed" your precious leads. They won't turn into sales unless someone telephones when a call is requested, sends out literature or samples, and makes sure that customers' needs are met.

This process works for The Perfect Kernel. A few days after announcing her own list, Jane watches it begin to grow. When she reaches 100 members, she posts some of her previously created info-tools and starts to participate actively. Over time, her list increases to more than 3,000 people and the volume of retail sales goes up by 10% due to electronic orders.

You now have several distribution channels for your info- tools: standard e-mail for manual responses, mailbots for automated responses, public e-mailing lists, and your own list on an automated listserver.

Scheduled Task	Description	By	Date Created	Date Posted	Location & Notes (e.g. # responses)
Signature File	J. Ogilvie; master	jo	11/14/99		
Signature File	P. Piper for CompuServe	jo	11/17/99		
Signature File	E. Taylor for Web	jo	11/17/99		
Blurb #1	healthy value	jo	12/1/99		
Blurb #2	short #1 for news groups	jo	12/3/99		
Report #1	Native American cultivation	jo	12/5/99		
Report #2	Corn species	jo	12/5/99		
CompuServe	Subscribe ($21.95/month)	jo	12/6/99		
Report #3	Popcorn manufacture	jo	12/8/99		
Blurb #3	New flavor announcement	jo	1/6/00		
Signature File	Modify Ogilvie, Dept QA, for news groups	jo	1/6/00		
Press Release	Corporate backgrounder	jo	1/12/00		
Press Release	New flavor announcement	jo	1/14/00		
Report #4	Flavored popcorns	jo	1/14/00		
FAQ	Where to find The Perfect Kernel's products	jo	1/15/00		
FAQ	Making good popcorn	jo	1/15/00		
E-mail	cover response	jo	1/16/00		

Figure 3.11. Chronological infolog. (*Continued on next page*)

Scheduled Task	Description	By	Date Created	Date Posted	Location& Notes (e.g. # responses)
Upload reports	Gourmet Food Forum, CompuServe	jo	1/20/00		
Newsletter	January issue	jo	1/23/00	1/23/00	
Subscribe RITIM-L	mailing list on information marketing	jo	1/26/00		
Check news group	alt.college.food	jo	1/27/00	1/27/00	
Answer e-mail		jo	2/2/00		
e-mail response	franchisee response	jo	2/9/00		
Answer e-mail		jo	2/9/00		
FAQ	franchising	jo	2/13/00		
Answer e-mail		jo	2/16/00		
Check news group	rec.food.recipe	jo	2/18/00		
Answer e-mail		jo	2/23/00		
New mailing list	healthy snack food eaters	jo	2/26/00		
Announce list	at mail-list.com	jo	2/26/00		
Post Report #1	to mailing list	jo	2/27/00		
Answer e-mail		jo	3/2/00		
Create mailbot	for auto-response to list	jo	3/4/00	3/4/00	
Press Release	new franchise open	jo	3/5/00	3/5/00	

Figure 3.11. Chronological infolog. (*Continued from previous page*)

Whenever you change or add to your info-tools, be sure to post them to the various lists and news groups you've joined. Record these postings in your activity log. If you have a listserver address, don't forget to show it in your signature file, all info-tools, traditional promotions, business cards, and letterhead. Now let's turn to another inexpensive way to establish an electronic presence on the Internet.

News Groups

News groups are virtual communities of people who choose to discuss a shared interest on the Internet. Called USEnet, this portion of the Internet hosts discussions on over 30,000 topics, with millions of people participating worldwide. A given news group that reaches even 0.1% of the Internet population is extraordinary—that's over a hundred thousand prequalified prospects interested in something related to your business. About 1 **gigabyte** (**billion** bytes) of new information is circulated every day through this Internet function.

To find a list of news groups, point your browser to one of the following sites:

- *http://www.liszt.com/news*

- *http://www.dejanews.com*

- *http://www.reference.com*

- *http://tile.net/news/viewlist.html* (seen in Figure 3.12)

At these sites you can search for news groups by keyword. In most cases, you don't even need to subscribe; just click to read the messages that interest you. Try one or two that appeal. As an exercise, try out the biz.general news group shown in Figure 3.13. You can find out which of the biz newsgroups allow advertising by looking at their FAQs at *http://www.bizynet.com/faq-news.htm*. The Internet changes so rapidly that you should search for relevant news groups at least every six months. Put that task in your info-log! You can even buy special software, such as News Rover (*http://www. newsrover.com*), to search news groups for you.

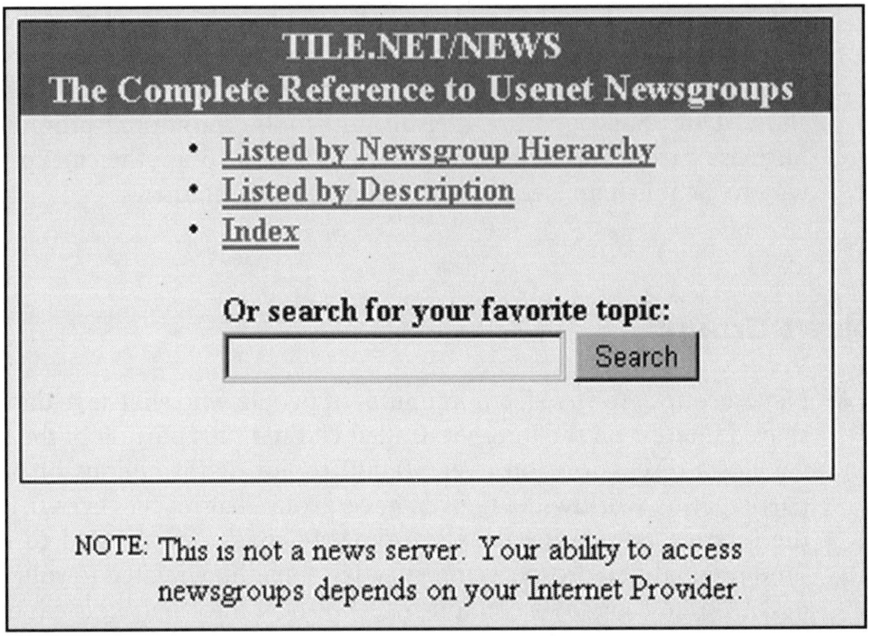

Figure 3.12. News group source site, *http://tile.net/news.* © 2000 List-Universe.com.

In a news group you can post a message of your own or respond to a message someone else has submitted. The former is better because everyone in the group will receive your response. An answer to a message on a prior topic, called a **thread**, is sent only to those who have read the prior message.

The information you distribute online, called a **posting**, can be as short as one or two sentences or as long as a multimedia presentation. If you post a message that is nothing more than an ad on an inappropriate news group, you will be considered a spammer and may be asked to leave the group. Generally, your postings will be effective as long they as contain real information of value to readers. Press releases and product announcements are acceptable in some news groups.

Major news group categories are shown in the table in Figure 3.14. Each of these categories is divided hierarchically into minor groups and then into more detailed subgroups, like an outline. Groups are named by continually appending other words to the right of the prior word,

Biz Heirarchy	Long Title	
FAQ - biz Hierarchy Charters	Listing of biz Charters	
Biz.* Frequently Asked Questions	Primary biz.* FAQ	
biz.books.technical	Technical Books - Offers & Requirements (Moderated)	GO
biz.caucus	Business Related Political Discussions (Moderated)	GO
biz.comp.accounting	Accounting Software & Procedures (Moderated)	GO
biz.config	Biz UseNet Configuration and Administration	GO
biz.general	Business operations and offerings. (Moderated)	GO
biz.healthcare	Discussion for healthcare professionals (Moderated)	GO
biz.marketplace.computers.discussion	Computer Market Forum (Moderated)	GO
biz.marketplace.computers.mac	Macintosh hardware/software (Moderated)	GO

Figure 3.13. BIZynet.com FAQs, *http://www.bizynet.com/faq-news.htm.*
Courtesy BIZynet, Inc.

BIZ	Business	SCI	Science topics
COMP	Computer-related topics	SOC	Social issues
MISC	Miscellaneous topics	TALK	Like Talk Radio—anything goes
NEWS	Current events	ALT	Other topics not covered above
REC	Recreation-related topics		

Figure 3.14. Major news group categories.

separated by a period. The longer the name, the more focused the group. You can often check all the FAQs in a news group category at once. Jane Ogilvie might find news groups related to The Perfect Kernel at rec.food.recipes or alt.college.food.

Some news groups are moderated by people who review messages for relevance before posting. Many readers prefer moderated groups because they tend to have higher-quality, less-repetitious content. Even unmoderated news groups have rules about what you can and cannot post; be sure to check their FAQs. In general, the best way to gain attention in this environment is to participate actively in a good discussion thread. As always, play observer initially. Stay in the background (**lurk**) for several weeks, reading messages without sending any of your own.

Once you find a few appropriate news groups, post messages asking for names of related groups. The members themselves will lead you to more- and more-focused news groups. Take their leads until you think you have located the majority of news groups appropriate to your business. Don't forget that asking questions enables you to leave your signature file, which builds recognition for your business.

To manage your news group participation, create a series of folders and mailboxes using programs such as Eudora Pro (*http://www.eudora.com*) or Outlook 98 (*http://www.microsoft.com/outlook*). They will automatically place news group postings or incoming newsletters and listservers into appropriate folders so you can **scan** (view subject lines without opening a message) them quickly each day.

Some people advocate using fake names in signature files and "From" lines of newsgroups to avoid receiving junk mail, but you may regret it from a business perspective. As Chris Gunn of BIZynet puts it, "that's like trying to do business with an unlisted phone number." For more general information on news groups and mailing lists, go to the Internet FAQ section at *http://www.bbn.com/support/resources/internetfaq.htm*.

Net Courtesy

When you participate in the non-Web portion of the Internet, especially news groups, you're invading areas of cyberspace that people guard avidly against commercialization. If you don't honor the rules, you may get **flamed** (sent derogatory messages), receive spam, or be ousted by your ISP. Here are a few basic rules:

- If you use news groups or public mailing lists, be subtle.

- Never post blatant advertising in news groups. Use the third-party technique of a satisfied customer talking about your products or services in a positive way. If you have a satisfied customer, ask for a testimonial in the appropriate news group. You can also answer a question asked by someone else in the group.

- Keep your contributions full of real information.

- CAPITAL LETTERS are considered rude.

- Distribute information through e-mail only to those who have expressed an interest in receiving it.

- Always let customers remove their names from your e-mail address book (unsubscribe).

Marketing on Online Services

About 23 million people currently subscribe to one of the "Big Three" online services: America Online (AOL), 19 million; CompuServe, 2 million; or Prodigy (1.5 million). Besides providing Internet access, the online services offer a self-contained online universe, complete with shopping, news, and personal communications services, such as chat rooms. Subscribers who are timid about the Web or who have slow modems may use only an online service. Since the majority of subscribers to these services are families at home, the online services may represent a significant market for you.

Broadly speaking, CompuServe, which was acquired by AOL in 1998, has a reputation for having more business customers, whereas Prodigy aims at the home market. AOL has the largest customer base, easiest user interface, and best graphics, but has problems with busy signals to local servers due to rapid growth. If you choose to market directly to online service customers, be aware that membership changes rapidly and that demographics can be difficult to nail down. Web portals have to some extent replaced these services as destination points and gateways. Online services are fairly competitive with ISPs, averaging $20 to $22 per month for unlimited user access.

Depending on your business, you may want to subscribe to all or none of these services. Of course, you will drop any online service whose marketing results after several months do not cover at least the monthly expense of that service. As with everything else on the Internet, the best way to learn about an online service's customers and culture is to observe quietly in the background.

Online Communities of Interest

Online communities cover everything from aquariums to zoology, from politics to pop stars. Major computer companies, such as IBM and Microsoft, also maintain user communities on the online services, and, of course, Web-related communities are very popular. Search the available topics for the ones most likely to attract users who fit your profile of a good prospect. Each community has a system operator, or **Sysop**, who is responsible for managing its activities and publicizing it on the online service. Each time you move to a new community, study it until you understand its style and the quirks of its Sysop. If you are an expert on a subject, you can use these communities to become better known, to establish credibility, and by extension to promote your company.

You'll find three elements to a community:

- **Conferences** (called **Forums** on AOL), which are moderated, scheduled chat rooms in which people communicate simultaneously

- **Message boards,** which operate like news groups, with people posting comments or queries on a topic and others responding at different times. Message boards can be thought of as a no-host radio call-in program, limited only by the topic.

- **Libraries,** sections packed with files uploaded by others, including both useful shareware programs and informative reports or white papers. You can obtain a count at any time of how many people have downloaded your report from the library. If your report is interesting, expect hundreds of downloads per month.

To see a list of relevant communities on AOL, type in the keyword BUSINESS KNOW-HOW. Choose Message Boards or Forums, and select a relevant topic from the list, as seen in Figure 3.15. You might also want to check the keywords SOHO (small office/home office) or ONLINE BUSINESS. On CompuServe, select "GO FORUMS" from the

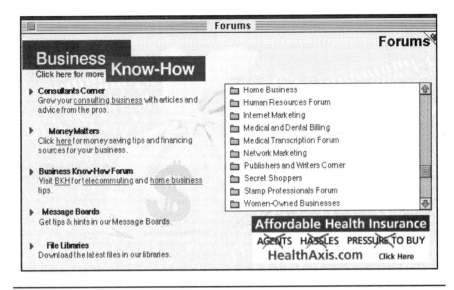

Figure 3.15. Business forums on AOL. AOL screenshot © 2000 America Online, Inc. Used with permission.

Main Menu. The Public Relations and Marketing Forum on CompuServe is particularly valuable because you can upload a press release. Prodigy, which has no ability to store info-tools, strongly discourages advertising and promotion. You might try the Small Business/Home Office board, as long as you are subtle. Otherwise, your Prodigy marketing will be restricted to purchased advertising.

Remember, the purpose of all this is to create easy pathways to the largest possible number of potential customers. At The Perfect Kernel, Jane decides to start with CompuServe, then add the other online services, and finally build a Web site. First, she uploads her previously created reports to the library section of Cooks Online on CompuServe, selecting keywords carefully to make it easy for others to find her files.

Message Boards

Once you contribute a report or any other info-tool to an appropriate library, announce it in the message board for that community and on any other appropriate (meaning on-topic) message board. Then start reading postings regularly, respond to questions if you know the answer, and comment on the messages posted by others. Always include your signature file so that members will be exposed to your company name and know how to reach you.

If people ask for information about your products, forward a blurb and tell them where to find other info-tools you have uploaded. If their request appears in the message section, post your blurb there. If the request comes from private e-mail, send your blurb to the individual's e-mail address only. Be sure to track all these actions, as well as the number of responses from each source, in your info-log.

At The Perfect Kernel, Jane sends a notice about her report to participants in Cooks Online and begins to respond to queries. As her e-mail inbox fills with requests for information from CompuServe subscribers, Jane responds with her blurb. Jane cycles the questions she gets into more info-tools, blurbs, and reports, which she adds to her online marketing arsenal.

She finds several other areas indirectly related to her marketing needs. The section Building Your Business draws participants looking for business opportunities. As it happens, The Perfect Kernel offers franchises to qualified people who want to distribute its popcorn or open a storefront of their own. Jane creates a report and blurb related to franchising and spreads the word online. As a result of her online activity, Jane sells six franchises around the country over the next few months—excellent results from these early online marketing steps.

Conferences or Forums

Conferences on CompuServe or Forums on AOL allow you to showcase your own and your company's experience. (Prodigy has no facility for conferences, although you can become an Information Associate.) Conferences are like chat rooms, but they have a focal point—you.

You can always participate in conferences arranged by others, which at least permits you to leave your signature file. It's better, however, to host a conference in your area of expertise. The Sysop of the particular forum or board arranges conferences. Sysops may be hard to reach, and it can be difficult to schedule a conference on a particularly busy forum.

As the moderator, you will make a presentation, with files delivered before hand to conference attendees. Participants could number from several dozen to several thousand. During the conference, any attendee can type in a comment, which is then commented on by the rest of the group.

Make sure all attendees know how to reach you afterward, since you can't market your services directly during the conference. Conference participants are a self-selected list of likely prospects. You're on your own, though, to follow up on leads from people who contact you later.

Classifieds

Classified ads, ads that appear in a section organized by subject, are available on all the online services and USEnet, as well as on the Web. Ads like the AOL ClassifiedPlus in Figure 3.16 can be one of the best advertising buys in the world. They are relatively inexpensive—often

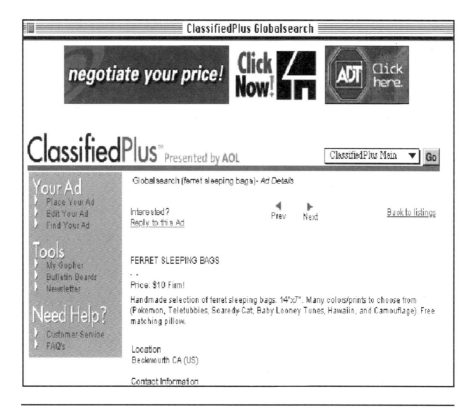

Figure 3.16. AOL classified ad, *http://classifiedplus.aol.com*. AOL screenshot © 2000 America Online, Inc. Used with permission.

free or just a few dollars per week—and can reach a potential audience of millions. (AOL claims a potential audience of 45 million viewers/week for 2 million listings in 10 categories across all its properties including AOL, AOL.com, Compuserve, Digital City, and Netscape.)

Depending on your target audience, classifieds may be a better buy than display ads; viewers of classifieds preselect themselves by searching specifically for the category that interests them. Most people who read classifieds are ready to buy: They are the ultimate in prequalified customers.

AOL's classified charges, which are category based, range from $2 to $22 for two weeks for a multiline ad, depending on category. Monthly and annual rates are also available. By comparison, print classifieds may run from less than $1 per day for a 3-line ad in a paper with a circulation of under 100,000 to $213 per day for the same ad in a paper with a circulation of several million, like the weekend edition of USA Today. Most print outlets, including the Los Angeles Times, now include an online ad (or at least a link) for free when you purchase a print classified. The LA Times also offers online-only classifieds for $35 per week.

Writing a good classified ad is an art. You'll need a good headline as well as concise body copy. Study the ads that appear online, check out the tips for writing an ad at AOL Classifieds, get a book from the library, or run a comparison ad in a newspaper. Remember to track your ads so you know which ones work best. You can do this by coding e-mail response addresses, or even by creating a separate Web entry page for each ad. You'll know within several days if your classified ad is successful. Change the language if it doesn't draw.

Most people get an excellent response if they offer anything worthwhile. If you sell only several items, you may break even; a few more and you've made money.

USEnet and Web Classifieds

If your budget is really tight, consider USEnet classifieds, which are free to both buyer and seller. USEnet classifieds are found mainly in the .forsale news group, but some other news groups accept them (check, for example, .wanted, .jobs, or .marketplace). Starting with the .forsale news groups, ask members for their help in locating others that accept classifieds.

You can localize your ads by going to regional news groups. For example, if you want to sell your old family car in Chicago, the chi.forsale news group would be the best place for you. All you do is join the group and type an article that becomes your ad. As always, post only items for sale that are relevant to the subject of a news group. Use a news group search program like the one at *http://www.liszt.com/news* or *http://tile.net/news/viewlist.html* to locate good "for sale" sites.

Web-based classifieds, such as Classifieds 2000: The Internet Classifieds (see Figure 3.17) have more features than those on USEnet. Most, for instance, have the capacity for photos and parameter searches. Classifieds 2000 is free. On the high end, the WebTrade Center (*http://www.webtrade.com/*), charges $80 for a three-month ad, with a $50-$60 charge for each additional category.

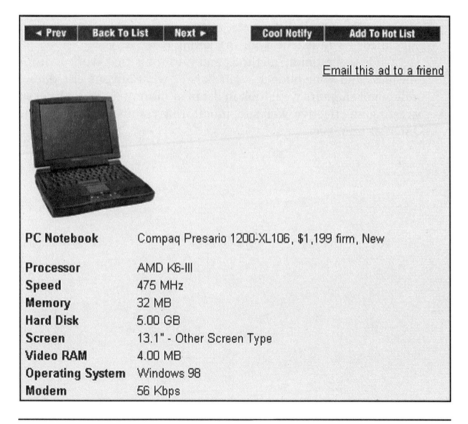

Figure 3.17. Internet classified ad from Classifieds 2000, *http://www.classifieds2000.com.* © 2000 At Home Corporation. All rights reserved. Excite, Excite Shopping and Classifieds 2000 are service marks or registered service marks of At Home Corporation in the United States and other countries.

Advertising on Wireless Services

A brand new advertising opportunity has arrived with wireless services delivering information to hand-held devices, such as pagers, cell phones, and **PDAs** (personal digital assistants). Brief one-line ads can be used to draw immediate attention to your product or Web site. "Hot? Click here for the closest Frozen-Freezee." Or they can tickle users to visit a site: "Have you checked your stocks today?" with a link to "Easycome-Easygo.com." Ad rates for such advertising are in great flux—negotiate!

As you review your marketing plan in light of all this information, you may decide that these off-the-Web methods alone will consume your time and financial resources. If they achieve your marketing objectives or produce sales, that's terrific. If you later decide to go on the Web, these tools—e-mail, listservers, news groups, online communities, and classifieds—will extend your marketing reach.

Choose the online methods and info-tools that work best for your business and your budget, regardless of what anyone else does. In the following chapters we'll look in detail at more steps to Internet success: creating an effective Web site, monitoring results, and promoting your Internet presence.

4

Setting Up Your Web Site

As you've realized by now, the World Wide Web is a sinfully rich marketing and sales tool. To truly take advantage of the Web, however, you must develop a Web site that meets your goals while implementing the essential back office functions that ensure customer satisfaction. In this chapter we'll explore the logistics of site setup, from estimating costs and registering a domain name to accepting payment and shipping product. These issues, along with the design considerations discussed in the next chapter, will enable you to complete the fifth step of Internet success: creating or upgrading your Web site.

Although you will most likely contract with other companies for Web design and hosting, we will also consider whether it's reasonable and cost-effective for your company to execute those responsibilities itself. Most of all, we will focus on the importance of planning and research before you start spending money. In this chapter you'll learn about

- Planning your site, including budget, timeline, staff, and infrastructure.

- Hiring service providers: ISP, Web host, designer and/or engineer.

- Registering a domain name.

- Accepting payment online.

- Back office preparation for order fulfillment and customer support.

- Ongoing site management.

Preplanning Pays Off

A strategic Web plan includes the standard elements of any project management task:

- Budget

- Timeline for development

- Identification of key personnel and tasks for site development and upkeep

- Analysis of internal resources and needs, in this case for hardware, software, and telecommunications infrastructure

Before handling these elements, return to the initial plans for your Web site in Chapter 2. Transfer your goals and objectives onto a concise Web worksheet, like the sample in Figure 4.1. You will use this worksheet to

- Conduct internal planning.

- Form the basis for a **Request for Quote (RFQ)** from various designers and Web service providers.

- Establish the tone, content, and "personality" of your site.

The most important function of the worksheet is to ensure that your business "dog" wags your Web site "tail," not the other way around. The worksheet is a useful tool to encourage team buy-in, forge consensus, or justify the project to higher-ups. When you look for people to assist with the site, either inside or outside the company, the Web

WEB SITE PLANNING WORKSHEET

Web Site URL: _____

Page Name: _____ Date: _____

Goals: _____

Objectives (quantifiable) in the form of:

1. _____ (units) within _____ (time frame)

2. _____ (units) within _____ (time frame)

3. _____ (units) within _____ (time frame)

Target Audience:

Call(s) to Action:

Site/Page Description (Include estimated number of pages, number of multimedia elements, i.e. animations, audio, video. Specify whether live, downloadable or streaming technologies will be used. Indicate frequency of live events.)

Resources

	Needed for Development	Avail? Y/N	Needed for Operation	Avail? Y/N
Hardware				
Software				
Server				
Communication				
Client	Not Applicable	N/A		

Content Sources:

Development Staffing:

Maintenance Staffing/Frequency:

Estimated Costs:

$ _____ Start-up $ _____ /mo. Maintenance

Figure 4.1. Web site planning worksheet. © 1997-2000 Watermelon Mountain Web Marketing.

worksheet provides a succinct recruitment message. When you come to the inevitable decision forks in design, the worksheet will help you maintain focus.

Do you remember cereal box contests? The ones where you had to complete the phrase "I like fruity SugarOhs because..." in 25 words or less? Writing the summary for the worksheet is much like that. If you can't say what you want your site to accomplish and how you will do it in less than one page, you haven't fully thought it through.

A Web worksheet starts with the goals and objectives for the site. It should include a description of the target audiences and the methods to be used to attract them. Specify the payoff and/or calls to action. As you go through various planning steps, complete the sections about resources, revenue, staffing, and budget. The worksheet and all the cost estimates belong in your Web notebook.

Preliminary Budget

A budget not only allows you to manage expenses for the Web site, it allows you to compare estimated costs for this form of advertising, sales, and/or customer support against offline forms. It ensures that you have thought through potentially hidden expenses and forces you to set priorities in terms of features and time. Thinking about money makes you ask whether the investment of time and dollars for a Web site will produce the desired results, or whether there are better ways to expend limited financial and personnel resources.

Prices for Web development vary by size and complexity of the site, geographic region (vendors on the coasts are more expensive), and the size and reputation of the design house you select. Some businesses have found that Web developers outside the country are less expensive than those in the United States. Given that vendors' estimates for developing and maintaining the same Web site may be separated by several orders of magnitude, one approach is to start with an internal estimate of how much you are willing to spend. After your first round of bids, finalize a budget—and stick to it. If you don't establish a limit, Web expenditures can quickly balloon out of control.

Costs for Web development have risen rapidly as the demand for the services has grown. The price for a small site is now about twice what it was in 1997, while a medium site runs about 50 percent more and a large site has increased by about 25 percent. How much?

According to Cyberatlas *(http://cyberatlas.internet.com/big_picture/ hardware)*, the *average* budget for an e-commerce site is in the mid-$20,000s for a small retail or B2B site, $37,000 for a medium site, and $68,000 for a large site selling exclusively online. A media or portal site averages $10,000 more. These budgets include only development and hosting, not the additional costs of internal labor, maintenance, infrastructure, or site promotion. Sites that are database driven, involve real-time transaction processing, or include multimedia cost more than the average marketing site. The chart in Figure 4.2 indicates, however, that the spread in Web site budgets leaves room for businesses of any size.

Before you panic, most small businesses can put up a modest site with a little custom design and some basic marketing for $1,000 to $2,500 plus internal labor. You can create even less expensive Web pages using low-cost, off-the-shelf templates from a Web host or provider (for example, see *http://www.Netopia.com/software/nvo* or IBM's HomePage Creator at *http://www.ibm.com/hpc*). A well-organized, simple site that offers value and is well promoted may suffice to make sales or draw people to your business.

The table in Figure 4.3 provides some rough estimates of startup and annual maintenance costs for mini, small, medium, and large sites. Except for the mini site, which is done by modifying a template offered by a Web hosting service, the table assumes contracting with a Web designer to build and maintain the site. The mini, small, and medium

	Type of site		
Budget	Total Sample	Media/Portals/ Info/Publishers	Exclusively Online Sales
None	4%	7%	4%
$1 to 100	2%	3%	1%
$100 to 500	9%	10%	6%
$501 to 1,000	10%	5%	11%
$1,001 to 5,000	34%	20%	31%
$5,001 to 10,000	13%	11%	7%
$10,001 to 99,999	22%	28%	27%
$100,000 to 999,999	8%	15%	9%
over $1Million	1%	2%	3%
Average	$36,579	$77,788	$67,858

Figure 4.2. Budget for Web site investment, *http://cyberatlas.internet.com/ big_picture/hardware/article/0,1323,5921_234331,00.html*. Reprinted with permission. © 2000 Internet.com, LLC. All rights reserved.

sites use a Web hosting service, while the large site is self-hosted. Both the mini and small sites are text and graphics only. The medium site adds multimedia in the form of limited animation and sound, while the large-site budget includes some streaming media.

In this model, all except the static mini site do some form of online sales. The small site starts selling online, adding a small, free catalog and shopping cart from its Web host, and paying for access to a secure server. The medium site adds real-time payment processing and a merchant card account. Note the oft-ignored line item for in-house labor to service the site, from providing content updates to communicating with the Webmaster and customers.

One of the most difficult numbers to estimate is the cost of marketing. How much are you willing to spend to acquire visitors to your site? Some venture-funded dot-coms are spending anywhere from 70% to 125% of revenues on marketing! We'll talk more about this in Chapters 7 and 8, but for now expect to spend about 20% to 40% of your *total* budget for marketing if you're a Web-only business. You may get away with as little as 5% if you have an established offline marketing program already in place. Another way to think about it is to allocate 60% of what you're budgeting for Web site development to your Web site marketing effort. That level of effort should enable you to earn back your investment. It makes no sense to spend a small fortune on a Web site that receives no traffic.

Think long and hard about how many visitors you expect on your site. Divide marketing costs by anticipated unique viewers (in thousands) to estimate your CPM (cost per thousand). How does this CPM compare to your existing advertising, whether by newspaper, direct mail, or TV?

Perform a similar analysis if you're selling online or providing customer support. Estimate your cost per sales transaction (or per service inquiry) and per dollar of sales (i.e., total online revenue). How much in online sales would be required to break even on the Web site? How does your cost per sale online compare to other means of selling? How many people do you expect to obtain customer support from your site instead of from telephone or in-store service? How much traffic needs to shift to the Web to save money on support staffing?

Use the categories and numbers in Figure 4.3 as a guide to create your own spreadsheet. Fill out your cost estimates as you proceed through the development process. Be careful: A 1999 Gartner Group study found that most companies budgeted only 50% to 75% of what their site eventually cost. The most often underestimated factor was labor, which ac-

Item	Mini Site Setup/Annual	Small Site Setup/Annual	Medium Site Setup/Annual	Large Site Setup/Annual
Hardware	$1,500 optional 1x	$3,000 optional 1x	$7,500 optional 1x	$15,000 optional 1x
Software	$200	$600-$2,000	$2,000-$5,000	$5,000-$50,000
Register Domain	$70/$35	$70/$35	$140/$70 (2 names)	$140/$70 (2 names)
ISP	$25/$300	$25/$300	$25/$480	$25/$480
Web Host	$25/$240	$50/$360	$50/$720	Self-host
Web Design inc. 1 yr updates	5-8 pages free template	20 Pages $1,800	50 Pages $5,000	100 Pages $10,000
Telecomm	$0/$600 @ $50/mo POTS 56K	$60/$480 @$40/mo POTS 56K; new line	$60/$900 DSL @ $75/mo	$1,300/ $6,000 partial T1 @ $500/ mo
Multimedia and extras	None	cgi-script $25/included	audio/animation $4,000	streaming media $12,000
Shopping Support	None	inc. by Web Host +$120 for secure server @ $10/mo	$150/$1,200	$6,000 (software)/NA
Monitoring	From Web Host	From Web Host	$700 software	$700 software
Create Banner Ads	Free	$300 for 6 ads @ $50/ad	$600 for 12 ads @ $50/ad	$2,400 for 24 ads @ $100/ad
Set-up Costs				
Annual Outside Cost				
In House Labor	$10K /yr	$25K /yr	$40K-70K /yr	$70K–120K /yr
Total Site Cost				
Marketing @ $20% Site Cost				
Estimated # Visitors				
Estimated CPM				
Estimated Sales (#/$)				
Cost of Sales				

Figure 4.3. Web site budget worksheet. © 1997-2000 Watermelon Mountain Web Marketing.

counts for 79% of total site expenses, followed by hosting fees and servers. Except for the easiest template-based sites from a Web host, expect a site to cost twice as much and take twice as long as initially budgeted!

Timeline

You must establish the initial timeline just as you do the budget. If you don't set a deadline and a schedule for achieving it, your Web project may never be done! Obviously, a timeline will vary with your situation and with the complexity of your site. For instance, you may require an introductory site in conjunction with a scheduled event or product launch. One criterion for selecting Web designers will be their availability to work to your timetable, but be realistic: Good sites take time. If you have a deadline, give everyone enough lead time to do a good job. Even the simplest sites usually need at least a week of planning, although putting them up may take only a day. Many sites take months.

As you can see in Figure 4.4, you should expect to spend about half the time available for your project in the planning and design phase. The remaining half will be split almost equally between development and testing. These ratios, which are typical for both media production and programming, may seem excessive on the front end. They aren't. The time you spend planning will save you dollars in the end.

You don't have to launch all the pages on your site at once. It's better to get a site up and begin to establish your online presence than to wait until everything is perfect. Continue to build, test, and publicize pages over time. Sequencing development not only spreads out the costs, it also enables you to see how well a specific page works. If you're not sure how to accomplish this, prioritize goals in your business plan. Develop first by target audience, then by page or feature for that audience. You may want to delay all multimedia until the basic site is up. Since it is difficult to recover from a botched launch, ensure that you have a well-functioning small site with core products and features before you start a publicity campaign.

You should also create a schedule for additions, monitoring, and updates. Depending on the purpose of your site and the nature of your business, some element of your site should probably change at least once a month to keep it fresh and interesting to viewers. New content might be a press release, a product announcement, a special offer, or simply different graphics. Unless your business is completely static, your Web site won't be

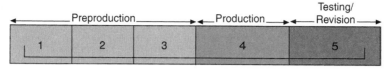

Preproduction
1. Establish needs, goals, objectives
   Setup team
   Establish budget and time frame
   Research other sites
   Survey internal resources
   Select providers
   Write treatment
2. Select and register domain name
   Prepare storyboards and flowchart
   Write script
   Create comp designs
3. Feedback cycle and design revision
   includes focus groups and internal review

Production
4. Collect and prepare content elements
   Write all text
   Produce all graphics
   Write Web site programming
   Produce any multimedia elements
   Research and create links
   Sell and obtain electronic art for ads and sponsors

Testing/Revision
5. Test programming, including syntax and links
   Test user interface/acceptability (internal)
   Review content for accuracy
   Test trial site with limited number of users (external)
   Launch

Figure 4.4. Development timeline.

either. There is a fine line between adding new information to draw repeat visitors and making changes for the sake of change. If your site successfully provides service to repeat customers, leave key functions well enough alone.

As you'll learn in Chapter 7, changes on a site offer opportunities for promotion. By spreading out development and updates, you'll generate multiple promotional announcements, drawing new or repeat viewers each time.

Set Up a Team

Developing a Web site can be daunting. Leonardo da Vinci was probably the only person who could have done it all himself—from stunning graphic design to elegant code, from mastering the aesthetic vocabulary of six different media to computing bandwidth requirements. Ordinary mortals need to designate a team and team leader (unless that's you) to select and meet with various Web providers. The team will also evaluate and test designs, provide content, suggest site structure, schedule material for updates, and coordinate with other business operations. "Team" notwithstanding, you still need a senior person with decision-making authority who has the final say and who signs off on everything.

Besides those involved with information systems, the team should include representatives from any department that will provide content and/ or is expected to interact with users. This may mean representatives from corporate communications, human resources, customer service or marketing. If you plan to generate revenue from your site, include staff from sales, order processing, shipping, accounting, and catalog development.

Launching and publicizing your site when it is ready may be an in-house marketing responsibility, or it may be handled by your Web designer, Web host, PR firm, or advertising agency, depending on what you've decided. In any case, you'll want a marketing person to oversee the activities conducted by these contractors.

There are no fixed roles for participants in a Web project, nor are there rules saying what must be done in-house and what should be done by an outside provider. Even the distribution of labor among outside providers is in flux. Both hosting services and designers, for example, may offer to do such initial promotion tasks as submitting to search engines. Unless you already have a skilled programmer in-house, you may find that outsourcing actually costs less than hiring in-house talent.

A Web site is not a one-time project. Like Tennyson's river, it goes on forever. In your staffing plans, be sure to identify who will be responsible downstream for

- Managing the site.

- Ensuring that users receive technical and customer support.

- Updating the site.

- Responding to communications from users.

- Monitoring and analyzing site traffic and providing feedback.

Consider preexisting workloads before tasking members of your team. What you think will be a one-time, 20-hour task completed within a month may easily turn into a task that takes 20 hours a week indefinitely.

Assess Infrastructure

As part of determining your budget and timeline, survey your internal resources. This is critical if you expect to host your own site, sell online, offer customer support, or receive a large number of new e-mail messages. You may need to budget for new equipment or allow time to install additional phone lines or train staff on new software. Some of the items come with a substantial price tag, so be sure they are included in your budget.

Hardware and Software In-House

Survey the hardware, operating systems, and browsers currently in use. Are you irrevocably tied to what you currently use? If so, that constraint may affect your selection of a Web host and developer. Will you need more equipment if you bring on additional employees to handle demand generated by the site? Will you need to install plug-ins or other software to create content files or play back the contents of your Web page? If so, make sure your equipment has the capacity for them. You may need to upgrade your computers to communicate with the server hosting your site. Before buying any additional equipment, check with the Web hosting service to make sure what hardware, software, and operating systems will be compatible.

If you plan to host your own site, it's critical to select the correct **server**, a computer with the software and telecommunications capacity to act as a host. This decision is affected by the complexity and size of your site and the amount of traffic you anticipate. At a minimum, expect to pay at least $4,000 to $6,000 for an in-house system, plus staff time for programming and maintenance. The operating system you use will affect other decisions downstream, including selection of Web development and server software, whose costs range from free to thousands of dollars. Your choice of other application packages, such as security, catalog, or multimedia software, will also be affected. Consult with your information systems manager about your plans.

The general guideline for buying hardware definitely holds with purchases for the Internet. As a top priority, maximize the speed at which you can access the Web. Get the fastest method that your infrastructure will support, such as ISDN, DSL, or cable. After that, buy the machine with the fastest processor and most memory that you can afford. Any VGA monitor will do, although larger screens make it easier to see Web images without scrolling.

Internal Telecommunication Needs

If your company is on a network, discuss your Web project with your system administrator to see if additional equipment will be needed. You may require more routers, for instance, if many more people will be online at the same time. If you expect increased Internet traffic, also check the capacity of your Internet connection and its server to make sure that it can handle more simultaneous users without slowing down.

Especially if your server is located in-house, consider upgrading to a dedicated DSL or a fractional T1 or T3 line instead of a regular telephone connection. The table in Figure 4.5 shows the different types of lines, with sample rates, setup fees, and purposes. The rates for these lines vary around the country. They may run anywhere from tens to several thousand dollars per month, depending on your needs and usage.

Establish User Hardware/Software Requirements for Your Site

You rarely have a guarantee about your users' computer skills, equipment, software, or navigational savvy on the Web. It may be helpful to include several questions about such matters on the survey you use to build your audience profile. Will your viewers have the latest version of a browser? (If you are upgrading an existing site, you may have statistics showing the platforms, browsers, and browser versions that your visitors currently use.) Will your site be compatible with multiple browsers? Be sure to discuss your expectations with your Web designer. Plan

Type of line	Typical Monthly Rate	Set Up Fee	Purpose
Dial Up 56K	Free-$40	none	low volume, one person, dial up connection, unlimited time, email
DSL or Cable	$20- $250	$40-$250	Small-medium sized business or residence, low security, always on
Dedicated ISDN line 64kbps	$100-$200	$100-$250	Permanent Internet connection for LAN, email and/or low volume server
Burstable T-1 line	$500-$2000	$1000-$1500	Average to large sized business using multimedia, point-to-point access
Full T-1 line	$1000-$1500	$1000-$1500	Large, high volume business, full time access, fastest

Figure 4.5. Telecommunication rates.

to have in-house whatever hardware and software you expect most of your customers to have.

Remember that the more multimedia you put on your site, the more sophisticated the user software and hardware required, and the more likely some viewers will be shut out. Is your audience really likely to download and install plug-ins for multimedia? Too much animation, too much Java programming, too much streaming media for movie clips, and your viewers will click away to another site. Although the majority of testing will be the responsibility of your Web designer, you should duplicate a typical viewer's experience before signing off and accepting the work.

At this point, you're ready to search for service providers. Put the planning worksheets and budgets into your Web notebook—it will soon be filled with detailed schedules, cost estimates, task lists, RFQs, bid responses, contracts, design documents, and written sign-offs.

Selecting Service Providers: ISP, Web Host, Designer and/or Engineer

The first decision is whether to handle your site in-house or to hire others. It is certainly possible for a large company, with the right resources and skilled personnel on staff, to become its own ISP, host its own site, and handle all design and promotion internally. Many do. Some corporations staff their Web unit with 6 to 12 people; others create an entire online division as an independent profit center to market and sell products on the Web.

Small high-tech companies may have the in-house skills to create, maintain, and host a modest site, growing staff as the need arises. They may contract out only for ISP and graphic design support. Other small companies decide their Web plans are so modest that they hire an owner's teenager or send an administrative assistant to take a class in Web design, locate a Web host, sometimes selecting their phone company for sheer convenience, and decide they're finished. Still others use the site-building template on an online service to start a one-person, Web-based, home business. Sometimes the results are great; sometimes self-created Web sites resemble the early newsletters produced when people decided they were skilled with desktop publishing software.

However, most small companies don't have people with necessary Web skills in-house, and their staff is often stretched thin. Their options are to use a one-stop template-based shop, to hire a Webmaster to manage the process, or to outsource the entire project. Even an outsourced project will require an internal coordinator and draw on more staff resources than you expect. There are ways to do a good site with relatively little money, but there is no way to do a great site without a significant investment of time.

There is no one right solution. In business you usually have to spend money to make money. That may mean going with a pro, either in-house or outside. The more complex your site in terms of transactions, multimedia, or size, the more you need professional guidance. If you are serious about the Web, it is worth an investment to make the site easy to use, graphically appealing, and effective for marketing and sales.

Otherwise, it may turn out to be an expense that never returns cost savings or increased revenue.

Web sites are subject to a truism that affects all forms of media production: "You can have it good; you can have it fast; you can have it cheap. Pick any two."

Selecting an Internet Service Provider (ISP)

Chances are you long ago selected one of the more than 8,800 ISPs to connect your business or home to the Internet. (Point to *http://www.thelist.internet.com* for a directory sorted by country, state, and area code.) How else could you have done all this research? You may also have established accounts with one or more commercial online services that you want to keep for marketing reasons.

Criteria for ISP selection are a subset of those used to select a Web hosting service. To obtain Internet access for your company, you probably looked at such factors as

- Rates for connect time; unlimited service is best for a business.

- Free local access numbers and cost-free, dial-in access when out of town. Most ISPs support Internet mail access at the very least. Many regional or local ISPs charge for access when you use a toll-free number; this can add up if you travel a great deal. Otherwise travelers have to find a cyber-cafe with Internet access by the hour.

- Reliability and speed of access to the Internet and to your office. POTS (Plain Old Telephone Service) may be a limiting factor. Not all ISPs can bring you in on leased lines, T1, or DSL service. Other limitations include the number of customers (the average ISP has several thousand) and the connection speed between the ISP and the Internet backbone.

- The number of e-mail boxes provided under one account.

- Convenient installation of browser software, plug-ins like Real Audio, Real Video, or Shockwave, and extras like Adobe Acrobat Reader.

- Support, security, and backup procedures, including redundant servers.

- A free trial period or month-to-month contract option so you can assess your satisfaction before signing a long-term contract.

- Compatibility with existing and planned hardware and telecommunications capabilities.

The graph in Figure 4.6 from *http://cyberatlas.internet.com/big_picture/ hardware/reasons.html* shows what factors influenced ISP choice by over 1,000 businesses and 6,000 business users in 1999. Businesses still say they are satisfied no more than 35% of the time, citing as their the most frequent complaints with ISPs as

- Slow log-ins, 45%

- Busy signals, 26%

- Too expensive, 26%

The ISP marketplace is changing rapidly as large companies merge and/or acquire smaller firms. Nationwide providers like AT&T or MCI Worldcom and regional suppliers like the Baby Bells have begun to displace mom-and-pop ISPs, and the field is rife with mergers. Figure 4.7 (*http://www.internet.org/cgi-bin/genobject/connectivity*) shows the market share of the largest ISPs in the United States.

ISPs are entering an era of commodity pricing similar to that of long distance. There is additional price pressure from "free" ISP services, which are advertiser-supported. Most ISPs now offer unlimited Internet access for $15 or less per month for basic service, including one e-mail account and 3 to 5 MB of free Web space. However, they vary widely in the availability of free local access numbers, the number of calls they can handle at any one time, the nature of their own connection to the Internet, and the space for personal home pages.

For serious marketing, look for an ISP that can provide multiple e-mail addresses, mailing list programs (listservers), mailbots, news group access, and **FTP (file transfer protocol)**. The provider must give you a **SLIP/PPP** account (Serial Line Internet Protocol/Point-to-Point Proto-

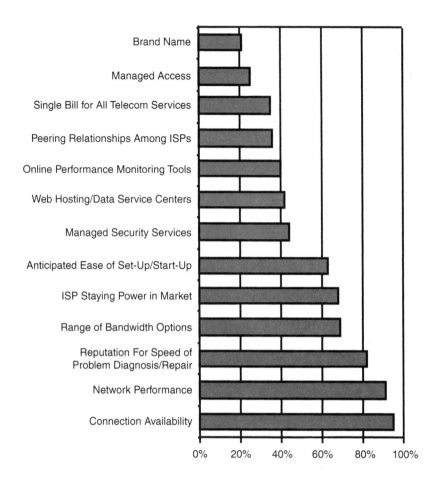

Figure 4.6. Reasons customers choose an ISP, *http://cyberatlas.internet.com/ big_picture/hardware/reasons.html*. Reprinted with permission. © 1999 Internet. com, LLC. All rights reserved.

col—the Internet protocols that support Web and FTP servers). If an ISP can't provide all or most of these functions, keep shopping. Some, but not all, ISPs also host Web sites.

Some ISPs have a start-up fee; others offer a discount for year-long contracts; some charge extra for services like mailbots and listservers. Compare costs for start-up, first year, and subsequent years of service, as well as connection track record, business history, and customer rat-

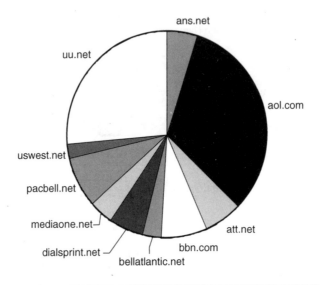

Figure 4.7. ISP market share, *http://www.netsizer.com/daily/isp.html.* Source: Netsizer.com/*www.netsizer.com*

ing. The lowest-priced service may not be the best bargain; sometimes you get what you pay for.

For references, check with existing customers or review customer rankings of ISPs in your area at *http://www.cnet.com/Content/Reports/ Special/ISP/index.html?tag=st.cn.sr1.dir.* Figure 4.8 provides an ISP selection checklist. Based on your online marketing plan, decide on the services you will need, customize this checklist, and request bids from several providers based on the same set of services.

Selecting a Web Host

Not all ISPs host Web sites, and not all Web hosts provide Internet access service. Depending on your choices, you may end up with two different providers or you may find some, such as Planet Systems Network *(http:/ /psn.net/business),* or Earthlink *(http://www.earthlink.net/business),* that offer an integrated business package encompassing both. In this virtual world, a Web host with a server thousands of miles away may host your site, but a local ISP with a free access number may be used for e-mail and

ISP Name _____ Date _____

Item	Y/N	Description	Cost
General			
Length of time in business?			
Staff qualifications/turnover?			
Client references? (get 3)			
System			
Local access numbers?			
Access numbers nationally?			
800-number access? Surcharge?			
Type of Internet connection?			
What connection speeds does the ISP cater to/handle?			
How much traffic at once?			
Security, e.g. firewalls?			
What % of time was server available during past 3 months?			
Server/connection redundancy?			
Back-up policy?			
Pricing			
What is the pricing structure?			
Monthly Flat Rate?			
Hourly?			
Add-on and over-quota rates?			
Long-term discounts?			
On/off connection fees?			
Technical Services			
Software pre-configured for use on your end?			
Will they support reconfiguration of your existing set-up, if needed?			
Can they support mailing lists? News groups? Mailbots?			
What level/hours is technical support provided?			
What are the charges for technical support? Set-up? Troubleshooting?			
Other			
Free personal Web space? Size?			
How many free mailboxes with account? Cost for additional?			

Figure 4.8. ISP selection checklist. © 1997-2000 Watermelon Mountain Web Marketing.

Internet searching. If your ISP and Web host are different companies, decide whether you want the Web host to forward mail received at your site address to another e-mail name (called an **alias**). Figure 4.9 *(http://www.internet.org/cgi-bin/genobject/hosting)* shows the market share for the 13 largest Web hosting companies in the United States.

You will need to communicate directly to your site, perhaps via FTP, for uploading new content files, downloading transaction records, or checking statistics. Your Web host should provide you with directions for doing this. Some of the statistical analyses discussed in Chapter 6 should come with your hosting contract at no additional charge. Hosting services may not support all Web development packages equally. If a certain site development package is critical, perhaps due to an existing **legacy site**, that must become a selection criterion.

Depending on your needs, there will be additional technical questions, such as

- The bandwidth available, which determines the number of hits your site can handle at once. Approximately 1500 Kbps bandwidth (a T1 line) will handle 50K hits per month, assuming traffic

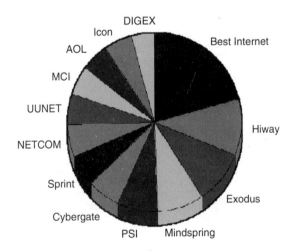

Figure 4.9. Web hosting market share, *http://www.internet.org/cgi-bin/genobject/hosting.* Courtesy Michael Bauer, Internet.org.

is spread evenly. Remember, though, that traffic spikes may occur with special offers or events and other forms of site promotion.

- What operating system the host uses/supports. Of the two most commonly used operating systems, UNIX is generally used for large sites that expect high traffic volume, while Microsoft NT is acceptable for smaller sites.

- The connection between the host server and the Internet backbone, especially if you need high speed and wide bandwidth for multimedia.

- Whether you need a server solely for use by your company (**dedicated server**) instead of a **shared server** used by many other companies. Dedicated servers are faster and more flexible; shared servers are less expensive and generally used for smaller sites.

- Whether the Web host has redundant equipment in case a server goes down.

- The Web host's provisions for backups and data security.

- What statistics will be available to analyze traffic to your site.

- Which catalog, shopping cart, and checkstand packages are supported, and what provisions exist for secure credit card processing.

- Whether the site supports **CGI** (Common Gateway Interface) programs that allow non-Web information to be turned into a Web document on the fly. These are frequently used for on-site registration, electronic order forms, and surveys.

- What other services are offered, such as Web design, Web mall operation, site promotion, or audited statistics for advertising traffic.

Most companies have an initial setup fee plus monthly charges and add fees for special services, such as automated fax-back. Most offer discounts for long-term contracts. Prices vary widely—from tens to hundreds of dollars per month. Identify several Web hosts that can provide the services and space you need, then compare prices on a spreadsheet. Web hosting fees may be based on

- The amount of space needed on the server (estimate 10 KB per page of Web text; graphics or multimedia will take more space).

- The amount of traffic you estimate per month.

- The frequency and size of data transfers.

- The number of domain names supported.

- Support for specialized programs, such as streaming video, database software, animation, or particular e-mail or security programs.

- Support for specialized electronic commerce services, including access to a secure server. Some Web hosts specialize in transaction-intensive sites, with prices based on catalog size.

- Additional statistical analysis.

As with ISP selection, analyze start-up costs, first-year total costs, and subsequent-year costs independently. A small business should be able to find a solution for between $10 and $250 per month, depending on the size and complexity of its site. Cost, however, should be only one factor in your decision. Pay particular attention to business history, performance history, technical support, and customer service. There are already many sad stories of Web hosts and developers going out of business leaving their customers stranded. Almost all Web hosts provide a list of customers on their own site. For references, e-mail the Webmasters of several sites similar in scope to yours.

You can check the monthly ratings of the Top 25 Web Hosts and find other information at such sites as

- *http://www.hostindex.com*

- *http://www.hostcompare.com/checklist.htm*

- *http://www.tophosts.com*

The checklist in Figure 4.10 summarizes selection criteria for a Web host. Before you start the process, check off the items you need and estimate quantitative entries, such as the number of expected hits per month (average and maximum) and the total space needed in megabytes. You may need assistance from your Web developer to fill in some of these blanks.

The Mall Alternative

Malls are virtual shopping areas on a server or online service that host or link related commercial sites. Some Web hosts define their own mall as a package of services that includes hosting, design, store building, transaction processing, and promotion.

Like every other Web service, rates vary widely depending on the mall and the benefits it provides. For example, The Great Internet Mall of the Americas at *http://www.intermallamerica.com* shown in Figure 4.11 offers a turnkey solution including hosting, template-based store building, transaction processing, banner advertising on the mall, and assistance establishing a merchant card account through *http://www.ccnow.com*, an online reseller. (As you'll see later, the last option can be helpful if you have a new small business.)

Another Internet mall, *http://merchant.shopnow.com/list.jsp*, acts more like an advertising site. Its service consists of home page links with promotional and merchandising opportunities. Rates start at $29.95 per year for an "entry tenant" with a 20-word directory listing and a link. Other tenant levels, from "standard" to "anchor" at rates of $509 to $2,999 per year, offer a longer description, keywords in a search engine, and other features. Some malls offer additional on-site advertising, ranging from $9 to $30 CPM based on location within the site.

Selecting a Web Designer and/or Engineer

Web design has become the latest career fad for computer whiz kids, hackers, and underemployed artists, but a business site requires a great deal more skill and sophistication than a personal home page does. Not all Web designers are created equal. Highly skilled programming houses don't always have graphics and marketing communications

Web Host Name _____ Date _____

Item	Y/N	Description	Cost
General			
Length of time in business?			
Staff qualifications/turnover?			
Client references? (get 3, preferably on the Web)			
System			
Type of connection to the Internet?			
What connection speeds does the Web Host cater to?			
How much traffic can they handle at a time?			
What provisions do they have for security, e.g. firewalls?			
What % of time was server available during past 3 months?			
Server/connection redundancy?			
Back-up policy?			
Pricing			
What is the pricing structure?			
Monthly flat rate? for space in MB? Hits in K?			
Add-on and over-quota rates for space or hits?			
Long-term discounts?			
On/off connection fees?			
Technical Services			
Predominantly UNIX or NT shop?			
What level/hours is technical support provided?			
What are the charges for technical support? Setup? Trouble shooting?			
Can they handle streaming media, if applicable?			
What kinds of monitoring/server and site reports are available? How often?			

Figure 4.10. Web host selection checklist. © 1997-2000 Watermelon Mountain Web Marketing. (continued on next page)

Web Host Name _____   Date _____

Item	Y/N	Description	Cost
Do they do routine link verification? Syntax checking?			
What Web development packages do they support?			
How easy will it be to make changes to the Web site?			
Frequency and fees for updating?			
Web Development Services			
Do they provide design support? Custom or template?			
Do they bill by hour or by job?			
What kinds of multimedia can they create/support?			
Do they develop/support interactive pages? CGI? or perl?			
Do they handle SQL or other database programming?			
Do they have in-house copywriters?			
Web Promotion Services			
Do they offer Web marketing consulting? (by hour or job?)			
What kind of Web promotion is available/included? (e.g. submissions, What's New?)			
Transaction Support			
Catalog, shopping cart, and/or checkstand software?			
Secure server (SSL minimum)			
Real-time transaction processing? (e.g. Cybercash)			
Digital ID and/or encryption?			
Are they tied to any specific providers? If so, which ones?			

Figure 4.10. Web host selection checklist. © 1997-2000 Watermelon Mountain Web Marketing. (continued from previous page)

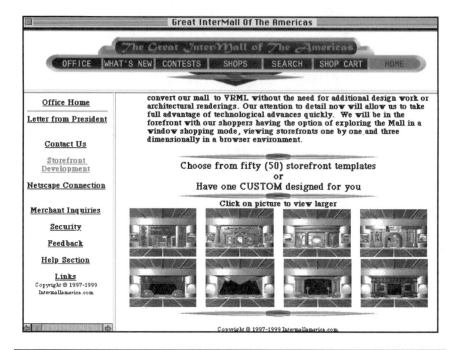

Figure 4.11. Turnkey mall site, *http://www.intermallamerica.com/flowbar/office/start.html.* Courtesy Intermallamerica.com.

know-how. Wonderful graphics artists and ad agencies don't always understand the Web implications of their designs in terms of download speed or navigation.

Not all developers have the knowledge to build effective order-taking mechanisms; not all are familiar with specific feature modules; not all have business experience. You are more likely to find providers with excellent technical and/or graphic skills than with a marketing background. *You* must add the marketing insight to the process. Be sure that the developer you hire has

- References and a portfolio of existing sites.

- A reasonable business history.

- The skills and experience to do the job you need, including specific expertise in e-commerce if needed.

- The time and staff to produce the work according to your timeline.

- The flexibility to work within your budget.

- The willingness to contract for site updates on a regular basis.

- Experience with standard business and programming practices, from business contracts to commenting code.

An ISP, Web host, or advertising agency may offer design services, or you can check for Web designers in your city's creative directory or with an Internet professional association. On sites you like, look for the developer's name at the bottom of a home page or on the "About Us" page. You can always ask for a referral from a business whose site you want to emulate. Finally you can search for design companies online at such sites as

- SiteMine.com Developer Directory: *http://www.sitemine.com/developer.asp*

- Yahoo Design Referral Program: *http://www.viaweb.com/vw/partdir.html*

- Web Designer Directory: *http://www.eg-web.com*

- Digital Spinner's Web Developer Directory: *http://digitalspinner.com/directory*

Always, always, always look at designers' work online; almost all have a portfolio of links on their own site. (If they don't, ask yourself, "Why not?") Call or e-mail several of their clients to check references. (E-mail addressed to Webmaster often forwards to the designer, so contact the clients' marketing or communications department directly.) While a Web host may be located anywhere, a local Web designer may be more convenient for face-to-face meetings. If you can't find the skills you need locally, look for companies adept at combining audio teleconferencing with online posting to work with clients long distance. Design costs may be lower if you select someone away from either coast. Only you can weigh the factor of convenience versus cost.

If you're satisfied with a basic site, you can short-circuit the design process by signing up with a Web host such as Hiway Technologies (see Figure 4.12, *http://hiway.com/expresstart*) that offers a template tool for Web design. For a low-cost, high-quality compromise, identify a local graphic artist with the skills to customize a template. An experienced eye can quickly select colors, typefaces, and buttons that add a sophisticated veneer to an otherwise pedestrian design. (See the Freebies section at the end of Chapter 5 for other template sources.) Your needs, as well the designer's rates, skills, and availability, will determine the best provider for you.

Selecting a Web designer is a multistep process. First, assemble a list of 8 to 12 potential providers based on referrals, sites you've collected, and/or directories. After looking at their on-site portfolios, select no more than 6 whose work you like. Then use the questionnaire in Figure 4.13, modified according to your Web plan, to prequalify potential Web designers by phone or e-mail. At this point, narrow your list to 3 or so that you will ask to respond to a request for quote (**RFQ**).

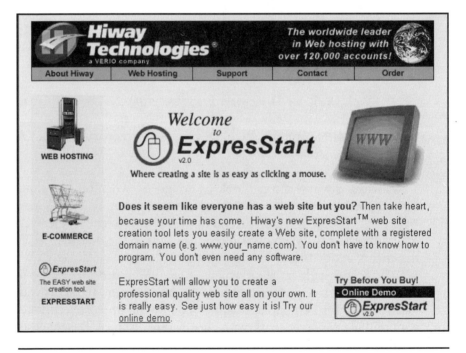

Figure 4.12. Templates for Web design, *http://hiway.com/expresstart*. Courtesy Verio, Inc.

Requests for Quote

An RFQ may consist of

- A cover letter requesting a bid and the due date for a response.

- A brief description of how you envision the site.

- A list of features.

- A tentative site index.

- A list of deliverables (e.g., do you want JPEG illustrations? HTML code?).

- A timeline for development.

The more detailed your RFQ, the more accurate the bids you will receive. Three fictional RFQs, shown in Figures 4.14 to 4.16, will give you an idea. Unless you use a standard RFQ for your site, it may be impossible to compare prices and services from different designers. With answers and bids in hand, you should have the information to make a selection.

To solicit more bids, you may e-mail your RFQ to a number of Web developers or post your RFQ on business association, local ISP or Internet organization sites, or on your own purchasing pages. Many large corporations and government agencies are required to do such postings as a matter of purchasing policy or law respectively.

You may choose to split the RFQ for your site in two and double your search effort to provide two separate sources, one for design and one for programming. If one provider designs the "look-and-feel" of your Web site and another handles the engineering, insist that they communicate closely. If artists are not familiar with the exigencies of the Web, their designs may take a long time to download or be hard to navigate. They may deliver art that appears completely different on a low-resolution monitor with the limited color palette of the Web, or that is difficult for programmers to execute. Similarly, Web engineers may not understand the importance of a particular graphic element and give it short shrift.

If you haven't already done so, try to meet local finalists at their office to discuss your RFQ. That way you can confirm the designers have the equipment you'd expect and that the personal chemistry exists.

Web Developer Questionnaire

1. How long have you been in business?
   How long have you been designing Web sites?

2. If not already available, please provide the URLs and client references for at least three sites you have designed, preferably ones similar to ours. Describe what services you performed for each of these sites.

3. Which Web services do you offer?

   a. Graphic design and page layout?
   b. Copywriting?
   c. Basic HTML programming? (What software/package do you use?)
   d. CGI scripting?
   e. Java/Shockwave (for animations)?
   f. Database programming?
   g. Other (e.g. Perl)?
   h. Site updates? Frequency and cost?

4. Do you design banner ads?

5. What is your policy on site updates?

6. Do you perform site testing? If so, on which browsers, which versions, which platforms?

7. Will you do site verification, e.g. code, dead links, spelling etc.? How often?

8. Do you offer any promotional services?

9. Do you work with a team or alone? If a team, who would be our contact point? Who are the other members of the team?

10. What is your process for working with clients? e.g. comps? Review stages? Testing?

11. Our development schedule is:_____. What is your availability?

12. Do you price by job, page, or hour? What are your basic rates and/or rates for each service you offer?

If applicable, add:

13. We are thinking of adding multimedia (specify type) in the future. What relevant multimedia production experience do you have? (Get URL and reference)

14. We are thinking of adding a special feature (e.g. chat line, forum) in the future. Have you done this before? (Get URL and reference)

15. This will be a transaction site, with X (number of) products that are paid for by (Y) payment processes. We expect Z (number of) purchases per week. What access to and experience with storebuilding, checkstand and payment software modules do you have? Are you tied to development and/or support of particular products?

16. Do you understand that this will be a work for hire and copyright will belong to us?

Figure 4.13. Web developer questionnaire. © 1997-2000 Watermelon Mountain Web Marketing.

Old McDonald Web Site

This site will be Soybean Brothers' informational tool for farmers and ranchers with small-to-medium holdings. The objectives are to record 7,000 hits per week, with a minimum of 25% of the visitors returning at least four times within a three-month period. The site will provide real-time commodity and livestock prices direct from the Chicago Board of Trade; farm news; weather reports by region; live chat "Ask the Aggie" discussion sessions; and a bulletin board for farmers to seek advice from one another. Support for this project will be required from the MIS, sales, and marketing departments. Formal content sources, such as commodity prices and weather reports are available on a contractual basis; members of the School of Agriculture at Landgrant U. and employees of County Extension have agreed to participate in "Ask the Aggie" discussion sessions. Initial development costs of $20,000 and $2,000 per month maintenance costs will be supported by paid advertising and online sales of soy additives. The site is expected to generate $4,000 per month in revenues, breaking even after 11 months and earning a profit thereafter.

Figure 4.14. Fictional RFQ: Old McDonald.

Humble Pie Web Site

The Humble Pie Web site will be established to create a corporate Web presence while allowing customers to place pie orders for delivery or pickup at any of our 234 nationwide franchise locations. The site will incorporate contests, games, and client-printed promotional coupons. The objectives are to generate 20,000 hits in the first two months after launch, with purchases by 3% of the viewers.

This first module will later be augmented with an **Extranet** (a Wide Area Network with Weblike operations) to facilitate franchisee communication with headquarters for such purposes as ordering supplies, learning about new promotional campaigns, and training.

The advertising agency for Humble Pie will handle site construction and maintenance with input from our own marketing department. The $30,000 development expense and $6,000 monthly expenses will be offset by cost savings in training and order processing after one year of operation.

Figure 4.15. Fictional RFQ: Humble Pie.

My Favorite Guru Web Site

My Favorite Guru will be an infotainment Web site constructed as a psychic mall for alternative religions. The objective is to generate 60,000 hits per month, with each visitor linking to at least three sites in the mall per visit.

To attract visitors to mall sites, My Favorite Guru will offer streaming audio of new age music, streaming video of blessings by religious leaders such as the Maharishi Maheesh Yogi and Baba Ram Dass, audio clips of mantras, and downloadable video clips of ever-changing Sufi patterns. When their psychic energy is low, users can communicate with one another through text and audio chat rooms. Response levels will be monitored for each mall tenant and for each multimedia activity. If an activity generates fewer than 2500 hits per month, it will be replaced.

Sixteen organizations have expressed preliminary interest in the mall. We will need to hire a programmer/Webmaster to program and maintain the site, with additional specialty work contracted out under supervision of the sales and marketing department. Mall lessees will pay a monthly fee of $1,000, 50¢ per hit, or 5% commission on sales referrals from this mall, whichever is greater, to cover development and maintenance costs.

Figure 4.16. Fictional RFQ: My Favorite Guru.

Before signing with your choice of design and/or Web engineering firm, ask to see a sample contract. A contract may include as attachments the design description from your RFQ, a schedule of interim deliveries and review dates, and a schedule of payments. Make sure that you will retain password control and access to the site to make at least some changes yourself. Confirm that your company will own the copyright and that you will have physical ownership of commented programming code for the site (i.e., offline backup disks or download and hard copy produced several times a week). Having the code will make it easy to move your site, its development, or its maintenance to another provider, if necessary. This is particularly important if your designer is also your Web host.

Some companies offer an introductory package as low as $275 to $795 for a for a basic 3- to 5-page site including hosting. Others price by the page ($60 to $200 for roughly an 8.5" × 11" page), with add-on fees for custom design and multimedia. Still others charge only by the hour, though you can set a limit on the number of hours, prioritizing what will be eliminated if you run out of money.

Don't be surprised to find that hourly rates vary not only by region of the country ($50–$150/hour), but also by task complexity. Basic HTML programming is at the low end of the scale, with Java, database programming, and strategic planning at the high end.

As we've discussed, costs for Web development range from free (see "Freebies and Features" in Chapter 5) to tens of thousands of dollars. As you can tell by looking at some of the sites in this book, there is no upper limit. A Fortune 500 company may spend anywhere from $500,000 to more than $5 million to create a transaction-intensive, electronic commerce site! As a rule of thumb, estimate an average of $100 per page.

Domain Name Registration

If you haven't done so already, you must select and register a domain name. As you can tell from their presence in all advertising media, URLs have become ubiquitous.

A Site by Any Other Name Might Not Smell As Sweet

How important are names? Very! Your Web identity and self-promotion start with your domain. Be as careful choosing your URL as you were selecting your business name; it's an absolutely critical Internet marketing decision. Make the domain name easy to remember, easy to type, and/or self-descriptive for easy searching. The appellation *.com* immediately signals that you are a commercial enterprise; *.net* and *.org* are considered less desirable, although some businesses register the same name using all three extensions.

Company names work particularly well whether you already have brand recognition (e.g., Sony.com) or a preexisting customer base. It's the first name most people will try online; many will never bother to use a search engine to find you. If the nouns in your business name are already taken, try adding "inc" or "company" or keywords describing what you sell, such as HealthyPlanetNaturalFoods.com. Or try hyphenating your business name: Healthy-Planet-Market.com.

If your business name isn't descriptive (Petunia's), perhaps your product description is artsupplies.com. You can also try for "clever." A name like eat.com, which Lipton Inc. uses on its Ragu Sauces site, draws attention from the curious. Portals and businesses with an expansive online mission aim for short, flexible names that are easy to remember but won't limit them to specific products (e.g., Amazon.com, go.com, or snap.com.

With the recent expansion of URLs from 22 characters to 63 (plus extensions), many more names have become available. That's a good thing: 97% of the single words in Webster's dictionary have already been taken by "name prospectors," even though less than half are active sites! Stumped? Network Solutions (*http://www.network solutions.com*) now offers "My Name Finder," a feature that generates available multi-word domain name combinations from a list of business synonyms you have entered.

To open up more URLs, **ICANN** (Internet Corporation for Assigned Names and Numbers) is considering creating additional domain extensions, such as *.info* or *.shop*. There is even talk of a *.xxx* extension for adult sites. Be cautious about using new domains. Both users and search engines will have trouble finding your site until new extensions are well-established. Beware, too, of companies promoting domains like *.ws* (Western Samoa) or *.cc* (Cocos Islands). These are not easily recognized and will leave your site stranded in cyberspace, alone and visitor-less. As you'll learn in Chapter 10, there are legitimate reasons to register in different countries you have targeted in your global marketing plan. Registering with a specific country's domain extension may make it easier to be found by search engines that serve that nation.

Your domain name is actually converted into a numerical Internet Protocol address. All computers on the Internet are instructed that this address is found on the server where your domain resides. After it has been assigned, no one else can use your domain name. Needless to say, once your name is registered, you'll be besieged by a "welcome wagon" of companies offering Web-related products and services.

Registration Process

To reserve a name, registrants previously had to use Network Solutions, Inc. at *networksolutions.com*, which had an exclusive, five-year contract with the U.S. government to manage domain name registration. Now 124 companies are accredited by ICANN to register top-level domain names (*.com*, *.net*, and *.org*), all using the expanded Shared Registry System. This central database is currently stored at Network Solutions and at the Internet Network Information Center (InterNIC). For a list and more information on registration companies, go to *http://www.icann.org*. For more information on InterNIC policies, go to *http://rs.internic.net*.

Domain registration costs $70 for the first two years, with an annual $35 renewal fee thereafter. You can register yourself at any of the ICANN sites, or let your Web host or ISP handle domain name registration for you. This service has become so competitive that you should not have to pay any charges beyond the regular registration fee. If you are hosting your own site, you will need to register your server first and then your name.

Standard registration procedures are easy. First, see if your desired name is available by searching the WhoIs database at *http://whois. internic.net/* or on any of the registration sites. After you have selected a name (as long as it doesn't use anyone else's trademark), apply online through one of the registration services.

If you want to reserve several names until you make a final decision, you can "park" a name on someone's server temporarily. Some Web hosts will "park" names for free (e.g., *http://www.domain save.com* at WebHosting.Com) or a modest fee (e.g., *http://www. abidingweb.com)* until you are ready to go online. This is an enticement to use their service, but you can easily transfer the name elsewhere (sometimes with an administrative charge). If you've paid a "parking fee," the Web host will often apply the amount to your account if you select it as your host. A "parked" name is reserved until the payment period expires, 30 days after the date on the invoice you receive from InterNIC. Once you've paid for the name, of course, it's yours as long as you renew it.

Many companies advertise reduced registration rates as a loss leader to win clients for other services, such as hosting, design, or promotion. For instance, some companies offer a one-page Website and registration for as little as $35 per year (plus personalized hat!) at *http:// www.register.com*. Website University claims to offer free registration and a six-page design by its students in exchange for a year-long hosting agreement *(http://www.websiteuniversity.com)*. A number of others, including Network Solutions and *http://www.bulkregister.com*, offer discounts for bulk name registration.

Within the "name" marketplace, you can find supplemental name services. You can "wait-list" your first-choice name at *http:// www.mymonitor.com*, which will automatically register it for you at no additional charge if the name becomes available. At *http://www.my domain.com* you can arrange to mask a long domain name with your preferred one, forward visitors from your preferred domain name to a free site, or forward e-mail from one address to another. For a fee, RealNames will direct users from your business name to your URL at *http://www.realnames.com.*

What's in a Name? Money and More

Names are important enough that some companies buy up any possible spellings (and misspellings) of their name, as well as any derogatory terms that could refer to them. Businesses may find themselves paying to reclaim their own brand names unless they have reserved them through trademark. Courts have held that **cybersquatting**—using someone else's trademarks within a domain name—is illegal. This happened to Compaq, owner of search engine AltaVista, which paid $3.35 million to reclaim altavista.com in 1998. If your desired name is taken, you may be able to negotiate a purchase with the owner, whose name you will find in the WhoIs database. If a site is already active, the price may be higher.

Some companies and individuals have simply gone into the name game, buying up as many names as they can think of and then licensing or selling them. It can be lucrative! The name WallStreet.com was auctioned in April 1999 to a Venezuelan company for over $1 million. Business.com sold for $7.5 million in November 1999, and America.com was on the block for a cool $10 million. Most names sell for much less; even popular ones like tv.com or internet.com sold in the $15,000 to $150,000 range. Over 100 Web sites now broker names, either by auction or by soliciting private bids. For example, check out *http://www.bestdomains.com* or *http://www.greatdomains.com.*

Managing Transactions

Before you "go live" with your Web site, put in place the "back-end" processes you need, like accepting payment and fulfilling orders. If you host your own site, you may find that you need to purchase software to support specialized functions; if you host elsewhere, your selection of a Web engineer and host may well depend on their ability to provide such services as

- Automated payment processing.

- Automated e-mail for order verification and tracking.

- Feeding transaction data to your inventory and accounting software.

- Interface to customer support.

- Communication with warehouses and shippers.

Depending on the size of your operation, payment processing may a range from simple credit card processing through a secure server to full integration with inventory, warehousing, shipping, accounting, and other management information systems. The more sophisticated your financial processing, the greater the cost will be. Web hosts that specialize in online stores are best able to assist with handling transactions, especially for medium-to-large sites.

If you host your own site, you'll need to buy and install transaction software, which can be quite expensive. Hosting your own e-commerce site usually is viable only for large companies.

Accepting Payment Online

Just how sophisticated should you get when it comes to accepting payment? WebCom *(http://www.webcom.com)*, a transaction-based Web host, recommends assessing your needs as shown in Figure 4.17. Keep this model in mind as you read through the software options that follow.

For the smallest businesses in the first column, hand-processing transactions is a cost-effective option. **Electronic funds transfer (EFT)**, shown as a payment method, is the preauthorized transfer of funds from one bank account to another. It will be discussed in detail later.

Almost any Web software package can create an **electronic order form**, seen in the second column, for order and payment information; just be sure your Web host can handle CGI scripts. If you accept purchase orders or maintain open charge accounts for your customers, such a form is an excellent, low-cost alternative to credit cards. The completed form can be e-mailed back through a secure server, set up for automatic fax-back, or returned by mail with a check or money order.

Real-time credit card processing follows the checkstand process with credit card authorization, the equivalent of running a card through an

	1- 2 Products < 50 transactions per week	2-10 Products < 50 transactions per week	> 10 Products < 50 transactions per week	> 10 Products > 50 transactions per week
Order Method	Phone, fax, e-mail	Electronic order form	Shopping cart with checkstand	Shopping cart with checkstand
Payment Method	EFT or credit card by phone, fax, e-mail, check Money order	EFT or credit card by phone, fax, e-mail, check, Money order	EFT or credit card by phone, fax e-mail, check, Money order	CyberCash (real-time credit card processing)

Figure 4.17. Transaction needs by volume, *http://www.webcom.com*. Courtesy WebCom, worldwide host to small business. A member of the Verio Group.

electronic swiper at a storefront. The customer is not charged until the product is shipped, while the merchant is assured that the card number is valid and the account holder has credit available to cover the transaction.

Let's look at these options in greater detail. In most cases, payment is made by credit card, but taking that number and processing the payment may be handled several different ways. Credit card data may be delivered offline, faxed, or e-mailed after completing a form on the Web, or processed directly by a bank.

In spite of the perceived risk, credit cards are actually one of the best ways for individuals to make payment online. A cardholder's liability for unauthorized online use is now *zero*, and most cards act as a guarantee of satisfaction. That is, a consumer can easily cancel a credit card purchase and return unacceptable goods. Your risk as a merchant is far greater than your customers' risk.

Phone, Fax, and Snail Mail

Old-fashioned ways are both safe and inexpensive, allowing customers to mail a check, call an 800 number, or fax a printed form with a credit card number. Preferably, you want to offer customers a toll-free number to place an order by phone or fax. The rates for setting up and running inbound toll-free numbers vary by vendor and location. As you can see in Figure 4.18, it's worth a few calls to get the best price.

Provider	Setup Fee	Monthly Fee	Per Min. Charge
AT&T	None	$5	.09-.16¢ per min depending on state
Worldcom	None	$5	.07¢ anytime. state to state 10¢ in state
Qwest	None	$25 monthly minimum	6.7¢ state to state 5¢ local 5.9¢ instate

All prices vary from state to state

Figure 4.18. Sample rates for toll free numbers.

For a monthly and/or per transaction fee, some Web hosts will establish an automated fax-back system. This allows consumers to fill out their form online (without bothering to print it out), but the information is faxed rather than sent over the Internet. This method also works for individual customers with established accounts who receive monthly bills. You can accept an online purchase order from business customers without requesting sensitive credit card information.

Even if you accept credit card information online, always offer at least one alternative for customers who don't trust electronic methods. Given that 82% of small businesses themselves worry about credit card security and privacy on the Internet, it's not a surprise that 80% of their customers do. Resolve your concerns and theirs the way EyeWire does. This company, which sells images and tools to graphic designers, emphasizes its 800 number on its order information page at *http://www.eyewire.com* in Figure 4.19. The easier you make it for people to buy, the more sales you will make.

Credit Cards

In 1999 over 19 million people charged an average of $244 using a credit card online for a B2C transaction. That's over twice the number who charged in 1998 and represents $4.6 billion out of $3 trillion worth of total credit card transactions. By 2002, an estimated 120 million people will have purchased online, and 80% of those purchases will be

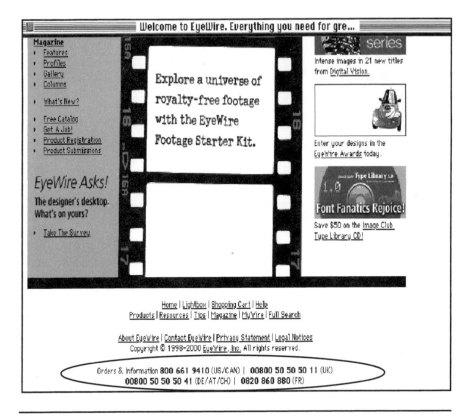

Figure 4.19. Offering the 800-number option, *http://www.eyewire.com.*
Courtesy Eyewire, Inc.

by credit card. By contrast, the average B2B online order was $800, as
seen in Figure 4.20.

After customers place an online order using their credit cards, their
payments (minus a transaction fee) are transferred by the card issuer to
your **merchant account.** Most card issuers provide free software to transfer information directly from your computer to theirs.

Although over a billion credit cards are in circulation, not all your
potential customers will use one online, especially if they are buying
internationally. (Europeans, for instance, prefer to use debit cards, checks,
or COD.) In the case of unauthorized transactions, such as children
using parents' cards without permission, the cardholder may refuse to
pay and/or you may end up with the expense of processing returns.

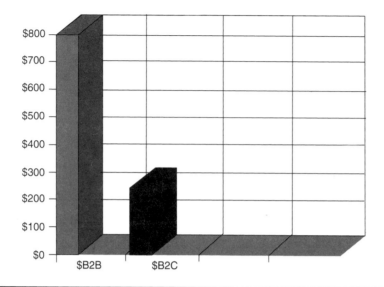

Figure 4.20. Comparison of B2B to B2C average online transaction by credit card, *http://www.emarketer.com/estats/112999trans.html.* Courtesy eMarketer, Inc.

In spite of these caveats, you could miss many sales if you don't take credit cards. Even the federal government now pays for most purchases under $2,500 (in some cases up to $25,000), using its own credit card equivalent, the IMPAC purchase card.

Setting Up a Merchant Account

Credit cards can be costly to you as a merchant. If you are not already set up to accept credit cards, research costs thoroughly. A card issuer may ask you to estimate the percentage of credit transactions to be handled electronically, by phone, or in person; your anticipated annual dollar volume on credit cards; and the average charge amount. While there are only four major providers (American Express, Visa, MasterCard, and Discover), card accounts are offered through a variety of sources.

Most, but not all, commercial banks offer merchant card accounts. You will have to provide basic business financial data and possibly personal financial information, especially if you are a sole proprietor or have only recently established your business. You may also be required to create a second checking account into which all your revenues from credit card sales will be deposited and against which all charges will be debited. Some banks are reluctant to establish merchant accounts for new, mail-order, or Web-only companies. If your local banks don't come up with a reasonable rate, try one of the national commercial banks or a company like EMS Global that specializes in setting up merchant accounts *(http://www.eft.com)*.

Most card issuers charge some combination of a one-time setup fee, a monthly fee for electronic swiping devices, a percentage of credit card sales, and/or a fee per transaction. All these fees vary, with the percentage of sales ranging from 1.2% to 6%. Generally speaking, the lower the value of receipts and the lower the volume of transactions, the higher the percentage rate you will be charged for each transaction. The table in Figure 4.21 shows some sample transaction rates for credit cards.

Given the highly variable fee combinations and percentage rates, it is definitely worth shopping around for the bank or service company that offers you the best rates for the type and amount of business you expect to do. For instance, American Express now has a flat fee of $5 per month for small businesses, as long as their annual charge volume is less than $5,000.

If these rates are too high or if your transaction volume is too low to qualify for a merchant account, consider using the services of CCnow *(http://www.ccnow.com*, shown in Figure 4.22). For a 9% transaction fee and no start-up or monthly fees, CCnow acts as a reseller to process credit charges for you. When they reach the checkstand, customers transfer invisibly to the CCnow secure site. A similar service is offered by *http://www.paypal.com, http://www.paybutton.com* or *http://www.ibillcom*.

Now that you have a merchant account, you need to arrange to handle credit card transactions online. CyberCash (see Figure 4.23) at *http://www.cybercash.com* is one of many providers of server software designed to manage electronic transactions securely in real time. Their add-on module, which is available from many Web hosting services (sometimes for a monthly fee), automates all credit card processing and provides immediate confirmation that the cardholder has an adequate limit to make the charge.

The CyberCash site lays out six steps to become a CyberCash merchant. The process is simpler if your Web hosting service already offers the module. In any case, note that you must already have a merchant card account.

The amount from a sale that goes to the card issuer (called the Monthly Discount Rate) depends on your transaction volume, average transaction amount, and means of reporting transactions. Merchant Accounts have additional fees for initial application, monthly statement, equipment rental or purchase, and supplies. There are also differences in minimum monthly charges and how quickly payments post to your account. Shop around! For additional information, try these sites: *http://merchant creditcard.com/rates.html* or *http://www.wilsonweb.com/articles/merch-cc.htm*.

Card Issuer	Monthly Discount Rate (% to Issuer)
MasterCard/Visa	1.59-2.35%
Discover	2.12-2.82%
American Express	2.95%-3.75%

Figure 4.21. Sample merchant account fees.

Figure 4.22. An alternative to your own merchant account, *www. ccnow.com*. Courtesy CCNow.

Figure 4.23. Provider of real-time transaction software and services, *http://www.cybercash.com*. © 1999-2000 Cybercash, Inc.

1. Notify your bank that you want to accept credit cards via CyberCash.

2. Execute a service agreement and complete the online registration form.

3. Download Cash Register software from the CyberCash Web site and execute the Software License agreement.

4. Generate a public/private encryption key using the utility provided, and e-mail the public key and your merchant name to CyberCash.

5. Install and integrate the Cash Register software into the Web store on your server.

6. When you are ready, e-mail CyberCash that you are ready to go live with online transactions.

Payment Alternatives

Credit cards aren't the most appropriate vehicle for all transactions. Another approach operates like a debit card, taking advantage of a digital wallet to create digital cash or e-money. A digital wallet is a secure, encrypted envelope that seals personal information, including bank accounts, credit card numbers and expiration dates, shipping and billing addresses, and digital IDs.

Customers, who must purchase digital cash before they can spend it, tuck the "cash" into their wallet as an encrypted data file. Entrypoint *(http://www.entrypoint.com,* shown in Figure 4.24) utilizes its own wallet technology for this service, which is particularly handy for small purchases, such as game playing time, database searches, and downloads. Microsoft bundles its wallet with newer versions of browsers.

Depending on your product, you could consider following the example of NewsLibrary *(http://www.newslibrary.com,* shown in Figure 4.25). Customers first set up a "passport" guaranteed by credit card. NewsLibrary bills the account monthly for any articles downloaded from its worldwide newspaper archives at prices ranging from $1.95 per article to $77 per month for 100 retrievals.

EFT on the Internet

Electronic Funds Transfer (EFT) refers to electronic payments transferred between two checking accounts. It covers both an automated deposit to and a withdrawal from an account. EFT can be accomplished as part of Electronic Data Interchange (described later), or independently.

Many people are familiar with EFT without knowing the term. Applications include the automated deposit of Social Security or payroll checks and automated withdrawals for such payments as dental insurance, gasoline credit cards, utility bills, or donations to a local public broadcasting station. Perhaps you have received a letter asking whether

Figure 4.24. Digital wallet, *http://www.entrypoint.com/cgi-bin/index.cgi.*
Courtesy EntryPoint, Inc.

you want such a service instead of paying by check. By the year 2002 almost all businesses and over 15 million households are expected to do some form of EFT. The Federal government plans to make all its benefits payments via EFT starting in 1999.

EFT is extremely effective for the billing company because it guarantees payment (as long as there is money in the account!). It saves the individual customer the time and effort of writing and mailing a check while saving the merchant the cost of bill processing, mail and deposit delays, and bad checks.

This works particularly well with customers who buy from your Web site on a regular basis, and it is also cost-effective for one-time purchases over several hundred dollars from a number of different customers. With cost and labor for processing a standard check now running up to $4, it's worth seeing if you can save several dollars (or more) per transaction. If your company receives hundreds of checks on a regular basis, as do fitness centers, Internet service providers, online newsletters, or cable companies, this may be an excellent option on or off the Web.

To explore this alternative, first survey your primary customers to see if they would be interested. Then talk to your bank. Most commer-

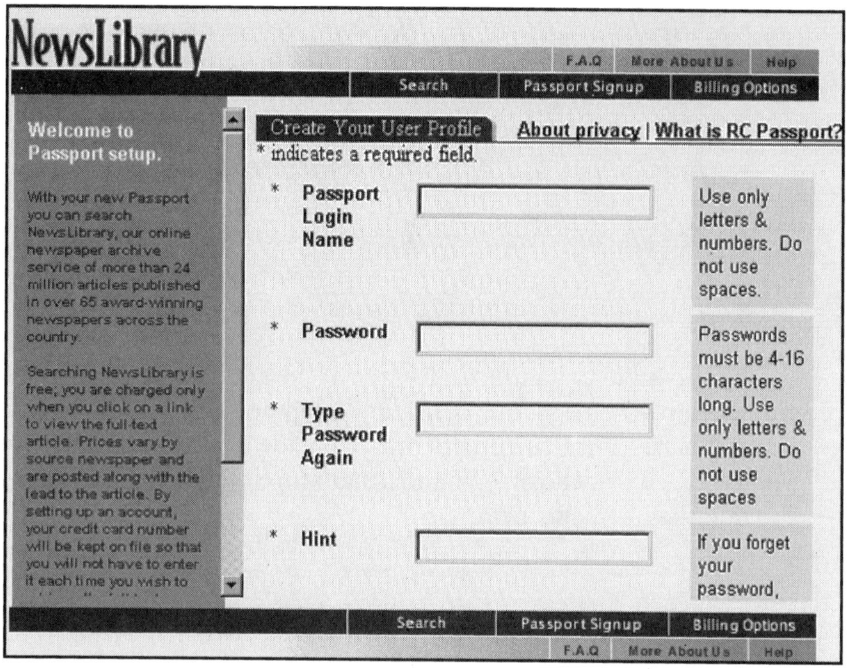

Figure 4.25. Guaranteed accounts for small purchases, *http://www. newslibrary.com/passports.htm*. Courtesy NewsLibrary.

cial banks are capable of handling EFT through the Automated Clearing House (ACH), which facilitates the transfer of funds between member banks. Bank of America, for instance, already has about 700,000 customers for its online bill payment system. In addition to a bank setup cost of $100 to $200, expect per transaction costs of 5 to 50 cents. Some banks charge a monthly fee and/or a per file transfer fee instead of, or in addition to, setup and transaction fees. Besides the bank's fees, there will be a charge for the software for your Website, generally starting around $900. You'll find general information about EFT at *http:// www.pulse-eft.com* or *http://www.transact.com/info/redieft.html*.

Often called interactive online billing and payment software, some EFT products can be integrated into shopping cart/checkstand software. This option is available as a turnkey solution for your Web site and/or as a service from

- *http://itransact.com/index.html* (seen in Figure 4.26)

- *http://www.cybercash.com/cybercash/services/paynow.html*

- *http://www.electronicfunds.com/index.html*

- *http://www.checkfree.com/index-ecommerch.html*

- *http://www.electronicfundtransfer.com*

It is possible to handle EFT without the automated software. If your transaction volume is low, consider an online form that users either fax or mail back. Since customers must provide a bank account number, a voided check or deposit slip, and a signature, they will need to print out the initial agreement form.

Figure 4.26.   Sample EFT site, *http://www.itransact.com*. Courtesy iTransact.com, Inc.

EDI on the Internet

Businesses that consistently trade with each other have one more option for secure financial transmission. **Electronic Data Interchange** (**EDI**) is the computer-to-computer exchange of structured business data, including invoices and payments, between two trading partners. With EDI, companies send each other business messages in a fixed format that moves information from one application to another without ever being rekeyed. This format is quite different from the unstructured nature of an e-mail message, as shown in Figure 4.27. Because it affects so many aspects of order taking, fulfillment, production, inventory, and bookkeeping, EDI has a major impact on business structure and processes.

Traditional EDI can be costly, running seven to ten times more than Internet-based forms of electronic commerce. Recent advances in EDI over the Internet have begun to make it more cost effective for small businesses. For some sellers, EDI speeds payment and thus improves cash flow. You can expect EDI costs per transaction to range from 1 to 2 cents per data line plus start-up costs.

In the past, both the buyer and seller, called **trading partners** in EDI lingo, had to subscribe to a **VAN** (**Value Added Network**), a private electronic network independent of the Internet, to act as the switchboard for transmit-

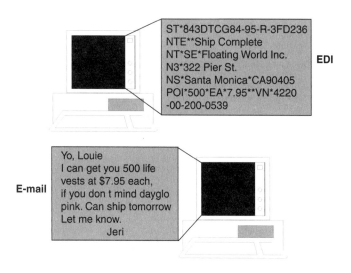

Figure 4.27. EDI vs. e-mail information format.

ting messages between them. Many EDI software vendors now offer products that integrate a Web site with EDI applications, avoiding VANs entirely.

The latest advance in making EDI available over the Web is the creation of **XML (eXtensible Markup Language)**, which packages Web data in a way that can be understood by EDI software. Since the latest version of Microsoft Office is XML enabled, EDI on the Internet is likely to receive a significant boost. Sales made using EDI over the Internet are now expected to reach $800 million in 2003, out of a total of $2 trillion in B2B sales.

Some large companies, particularly discount retailers and manufacturing firms, now require their suppliers to use EDI. For small businesses who want to sell to the WalMarts and General Motors of the world, an alternative solution is a Web-based EDI service offered by some of the main EDI vendors, such as Sterling Commerce, Harbinger, and GEIS. Small businesses enter required information at the EDI vendor's Web site. The vendor translates the information into EDI format and then transmits it to larger trading partners. Although small businesses must rekey the data into their internal systems, this approach makes EDI accessible to companies that cannot afford other EDI models. Figure 4.28 shows the site of 1EDIsource (*http://www.1edisource.com*), one of several companies that sell software for EDI on the Internet and off.

For more information on EDI, see these Web sites:

- *http://geocities.yahoo.com/cgi-bin/hood/geo?hood=WallStreet*

- *http://www.edi-info-center.com*

- *http://www.commercenet.com*

For selling to the government with EDI, try

- *http://www.acq.osd.mil/ec*

- *http://www.sba.gov/gopher/Ecedit/Facts*

Selecting a Payment Option

In the unpredictable world of the Internet, one trend is predictable: More and more business transactions will be handled with some combination of electronic technologies, whether it be the Web, EFT, or EDI. In 1998

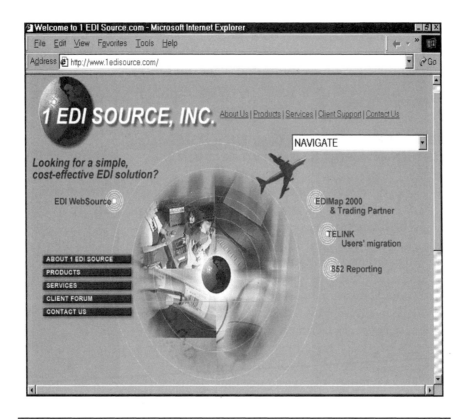

Figure 4.28. Vendor of EDI software on the Internet, *http://www. 1edisource.com. Courtesy 1EDISource, Inc.*

only 6% of sales transactions by volume came through electronic means, but projections are that this will increase to 24% by 2003.

As part of your online business plan, you need to weigh payment methods and their associated costs to decide which are best for you. If need be, make up sample spreadsheets estimating costs for transactions at various volume levels and average amounts. If it doesn't complicate your bookkeeping too much, you may want to hedge your bets by offering several payment options.

Make it clear on your site that you use secure transaction methods. Advertise on your Web page which payment methods you accept, just as merchants on Main Street place Visa, MasterCard, American Express, and Discover logos in their windows.

Make it as easy as possible for consumers to buy on your site with confidence. Try to allow customers to select a payment method based on their level of comfort and what their browser will accept.

Back Office Preparation for Order Fulfillment and Customer Support

Web development may seem simple compared to getting product out the door and into customers' hands. Some 25% of online transactions last Christmas were never completed! There's a high price to pay for failure: According to its study in the first quarter of 1999, BizRate.com found that online shoppers who experienced trouble were 73% less likely to buy from that Internet merchant again. A pretty Web face is simply not enough: Customers expect cyber-service levels to match the level of service in the real world. Figure 4.29 shows the high correlation between customer satisfaction functions and repeat purchases.

An order fulfillment process that satisfies customers must encompass everything from order taking and managing e-mail to warehousing and shipping. It may require that you establish

- Drop-shipping from a supplier.

- Accurate online inventory information so customers don't order out-of-stock items.

- Adequate server capacity to handle maximum traffic loads without crashing or slowing down the site.

- Order tracking, either online or by well-trained customer support representatives.

- A method for handling returns. **Click-and-mortar** businesses with a physical storefront have an advantage over pure "e-tailers" here, since customers can more easily return a product and pick out a replacement.

- A transportation network for immediate home delivery, such as Blockbuster's arrangement with Food.com (a take-out restau-

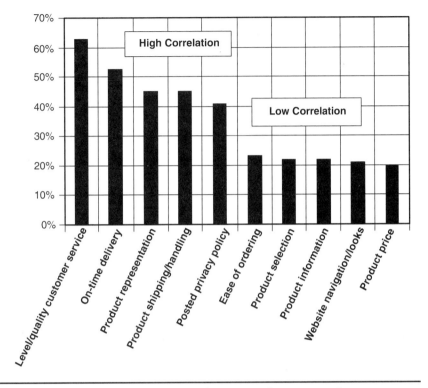

Figure 4.29. Why e-shoppers return, *http://www.bizrate.com.* Source BizRate.com, Consumer Online Report, First Quarter 1999.

rant service) to deliver a video and dinner ordered online within a short time frame.

- Local outlets for packaging orders for customer pick-up (e.g., Furr's online grocery shopping service in the Southwest).

- Large warehouses with bar code scanners and inventory management systems that package and ship items quickly and accurately (whether run by your company or outsourced).

- Online shipping and tracking services via common carrier.

Shipping

Shipping can be easily integrated into a Web site. If your Web host doesn't offer shipping with your online storefront (see Chapter 5), ask about incorporating applications from Federal Express, the U.S. Postal Service, or UPS. Generally, a shipper is happy to provide free software and technical support to guarantee that it will get your business. When the customer selects a delivery date and method, the data is transmitted to the shipper, who generates a bill of lading, schedules a pickup, and forwards the information to you, all automatically. Some shipping software allows customers to track their orders from your Web site or provides e-mail notification before delivery or confirmation after. For more information, check out

- *http://webapi.fedex.com*

- *http://www.ec.ups.com/ecommerce/solutions/index.html*

- *http://new.usps.com*

Warehousing

Preexisting distribution networks geared to moving large truckloads of items from warehouses to retailers just don't cut it! Web e-tailers are taking advantage of knowledge that offline catalog companies figured out long ago. For instance the Keystone Internet Services unit of Hanover Direct, Inc. *(http://www.keystonefulfillment.com)* provides fulfillment service to KBkids.com. Museumshop.com, which sells products from a multiple museum gift shops, outsources to Fulfillment Plus *(http://www.ffplus.com)*. Other fulfillment companies include Rush Order Inc. *(http://www.rushorder.com)* and Young America *(http://www.young-america.com)*.

It may cost more per order to outsource, but it's worth it if you don't have the capital or expertise to manage the process yourself. When selecting a fulfillment house, check references from their other clients and make sure that

- Their software management systems, such as database or accounting, will be technically compatible with yours.

- The fulfillment house has experience packaging your type of product.

- The company offers high quality customer service.

- The warehouse is close to a shipping hub and the company maintains good relationships with shippers.

Ongoing Management

Once you have a Web site, management extends far beyond your online presence. If you are a manufacturer or wholesaler, you may find that your site creates new problems with distributors or dealers, who are threatened by direct sales online. New sales policies and incentives may be required to avoid cannibalizing your existing sales channels.

We discussed the importance of e-mail response in the last chapter. As part of your customer support efforts, reconsider automating e-mail when you reach the point that you can no longer respond within 24 hours. Consider outsourcing or buying software like Kana Communications *(http://www.kana.com)*, which uses keyword scanning to direct messages to the right party or to handle simple responses instantly.

Software to synchronize a phone conversation with a representative while the customer is on the site is available from Webline at *http://www.webline.com/default.com*, *http://www.iaexpress.com*, or *http://www.click2talk.com* among others. For real-time chat features that allow customers to connect with responsive support online, try free services from *http://www.humanclick.com*, or for-fee services from such firms as *http://neteffect.com*, *http://www.etetra.com*, or *http://corporate.ask.com/press2.asp*.

These methods are all designed to increase the number of visitors who actually close a sale online: A Forrester Research study showed that as many as two thirds of all buyers abandon purchases at checkout! Consider e-mail, FAQ pages, natural language search engines on-site, and other forms of online service to reduce the incidence of telephone calls, the most expensive method of customer support. For some businesses, of course, telephone support is the best solution. People like to speak with a real human being for financial services, for instance. Even with automated systems, be prepared to hire support staff to handle e-mail or phone calls; if your site is working well, you will have more customers, not fewer!

As your site moves into its next iteration, you may discover that many internal policies need review. Has the site become incoherent? Cumbersome? Are there central policies regarding privacy? Design standards? Compliance with legal or regulatory requirements? Do you know who is responsible for the content of each page, when it was last updated, and when it should be reviewed? Many owners of large sites create a parallel database tracking system to monitor the status of each page and ensure that the proper staff receive feedback on page performance. Figure 4.30 shows one such database developed by in-house MIS staff to support a Web redesign effort.

There's a lot to think about already, and we haven't even talked about your actual Web site yet! In the next chapter, we'll consider that additional piece of your Internet marketing jigsaw puzzle. We'll focus on how to design a site for marketing effectiveness including concept, appearance, ease of use, catalogs, and merchandising.

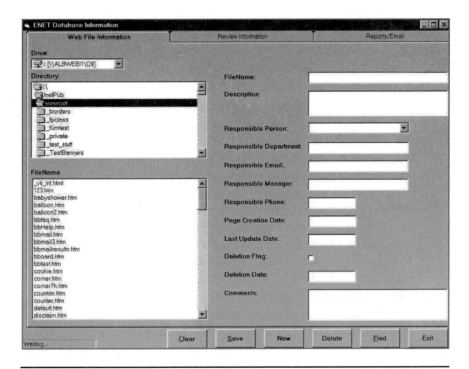

Figure 4.30. Example of a database management system for a large Web site, *http://www.pnm.com.* Courtesy PNM.

5

Designing an Effective Web Site

Good Web design engages visitors; it keeps them on the site and brings them back as repeat viewers. Accomplishing this is not easy. Competition from 3.6 million other Web sites ensures that "a greener screen" is just a click away. You have only 3 to 8 seconds to grab viewers' attention and convince them they'll receive a benefit from remaining on your site. That's about as much time as it takes to roll a grocery cart down the cereal aisle!

In this chapter we'll look at design techniques for netting visitors and making your site "sticky" so they stay. We'll explore ways that design enhances the marketing effectiveness of your site, delivers a clear marketing message, and reflects your commitment to customer service. You'll learn

- how to analyze Web site design

- the basics of writing for the Web

- how to select, structure, and assess storefronts, catalogs and auction sites

- the steps of the design process

- helpful hints for a successful site

- free features and resources to enhance your site

There's More to a Site Than Meets the Eye

Before you can create or upgrade your Web site, you need to understand how to evaluate the design of other sites. As with art, you can move beyond the perspective of "I don't know anything about it, but I know what I like." The better you can articulate what makes a particular Web site effective, the better you can communicate with your Web designer, colleagues, customers, and even your boss.

Start a collection now of sites that you like or dislike. Bookmark these sites whenever you're surfing the Web and print out pages to save in your Web notebook. This collection will be of invaluable assistance to your developer. By the end of this section, you should be able to analyze five elements of a site, identifying what features of each are worthy of praise or need improvement:

- Concept

- Content

- Navigation

- Decoration

- Marketing Effectiveness

Concept

Concept is the beginning, but not the end of a Web site. A clear concept or unifying theme enables you to decode the audiences and purposes the site is intended to serve. What message is the audience expected to take away? What actions does the creator want the audience to execute? Only in the context of its goals and audience can you evaluate how effective a site is and whether the most appropriate means of communication have been used.

Keep in mind the dictum "form follows function." In Chapter 2, you defined the purpose(s) your Web site will serve (its function) and what audience(s) you want to reach. Your concept (form) needs to be "in sync" with your function and audiences. One easy way to start is to make up a list of adjectives (use a thesaurus if necessary!) like those in Figure 5.1. Describe the *feelings of* your audience before they arrive at your site and how you want them to *feel about* your site and your company. These adjectives will help your Web designer convey the personality, tone, and character of your business. Your creative team plays an essential role here, transforming your marketing message into a visual metaphor that carries through all the pages of your site. Effective mar-

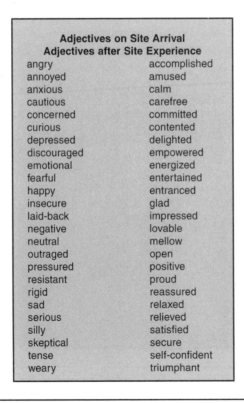

Adjectives on Site Arrival	Adjectives after Site Experience
angry	accomplished
annoyed	amused
anxious	calm
cautious	carefree
concerned	committed
curious	contented
depressed	delighted
discouraged	empowered
emotional	energized
fearful	entertained
happy	entranced
insecure	glad
laid-back	impressed
negative	lovable
neutral	mellow
outraged	open
pressured	positive
resistant	proud
rigid	reassured
sad	relaxed
serious	relieved
silly	satisfied
skeptical	secure
tense	self-confident
weary	triumphant

Figure 5.1. "Lizard brain" adjectives.

keting reaches into our "lizard brain," the emotional, irrational core from which many decisions are made.

As you surf Web sites, you'll quickly realize that the good ones maintain the same visual concept throughout. This consistency not only reinforces the chosen message and image of the company, it also makes it easier for viewers to navigate the site. The concept may be a concrete metaphor, like that of *Grant's Ale (http://www.grants.com,* shown in Figure 5.2), or a matter of style, as with New York Cabbie *(http://www.nycabbie.com,* shown in Figure 5.3). Or consider *http://www.supplierlink.com,* shown in Figure 5.4. You know the purpose of the site immediately from the opening graphic. The home page instantly defines the target audiences and functions available.

The concept for a Web site can be folksy or formal, avant garde or retro, academic or playful, sophisticated or slapstick, droll or determined. It only matters that it's consistent throughout the site and congruent with your purpose and audience. If the concept of the site contradicts the message you want to convey, it will not achieve your marketing goals no matter how beautifully it is executed.

Figure 5.2.   Concrete metaphor, *http://www.grants.com.* © 1999 Yakima Brewing and Malting Co.

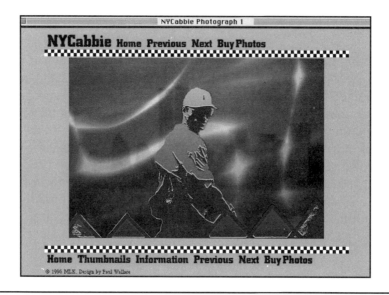

Figure 5.3. Style metaphor, *http://www.nycabbie.com.* © MLK (tps), Paul Wallace, Webmaster; Frank Palmenta, Digital Artist.

Figure 5.4. Sample site, *http://www.supplierlink.com.* Courtesy POD Associates, Inc.

Content

A site unfolds for a viewer not just on the screen, but in time. Like a story, a site should have a beginning, a middle, and an end. This may seem counterintuitive given all the links and random navigation on the Web, but if you think about time, instead of space, it makes sense. The beginning grabs viewers' attention, the middle is the value-added, content portion of the site, and the end is the payoff (when viewers' needs are satisfied, e.g., by downloading a file) or the **call to action** (a specific suggestion of what step to take next, e.g., register now.)

To fulfill the purpose of a site, content—the words, pictures, and multimedia on the screen—must be relevant, stated clearly, and communicated quickly.

Sites can be grouped into four general stages of development:

- **Informative:** a static site that presents passive material or advertising about a company or product; the Web equivalent of a brochure

- **Interactive:** a site that engages viewers to take action online, such as searching a catalog or checking the status of a shipment

- **Transactive:** a site that sells product or services and accepts payment online

- **Transformative:** a site that affects basic business processes, such as accepting bids from vendors or providing service to existing clients

While some sites cycle through these stages in sequence, many fit contentedly into only one category for their lifetime. Go back to the goals you stated for your site in Chapter 2. Where do your goals place you on the art shown in Figure 5.5? Is your content appropriate for the type of site you're creating?

Whatever the Web site, someone must conceive the initial content; almost always that someone will be within the business, not a contractor. An outside developer rarely knows a company's products or services well enough to start writing content from scratch. Inside staff will probably also suggest external links and provide an initial hierarchy of information (the **site index**), structuring what should be on the surface, and what belongs several clicks down.

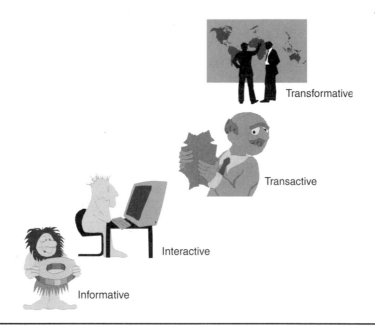

Figure 5.5. Stages of Web development.

Sometimes you can tell that the content of a site consists of a preexisting ad or brochure copied without change. Often, this doesn't work. The copy may be too wordy, too long, or too passive for the inherently interactive Web. (We'll discuss writing for the Web specifically later.) As Marshall McLuhan noted long ago in his analysis of media, the initial tendency is to make previous media the content of the newest one. (For example, people tried to read print ads on radio or put theater-style stage productions onto television.)

While you can sometimes adapt older content to save time and money, almost always you will need to tweak or "re-purpose" it for the Web. Graphics may not transfer well to a lower-resolution screen; photos may take too long to download. You'll want to reorganize content, creating links or putting some information farther down in the site.

Don't feel that you have to overwhelm visitors with every single bit of information ever created about your company. In fact, a site that stays tightly focused on your marketing mission will be more satisfactory to both the viewer and your bottom line.

Navigation

How well can the viewer get around a site? Is it obvious? Intuitive? Does it leave a trail of "pixel crumbs" so viewers know where they've been in case they want to go back? Does the site provide clues to what users will find at future destinations? Are they led gently along a garden path to the next panorama or left to wander through a maze?

Most Web sites follow one of five basic structures seen in Figure 5.6:

- Sequential

- Grid

- Tree

- Hub

- Web

A sequential arrangement, best suited to a site with only a few pages, presents information linearly, organized by time, logic, or alphanumerically. A grid or table structure aligns topics and subtopics, taking ad-

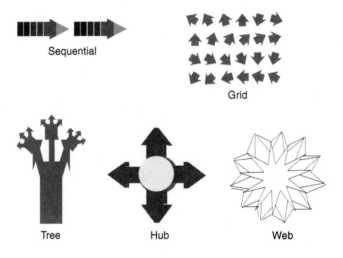

Figure 5.6. Five basic site structures.

vantage of internal links to move experienced users through a relatively small site. Think of information arranged in a spreadsheet or database, tightly structured but with each cell of roughly equal importance. The hub structure also treats all information as equivalent in importance, with "spokes" to different pages radiating out from a center point and the user always returning to the hub (home page) to go elsewhere.

By contrast, a tree or hierarchical approach divides content by degree of importance, with the most important (home page) as the root and all other pages branching off into progressively greater detail. The Web structure is the most free-form, allowing links from page to page as needed, without any predetermined hierarchy of information. While some sites use only one structure, you may find that information must be organized differently on different pages. Establish those needs in your site index before your Web developer begins work.

Site designers can facilitate navigation in many ways:

- Offer a clear, complete home page that is always accessible with a link from other pages. Make sure it downloads quickly: a maximum of 15 seconds, and preferably 10 at your users' most common connection speed.

- On the home page, let users know how the content is organized, much like the table of contents in a book or the outline of an essay.

- Restrain the number of main on-screen options to no more than 6 to 10. Keep any point on the site reachable within two or three clicks.

- Use pop-up or pull-down menus or **mouse-overs** to provide additional detail. Mouse-overs, which bring up a secondary menu when the cursor hovers over a selection, are not available with older versions of browsers.

- Guide users with consistent visual cues such as buttons, layout, and prompts. Develop an identifiable menu structure, such as Envirolink's icons (*http://www.envirolink.org*, shown in Figure 5.7). The menu should remain available on every page.

- Change the color, shape, orientation, or type style of links on the menu and index so users can always tell where they have

Figure 5.7. Clear menu and structure, *www.envirolink.com*. Courtesy of The Envirolink Network.

been and where they currently are. Hypertext links are generally in blue, though users can actually change this in their browser preferences.

- Structure the site consistently, with similar elements always appearing in the same place on different pages.

- Take advantage of click actions to reinforce messages (i.e., ask viewers to request something specifically by clicking).

- Always provide a site index (sometimes called a map or directory) that affords an overview of the entire site in terms of both structure and content. Make the site index available from every page and ensure that it contains active internal links to the desired page(s).

- Consider a site search engine so users can enter keywords to maneuver through a large site (see *http://www.teefinder.com*, shown in Figure 5.8). Select your search engine carefully; some, like the one in Microsoft's Front Page, are less than pretty and the results are inadequate. You can use a free search engine algorithm, or contract with a Web-based service to index your site for you. Some

Figure 5.8. On-site search engine, *http://www.teefinder.com*. ©1998 Teefinder; Web design and development by Circle-R Designs at *http://www. circle-r.com/webdesign*.

of these are free if you allow advertising on your search results page. (See "Freebies and Features" later in this chapter.)

- Assist users with on-screen help, especially for complex, information-dense sites.

Of course, like anything else creative, there are reasons to break all the rules. If the purpose is to entertain users and create an on-the-Web experience, a designer may choose to amuse, confuse, confound, and mystify the viewer, as the Haring Kids children's site does on its menu at *http://www.haringkids.com*, shown in Figure 5.9.

Decoration: Backgrounds, Buttons, and Bars

The unique style of a site—what most people think of as Web design—is actually the servant of concept, content, and navigation. Decoration

Figure 5.9. Unusual site menu, *http://www.haringkids.com*. Created by Daniel Wiener and Riverbed. © Estate of Keith Haring.

refers to the graphic and multimedia elements that are as unique to your site as your logo is to your name.

A designer has almost infinite options for color, buttons, backgrounds, textures, rules, typefaces, illustrations, photos, and multimedia. Should the buttons be three-dimensional, flat, or beveled? Should the imagery be realistic, abstract, or a combination of the two, like the surreal paintings of Magritte? Are cartoons or logotypes appropriate? Imagination is the only limit. Corporate colors, logo, and/or standard typefaces should be repeated on a site. Be sure, however, that your developer uses computer-friendly typefaces and a Web-safe palette, which optimizes colors for Web sites viewed on different platforms.

Designers are fond of a saying by the architect Mies van der Rohe, "God is in the details." Make your company image sparkle through the decorative details on your site. Take a look at the five screenshots in

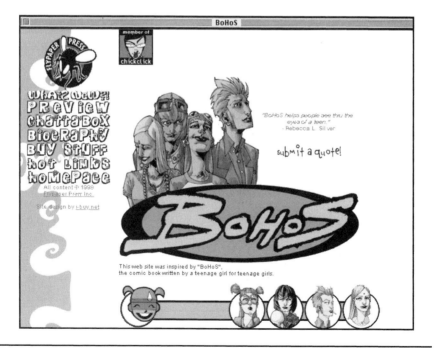

Figure 5.10. Unique style, *http://www.bohos.flypaperpress.com*. Trademark and © 1999 FlyPaper Press at *http://www.temp24-7.com*.

Figure 5.11. Unique style, *http://www.flaxart.com.* Courtesy Flax Art & Design.

Figure 5.12. Unique style, *http://food.epicurious.com.* Courtesy Epicurious Food © 1999-2000 Conde Nast, Inc. All rights reserved.

Figure 5.13. Unique style, *http://www.finecoffee.com* or *http://www.alvan houtteusa.com.* Courtesy Fruba, Inc. dba College Hill Coffee Shop.

Figures 5.10 to 5.14 (*http://www.bohos.flypaperpress.com, http:// www.flaxart.com, http://www.food.epicurious.com, http://www.fine coffee.com, http://www.beadgallery.com*). Would you be likely to confuse the corporate identity of any of these sites, each of which has its own unique Web style?

Marketing Effectiveness

Marketing effectiveness is a summary assessment of how well a site conveys a central message, addresses the needs of its target audiences, and moves the audience to take action. It takes into account the appropriate use of features for promoting a site within its own pages, which we'll address in Chapter 7. Figure 5.15 is a rating sheet that you can adapt to evaluate your own or others' sites.

Figure 5.14. Unique style, *http://www.beadgallery.com*. Courtesy The Bead Gallery. Web designer, TacWeb (*www.tacweb.com*).

Writing for the Web

Writing Web-style is an art in itself. Since viewers scan the screen, rather than read it, text on the Web needs to emphasize quick pickup of keywords. When viewers see something of interest, they stay on the page. Otherwise, it's "hasta la vista, baby." Your writing task is complicated by the reality that viewers may enter the site at any point and may jump from one page to another with no thought to linear sequencing.

Based on the imagery and the content, who is the audience for this site and what purposes does the site serve? Rank each item below from 1-5 with 5 being best. Subtotal each category, then total the site overall.

CONCEPT

How well is a coherent visual metaphor carried through the site?	1	2	3	4	5
How well is that metaphor carried through on each screen?	1	2	3	4	5
How well does the metaphor fit the company image?	1	2	3	4	5
How well does the metaphor suit the purpose of the site?	1	2	3	4	5
How well does the metaphor suit the target audience?	1	2	3	4	5

Concept Subtotal_____

CONTENT

How appropriate is the text-intensiveness of the site?	1	2	3	4	5
How well does the site answer any questions you may have?	1	2	3	4	5
If you have unanswered questions, how easy is it to ask questions via e-mail and/or phone? How prompt is the response?	1	2	3	4	5
How well does the content suit the purpose of the site?	1	2	3	4	5
How well does the content suit the target audience?	1	2	3	4	5

Content Subtotal_____

NAVIGATION

How consistent is the navigation?	1	2	3	4	5
How obvious, simple, or intuitive is the navigation?	1	2	3	4	5
How easy is the access to the menu, site index, and home on each screen?	1	2	3	4	5
How accessible are navigation tools (screen visibility/position)?	1	2	3	4	5
How effectively are internal links used to move through site?	1	2	3	4	5
How well arranged is the content (e.g. number of clicks needed)?	1	2	3	4	5

Navigation Subtotal_____

DECORATION

How attractive is the decoration?	1	2	3	4	5
How well does the decoration support the concept?	1	2	3	4	5
How well does the decoration support the content?	1	2	3	4	5
How well does the decoration support the navigation?	1	2	3	4	5
How well does the decoration suit the purpose of the site?	1	2	3	4	5
How well does the decoration suit the target audience?	1	2	3	4	5

Decoration Subtotal_____

MARKETING EFFECTIVENESS

How well does the site convey its central value message?	1	2	3	4	5
How well does it meet the buying needs of its target audience?	1	2	3	4	5
How effectively does it use calls to action?	1	2	3	4	5
How well does the site promote itself withing its own pages?	1	2	3	4	5

Marketing Subtotal_____

Site Total_____

Figure 5.15. Web site evaluation form. © 1997-2000 Watermelon Mountain Web Marketing.

It's always hard for writers to throw out words; they need to throw out even more of them for the Web. The low resolution of a computer screen presents a physiological challenge for readers—text on a screen is hard to read and tires the eyes. In fact, it takes 25% longer to read the same passage on the screen than it does in print. To make things easier for your viewers, surround text with plenty of white space and keep line lengths to less than half a screen width. That means only 8 to 12 words per line! Viewers might not know why, but they'll reward you for saving their eyes by staying longer on your site.

There are a several other quick tips to tailor writing for the Web:

- Go for an interesting "hook" in the lead sentence to grab the reader: Say what's in the page for them. It improves search engine ranking to style your first paragraph like an abstract and load it with keywords, but that can make for stilted writing.

- Use the journalistic convention of the inverted pyramid, shown in Figure 5.16, on every page; put the most important information at the top of each page and the least important at the bottom.

- Use lots of bulleted phrases, much as you would in a presentation. If viewers want more detailed information, link them to a page they can download and print out for offline review.

Figure 5.16.   Inverted pyramid style of journalism.

- Think short: short words, short sentences, short paragraphs of three sentences. "Chunk" text into packages of less than 100 words and link them together, rather than having long pages that require scrolling. Many short pages are better than one or two lengthy ones.

- Use the active voice. "The dog chased a car," not "A car was chased by the dog." Grammar checkers in most word processors can be set to highlight the passive voice (not perfectly, but better than nothing). One easy clue that you're using the passive voice: forms of the verb "to be."

- Write for an emotional jolt, humor, or entertainment on every page; the viewer wants a payoff for visiting your site.

- Keep your tone conversational, rather than authoritative. Some of the "no-no's" in standard written English are okay on the Web: contractions, colloquialisms, slang, sentence fragments. Depending on the nature of your site, writing in first person ("I") or second person ("you") may be fine.

- Viewers first scan the upper right corner, then the upper left. After that, their eyes move left to right down the page. Place your information accordingly. The most important material on a page should appear without scrolling, the equivalent of "above the fold" in the newspaper world.

Typographic Tips

How words "look" on the screen is as critical as the words themselves. Since you don't have the control of a Web page the way you have control of a print page, this can be quite frustrating. Page appearance will vary on different browsers, different browser versions, different platforms, and different monitors. If users don't have the typeface you specify, their machines default to standard fonts preset only for large, medium, and small. You can treat the text as a graphic to avoid these problems, but that will increase download time. What's a writer to do?

- Avoid italics and underlined text, which by Web convention is used only for links. Stick with normal and bold type.

- Use color contrast and unusual type position for emphasis (as long as the type is not vertical).

- Design for a 640 × 480-pixel screen for 14" monitors.

- Keep your lines less than half a screen wide with hard returns.

- Select a typeface that's been optimized for the screen, such as Arial.

- Keep your headline size proportional to your type size.

Many sites provide suggestions for good Web design and writing. Check out some of these, but don't forgot the best book on writing, *The Elements of Style* by William Strunk and E. B. White.

- CERN Style Guide: *http://www.w3.org/Provider/Style/Introduction.html*

- Jakob Nielsen: *http://www.useit.com/papers/webwriting*

- Yale Center for Advanced Instruction Media Web Style Guide: *http://info.med.yale.edu/caim/manual/*

- Web Wonk: *http://www.dsiegel.com/tips/index.html*

- Joe Gillespie's Web Page Design for Designers (great tips on typography): *http://www.wpdfd.com/wpdhome.htm*

To get an idea of good writing, look at the IRS site at *http://www.irs.gov* in Figure 5.17.

Effective Storefronts

Storefront sites that handle financial transactions can be an order of magnitude more expensive than an ordinary Web site. A recent survey by NetMarketing *(http://www.net2b.com)* priced development of a 7,500-item catalog site at anywhere from $30,000 to $1.2 million, with

Figure 5.17. Sample site with good text, *http://www.irs.gov.*

a median price of $479,000! There are less- expensive options—in the $50 to $500 range—so the adage that it pays to shop around holds as much for building Web sites as for buying on them.

In addition to the transaction software discussed in the previous chapter, several other pieces of turnkey software are required to construct a shopping-intensive site:

- Catalog or auction display

- Shopping cart

- Checkstand or register

Catalog or auction software allows you to display your products. **Shopping carts** let customers click on products they might like to buy as they review a catalog. They can view or change the contents of their cart at any time. To pay, a customer goes to a virtual **checkstand**. A checkstand totals the order, adds taxes and shipping charges, accepts shipping and billing information, and transfers the user seamlessly to a secure server for the payment steps discussed in the previous chapter. This suite of functions is sometimes called a **store-building** program.

Catalog Software

You must stock your virtual shelves, setting up your products to be viewed in an organized fashion. Many Web hosting services now offer packages to create an online catalog. You enter the specifications and price of each product on a form that is included in a single table (called a **flat-file database**) and add thumbnail digital art if appropriate.

More expensive packages, required for larger stores, use **relational databases**, which have related tables for different types of information. This approach allows sophisticated searches on multiple fields to present customized results on the fly. Databases are easy to update (e.g., if you change the supplier on all the coffee mugs you sell, you enter the new information just once).

Depending on the software you select, you may be able to

- Choose one of several prepackaged styles.

- Modify colors, fonts, background, and layout.

- Have your Web designer completely customize your catalog.

- Search the database of products by name, type, or other variables.

- Import product data, and sometimes imagery, from a preexisting print catalog or inventory in electronic form.

Catalog software ranges in price from free inclusion with Web hosting deals, to several hundred or several hundred thousand dollars. The variables are catalog size, capabilities, searchability, flexibility, and operating system. As you would expect, the most complex and expensive software searches in real time through an ever-changing inventory for products like concert tickets, airline flights, or stock. Figure 5.18 shows

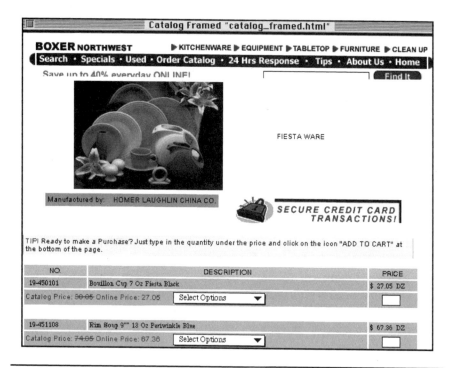

Figure 5.18. Catalog software from Custom Catalogs Online, Inc. seen at *http://boxernw.com/boxernw/images-f/b19-450.jpg.* Courtesy Boxer-Northwest Co.

the catalog software from Custom Catalog OnLine, Inc. *(http:// www.customcatalogs.com)* in use by Boxer-Northwest, a wholesale restaurant supply company, for over 5,000 items, at *http://boxernw.com.*

As an alternative to creating a database or entering individual items, Infosis Corporation *(http://www.infosiscorp.com)* allows you to import your print catalog in Quark or PDF (Adobe Acrobat) format directly onto your Web site. Their software preserves existing layout, photos, and graphics while adding a zoom-in capability, thus speeding the development of large or frequently changing online catalogs.

If you have a modest-sized catalog (10 to 1,000 items), you can usually find a Web host that includes catalog software as part of its hosting package for $25 to $125 a month. Pre-existing software from a host may reduce design flexibility, but it dramatically simplifies and speeds the development process. The larger your catalog, the more expensive your solution will be.

Sources for catalog software include WebCom at *http://www. webcom.com* and Catalog.com (*http://www.catalog.com*), both of which include catalog and shopping cart software as part of their Web hosting service. Catalogs and shopping carts can also be purchased from these sources as an add-on product for a freestanding site, with the price depending on the number of items. For a list of catalog software, check out *http://www.webcrafts.com/ShopCartF.htm#shop*.

Auction Software

The increasing popularity of auction sites has led, not surprisingly, to the development of prepackaged software to run auctions on your own site. Vendors include Microsoft (*http://www.microsoft.com*), which has an auction extension to Site Server 3.0, and Beyond Solutions (*http:// www.beyondsolutions.com/products.html*). Beyond Solutions offers an add-on Flash component for three-dimensional product display. Running your own auction site can be profitable: Goodwill's Internet auction site, *http://www.goodwill.org*, has sold more than $100,000 worth of items.

Shopping Carts and Checkstands

Shopping cart programs generally incorporate checkstands. Like catalog software, cart programs have a tremendous range in price and capability, and are often incorporated with a Web hosting package. Elaborate shopping cart software may allow you to create a registration database of shipping and billing information so that repeat customers need not reenter their data.

Depending on the nature of your product (fruit? flowers? medicine?), shipping volume, and customers' needs, you may want to automate shipping options from UPS Ground or Federal Express as described in Chapter 4, and/or generate shipping labels as part of the process. Free shipping is becoming a competitive pricing feature on many merchandise sites. Since the costs are generally integrated into the overall price, you may want to adjust your own pricing to follow suit.

If you plan to sell internationally, you need software that supports international currency exchange and shipping requirements. If your Web host offers a shopping cart, check out the cart supplier's Web site to confirm that the product will meet your needs.

A sample shopping cart from Hassan Shopping Cart (*http://www.irata.com/products.html*) is shown in use at A. L. Van Houtte Fine Coffee (*http://www.finecoffee.com/cgi-local/shop.pl/*, shown in Figure 5.19). The Hassan Cart is a UNIX-based solution that supports UPS shipping. Costs range from $200 for a single license to $1800 for a site license, plus per module charges of $200 to $300 for CyberCash or other secure transactions. For comparison with other cart programs, take a look at

- Precision Web (*http://precisionweb.net/shop.html*). This hosting service offers its free Ultrashop shopping cart software, otherwise priced at $200, with every site. Their shopping cart software is database driven, secure-server enabled, and customizable.

- Hamilton Associates (*http://www.hamassoc.com*). Their basic cart product is EZshopper, which runs $600 for the server software,

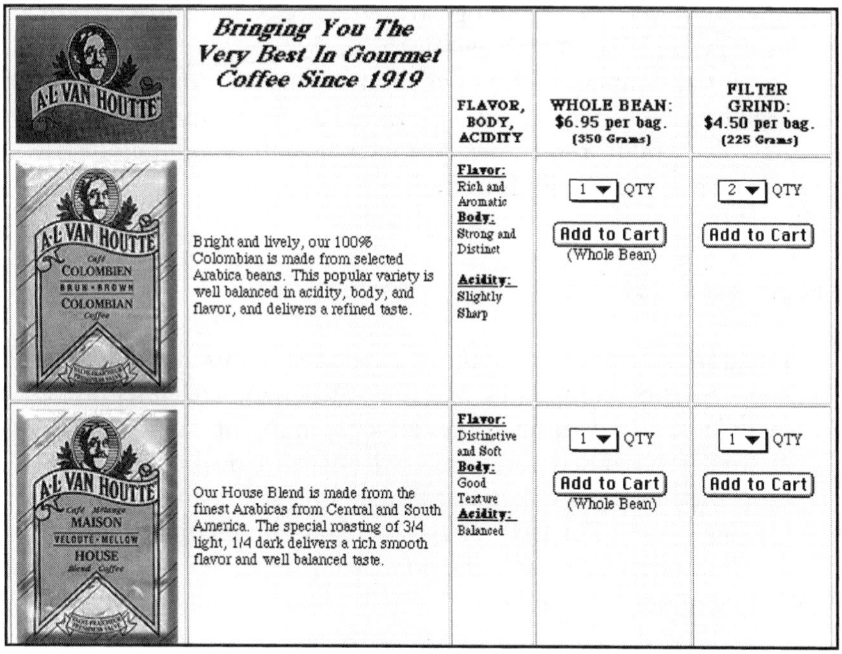

Figure 5.19. Shopping cart from Hassan seen at *http://www.finecoffee.com/cgi-local/shop.pl.* Courtesy Fruba, Inc. dba College Hill Coffee Shop.

plus $75 per ten-item page. It has optional modules for real-time integration at $195 and database administration/statistics for $250. Their Minicart option for $200 is useful for companies with only a few items. After calculating the sales total, shipping costs, and tax, their products send both company and customer a sales confirmation receipt with the individual order number.

- GTA NetOrderForm *(http://www.gta-tech.com/)*. This free, simple-to-use, turnkey shopping cart system comes complete with online administration features, online credit card verification, customer feedback forms, and secure server capability.

You might also check out *http://www.pdgsoft.com*, which sells its cart for $750 or *http://www. macrotec.com*, which "rents" cart software.

If one store is not enough, perhaps you would like to build your own shopping mall! The Mallsurfer turnkey solution *(http://www. mallsurfer.com/)* includes shopping cart, checkout stand, and store departments. It runs from Windows 95/98 or NT and can be uploaded to any Web site. The shopping cart and checkstand software are available as freeware or shareware, while the mall software itself starts at $189.95 for initial setup and $9.95 per shop per month. Mallsurfer also offers a mall hosting service. If you've decided to open your cyberstore on someone else's mall, remember to join one with similar industries or one where you'll be easily found.

Integrated E-Commerce Solutions

Integrated e-commerce solutions are usually purchased by Web hosting services or by companies that host their own site. Integrated packages include standard modules for catalogs, shopping carts, and checkstands, as well as expanded administrative and statistical options. Most important, they provide linkage or export options to inventory, accounting, mailing list, and/or EDI (electronic data interchange) systems.

Web hosts may offer the complete package in one of their monthly pricing options. The following sites are just a few of the vendors available:

- Free is a good price when you have a tiny, niche store with only several products. Several sites—*http://www.bizland.com* (seen in Figure 5.20), *http://www.freemerchant.com*, and *http://*

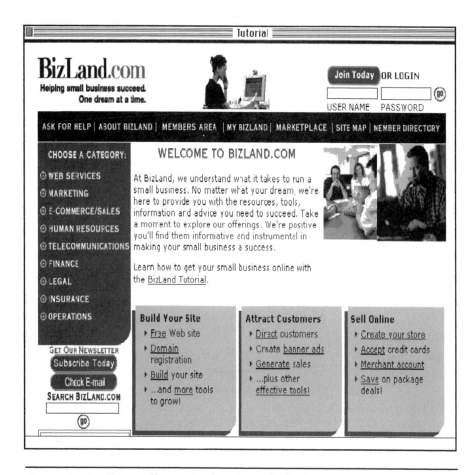

Figure 5.20. Free small store site, *http://www.bizland.com*. Courtesy BizLand, Inc.

www.bigstep.com—offer free 35 MB sites with shopping cart, customer e-mail, tracking reports, and credit card acceptance services. They make their money selling advertising space and from transaction fees on credit card purchases. For card services Bizland, for example, charges $15 per month, plus 15¢ per sale and 2.67% of the sales price. Store "rental" starts at $50 per month if your site goes beyond the free space.

- Advanced Internet Technologies, Inc. (*http://www.aitcom.net*) is an e-commerce Web hosting service that offers a card verification service, as well as store-building and statistical tools. Setup costs range from free for a 20 MB starter site to $95, with monthly rates ranging from $7.95 to $299.95.

- Web Store, from Intel's iCat Division (*http://www.icat.com*), runs $9.95 per month for up to 10 items, $99.95 for up to 100 items, and $249.95 for up to 1,000 items.

- Webhosting.com (*http://www.webhosting.com*, shown in Figure 5.21) offers a fairly typical e-commerce turnkey selection starting at $19.95 a month, with prices increasing by catalog size and features. A similar package from NetNation Communications (*http://www.netnation.com*) runs $30/month including shopping cart and secure server for an unlimited number of products.

- The Yahoo! Store (*http://store.yahoo.com*) offers electronic commerce Web hosting. Prices start at $100 a month for up to 50 items or $300 a month for the first 1,000 items; each additional 1,000 items is another $100/month. This site offers fast point-and-click store building, lots of statistical and tracking tools, and great promotional tips. Since it's Yahoo! you can count on

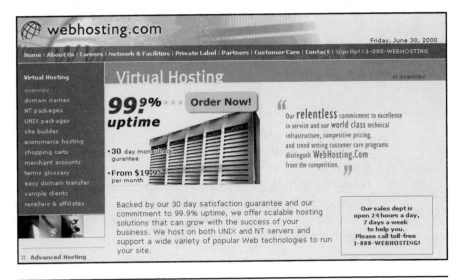

Figure 5.21. Sample Web commerce solution, *http://www.webhosting.com*. Courtesy Webhosting.com.

server reliability and traffic generation. Yahoo! stores are listed automatically on its online mall (Yahoo! Shopping), its shopping search engine, its directories, and its main search engine. Optional listings are available on Yahoo!'s auction and classified sites as well. The downside of this store builder is that you have to enter items individually and process credit cards manually unless you have CyberCash. Yahoo! prescreens merchants' customer service standards to reassure buyers. AOL.com and Excite's Express Order offer similar store-building services.

- Amazon.com's zShops work like eBay, with postings that expire after a certain time, but you can set a fixed price. The cost is a $10 setup fee, a 2% to 5% fee per sale, and $9.99 per month for up to 500 items. The zShops fee for credit card transactions is 4.75% plus 60¢ per transaction.

- INEX Corporation (*http://www.inex.com*) operates a little differently: You buy software to create your store and upload the finished store to one of the ISPs that supports the INEX package. Although you start development with canned templates, these options require technical skills. Commerce Court Light ($595) handles up to 500 items, while Commerce Court Professional ($995) has no item limits and will interface with accounting and other systems. A similar approach is used by Boomerang (*http://www.boomerangsoftware.com*), but the site is uploaded to Boomerang's own server starting at $9.95/month, plus the cost of the software. Its software includes automatic e-mail response, marketing surveys, order processing, a customer database, and secure credit card transactions.

If you plan to host a huge site in-house, you'll want to look at an integrated hardware and software solution from one of the major companies. At this point you'll need not only dollars, but in-house technical staff to maintain the system. E-cats (*http://www.e-cats.com*) sells a turnkey online store for $10,000. IBM (*http://www.ibm.com/ebusiness*) offers NetServer and Net.Commerce for $9,000 to $38,000 through value-added distributors. The ubiquitous Microsoft has an integrated electronic commerce solution called BizTalk (*http://www.microsoft.com/ WINME/030499com/clark28k/html/BizTalk_default.htm*). BizTalk not only sells products online, it tracks supply and demand and communicates with vendors. It has been tested by such huge sites as 1-800 Flowers, barnesandnoble.com, Best Buy, Dell Computer, and Eddie Bauer.

Criteria for an Effective Online Store

To provide a positive shopping experience for customers, you must pay attention not only to the back-end issues described in the last chapter, but also to the online shopping experience itself. It goes without saying that no matter what size your store is

- Your online payment process must be secure and easy to access.

- Privacy must be guaranteed.

- You must notify customers, preferably online, when items are out of stock or have been removed from your catalog.

- The return policy, warranties, and guarantees must be clearly stated on the site.

- Shipping options and cost must be easy to access.

- The site should prominently display your toll-free number, as well as e-mail, fax, and regular mail so customers can reach you easily.

From an online perspective, a good search engine is essential, especially if you have a significant inventory. The search function should be available on every page and allow users to find products quickly by category or name. With a large number of stocked items, include a more advanced search function to sort by multiple criteria, such as price, size, and color. Be sure you select software that provides order confirmation by e-mail and/or a detailed summary page the buyer can print out.

You may want to choose a storefront product that allows you to set up a special sale area. Do you want one with features like customer reviews and product comments? What about a FAQ section that gathers browsing and purchasing information in one place? If your product lets users elect to receive e-mail notification of sales or other news, be sure they can "opt-out" simply.

Some packages offer sales reporting tools and customer-service features, such as recommending related products. Such **intelligent agents** act like knowledgeable store clerks who **upsell**, encouraging additional purchases or suggesting that buyers upgrade to a more expensive model.

Some store sites place **cookies**, small data files with unique identification numbers, on users' machines and/or require a log-in with user name and password. Either method allows a site to personalize users' experience on follow-up visits. In theory, personalization makes for a more emotional connection with the viewer. It can be as simple as welcoming visitors by name or as complex as maintaining a database that presents products or information prearranged to be relevant to the viewer. For instance, the alternative news site Slashdot (*http://www.slashdot.org*) allows users to tailor the news they receive by topic and connection speed.

Cookies are a mixed blessing. Some cookies still require that viewers enter their name and password each time, which can be a nuisance. Some people resent cookies as an intrusion on privacy. (Although users can turn off cookies in browsers' Preference sections, many do not know how.) Other viewers prefer the convenience of prerecorded shipping and charging information, an address book, a datebook of upcoming birthdays or events, or a list of past purchases. Most developers know how to do cookies, or you can purchase packages like GuestTrack that integrate customer information databases with your Web site (*http://www.guesttrack.com*). In any case, if you collect personal information, post and follow a privacy policy to reassure your users (see Chapter 9). For more information on personalization, check out *http://www.personalization.com*.

If you are a member of organizations that vouch for privacy or reliability, such as Trust-e (*http://www.truste.com*) or the Better Business Bureau Online (*http://www.bbonline.org*), be sure to include their logos on your site.

As in the mall, attractive presentation is essential. Are product descriptions easy to read? Are photos clear? Can thumbnail images, presented for quick downloading, expand with a click to permit a better look? Do you make it easy for buyers to navigate through your site, removing any online obstacles to purchase?

A word about merchandising: Products that sell well in a store don't always sell well online and vice versa. You may decide not to offer identical inventory or to alter your online pricing. You can choose to feature different items prominently on your home page or secondary pages, just as you would rearrange the display in your store window or place items for shoppers to see when they first walk through your door. Given the price pressures on the Web—someone will always undersell you—it's critical that small businesses provide the service or after-sales support that distinguishes them from large discounters.

For shopping sites to learn from, look again at Amazon.com; Land's End (*http://www.LandsEnd.com* seen in Figure 5.22), which is a great site for those with dial-up connections; or The Sharper Image (*http://www.SharperImage.com*), a multimedia feast for those with wide bandwidth Internet access. To see how a cluttered design can suggest "great buys," check out ZDnet's Computer Shopper site (*http://www.Computer Shopper.com*). With 8.5 million visitors each month, this site's aggressive point-of-sale display must be the right approach for its customers.

The Design Process

While it may vary according to circumstances, the design process for a Web site generally incorporates the following steps:

Figure 5.22. Good major catalog site, *http://www.landsend.com*. Permission granted by Lands' End, Inc.

1. Initial design conference and schedule

2. Design "comps" for you to choose from

3. Navigation storyboards or flowcharts

4. Element creation

5. Programming and integration

6. Testing and corrections

As described in the timeline section earlier, the first four steps, along with your other preplanning, will absorb about half the time before launch. Steps 5 and 6 will each take roughly one quarter of the time.

Initial Design Conference and Schedule

Your RFQ provides the designer with an excellent starting point for discussion at your initial design conference. Bring your statement of site goals and objectives, your collection of site printouts, the URLs of sites you like and dislike, and your list of adjectives about user feelings. To the index in your RFQ, add a list of desired internal and external links and where they belong. The more concrete your concept and expectations, the more likely you will be satisfied with the results. The more specific the information you provide, the easier it is for the designer to deliver what you want and the less expensive the design process will be.

Bring your calendar to schedule when deliveries from the design team can be expected and when you plan to launch the site. Indicate clearly at what points you want to see material and how long you will need for approval. Finally, review your budget with the developer to ensure that your expectations are still within the price quoted and that the level of effort will be adequate to meet your requirements.

Although it may seem like a nuisance, the earlier and more often you seek internal and external review, the less difficulty you will have with implementation and operation. Ensure that all appropriate members of your team (and others if necessary) have an opportunity to sign off on decisions before major funds are committed.

A review cycle is also an opportunity to confirm that content is ready and accurate. This is particularly true if others are providing technical information, bibliographical references, or up-to-date databases. Checking content from internal sources is just as important. You might discover that the Human Resources Department updates the Job Openings database daily, but the Web designer expected updates weekly.

As part of the review cycle, you may want to conduct focus groups with potential users of the site. Try to find people who match your expected audience profile closely and who have a range of computer or content knowledge. You can use focus groups online through a scheduled "conference chat" at any point in the design process, or you can interview a "live" group. Focus groups can serve as independent testers throughout the development process.

Design Comps

As with print, a designer will generally provide several different graphic concepts (comps) for your Web site. The designer may use presentation software or Photoshop to generate individual screen images that provide a "look-and-feel" sense of your site. Be aware that images may not transfer exactly from Photoshop or other formats to HTML for the Web. The designer may include the layout for secondary and third-level pages, and/or a block diagram of screen elements (see Figure 5.23) for different types of pages. At this point, the designer uses "fake" text as a placeholder to show how a page will look.

After you select one approach and make suggestions, the designer will provide a final comp to confirm the look and feel of the site. Once you sign off on the final design, additional changes are likely to increase the cost. If the site is large, the lead designer or project manager should establish a standards book for the creative team to follow, especially if multiple contractors will be involved. A standards book establishes consistent icons, layout, typography, colors, graphics size, tone, style, and ad placement.

Navigation Storyboards or Flowcharts

Your Web designer might present the navigational elements of your site as a storyboard or a flowchart for your approval. A storyboard, which

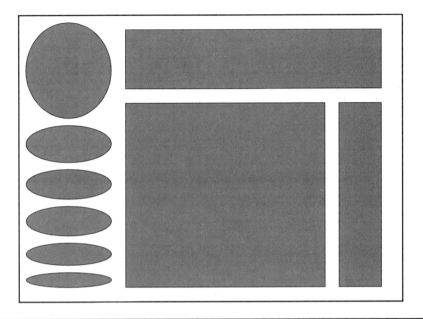

Figure 5.23. Block diagram of sample screen layout.

looks like the cels from a cartoon, depicts activity using pictures of each page. You can easily rearrange these individual pages on a wall or table to experiment with different ways of moving through a site. Many Web development packages can supply a navigation flowchart that provides context, showing where users are, where they might have been, and where they are able to go.

Check the proposed structure against the suggestions listed in the "Helpful Hints" section. Try to imagine how different visitors might experience it. Would navigation be obvious to someone who stumbled on the site by accident? Would an experienced, repeat visitor get frustrated at information buried too deeply? Will links keep visitors on the site or take them away? How many clicks does it take to get from one piece of information to another?

Depending on the complexity of the site, your designer may build a prototype or shell before proceeding to actual programming. If the designer posts this prototype site on his or her own Web site, other members of your team can review it. This might be a good time to bring in members of a focus group for comment. Remember, most people don't want to play an adventure game, hunting high and low for information.

Don't wait until right before launch to find out that users haven't got a clue how to navigate the site.

Strong visual cues help viewers find data and orient them in virtual space. Good structure is obvious and intuitive, such as in the Epicurious site at *http://food. epicurious.com/c_play/c00_home/play.html*, shown in Figure 5.24. Again, changes in structure after signing off on the prototype will probably incur additional charges.

Make sure the site organization is optimized for marketing, too. You may want the site divided so that different pages use different keywords, giving you better exposure in search engines. You might want a splash page designed with specific keywords in mind. If there are messages you want to reinforce with a click action, be sure the page with that call to action and the result are separated.

You need to balance conflicting goals when it comes to outbound links. Every time you link outside your site, you risk losing your viewer.

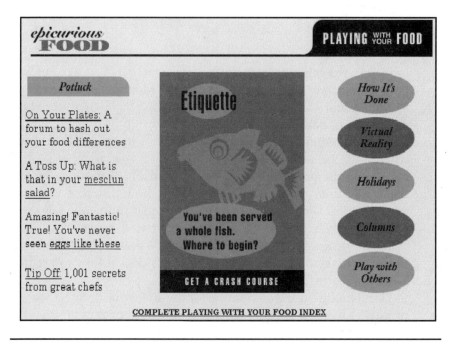

Figure 5.24. Visual navigation cues, *http://food.epicurious.com/c_play/ c00_home/play.html*. Courtesy Epicurious Food © 1999 Conde Nast, Inc. All rights reserved.

Not all are familiar with the Back button or pull-down history features of their browsers. On the other hand, many outbound links will generate a reciprocal inbound link, which can help improve the visibility of your site. If possible, have your designer open a new window when a viewer clicks on an outbound link; that way, your page remains on the user's screen.

If you are relaunching an existing site, it's also useful to know who already links to your old site. You can find this by running a spider. Free spiders can be found at *http://linkstoyou.com/CheckLinks.htm* or *http://siteowner.bcentral.com/sitecheck.cfm*.

Element Production

Some of the elements—text, graphics, and photos—for the site can be collected from company files; others will need to be created fresh. The less the designer has to do from scratch, the lower your cost. Perhaps someone in your company can write, edit, and/or proof the copy. Whoever handles the copywriting must optimize it for marketing purposes, with calls to action placed at strategic locations. On pages intended for search engine submission, the copywriter should consider the precepts discussed in Chapter 8 for improving rankings, particularly the ratio between keyword occurrence and the number of words on the page.

Since poorly written, ungrammatical text is a turnoff to readers and a putdown of your company, remember to proofread all content and check the spelling. Use focus groups to review the content for comprehensibility. If you are aiming a site toward children, you might want to assess readability level as well.

Do you have staff who could collect and digitize existing photographs, art, or database material, or review some of the free sources for line art, sprites, or digital images? Do you need to arrange for other professionals to shoot photographs or create art? Will some content be contributed by other departments? Your designer should specify the format in which elements should be delivered. Generally, photos work best in JPEG format; graphics work best as GIFs.

The primary developer should have budgeted for the creation of any new multimedia material, such as animation or audio files, unless it was clear from the RFQ that material would be provided independently. Depending on the project, either you or the lead designer will be responsible for making sure those pieces are created on time and in the required format. A good Web designer will bring to this project his or her knowledge of how to optimize the various pieces to get the best quality in the fastest download time. The designer usually is also responsible for establishing file naming and version numbering conventions and backing up all the various elements.

Programming and Integration

A Web programmer decides how to code your site based on his or her familiarity with different development packages, which packages will be supported by your selected Web Host, and the server to be used. The programmer should also consider the skills, available Web time, and equipment capabilities of your target audience. It is sometimes tricky to put all the different elements together in a way that will be compatible with various versions of browsers, plug-ins, and computers.

Don't be surprised if your Web designer first programs your site with standard elements, such as preexisting video clips or photos, instead of using your specific material. Often, it is easier to debug the programming portion of the site independent of actual images and content.

Finally, elements will be inserted into the program structure and you will be able to see your Web site. Generally, one type of page element comes up at a time. Then the developer will insert your content on additional pages of the same type. Be sure to check that text and images are on the correct pages!

Testing and Corrections

Through internal testing and debugging, the designer should catch any obvious problems, such as images that don't fully download or pages that don't appear. Ask your designer to run a **syntax checker**, which confirms there are no errors in the code, and a link verifier to confirm that links on your site remain valid. (See Chapter 6 for more on testing and analysis tools.)

The designer's next task should include testing or emulating site performance (still on a local server not accessible to the public) on an assortment of equipment, with various plug-ins installed. Make sure that the site is tested with the minimal configuration your viewers might have: perhaps Windows 95, a 486 processor, a 28.8 modem, 24 MB of

RAM, and a 13-inch monitor. Then move up to higher-level operating systems and more powerful hardware. Test on a Macintosh or when running on a local area network under Windows NT.

Many sites that look beautiful on a large, expensive monitor can be cropped or distorted on a smaller display. Make sure the text font is large enough to be readable when viewed at high resolution. Test the appearance of the site under several versions of Netscape and Microsoft Internet Explorer browsers. Each browser operates slightly differently, so what looks great in Internet Explorer may not look right in Netscape and vice versa. Check the appearance of your site whenever a new browser version is released. Your designer will optimize the site for appearance on multiple browsers; be prepared for some compromises. You may find support for compatibility testing at *http://www.AnyBrowser.com* or *http://www.cast.org/bobby*. The latter site also analyzes pages to determine whether they are accessible to people with disabilities.

At this point, request testing from both those who are new to the site and those who provided feedback during the design stage. If you have a complex site, it is particularly important to see what happens in terms of user interface, site navigation, and content accessibility. Reproof content that may have been edited to fit on the page or around an image. Each round of corrections should be followed by a round of checking.

Finally, upload the site to the Web host's server, but don't publicize it yet for the world to view. Test again with different hardware, plug-ins, and browsers, running on modems at different speeds. It's impossible to check all the permutations, but keep a careful record of the configurations used for each test.

To pretest the site in actual operation, ask small audiences of existing customers, members of news groups, mailing list subscribers, or a professional society to help test your site. Although they may be more knowledgeable than a naive user, these testers can be very helpful. Post a notice with a password or special extension asking for testing assistance and feedback. You might offer a small freebie or discount to those who fill out an online survey about the site and something larger if they catch a serious bug or make a suggestion you use. Ask testers to

- Confirm that the directions, index, and structure are clear.

- Assess the value of the links and suggest others.

- Exercise any contest or user-response mechanism.

- See if there are problems with multimedia or plug-ins on any platforms.

- Check for errors in content, from spelling to facts.

If you're confident of basic operations, but need to test the site under a heavy viewer load, run a beta site like *http://www.jump.com*, shown in Figure 5.25. Once the site is up and running, you or the Webmaster should check basic operations daily and run an online checker like Site Inspector (*http://siteinspector.linkexchange.com*) at least monthly. Some of the tools described in Chapter 6 will allow you to emulate system performance under different load conditions.

Users decry slow download time as their chief complaint, and their patience is growing increasingly thin. If your site downloads too slowly, you may need to scale down, eliminate, or compress some images or multimedia. In the worst case, the designer may create a stripped-down

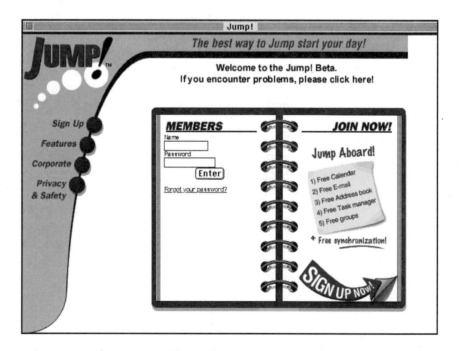

Figure 5.25. Beta test site, *http://www.jump.com*. Screenshot reprinted with permission from Microsoft Corporation.

version of the site as an option for those with less-capable equipment. When the site is stable and each page is optimized to download in less than 30 seconds on a 28.8 modem, you can announce your URL to the Internet universe.

One advantage of template-based sites is that much of this testing has already taken place. Minimum hardware configurations, plug-in versions, and software incompatibilities are well known; existing problems are usually documented. With a template, errors usually result from problems during the process of creating or integrating the elements, not from the program.

Helpful Hints for a Successful Site

What draws visitors to a site again and again? What enables you to build a relationship on the Web that turns a prospect into a customer? An existing customer into a repeat customer? A potential investor into a holder of your stock? According to a Cognitiative, Inc. poll, seen in Figure 5.26, ease of use and past experience are the biggest factors, but fast response time and frequent updates are important as well.

While this chapter focuses on the Web site itself, don't forget that the user's view of your site is often colored by the after-the-Web experience. Make sure that all your business operations can support the expectations for speed, service, convenience, and delivery that the Web creates. With that in mind, let's look at a few ideas for optimizing Web site design and operation. You might want to check your Web designer's work against the list that follows. Keep a running list of ideas as you research other sites.

Splash Screens

A **splash screen** is often displayed as a distraction while a Web site loads. It sometimes lists the browser version for which the site is optimized or includes information about what plug-ins are needed to run special features. Links to plug-ins or suggestions about how to speed up the Web site if you have a slow computer are often included.

A splash screen might dissolve into the home page or ask the user to click for entry. Multiple splash screens can be customized according to

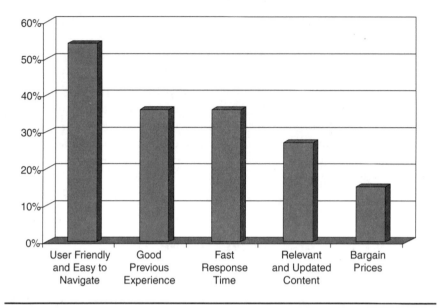

Figure 5.26. Factors affecting the decision of which sites to patronize, *http:// www.cognitiative.com.* Pulse of the Customer,[SM] Cognitiative, Inc.

source link, providing visitors from that link with a submenu of choices appropriate to their interests. Splash "doorways" with different URLs make it easy to track the effectiveness of promotional activities by counting how many viewers arrive via each entry point.

Splash screens, like the one for the multimedia site Monster Interactive in Figure 5.27 (*http://www. monsteri.com*) are an opportunity to make a first impression or establish a creative theme.

Home Page

Your **home page** is a welcome mat, main menu, and advertisement rolled into one. Whether your viewers consist of customers, suppliers, potential employees, or just casual visitors, your Web site makes a critical statement about your company. You have only one chance to make a first impression, whether it is your lobby, window display, telephone receptionist, brochure cover, splash screen, or home page.

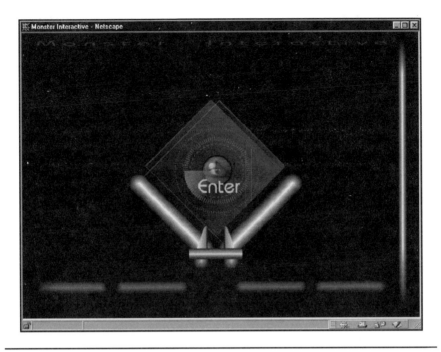

Figure 5.27. Good splash screen, *http://www.monsteri.com*. Courtesy Monster Interactive, LLC.

The best home pages arrange pictures and text artistically to catch the eye of the viewer and lure him or her to explore further, like the one shown in Figure 5.28 (*http://www.vivid.com/home.phtml*). Complex, yet simple, this site intrigues with a mysterious image of an eye floating within an oval. The oval itself is defined by contrasting color, not by a hard edge. The lack of clutter leads the eye to what's important. Another enticing home page is seen in Figure 5.29 at *http://www.scifi.com/set*. This streaming audio site uses visual images to "hook" listeners!

Requiring the viewer to scroll to see a complete image or description can be very distracting. If scrolling is unavoidable, try not to wrap text before and after an image. Instead, group text together so it will fit on one screen, with the picture on the next. In particular, try to avoid horizontal scrolling unless there is a valid aesthetic or display reason for doing so.

The disosaur home page at National Geographic (*http://nationalgeographic.com/dinorama*) is a great example of horizontal scrolling.

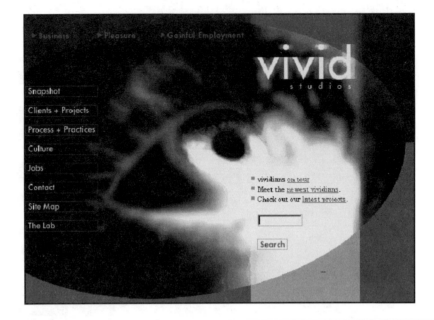

Figure 5.28. Artistic home page, *http://www.vivid.com/home.phtml.* Courtesy vividstudios.

Figure 5.29. Enticing home page, *http://www.scifi.com/set.* Courtesy USA Networks.

If it's too daunting to remember all this, use a Web host or developer that offers a gallery of templates you can customize, such as those from WebSites2Go at *http://www.websites2go.com*, shown in Figure 5.30. Additional template sources may be found in "Freebies and Features" later in this chapter.

Updates

Fresh content keeps your site interesting to repeat visitors. Updating your site daily, weekly, or monthly is an important consideration. Ask your developer whether you will be able to make changes on your own to page content, or even add and remove pages yourself. Many developers have an administrative form accessible from an ordinary word processor for changing text. Or you can buy a tool like Panasite Professional Web Content Man-

Figure 5.30. Template options, *http://www.websites2go.com*. Sullivan Creative, 9 Galen Street, Watertown, MA 02742, *www.sullivancreative.com*.

agement software (*http://www.panasite.com*) that lets you modify content, divide editing tasks among many staff members, and upload changes to your server. Cuesta Technologies' Web-N-Able package (*http://www.cuesta.com*) lets you add, subtract, and rearrange pages on sites they host without the delays or charges incurred by having the developer do it.

Multimedia Beware

Only some viewers—generally business users with high-performance Internet access at work—have the hardware, software, bandwidth, and patience to enjoy animation and sound, let alone video. Similarly, Java script creates problems for users of older browsers. Although this will change in the future, be cautious in the near term about including multimedia-intensive activities unless you also include an optional way for viewers to obtain information. If your audience is home or education based, you might want to make your "ordinary" site the default, so only viewers who select the version requiring plug-ins try to run the multimedia version.

Although the easiest way to deliver video and sound is to download files for future playback, users then need to move to another application for viewing. The alternative, streaming media, sends out video and audio signals while viewers are online, but this requires users to have the necessary plug-ins and fast access. Since it would take about two hours to download an uncompressed 60-second AVI (Video for Windows) file with a 28.8 Kbps modem, most online video is compressed, even though it makes playback somewhat jerky. Multimedia needs to be used with caution. It can generate more oops! than aahs!

Avoid Causes for Complaint

According to a recent survey by Cognitiative, Inc., the five most common reasons given by Web buyers for avoiding sites are

1. Outdated content, 25%

2. Slow response (download) time, 23%

3. Downtime and technical problems, 21%

4. Difficult navigation, 16%

5. Bad customer service, 15%

Note that only the last of these complaints has anything to do with the shopping process itself! One bad Web experience can turn a viewer off your site forever.

Reduce Download Time

As a rule of thumb, it takes one second to download one kilobyte of information with a 28.8 modem. Try to keep each page below 30 KB. If it's more than that, decide whether the image or information is really necessary. If so, compress large files, even if it means sacrificing resolution for speed.

For instance, a high-contrast, print-quality photograph may take as long as two minutes to transfer across phone lines. Most photos can be converted to a much smaller, low-resolution JPEG file that downloads in less than 20 seconds. Tools like Photoshop's WebVise further optimize JPEG and GIF files for the Web. Ask your developer about using size attributes to reduce perceived download time; attributes allow the text to download without waiting for the browser to figure out picture size on its own. If possible, reuse the same image more than once, since it won't need to be downloaded again.

Or consider using a series of thumbnail images, allowing viewers to click on the one or two pictures they would like to see expanded. Sometimes it is more effective to display an image unfolding as it downloads, instead of waiting for it to finish and pop on. As alternatives, consider line drawings or illustrations: GIFs download much more quickly than JPEG files. Keep in mind that a plain white background will download faster than a colored or patterned one.

Other tips to speed download time include avoiding Java and selecting Web development packages carefully. Many common **WYSIWYG** (what you see is what you get) packages, like Microsoft's FrontPage, Adobe's Page Mill, or Claris's Homepage slow down pages with irrelevant code.

Some 15 to 20 percent of users still turn off Web graphics so that pages will download more quickly, clicking on an image only if it interests them. Be sure that your text entices viewers to watch the image and that your layout and information flow works well without photos. You can check download time with commercial load-testing software such as SiteSweeper (*http://www.sitetech.com*) or Bang (*http://www.loadtesting.com*), or by using some of the free online tools discussed in the next chapter.

Since people can easily abort an image transfer and move to another site, try following Tetra's lead in Figure 5.31 (*http://www.tetra-fish.com*). Viewers build their own virtual aquarium on this site one fish at a time. By occupying viewers with decision making while an image downloads, Tetra makes the wait almost imperceptible.

Make Your Site Easy To Understand

Problems finding known information and organizing what is found can be addressed in several ways. Return to the principles of good navigation described earlier. The complexity of your navigation scheme will suggest presentation needs for your pages. For instance, secondary pop-

Figure 5.31. Virtual aquarium, *http://www.tetra-fish.com*. Courtesy Tetra/Second Nature.

up or pull-down menus or mouse-overs may keep pages from getting too cluttered and offer more choices to those who need them.

Since viewers linking to your site may enter on pages other than your home page, maintain consistent access to a menu and site index on every page, as Epicurious did in Figure 5.24 (shown earlier). Implement an on-site search engine if your site is large, and make sure that your site index contains active internal links.

Your page-naming conventions can help users organize information they collect. Use similar page names for similar information. Consider a call to action that reminds users to bookmark your site and to create an electronic folder for information they have gathered.

Avoid Problems with Testing and Maintenance

A viewer perceives as a "crash" anything that keeps the site from operating as anticipated, including those infamous 404 errors generated by a broken link. **Links** (internal and external) are enormously powerful because they lead users through a chain of related information with the simple click of a mouse button.

This problem is easily avoided by running verification software at least monthly to monitor links for valid connections and obtain referrals to a new address. (See Chapter 6 for details.) On a site that is link-heavy, a Webmaster should run this program weekly. If you can't be this religious about maintenance, ask yourself whether you really need all those links. Could you reduce the number to a few stable sites?

Don't forget that internal links (to other pages on your own site) can generate a similar problem if a page has been removed or renamed. This happens frequently on large sites with many stored documents. Development packages are supposed to handle page changes automatically, but don't always do so. Be sure to search your own site for any links to an altered page whenever you update content.

Visitors might also become frustrated if they can't use your link to a popular URL, such as the Mars Pathfinder images at NASA, because the destination site is busy. Instead, obtain permission to **mirror** the information on your own site with appropriate credit, instead of linking. You can use mirroring creatively to draw visitors to your site and away from a jammed site. In fact, a mirrored site closer to a viewer's physical location is often faster for them to access.

One of your criteria for selecting a Web host and developer was the extent of their backup systems, including redundant hardware and communications. Is there someone available around the clock? Are servers taken offline regularly for routine maintenance and software updates? Backups should be made very frequently: for high-traffic sites at least once an hour; while your site is in development at least once a day.

Don't short yourself when reserving server space: Leave of cushion of 40% more space than you need. Of course, when the unthinkable happens and your site goes down completely, you inform customers as soon as possible and offer refunds or coupons to make amends.

Want to make yourself feel better? You can check out the mistakes that others have made at

- *http://www.worstoftheweb.com*

- *http://www.webpagesthatsuck.com*

- *http://www.westegg.com/badpages*

Of course, there are resources for good design as well:

- *http://www.builder.com*

- *http://www.yahoo.com/Arts/Design_Arts/Graphic_Design/Web_Page_Design_and_Layout*

- *http://www.cnetbuilder.com*

- *http://www.lcc.gatech.edu/gallery/dzine*

Forget-Me-Nots

Check your design against this compilation of pointers and reminders.

- Web or no Web, many people still prefer tangible sheets of paper in a manila folder stuck in a filing drawer. Offer users a print-and-save–friendly version of each page on your site. Many people don't realize that frame-based sites print (or save) only the frame that contains the cursor. Test that your pages will print out properly; for instance, yellow text on a black background may be nearly invisible in print. Offer the option of reverse printing (black text on white) if your site uses a dark background and be sure that multihued sites will print legibly in black and white.

- Use many calls to action. In classic marketing terms, a call to action is the closing step in a sale. You can also ask viewers to demonstrate interest with smaller calls to action, moving them ever closer to a sale. On the Web, internal calls to action are almost always active intrasite links that ask users to take an action online, such as subscribing to a newsletter, signing a register, or bookmarking a page. They can also be used simply to move people through your site. External calls to action ask people to take an action off the site.

    Calls to action often use an active verb in the imperative: Save money, Get a free…, Learn about…, Check out our new…, Try…, Test drive…, For more information contact…. Be specific, but gentle, if you want users to take action. Don't bury a call to action three levels down. Make different opportunities visible at the highest level and on every page. Whatever the call to action, it should be tied to marketing goals and objectives.

    Take a look at the clever calls to action on Ragu's home page (shown in Figure 5.32) at *http://www.eat.com*. This site is loaded! Three external calls are found on the right: "Free" (an implicit call to action), "Fix Your Kitchen Up," and "Try Our Mac & Cheese Recipe." Can you find at least four internal calls to action on this page? (There are more than that). If you click through this site, you'll find dozens of calls to action, both external ("Don't forget to look under the Ragu Label…") and internal ("Go Peek!"). Keep a list of URLs or printouts in your Web notebook with great calls to action like these. We'll talk more in Chapter 7 about using internal calls to action as a method of promotion.

- Include at least one e-mail address and point of human contact on your site, preferably on every page. If there are multiple points of contact, try to put the specific, relevant e-mail address on the page instead of using a generic info@yourcompany.com. It will shorten the time for response, making it more likely that you can stay within a 24-hour window. It's a mistake to show an e-mail address only for your Webmaster (often your developer), who may not know enough about your business and staff to

Figure 5.32. Subtle calls to action, *http://www.eat.com*. Courtesy Lipton Investments, Inc. and Unilever USA, Inc.

forward mail appropriately or promptly. If the Webmaster's e-mail address is on every page as well, specify that it's for assistance or problems with the site.

- Even if your site includes a corporate phone directory, don't forget to identify the site on each page and include your street address, telephone, and fax number. If you are selling goods or services, be sure to include a toll-free number as well.

- Update the site frequently. For your own benefit and to indicate that your site is current, show the date of the last modification and the name of the person who made it.

- If appropriate for enrollment or payment purposes, make provision for passwords. Keep abreast of developments for protecting credit card numbers. (See Chapter 9 for more information on security protection.)

- A What's New section directs repeat visitors immediately to new content on your site. Note the fish icon on the Fishing Online site shown in Figure 5.33 (*http://www.pvisuals.com/fishing/whats_new/whats_new.html*).

- Watch This Space. If you must remove content and can't delete references to a page, post a construction icon. This may frustrate viewers, but it's better than an error message. Avoid posting frequent messages about coming pages that may never get built. To generate user interest in a return visit, announce an opening day for the page and include a call to action to bookmark the site for a return visit, perhaps with a chance to win something. If you use a site reminder service, as described in Chapter 7, encourage people to register so you can notify them when the new page is available.

Figure 5.33. What's new, *http://pvisuals.com/fishing/whats_new.* Courtesy Perspective Visuals, Inc.

Freebies and Features

As you've learned, developing a good site is a detailed and time-consuming process. The more you can acquire elsewhere, the shorter and less expensive your development cycle will be. Features that required custom programming several years ago are now easy to add to your site as links or downloadable code. You'll find sources for such site improvements such as maps and search engines in Figure 5.34. Figure 5.35 offers sources for free Web and Internet services, and Figure 5.36 provides places to obtain decorative items like backgrounds, buttons and bars. Sites for free tools may be found in Chapter 6; sites for free promotional options may be found in Chapter 7 and 8, and sites for multimedia plug-ins may be found in Chapter 9.

Features and Site Amenities

Use the added features and site amenities shown in Figure 5.34 only when appropriate as a way to encourage visitors to linger on your site. For instance, contractors or architects might include a map and direction service linked to photos of their buildings so potential clients can drive by their projects. A children's site might encourage youngsters to create and send free greeting cards. A company that offers hundreds of products or documents would benefit from a site-based search engine. A tourist-oriented company in San Diego or Puerto Rico might want to tout local weather, while one that sponsors conferences might create online forums for past participants. If you add features randomly, it will only detract from your marketing message and dilute the impact of your site.

Affiliate programs offer a relatively easy way to generate some revenue from your site. They offer a commission on viewer click-throughs (prospects), qualified leads, or sales referred from your site. Bookstore programs from sites like barnesandnoble.com and Amazon.com probably are the best known—Amazon.com has more than 430,000 participating associates; however, hundreds of such programs are now available. Since affiliate programs link viewers away from your site to make a purchase, be sure they provide an on-site Back button to increase the likelihood that viewers will return. Most affiliates provide code to "cut and paste" onto your page and allow you to select certain items to highlight or sell.

Type of Resource	URL	Free (✔)
Affiliate program	*http://www.amazon.com/exec/obidos/subst/ partners/associates*	5-15% to referring site
Affiliate program (established on your site)	*http://www.clicktrade.com*	✔
Calendar	*http://calendars.net*	✔
Catalog and shopping cart	*http://www.yahoo.com*	✔ up to 50 items
Catalog and shopping cart	*http://www.icat.com*	✔ up to 12 items
Catalog and shopping cart	*http://www.openmarket.com*	✔ up to 12 items
E-mail (offer on your site)	*http://www.zzn.com/informail/signup.asp*	✔
Games (trivia)	*http://www.uproar.com/webdevelopers/*	✔
Greeting cards	*http://www.regards.com*	✔
Guestbook	*http://www.guestbooks4free.com*	✔
Guestbook	*http://freeguestbooks.com*	✔
Guestbook	*http://www.miatrade.com*	✔
Hub (search engine) for affiliate programs	*http://www.refer-it.com*	✔
Hub for affiliate programs	*http://www.associateprograms.com*	✔
Hub for other free resources	*http://www.totallyfreestuff.com*	✔
Listbot	*http://www.linkexchange.com/index.html*	✔
Map & direction service	*http://www.aaa.com*	✔
Map & direction service	*http://www.vicinity.com*	✔
Map & direction service	*http://www.infospace.com/info/cbsite.htm OR specific map link at: http://www.in-100. infospace.com/info/kevmap/linktomap.htm*	(✔ with link; $ for co-branding)
Mutiple: chat room, message board, search engine	*http://freecenter.digiweb.com/index. cgi?action=FreeSearch*	✔
Multiple: banner ads, statistics, e-mail counter, intra-site search, guestbook, tutorials, polls, more	*http://www.hyperbanner.com*	✔

Figure 5.34. Free features and site amenities *(Continued on next page).*

Type of Resource	URL	Free (✔)
Multiple: cartoons, classifieds, counters, e-mail form processing, forum, greeting cards, guestbook, mailing list, polls, search engines, Web announcements, free links	http://www.bravenet.com	✔
Multiple: chat room, counters, e-mail list, guestbook, message boards, quizlet, search box, site submission, Web e-mail	http://www.beseen.com	
Multiple: games, greeting cards, screensavers, Web e-mail	http://www.maxpatch.com	✔
Personalized event & calendar service	http://www.when.com	✔ with link
Polls	http://www.pollit.com	✔
Scheduling service	http://www.scheduleonline.com	✔
Search engines, other search tools, scroll-able menus	http://www.smartlinks.looksmart.com/smartlinks?chan=home	✔
Search engine	http://www.atomz.com	✔ with ads up to 500 pages
Search engine	http://www.freefind.com	✔
Search engine	http://pinpoint.netcreations.com	✔ with ads
Search engine	htto://www.searchbutton.com	✔ with ads up to 2,500 pages
Surveys and forms	http://www.addaform.com	✔
Tools: Site statistical tracker	http://www.extreme-dm.com/tracking/?home	✔
Tools: spell checking, link verifier, syntax	http://www.siteowner.com OR http://siteinspector.linkexchange.com	
Topical search engine	http://abcparenting.com	
Weather	http://www.weatherlabs.com	✔
Weather	http://www.accuweather.com/wx/company/link.htm	✔ with link
Weather (local stickers)	http://www.wunderground.com/geo/BannerPromo/	✔ with link, selected cities

Figure 5.34. Free features and site amenities (*Continued from previous page*).

Commissions usually run 5%, but a few go as high as 20%. Some offer only a flat fee per click-through or lead. Usually, you'll receive a monthly statement with payment made when commissions reach a certain level. Unless you spend a lot of time and effort driving traffic to your site, don't expect to make a fortune. However, the right affiliation can be a convenient, value-added service for your visitors. Again, be selective. Choose no more than one or two affiliate programs, unless you want to be a virtual flea market!

If you prefer to have other Web owners drive buyers to your site, you can run your own affiliate program using software from *http:// www.clicktrade.com.*

As always, the Web reinvents itself. Several companies now offer the ability to build a little shop that appears to be within your site, but is really a link to another site. You select the goods you want to "cyber-stock" from the host company's warehouse, which might contain anything from games to office supplies. The host does all the transaction processing, shipping and customer service. Hiring a commerce provider like Vitessa at *http:// www.vitessa.com* or Iconomy at *http://www.iconomy.com* is very expensive, but it can save in other costs if you have enough traffic for the program to pay for itself.

There are conflicting opinions on the value of affiliate programs, with some forecasters arguing that up to 25% of retail sales on the Internet will originate on affiliate sites by 2002 and other forecasters persuaded that affiliate programs are on the way out because too many content sites lose their own viewers to retailers. Try it and see.

Free Web and Internet Services

If you're really strapped for cash, the resources in Figure 5.35 may be a reasonable alternative. They are certainly better than putting up a free site without your own domain name on a portal like *http:// www.geocities.com* or *http://www.tripod.com.* Supposedly these portals make some free domain name space available as long as you are willing to allow their advertisers to appear on your pages.

As an alternative, many ISPs now include 3 to 5 MB of Web space in their monthly fee. Check to see if they will allow you to use your own domain name, or if they permit only an extension (yourcompany. ISPname.net or ISPname.net/yourcompany). Some search engines no

Type of Resource	URL	Free (✔)
Brand naming guide	*http://www.namestormers.com*	✔
E-mail forwarding and Web site re-direction	*http://www.mydomain.com*	✔
Hosting	*http://www.homestead.com*	✔
Hosting and domain registration	*http://www.webjump.com*	✔ with banner ad
Hub for free Internet access sites	*http://www.lights.com/freenet*	✔
Internet access	*http://www.tritium.com*	✔ with ads
Site design and domain registration	*http://www.worldwidewebinstitute.net*	✔ 6 pages with paid hosting service for 1 yr
Site design, hosting, domain registration, search engine submission	*http://www.prosperitypromo.com*	✔ 5 pages
Template design (site builder)	*http://www.smartage.com/site_creator/index.html*	✔ with hosting service
Template design (site builder)	*http://desktoppublishing.com/template/web/sitekits.html*	✔ for non-commercial only

Figure 5.35. Free Web and Internet services.

longer index sites with such names. These small freebie sites may be useful as doorway pages to your main site, however.

Free Decorative Doo-Dahs

You'll have to decide whether the time it takes to search through the decorative resources in Figure 5.36 is worth it. You'll find many additional resources for free clip art and digital photos on commercial on-line services or by using a search engine.

In the next three chapters we'll cover the remaining steps to Internet marketing success. Chapter 6 deals with maintaining and monitoring your site, while Chapters 7 and 8 will discuss promoting your site effectively online and off.

Type of Resource	URL	Free (✔)
Animated GIFs, e.g. balls, buttons, bullets	*http://www.beseen.com/beseen/free/*	✔
Backgrounds, buttons, icons, rules, design tips	*http://dspace.deal.pipex.com/leuhusen/ graphic.shtml*	✔
Background patterns	*http://www.netcreations.com/patternland*	✔
Buttons and backgrounds	*http://www.freegraphics.com*	✔
Clip art	*http://www.clip-art.com*	✔
Clip art	*http://www.barrysclipart.com*	✔
Clip art, sounds	*http://www.maxpatch.com*	✔
Fonts	*http://www.fontsnthings.com*	✔
Fonts	*http://www.1001freefonts.com*	✔
Graphics (non-professional)	*http://members.tripod.com/~ GIFPRO/index.html*	✔ CD $10
Graphics	*http://www.graphics-by-celeste.com*	✔
Graphics, clip art	*http://www.arttoday.com/PD-0025148/ newfree/main.html*	✔
Graphics, clip art, Web sets, toon-a-day, and more	*http://desktoppublishing.com/free.html*	✔
Graphics, design sets, fonts, design tips	*http://www.geocities.com/siliconvalley/ heights/1288/index.html*	✔
Graphics generator for logos, buttons, and bullets	*http://www.cooltext.com*	✔
Sound effects	*http://soundamerica.com*	✔

Figure 5.36. Free decorative doo-dahs.

6

Maintaining and Monitoring Your Site

Your Web site is not finished when it first goes "live." A site is an ever-changing marketing tool. Art goes "stale" quickly online; good links appear and disappear; unexpected errors crop up when developers release new versions of plug-ins or browsers; your product line grows. As your business and cyberspace change, your Web site must change with them.

In this chapter, we'll explore Step 6 for Internet success: maintaining and monitoring your Web site. You'll want to determine how well your site fulfills the objectives you set for it. Is it attracting as many visitors as projected? Are they clicking away as soon as they arrive on your home page, or do they continue to view additional pages? Does your newest call to action draw more or less response than the prior one? Instincts and anecdotal evidence, although critical, can be deceptive. Let statistical data cushion your decision making.

Planning for a Web site must take into account the budget and personnel needed for ongoing maintenance, updates, and monitoring. If you are working with an outside Web designer and/or Web host, include questions in your selection survey about update frequency and available tools for analysis. In this chapter you'll learn about

- A site maintenance schedule to keep your Web site at its peak.

- Site and server statistics.

- Analyzing statistical reports.

- Available statistical tools.

- Using results effectively.

Maintaining Your Site

Include a regular maintenance schedule in the Site Maintenance section of your Web notebook. Identify the people both in-house and outside who will be responsible for each maintenance activity. Designate the frequency with which it will occur, and coordinate these activities with your Webmaster and/or Web host. Your schedule should cover at least three types of checking:

1. Operational errors

2. Links

3. Content

Maintenance Schedule

Schedules for maintenance depend on the type of site you run. A complex multimedia site that relies on plug-ins for accessibility needs to be checked more often than a simple, static site. One with dozens of links, particularly to sites that are new themselves, will need more monitoring than a site with a few links to well-established databases at educational institutions. A site that updates price lists or inventory should be verified independently every time a change is uploaded to confirm that the right data appear.

As obvious as it sounds, check that your site is up and running properly every day. You might keep a running list of priority applications or pages to add, based on customer requests or internal marketing needs. Run a wish list of less important but attractive options as well. Then develop a schedule to add one item every week, month, or quarter, or as time and budget permit. At a minimum, plan on monthly additions or changes to your page.

Some of your most useful feedback will come from users who e-mail messages and queries to the Webmaster. Be sure you receive copies of all those messages, good and bad; you can always include a "copy to" option on the e-mail form so both you and the Webmaster receive complaints and praise. Keep these e-mails in the Site Feedback section of your notebook, along with the results of user testing conducted in Chapter 4.

Check Syntax

Confirm that your Web designer uses a syntax checking program to catch the inevitable typos and errors in his or her code. This may be done in the form of an HTML editor, such as the free program HoTMetaL *(ftp:// ftp.ncsa.uiuc.edu/Web/html/hotmetal)*, which checks the structure of code (its syntax) as it is written. Syntax review can also be done with after-the-fact checkers, such as those available at the following sites:

- Dr. Watson: *http://watson.addy.com* (shown in Figure 6.1)

- Weblint: *http://www.weblint.com*

- Site Inspector: *http://siteowner.bcentral.com*

- Imagiware: *http://www2.imagiware.com/RxHTML*

- Web Site Garage: *http://www.WebsiteGarage.com*

- HTML Online Validation Service: *http://val.svc.webtechs.com/ index.htm*

Since these free services check programs online, the site must be up and running before it can be tested. If your designers use one of these, consider publishing your page with limited password access until it has been validated or having them check it on their server. Different checkers offer dif-

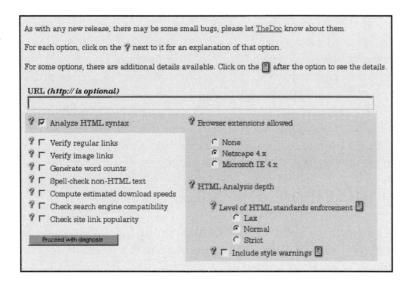

Figure 6.1. Syntax error checker, *http://watson.addy.com*. Courtesy Cliff Addy, Addy & Associates, Inc.

ferent features, so compare them carefully. For instance, Site Inspector checks for browser compatibility, while Dr. Watson generates word counts.

Verify Links

Web surfers complain frequently about dead links that yield the frustrating message "404 Not Found" or "URL unknown." Once you have more than a few links, verifying becomes a painstaking and tedious task. Let a computer do it! Software is available to check all links automatically on a regular basis. Generally you will need to ask your Webmaster or designer

- Whether they have such software.

- How often they run it (weekly would be good for links!).

- If there's a charge.

If the designer doesn't have these capabilities, see if your Web host will run a link verifier for you. You (or they) might try Linklint 2.1 at *http://goldwarp.com/bowlin/linklint/* (shown in Figure 6.2) for automatic link-checking software. It has a one-time shareware fee of $10 for individual use or $100 for commercial use.

A talented Web programmer can arrange for a dead link to generate an e-mail notification to the Webmaster so that the link can be removed even before a routine verification check occurs. A copy of the e-mail can be sent to viewers so that they know the problem is being handled—a nice touch.

MOMspider (Multi-Owner Maintenance Spider)

It's helpful to receive notification about links that have changed so that you can be sure their content remains relevant to your site. As you may recall, a spider is a program that automatically searches the Web for sites that link to yours, either inbound or outbound. MOMspider not only finds broken links, it also finds ones that have

Linklint 2.1 - Fast html link checker
Version 2.1.0 July 24, 1997 (recent changes)

Other pages:
Linklint Home | Inputs | Instructions | Specifications | Ordering

Linklint is a Perl shareware program that checks all local and remote links on a web site. It works with Perl 4 or Perl 5 on Windows and Unix platforms. Ftp sites for Perl can be found at http://www.perl.com/perl/.

Linklint has earned high praise from many users, including these comments:

... kudos on a fantastic application ... I'm definitely going to use your software from now on. It beats every other link checker I've tried, hands down.

Mike Simpson, Web Manager
University of Pennsylvania's Library
20,000 HTML pages, 2 gigabytes of content

Three Modes of Operation

Local Site Check:
Checks links on your site locally, looking for files on the local file system. This mode is ideal if you are developing on a system that does't have a web server, or to check a group of pages before posting them on your server.
input examples | output example

Figure 6.2. Link checking software, *http://goldwarp.com/bowlin/linklint*. Courtesy Bowlin Software.

moved, changed, or expired. It is free at *http://www.ics.uci.edu/pub/ websoft/MOMspider.*

Make Corrections and Fixes

Most programmers make and test changes offline and publish a finished page. A structured release of fixed, updated, or new pages allows your team to plan its work, at the same time providing a clear way to assess whether your designer is meeting contractual terms. Be sure to discuss how much maintenance and upgrading time will be included when negotiating your Web development contract. Most developers include several hours per month in their basic maintenance agreement and then charge an hourly fee for additional work.

In response to feedback from users or your own review process, you may have a collection of fixes that have been programmed and tested. Except for critical errors that must be repaired immediately, collect a small batch of changes for scheduled maintenance activity, perhaps weekly or biweekly. Every time you go into your site, you risk introducing an error. On the other hand, making too many changes at once may complicate identifying the source of a problem that occurs, and waiting too long to make changes suggested by the statistical findings doesn't make good marketing sense.

Be especially careful when more than one person makes changes. It is common in the software world to develop and test new modules independently and then integrate them into the existing structure. (A module can be a page, a database, or a function such as sound playback.) Your Web designer should enforce some form of version management so that all developers work from the same base. A systematic approach tests each new module with all the other revised modules in place to avoid negative interactions, particularly when the navigational structure changes.

Finally, each time significant changes are made or new features are added, retest site performance with different browsers, platforms, and monitor configurations, as described in the previous chapter. Emulation sites for download speed and appearance include

- *http://www.cast.org/bobby*

- *http://www.AnyBrowser.com*

- *http://siteowner.bcentral.com*

Update Content

Updating content maintains interest and draws repeat users. It keeps your site fresh and, as we'll see in the next chapter, provides a reason for past viewers to return to your site. Your update strategy will depend on the goals for your site. An online archival database needs less frequent updating than one pushing audio for a recording company's new releases. A sales site, on the other hand, may constantly offer new promotions, quizzes, or contests.

You may be able to automate some content changes by referencing or uploading a file that is regularly updated by others or is dynamically modified (e.g., an inventory of auto parts). Real-time information feeds are an obvious form of content updates. If you are carrying advertisements, a schedule for ad replacement will be negotiated in the advertising contract.

Many Web developers make it possible for their clients to modify site content on their own, either by filling out an "administrative form" or by uploading replacement text files to a particular location on the server. Some companies, like Cuesta Technologies, (*http://www.cuesta.com*, seen in Figure 6.3), enable customers to modify other aspects of their site, including adding or removing pages, without knowing anything about programming. The ability to modify pages on your own is extremely valuable: You can add time-critical information to your site without waiting for your developer to be available, and it saves the developer's charges. You may want to make "self-service" capability a criterion for selecting a developer in the first place.

Some event-driven updates, such as product announcements from a supplier, can't be prescheduled. Even if content updating doesn't apply to your site, schedule at least a monthly review to confirm that the information on your site is still accurate. At this time, you can also decide whether you want to incorporate any new links. Whatever method the updates take, be sure to **archive** (save offline) the old pages for record-keeping purposes. Companies with many people responsible for different pages on a large site may find it useful to create a content database that automatically (or manually) records such information as who is responsible for page changes, when a page was updated, and where archived versions are stored.

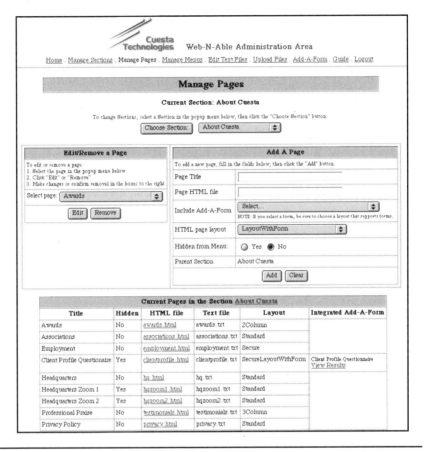

Figure 6.3.   Client tool for site management, *http://www.cuesta.com/webnable.html.* Courtesy Cuesta Technologies, LLC., Interactive commercial Web sites and sophisticated e-stuff.

Moving Your Site or Pages

Your URL may change if

- You change Web hosts and don't have your own domain name.

- Information is moved from one part of a server to another.

- Your company or Web host sets up a new server.

You may also decide to move information from one page extension to another, or even to another URL. As a result, links to your former address or bookmarks in user files will be incorrect. Be sure your Web host sets up redirection information in such circumstances.

Take a few other steps as well:

- Notify everyone with whom you have established a reciprocal or outbound link.

- Notify visitors who have registered on your site via e- mail.

- Run a spider to identify and notify everyone who has established an inbound link to your site

- Use the announcement, submit-it, and indexing services described in Chapter 7 to post your "moved" URL.

Monitoring Results

In Chapter 2, we talked about writing quantifiable objectives. To see if those objectives are met, you will need to specify ways to measure progress and decide how often data will be collected. In your selection survey for Web hosts, be sure to find out what statistical analysis tools they have and the types and frequency of reports you can expect. They should be able to provide you with reports showing both site statistics and server statistics. If you host a site on your own server, you may want to buy statistical software for your own use.

Most hosting services offer at least a limited set of statistical reports for free; a few charge for more extensive analysis or special reports. You usually access reports either on a hidden page of your site or by retrieving the reports with FTP. Before you select a Web hosting service, be sure to check out their sample reports! If your host does not provide statistical reports, you need to look for another host.

As more site owners become aware of the value of statistics, providing this information has become a competitive issue that differentiates hosts. Be sure to ask whether graphical presentations are available (these are much easier to understand!), how long data are kept, and the timeline for graphical comparisons. Find out whether you (or the host) can customize reports to meet your specific needs. Depending on the package used by the host, statistics may be available by minute, hour, day, week, or month. Don't be shy about asking your host to change reporting parameters to make it the report more useful. The worst they can say is no.

What you are trying to accomplish with your site will determine what you need to measure and how you measure it. Various hit counts are valuable for determining the percentage of visits that convert to sales, for assessing whether your strategy for launch publicity met expectations, and for measuring the advertising value of your Web site compared to other media. However, a high hit count does not always mean success. For instance, if your goal is to sell clear plastic lunch boxes online, the number of hits on your site is not the ultimate measurement—sales volume and profit margin are. Web site statistics alone can't give you those answers.

Hit Rate: Fact and Myth

Not all hits are created equal. The number of **raw hits** or visits to your site may be quite misleading. Raw hit counts dramatically overstate the number of visitors because each separate text, sound, image, or CGI file on a page is counted as a separate hit. A page with four images and a menu bar generates six hits; one for the link to the page, one for the menu bar, and four for the pictures. Often, those selling ad space on their sites will quote the raw hit number because it's the highest one available.

The number of unique visitors is far more useful for marketing purposes than hits. If you can't get this figure from your statistical reports, estimate it by (a) looking at the number of requests for the home page, (b) dividing the total hit count for a page by the number of files it contains, or (c) totaling the number of referrals by either URL or ISP. As a last resort, divide gross hit count by 6 to 8.

On the other hand, actual usage may be undercounted if a page is downloaded to a user's computer or LAN and then viewed multiple times by the same person or others. To measure the frequency with which pages are **cached** (saved in memory on a local computer or server), survey a representative sample of site users to see how often this occurs; then adjust your numbers upward accordingly.

Remember, too, that the number of hits on a counter or in a log doesn't indicate how many of those hits came from the same person logging in at different times. Did you give your mother your new Web address? Even the number of unique visitors who accessed your site really tells you only which computers called your server, not which people. Was it the 10-year-old surfing after school or the parent with purchasing authority?

To obtain more specific information, some Web sites place a **cookie** on the computer of users who register (and occasionally on any computer that visits the site). This short identifier file assigns a unique number to the machine, which is recognized each time the registered user logs in. Some cookies may have much more information: user name and address, purchasing history, shipping information, credit card numbers, reminder notes, e-mail address books, gift logs, or site preferences. Users don't have to re-enter duplicate information each time they make a purchase, while the site owner can personalize greetings or upsell by suggesting new items based on past browsing and buying patterns. The convenience of cookies, however, comes at a price in user privacy, which is discussed further in Chapter 9.

On-Site Page Counters

Some small companies install simple counters on one or more pages to track the number of hits. You can obtain free counters from many sources, generally in exchange for putting the supplier's icon on your site. If you use one, be sure to note the date you started counting, at least internally! Or you can try a free service like eXTReMe Tracking (shown in Figure 6.4), where the counter is invisible; you log onto eXTReMe at *http://www.extreme-dm.com/tracking/?npt* to see your statistics privately.

Before you implement an on-screen counter, consider its implications from a marketing perspective. First, it should not be used in lieu of statistical analysis—a page counter is a raw hit count. Second, think how it will look to your viewers. Low numbers may reduce the confidence of potential customers. Do you really want to advertise a lack of success? On the other hand, if you're selling advertising online and your numbers are high, an on-screen page counter may be a psychological selling point for an advertiser who wants a quick way to monitor impressions, however inaccurate.

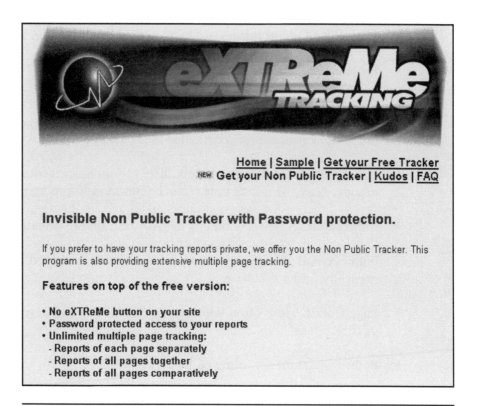

Figure 6.4. Free counter, *http://www.extreme-dm.com/tracking/?npt.* Courtesy eXTReMe Digital.

Analyzing Statistical Reports

Site Statistics

A good statistical package can provide a wealth of data about your site and its visitors:

- **Agent log:** which browsers, spiders, or link verifiers have been used by someone to check out your site.

- **Browser:** Estimated number of computers that visited site or page by type, version, and platform.

- **Click Rate:** Specific images or files requested by clicking on a link.

- **E-mail:** Feedback from users sorted into categories.

- **Entry Page:** Which page of your site did visitors see first?

- **File:** Number of times a particular file is accessed.

- **History:** Analysis (preferably graphical) of various features over time; in some cases a year-long history can be enormously important.

- **Impressions:** Number of times a logo or sponsorship was viewed.

- **Number and Demographics:** User registration compiled automatically into a database.

- **Page Count:** How often whole pages were requested; estimate of click count.

- **Path:** Page sequence followed by viewer.

- **Repeat Visitors:** Number of repeat visits from the same address.

- **Sales:** By frequency, volume, revenue item, buyer, or category.

- **Sessions:** Count of all the times the site is accessed by one user.

- **Time:** Time users spend on site and/or on a page.

- **Unique Home Page Hits:** Counts only one hit to home page per session.

- **User Survey:** Data compiled automatically into a database and/or report.

- **Visitors:** Number of unique addresses from which calls were made.

- **Which pages and files** are most heavily used.

Even these numbers may be somewhat inaccurate. Browser numbers don't tell you whether several people share a computer or whether the same person has called several times from an online service that generates multiple source addresses. Some statistical reports, for instance, eliminate AOL access from the totals because they can't be broken down to individual IP addresses.

Although you can determine how much time users spend on a page, you can't guarantee that they were actually looking at that page. They could have been chatting with a co-worker or talking on the phone. However, you can get a sense of relative use.

By following users' paths through your site, perhaps you'll detect patterns that show which pages or links within your site are least or most effective. Compare usage before and after a page is updated. Instead of just raw numbers over a month, look at access rates by specific date to correlate what happens after you have reworded a call to action, changed a headline, or substituted a new photo. Did any of these make a difference in number of visits, length of time spent, or how often visitors proceeded to an order page? Careful analysis can help you decide which parts of your site to delete, modify, or expand.

It is especially important to check how your visitors reach your site. A **referrer log** shows which URLs linked to your site. Try to correlate referrer URLs with the date that a new link went up; this will enable you to track the relative value of your reciprocal links. From an online marketing perspective, it's also extremely valuable to know which search engines were used to find your site and what keywords resulted in successful queries.

You also want to see whether other promotional activities successfully drove traffic to your site. If you don't usually obtain hourly, daily, or weekly statistics, ask your Web host to provide them following such events as new links, keyword changes, or the appearance of your site on a Cool Link list. After their TV ads aired on the Super Bowl, some advertisers actually monitored site access by the minute!

Server Statistics

Besides showing activity on your site, statistical reports can provide operational information about the server that hosts your site, whether it's on your premises or at your Web host's. These reports can help you monitor the performance of your Web host. Has the server been down? Is it able to handle the volume of hits? Are visitors being turned away?

Server data include such things as overall server usage by hour, day, and week, any network or communication problems, where errors were encountered, and comparative historical data. They can help you judge whether a site is so popular that access has become a problem, or whether some part of your site is generating many errors.

Amateur Statistics

In a pinch, you can download raw data files from the server as text, use the Find command in your word processor to search through it, and create your own reports. If the data seem incomprehensible, watch for a few key items in a long string of characters:

- A phrase that starts with "GET/..." This indicates the name of the first file requested by the browser.

- The referral source in the usual *http:// format*. If this is a search engine name, it might be followed by the keywords used to locate your site.

- The browser information, preferably including version number so you can see if most of your viewers are using current or out-of-date technology.

- The acronym **cgi** (**common gateway interface**) often indicates a search engine address, since it means something was typed in by the user. Use the Find command in your word processor to search for that term, the names of search engines, keywords, or browser names.

Comparing Sample Reports

Let's compare extracts of reports provided by two different Web hosts, seen in Figures 6.5 and 6.6. The extract of the server report for the host in Figure 6.5 analyzes server access by day, hour, and domain, but provides only the inflated number of requests or hits. The statistical report using Web Trends in Figure 6.6 includes the more useful totals of page

World-Wide Web Access Statistics
Last updated: Fri, 01 Jan 1999 05:13:31 (GMT -0700)

Totals for Summary Period: Dec 1 1998 to Dec 31 1998

Files Transmitted During Summary Period	765
KBytes Transmitted During Summary Period	36977.7
Average Files Transmitted Daily	26
Average KBytes Transmitted Daily	1275.1

Daily Transmission Statistics / Hourly Transmission Statistics

%Reqs	%KB	KB Sent	Requests	Date	%Reqs	%KB	KB Sent	Requests	Time
24.58	56.84	21018.4	188	12/1/98	6.01	8.61	3182.4	46	10
5.75	0.35	131.0	44	12/2/98	4.31	8.62	3188.3	33	11
1.05	0.14	53.0	8	12/3/98	11.11	21.02	7773.4	85	12
5.36	8.66	3201.6	41	12/4/98					

Total Transfers by Client Domain

%Reqs	%KB	KB Sent	# Reqs	Domain	Domain Name
1.70	0.94	346.2	13	cz	Czech Republic
0.39	0.13	47.2	3	nl	Netherlands
0.13	0.00	0.2	1	uk	United Kingdom
0.78	0.20	73.6	6	us	United States
48.37	60.06	22209.4	370	com	US Commercial
31.24	28.25	10447.6	239	net	Network
3.79	8.60	3178.6	29	org	Non-Profit Organization
13.59	1.82	674.6	104	unresolved	

Total Transfers by Reversed Subdomain

%Reqs	%KB	KB Sent	# Reqs	Reversed Subdomain
19.08	24.75	9152.1	146	com.aol.proxy
13.59	1.82	674.6	104	Unresolved
9.28	16.77	6202.6	71	com.nabisco
5.62	6.46	2387.4	43	net.psi.pub-ip.md.laurel
3.53	4.30	1591.8	27	net.flash.abq1.dialup.utc2
2.88	8.45	3126.3	22	org.frb
2.88	8.44	3120.2	22	net.uu.da.bos1.tnt3
1.96	0.33	120.5	15	com.intel.rr
1.96	0.21	77.3	15	com.aol.ipt

Total Transfers from each Archive Section

%Reqs	%KB	KB Sent	# Reqs	Archive Section
12.16	1.18	434.5	93	/
6.41	0.04	13.0	49	/blue_swirl3343.gif
8.24	4.18	1545.6	63	/chinapat.jpg
2.88	0.27	101.2	22	/client.htm
2.75	0.42	154.1	21	/open.htm
1.44	0.24	86.9	11	/ourstory.htm
2.09	0.27	98.8	16	/partner.htm
1.96	0.11	39.0	15	/philos.htm
7.06	0.05	16.9	54	/red_swirl12350.gif
1.70	0.06	22.1	13	/service.htm
6.54	0.32	119.8	50	/speckled_gradient1e3.gif
2.09	0.03	10.3	16	Code 404 Not Found Requests

Figure 6.5. Extract server report host 1. Courtesy ProcessWorks.

General Statistics

The User Profile by Regions graph identifies the general location of the visitors to your Web site. The General Statistics table includes statistics on the total activity for this server during the designated time frame.

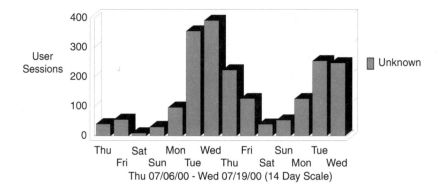

General Statistics	
Date & Time This Report was Generated	Wednesday July 19, 2000 - 14:51:09
Timeframe	07/06/00 00:00:00 - 07/19/00 23:59:59
Number of Hits for Home Page	N/A
Number of Successful Hits for Entire Site	75297
Number of Page Views (Impressions)	9386
Number of User Sessions	2044
User Sessions from United States	0%
International User Sessions	0%
User Sessions of Unknown Origin	100%
Average Number of Hits per Day	5378
Average Number of Page Views Per Day	670
Average Number of User Sessions per Day	146
Average User Session Length	00:09:15

Figure 6.6. Extract server report host 2. Courtesy American Hospital Association/Health Forum.™

views and user sessions as well. The report shown in Figure 6.5 provides only tabular data for a fixed time period, while the report in Figure 6.6 summarizes data graphically over variable selected time frames. Although not shown in the figures, both companies provide accesses broken down by files requested and by referrer URLs (same as "reversed subdomain"), but only the report in Figure 6.6 shows search words entered by the user. In other words, "you pays your money and you takes your choice." Knowing what reports you need and what various hosts provide may help you select the appropriate hosting service.

Available Statistical Tools for a Fee

There are many statistical packages, both fee and free. The fee-based ones include

- AccessWatch (free for individuals, $400 per server for service providers, discount program). This UNIX-based program generates statistics of server use by hour or day and computes access by page, domain, host, browser, platform, and referral source. For information, go to *http://www.accesswatch.com/license*. A sample report from this program can be found by a link or at *http://netpressence.com/aw-sample*.

- Accrue Insight (*http://www.accrue.com*) provides detailed user analysis software to assess purchase behavior and marketing effectiveness. The cost is based on network configuration and traffic levels. (See Figure 6.7)

- I/PRO (Internet Profiles Corporation) offers Netline for Web site measurement and analysis on both individual sites and Web hosts, starting at $750 a month. It also offers Velocity, which monitors sites' speed and performance from different users' perspectives.

- MarketWave's Hit List is a suite of real-time Web mining tools (*http://www.marketwave.com*).

- NetCount software, from Price Waterhouse at *http://www.netcount.com*, is one of the more detailed traffic analysis

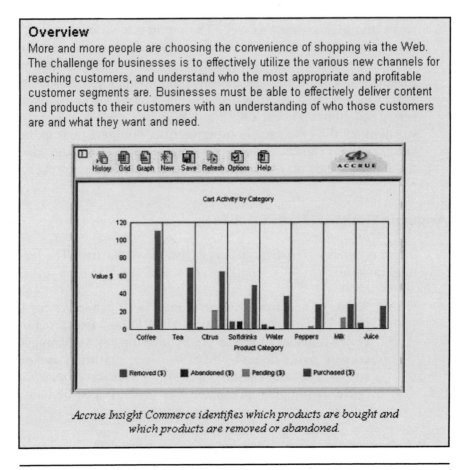

Overview
More and more people are choosing the convenience of shopping via the Web. The challenge for businesses is to effectively utilize the various new channels for reaching customers, and understand who the most appropriate and profitable customer segments are. Businesses must be able to effectively deliver content and products to their customers with an understanding of who those customers are and what they want and need.

Accrue Insight Commerce identifies which products are bought and which products are removed or abandoned.

Figure 6.7. Source for detailed user analysis software, *http://www.accrue.com/ products/commerce.html.* © Accrue Software, Inc.

tools, tracking such things as a viewer's path through the site and length of time on a page.

- WebTrends at *http://www.webtrends.com*, one of the most popular and low-priced packages ($299–$999 to purchase; $59–$199 to subscribe), offers a comprehensive package of server tools including traffic, link, streaming media, and proxy server analysis, as well as monitoring and alerts.

Available Statistical Tools for Free

If you're doing your own site development or hosting, check whether your tools already include management and reporting software. Microsoft's Front Page and Adobe's Page Mill both include reporting capabilities, as do Microsoft's Site Server and Commerce Edition. If your Web host or developer can't provide the analysis you want and you can't afford to install one of these packages, request the access logs for your site. Then apply one of the following free statistical tools to analyze the data yourself.

- Getstats (C language for multiple platforms) offers hourly, daily, weekly, and monthly summaries of use, sorted in a variety of ways. This is great for specific analysis. Documentation and directions for file access are available at *http://www.eit.com/software/getstats/getstats.html*. Graphing software for Getstats may be found at *http://infopad.eecs.berkeley.edu/stats* or *http://www.tcp.chem.tue.nl/stats/script*.

- Two free tools can be found at The Netstore at *http://www.netstore.de/Supply/http-analyze/findex.html*. Http-analyze 2.0 analyzes server logs in graphs and tables, while 3dstats 2.1 (freestanding or incorporated with http-analyze) provides a three-dimensional representation of statistics as seen in Figure 6.8.

- RefStats (freeware) summarizes the URLs from which users access your site. You can tell whether the user located you from a search engine, a sponsorship, an ad, or a link from another page. It is available at *http://www.netimages.com/~snowhare/utilities/refstats.html*.

- VBStats 3.1 (Windows freeware) offers standard reports and will build Top 10 lists, such as most-requested pages. It can be found at *http://www.tech.west.ora.com/win_httpd*.

- WebSideStory provides the HitBOX visitor tracker at *http://www.websidestory.com* and reports results on 45,000 member sites. Similar trackers are available at WebTracker (*http://www.fxweb.com*) and WebPal (*http://www.todico.com*), but they limit free use after a certain number of days or hits.

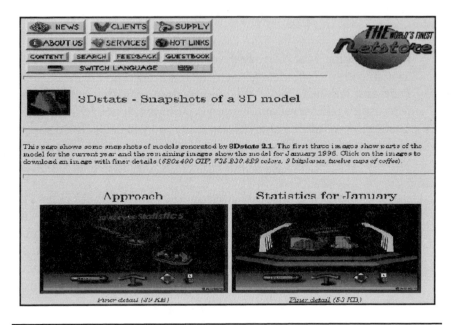

Figure 6.8. 3D statistical representation, *http://www.netstore.de/Supply/* *3Dstats/snapshots.html.* © 1999 Rent-a-Guru Æ, Heidelberg, Germany.

- Finally, WWWstat at *http://www.ics.uci.edu/pub/websoft/* *wwwstat* is another university freebie, offering basic log analysis, including graphics. Gwstat, a companion site at *http://* *dis.cs.umass.edu/stats/gwstat.html*, creates GIF graphs from the output of WWWstat.

For an up-to-date list of various log analysis tools, check Yahoo's list at *http://www.yahoo.com/Computers_and_Internet/Software/Internet/World_Wide_Web/Servers/Log_Analysis_Tools* or Ziff-Davis's tool review at *http://www.zdnet.com/yil/content/profit/soho/web1.html*.

Counting What Really Counts

Statistical analysis packages can't track where someone saw your URL offline and used that source to type it in. You can adapt a trick from direct mail marketing to analyze this yourself. Create a new page for each of your advertising campaigns and run a slightly different URL extension, such as www.maxpress.com/catalog/marketing.html or www.maxpress.com/Marketing5e, as a lead-in to your home page. Remember to install an automatic forward if you later take these pages down; who knows when someone might pick up an old ad! Or just publicize this address with an automatic forward to your real home page. Then you can use a standard package to monitor traffic on the lead-in pages.

Alternately, you could use your main URL but include directions to search on different words in each promotional campaign. Then track the search words used to reach the product page. By comparing the number of times each search word was used, you can estimate the effectiveness of different promotional campaigns.

Tracking Advertisements

Several companies now offer tools for advertising purposes that go beyond analyzing server and site logs. You may need to install such third-party auditing software to confirm viewership for advertisers or sponsors.

I/PRO in Figure 6.9, at *http://www.engage.com/ipro* verifies what percentage of visitors click on a banner. With click-through rates now around 1%, advertisers and others want independent confirmation that "clicks" are from their target audience. According to I/PRO's site, their audited reports account for over 70% of all audited reports issued for the Web. Prices start at $1250 a month based on the number of hits received.

Webwide comparisons of raw hits are also performed by software such as PC Meter (*http://www.pcmeter.com/usa/aboutus/background.asp*), which is available from the National Purchase Diary (NPD) at *http://www.npd.com* or Media Metrix at *http://www.mediametrix.com*. This software, similar to Nielsen's TV rating box, is installed on home computers to monitor the habits of Web surfers. The program extrapolates data to establish demographics and hit rates for top-rated Web sites.

Using Results Effectively

To make the most of the data you gather, use the information from registrations to establish a demographic profile and match that to cus-

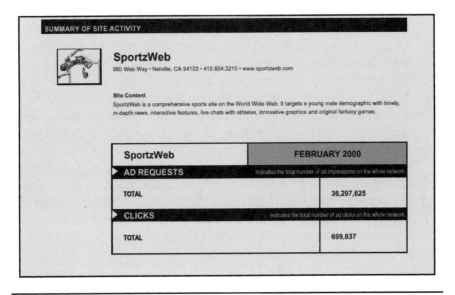

Figure 6.9. Source for audited ad statistics, *http://www.engage.com.* Courtesy Paul Schaut, CEO, Engage, Inc.

tomer profiles. Do younger viewers spend more time on one page than another? Which viewers are most likely to buy? Be aware that registration information is not always accurate and that optional registration may inaccurately represent your audience. On-site data collection has been drawing increased concern about user privacy, which is discussed in Chapter 9. Freeware for registration guestbooks is available at *http://www.toolzone.com,* seen in Figure 6.10.

If you hope to derive income from your site, whether by selling product, leasing space in a mall, charging subscription fees, or carrying advertising, it's critical to define the visiting audience. Without a demographic analysis and a reasonable estimate for the number of impressions you or your advertisers can expect, it may be hard to attract advertisers or set reasonable rates.

By structuring pages on your site carefully, you can discriminate among types of buyers, such as those more interested in a possible purchase than in the information presented. For example, requiring an additional click to obtain price information or print out a coupon could distinguish between those interested in incidental products, such as an online game, and those interested in buying your real product.

Figure 6.10. Free registration guestbooks, *www.toolzone.com*. Courtesy Urbanite Information Systems, Inc.

Some things you can measure only offline. For instance, how much coverage did you get in other media when introducing your Web site? Does your sales staff find a difference in the e-mail it receives from the Web versus calls generated from print or other media? Comparing on-line sales volume to offline ones is easy. If you're not selling online, it's more difficult, but worth the effort, to track the results of Web versus non-Web promotions.

For assistance with tasks like these, companies offer **data-mining** tools to help identify trends and patterns in your data. For example, Personify analyzes user behavior at Web sites (*http://www.personify.com*), while TargetSmart for Prospecting helps businesses analyze current customer data to establish a profile for good on-site leads (*http://www.targetsmart.com*). iMarket (*http://www.imarketinc.com*) matches site registrants with Dun & Bradstreet business data to prequalify sales leads.

Statistics, like your site itself, are a means, not an end. You must close the feedback loop by using the information to hone your online marketing efforts. Use the data you gather to improve your Web site, marketing strategies, products or services, and customer service.

For more information, check out the Internet Marketing Discussion List at *http://www.o-a.com* or LinkExchange Digest at *http://www.le-digest.com*. Both these moderated discussion groups cover site statistical analysis, tracking, click rates, and some of the Web promotion topics addressed in the next two chapters.

7

Marketing Your Internet Presence

The Web can be a field of nightmares instead of a field of dreams. You can build a site, but visitors may not come. They must know where to find you and why to look. Just as you reviewed long-term strategy before you began to design your Web site, you need to have a clear sense of where you're going before you start promoting it. Be sure to bring the right people into this decision-making process. You wouldn't ask marketing people to write HTML code; don't ask programmers to handle advertising. Some Web developers can do both, but many can't. If you don't have the time or in-house staff to handle Web promotion tasks, consider hiring outside help.

This chapter will review methods for promoting your Web site, as opposed to promoting your business. Unless you have an advertising site (which means your audience is your product), your goal is more than the greatest number of viewers. First, you want to bring your target audience(s) to your site and ensure they "get what they came for." Second, you want them to remain on your "sticky" site as long as possible, and third, you want them to return for multiple visits. Achieving these goals ultimately should improve your bottom line. Saving two topics—search engines and online advertising—for the next chapter, in this chapter we cover how to

- Research and write a Web promotion plan.

- Evaluate the effectiveness of promotional activities.

- Find marketing assistance.

- Launch a Web site, including an online PR campaign.

- Promote your site in the cheapest place of all—itself.

- Promote your site elsewhere on the Web.

- Use other Internet-based communications to market your site.

- Amplify your message with offline promotion.

Remember one of the basic laws of marketing: *When you find something that works, don't fix it!*

A Web Promotion Plan

Site promotion is no different from other online activities already discussed. You'll follow the by now familiar drill for Internet success: research, plan, execute, evaluate. You'll be adding many items to the Site Promotion section of your Web notebook. You may also want to create a Promotion subfolder for bookmarked sites. Save sites for potential links, announcements, and advertising, as well as sites whose techniques or ads you'd like to emulate.

Promotional Research

Go back online, ladies and gentlemen. Start researching the Web for examples of the advertising and promotional methods described in this chapter. Analyze lists of What's New, award-winning sites, and recommended Hot Sites/Cool Links. All these locations often drive a brief but intense flurry of activity to a site. Save examples of internal calls to action and banner ads. Check complementary sites for reciprocal links.

Run a spider (see Chapter 6) to see where your competitors place their links and who links to them. Collect promotional e-mail to see what others are doing. Research advertising rates and record the locations of your competitors' ads. For ideas on generating traffic on your site, check out locations such as

- Traffic Tribune at Submit It! *(http://www.submit-it.com)*

- Links:2000 Marketing and Advertising on the Net (*http://www.2000.ogsm.vanderbilt.edu*)

Writing the Plan

Unless you have a photographic memory, it will be impossible to track all the details of your promotional plan without a written schedule and record. A written plan helps you

- Communicate your objectives clearly to others.

- Delegate responsibility for implementation and monitoring.

- Outline related activities.

- Avoid repeating what has already been tried.

- Compare the results of different promotional methods.

- Have a basis for future changes.

- Recognize when you have achieved your objectives.

Your Web promotion plan should include all the standard elements of other plans:

- Goals and objectives, including target audience

- Implementation methods

- Budgets for time and dollars

- Required personnel

- Schedule of activities from prelaunch to at least six months post-launch

Goals and objectives for a promotion plan require a clear definition of the target audience(s) for your site and for each promotional activity. Your audience may include press, stockholders, and potential employees, as well as customers and prospects. It may be as narrow as 100 current business customers, if your new password-keyed pages are intended to shift them to electronic catalog ordering. Or perhaps you want to inform only owners of a particular product about a page that supplies warranty information, product upgrades, add-ons, customer feedback, and service data.

Different pages with different purposes need to reach different audiences, so it's no surprise that they need different promotional techniques. Plan to repeat promotional activities on a monthly basis, and whenever you add a new page or function to your site. After deciding on implementation methods, create separate logs to schedule and track each promotional activity. Such a log might look like the worksheet in Figure 7.1.

The One-to-Two Rule

The promotion plan, especially the timeline and budget, should be in place long before you launch your site. You must absolutely plan to spend money (or at least substantial sweat equity!) to let people know how to find your Web site in the haystack of more than 3 million others. The scary thing, according to a study by Alexa Internet, is that 80 percent of all Web traffic goes to only 15,000 sites, or less than 0.5 percent!

As a rule of thumb, reserve for marketing about half of what you spend on development. In other words, about one-third of your total Web budget should be allocated to marketing and promotion, with two-thirds for site development. Many dot-coms spend 40% to 70% of their total funding to brand their site, acquire customers and ensure their future loyalty! Whether they are content sites, B2C or B2B, we're talking millions of dollars!

Submitted to: Name & URL	Date Submitted	Appeared From/To	Cost $ & CPM	Results (if known)
Search Engines & Directories				
http://www.				
http://www.				
What's New Announcements				
http://www.				
http://www.				
News Group Announcements				
http://www.				
http://www				
Mailing List Announcements				
http://www.				
http://www.				
Hot Site/Cool Link Submissions				
http://www.				
http://www.				
Links (Specify Reciprocal, in-or Outbound)				
http://www.				
http://www.				
Link Exchanges				
http://www.				
http://www.				
Banner Ad Exchanges				
http://www.				
http://www.				
Paid Advertisements				
http://www.				
http://www.				
Sponsorships				
http://www.				
http://www.				
E-mail Promotions				
http://www.				
http://www.				
Off-line promotional activities				

Figure 7.1. Web promotion log. © 1999–2000 Watermelon Mountain Web Marketing.

Evaluating Results

You may already track the results of offline advertising and promotional activities with a code that identifies the source of inquiries or sales. You can do the same online. Create different **doorway** pages with different URLs or extensions to act as special "ports of entry" depending on how visitors arrive at your site. Like tracking return address codes on direct mail flyers, tracking doorway pages tells you which links and offline ads are most successful. You can also correlate hit rates with ads spread over a period of time or across a geographical region.

If you advertise on other Web sites, they should be able to give you click-through rates. If not, use referrer URLs in your statistics (see Chapter 6) to determine which online ads have the greatest pull. You can quickly optimize your advertising schedule for preferred sites, placement, graphics, wording, and special offers. Track results to see whether traffic builds and then drops off, whether it increases steadily, or whether there is no difference.

Monitor "query" strings from search engines to see what people are looking for and whether you should change your keywords. At the same time that you monitor your own success, monitor what's happening with your competitors. Set up a free account at TracerLock (*http://www.peacefire.org/tracerlock*), which monitors search engines automatically for new instances of a search term and informs you by e-mail.

Companies like DoubleClick have implemented sophisticated, and sometimes worrisome, programs for tracking exactly what viewers do on a site. They collect information entered in cookies and pass it along to clients who have placed Internet ads. (Although most viewers don't know it, they can opt out of advertising tracking on the DoubleClick site or by using certain privacy tools.) Other companies mine information gathered internally to "individualize" their marketing approach to customers, using such data as referral site and which pages are visited to vary banner ad placement or to **upsell** (suggest additional products) to a customer.

Since advertising and promoting your site may become expensive in both time and money, you want to know whether your expenditures bring results. Fortunately, on the Web it's fairly easy to tell!

Help Available

When there is a need, someone on the Internet pops up to fill it. Your existing Web developer, host, ad agency, or PR firm may already provide Web promotional services. The Web has spawned an industry of online promotional consultants, online agencies, and specialized Web marketing services.

Most marketing services aren't cheap. Hourly rates range from $50 to $250 an hour depending on the nature of the service, the size of the agency, and the type of contract you have. In many cases, the trade-off is between your money and your time. Online guerrilla marketing can be inexpensive, but you will need to commit the time of someone in your organization to plan, execute, and track the tasks. At the inexpensive end of the scale, look at services like Microsoft's bCentral.com, which offers marketing packages starting at $24.95 per month. If you are planning a major site with a large advertising budget, you might need the services of a major ad agency.

Lists of Net marketing companies may be found at *http:// www.lib.ua.edu/smr/ad0.html*. For additional research on marketing and advertising services, try *http://www.ad-guide.com*, the discussion group at *http://www.internetadvertising.org*, or *http://www.adresource.com*.

Launching a Web Site

If you've invested a lot of money developing a Web site, treat its launch as you would the opening of a new storefront or introduction of a new product, coordinating both online and offline efforts. The launch need not correspond with the day the site first becomes available to the public. In fact, it's better that the site run solidly for several weeks before you activate launch promotions that will drive traffic to it.

You may want to piggyback your site launch on another event, such as a trade show, a sales or stockholder meeting, a holiday promotion, or the introduction of a new product. Your goal for the launch is to create enough word-of-mouth and "word-of-web buzz" to generate good baseline traffic. You need to build a sense of anticipation and excitement. Here are some ideas drawn from the promotional concepts described in detail later:

- Coordinate press releases online and offline.

- Do several sequenced direct mailings and e-mails to an audience of customers, clients, suppliers, sales reps, and employees to announce your plans in advance of "opening" day.

- You can't control when your site will appear on a search engine, but you can time postings on What's New sites, as well as on appropriate news groups, mailing lists, and announcement services.

- Create special tag lines in your signature block, and write anticipatory stories for newsletters and e-zines about the coming event.

- Announce special "opening day" or "inaugural week" site offers, whether these are deep discounts, free gifts for every order placed online that day, or special contest drawings. Announce these offers on the Web, through other Internet venues and off-line.

- Offer a premium above your normal registration payoff (e.g., a discount coupon redeemable for several months) for those who register on your site during the first week or month. For an example see the Folgers site shown in Figure 7.2 at *www.folgers.com/cgi-bin/coupon.cgi.*

- Plan a live event for opening day (practice first), such as a chat with a well-known person; promote that event online and offline.

Figure 7.2. Coupon promotion, *http://www.folgers.com/cgi-bin/coupon.cgi.* Courtesy Procter & Gamble.

- If you have a storefront, put computers running your Web site on the show floor.

- Your formal inaugural week may be worth an advertising buy for a well-targeted audience; it might even be worth creating a special banner ad.

- If you are selling from the site, provide an incentive for both customers and sales reps who book orders online. (Be careful how you handle this; you don't want buyers holding orders while they wait for the big event.)

- Coordinate with offline publicity. Host a special event with a school or perform some community service that draws local or trade press while you unveil your site.

- Partner with a not-for-profit to make a contribution for each site visitor, thus encouraging the not-for-profit to help with promotional activities.

- Partner with suppliers or manufacturers for the event, asking them to assist with online promotion from their own sites.

Online PR campaign

There are no rules for a launch, but stealth won't help you drive traffic to your site. Besides using your regular offline press mailing lists, utilize online PR services as a cost-effective way to let your Web light shine. PR includes any technique that builds your company's reputation without a direct marketing message. Because stories are written by a third party, they are seen as more objective. Good publicity establishes your personal or company credibility as an expert or resource in the field and encourages others to spread the word.

There are both Web sites and listservers for distributing online PR. For instance, Online News, which has a number of readers in the press, is a good listserver for posting press releases. To subscribe, e-mail *majordomo@marketplace.com*. In the body of your note, say *subscribe online-news <your e-mail address>*. Note that this mailing list does not accept ads, just press releases.

Other online press outlets (most have a fee) include

- *http://www.businesswire.com*

- *http://www.digitalwork.com*

- *http://www.internetwire.com*

- *http://www.mediamap.com*

- *http://www.newsbureau.com*

- *http://www.partylinepublishing.com*

- *http://pressline.com*

- *http://www.prnewswire.com*

- *http://www.profnet.com*

- *http://www.prweb.com* (free)

For online media directories, try

- *http://www.mediainfo.com/emedia*

- *http://www.pressaccess.com*

- *http://www.mediafinder.com*

- *http://www.yahoo.com/News_and_Media/Newspapers*

As with other forms of online marketing, services exist to help you, either fee or free. DigitalWork (*http://www.digitalwork.com*) is a sample paid service; Multimedia Marketing Group (*http://www.mmgco.com*) has some free self-help resources.

If you plan a regular and extensive program of press releases and media outreach, it behooves you to set aside a **press page** on your site. It should include

- Current press releases.

- Recent stories about the company by others.

- A corporate backgrounder.

- A contact directory.

- Biographies of key staff.

- Digital photos of key managers, products, and processes.

- An archive of past press releases and stories.

You should also compile a hard copy equivalent called a **press kit,** which will add brochures, product spec sheets if appropriate, story reprints, and a business card. Since a mere Web site announcement is rarely newsworthy, try to tie your press releases to a new or unique element of your product or service, or something that will generate human interest. Information on how to write a good press release and other PR tips are available at

- *http://marketing.tenagra.com/releases.html*

- *http://www.netpress.org/careandfeeding.html*

- *http://www.netrageousresults.com/PR/prtemplate.html*

Other ways of obtaining publicity abound. Leave your signature block everywhere you travel online. Write articles for e-zines that link to your site. Produce an online and/or offline column and publicize that— with a link to your site, of course! Accept speaking engagements, attend conferences, run workshops.

Don't forget to take advantage of free publicity offered by organizations to which you belong. For instance, SouthWest Writers (*http://www.southwestwriters.org*) offers its published members free publicity for a period of time, including a link to the purchase location and a link to a personal Web site in exchange for carrying the SWW logo.

Promoting Your Site on Your Site

The following sections discuss ways to use your Web site itself as a promotional tool. Some of the techniques are designed to encourage people to remain on your site for a longer period of time, thus allowing you to reinforce your company name and increase perceived value. Others are designed to encourage repeat visits, gradually building a relationship with self-qualified prospects and preparing them to buy from you.

If viewers are current customers, so much the better: It's easier—and cheaper—to make repeat sales to satisfied customers than to acquire new ones. Existing customers have eliminated the risk of dealing with an unknown company online. They already know the quality of your products, the guarantees you offer, and the excellent service you provide.

Registration on Site

Registration is probably the most important call to action in terms of self-promotion. Use registration as more than a guestbook. Collect some brief information about the user whenever possible.

Use registration tools to build an e-mail list of self-qualified prospects. This is also an inexpensive way to establish a circulation figure, which can be useful when negotiating reciprocal links, bartering an ad exchange, accepting paid advertising, or recruiting sponsors.

On-site registration invites viewers to sign up for targeted e-mail or newsletters, such as the one in Figure 7.3 from BizBot at *http:// www.bizbot.net/lists.shtml*. You can also notify viewers of changes to your Web site, thus encouraging a repeat visit. You can even ask them to test changes to your site before you unveil them publicly.

A Four-Letter Word That Starts with "F"

There is no word more popular in marketing than free! Offer something in exchange for registration, completing a survey, or even just trying your Web site. Jelly Belly (*http://www.jellybelly.com* seen in Figure 7.4) gives away jelly bean samples in exchange for filling out a survey. HelloDirect.com offers anything from cordless phones to T-shirts for an on-site purchase over a certain amount. Television ads exhort viewers to

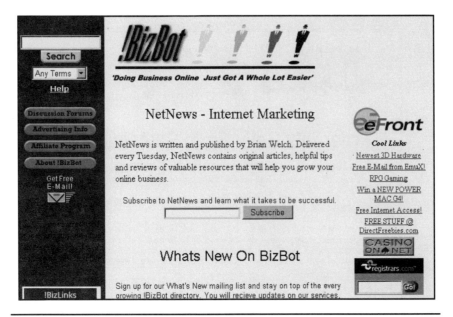

Figure 7.3. Subscription invitation for updates and multiple newsletters, *http://bizbot.net/lists.shtml.* Courtesy eFront Media, Inc.

visit Tiger.Buick.com to learn how to get a hat embroidered with Tiger Woods' signature. Freebies have an infinite number of variations.

Contests and Raffles

Offer free entry in a drawing or contest with an online announcement of the winners. You can pitch your contest offline, like Onstar's TV commercial: "Play the Batman Challenge at Onstar.com." For a sample Web site, see the sweepstakes at *http://www.delivere.preferences.com/ cgi-bin/dse/TV_DVD_Recliners.* If a minimum number of entries is required before an award is given, provide a registration counter that shows the number of entries. Raffles, drawings, sweepstakes, and other contests must meet certain legal requirements, including a disclaimer with eligibility, dates of entry, dates of delivery, number of prizes, and more. Have your attorney check the text before you put it online. Simple forms can be used for contest entry. Gift certificates or online shopping sprees are good prizes because the winner stays on your site and they

Figure 7.4. FREE is a 4-letter word, *http://www.jellybelly.com/sample_summary_frame.html*. © 1998 Herman Goelitz, Inc. All rights reserved.

encourage repeat business. Better yet, split the prize between the winner and a friend so you get two customers!

Coupons

Give free discount coupons for use online or offline. An NPD Group survey found that nearly one third of Web surfers utilize online coupons to save money. More than 50% say they find coupons just by surfing, while 27% use online ads and 7% get coupon information from word-of-mouth.

Furr's Supermarket site (furrs.com), for instance, has customers print out a "ValuPage" of coupons with online specials; when they purchase an item on the page, they receive certificates good for future purchases at the store. Coupons now travel the opposite direction as well, with hard copy coupons containing an offer code for online purchases distributed with in-store purchases or appearing in direct mail.

Be cautious, though. Computer glitches with coupons may end up costing you dearly. Coupon message boards, such as Infomedia's Deal of Day, Fat Wallet.com, and Ezboard.com, pass the word quickly among electronic coupon clippers when an error allows multiple uses of an online coupon, or when there are typos in the price or quantity of merchandise offered. Even the biggies get hit: Amazon.com, Buy.com, Staples.com, AltaVista, and eZiba.com were all targeted by bargain-hunting consumers taking advantage of programming errors. Be sure to test your coupon offer thoroughly on an offline server before posting it. Instead of, or in addition to, offering coupons on your own site, you can post them on such sites as ValuPage.com or CouponClipper.com.

Other Freebies

- A small sample of your product. FreedomZone.com decided to offer a million free CDs to create a fan base for new bands.

- A trial subscription to your fee-based e-mail newsletter or information service, or a free e-mailed report.

- The ability to download free software, from demo software to an animated greeting or a screen saver. You can purchase software to create screen savers from Postcard Software at *http://www.postsoft.com*, or you may be able to negotiate something with shareware developers who would like to attract customers to their products as well.

- A donation to a not-for-profit organization that your viewers care about.

Internal Calls to Action

If you don't suggest that viewers take an action, they may not think of it themselves. Earlier, we described external calls to action that move the visitor toward a sale, and we've talked about site registration as a powerful call to action. You can also move a visitor through or back to your site by using some of the following internal calls to action.

- **Bookmark This Site/Page.**   Make this site your browser home page. The Discovery Channel does this at *http://www. discovery.com/mydcol/yourhome.html*, shown in Figure 7.5.

- **Call us.**   Online users can now do this, even from a residence with only one phone line, using free software from Click2Talk (*http://www.net2phone.com/click2talk*).

- **Sign Up for a Service.**   Automatic site updates or a free newsletter are some services you can provide. Companies like Mind-It (*http://www.mind-it.com*) and NetMind (*http://www. netmind.com/html/webmaster.html*, shown in Figure 7.6), allow any visitor, whether or not otherwise registered, to request e-mail when site changes occur. (Individual users can configure their ownreminder systems for multiple sites by going to *http:// minder.netmind.com/mindit.shtml*.)

Figure 7.5.   A unique call to action, *http://www.discovery.com/MyDiscovery/html/ yourhome.html*. © 1999 Discovery Channel Online. Source: *www.discovery.com*.

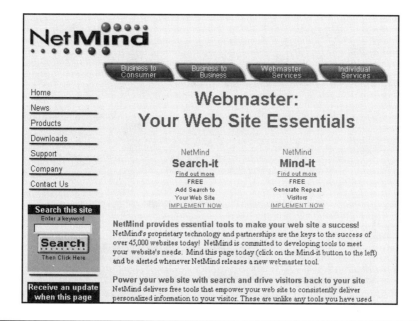

Figure 7.6. Site reminder service, *http://netmind.com/html/webmaster.html.* Courtesy Netmind Services, Inc.

- **Complete a Survey.** Offer something for free. Make the form easy to complete with drop-down menus or check boxes, not typing. You can use free software such as "Add-a-Form" (shown in Figure 7.7). Surveys can be used to help you improve your site, better understand your customers' needs, sign up members, or collect content information.

  The two most common problems with surveys are asking too many questions and asking too many people. Keep your survey to 45 questions maximum. Unless you need statistically significant data, you can probably stop after 100 responses to detect simple trends. Be sure to include screening questions so you know who your respondents are and make sure each question has a purpose. If you ask questions about things you don't plan to change, you'll only raise expectations and disappoint your respondents.

- **Attend Event.** Ask viewers to return for a scheduled special event, such as a celebrity chat or live concert, to increase site "sticki-

Figure 7.7. Free survey software for your site, *http://www.addaform.com*. Courtesy Cuesta Technologies, LLC., Interactive Commercial Web Sites and Sophisticated e-Stuff.

ness." If you want to set up your site as an interactive community, consider the various forms: standard chat, real-time groups, instant messaging, e-mail, and message board discussions.

Both free and commercial chat software is available, as well as services (some expensive, like PeopleLink.com) to manage chats, set up forum topics, monitor message boards, and suggest features like personal profiles. Chats can be publicized both online and offline; one television news program, "All News Channel," actually publicizes scheduled celebrity chats once a week.

Clever internal calls to action can be camouflaged as a poll or teaser or look like banner ads, as you can see from one of Ragu's pages (*http://www.eat.com.goodies/index.html*, shown in Figure 7.8). Three banner ads ("Mama's Soap Opera," "Learn Italian," and "Play") actually rotate on this screen. Each one takes the viewer to a different page on the site: funny stories, a RealAudio language lesson, or a glossary of Italian cuisine, respectively. (Besides the banners, there are at least three other internal calls to action and two external ones on this page. Can you find them all? Hint: Free is a call to action!)

Figure 7.8. Internal calls to action on Ragu site. Three oblong internal banners alternate in the lower left hand corner, *http://www.eat.com/goodies/ index.html.* Courtesy Lipton Investments, Inc. and Unilever USA, Inc.

- **Forward a link.** Invite recipients to forward your marketing e-mail to a colleague or send a friend a link to your site. The resource site HitBox does this at *http://www.hitbox.com* (shown in Figure 7.9). This last call to action is a subtle variant on one of the hottest trends on the Web, viral marketing.

Viral Marketing

Viral marketing is electronic word-of-mouth, the process by which viewers pass your message around. Viral marketing is inexpensive: The referral from a friend or colleague provides credibility for an ad, animation, photo, hyperlinked promotion, newsletter, game, press release, petition, or whatever else brings attention to your business. Studies have shown that 81% of recipients will forward a message to at least one other person and 49% will send it to two or more. (Speaking of bad infections, just think of all those urban legend e-mails that circulate on the Web over and over.)

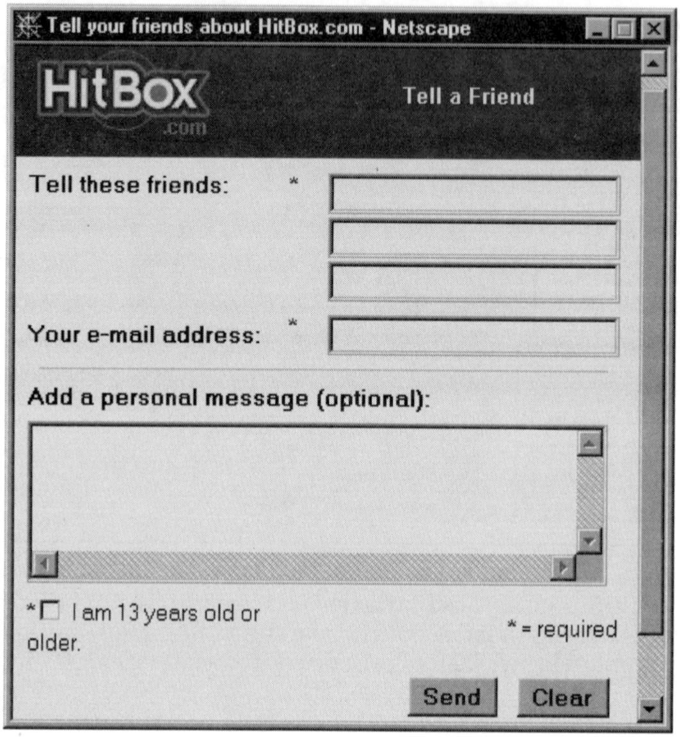

Figure 7.9. Send a friend a link, *http://www.hitbox.com.* Courtesy WebSide Story.

You've probably seen many examples. Any message sent from HotMail invites recipients to sign up for their own free account. Scope mouthwash invited consumers to e-mail a personalized, animated kiss to someone special, who in turn was invited to "pass it on."

Link requests can be tied to a freebie like GreenTravel.com's message: "Send this to a friend and you could win an Osprey backpack." ICQ (*http://www.ICQ.com*) instant messaging software works on the same principle. If someone wants to set up instant messaging with a friend who's not a subscriber, a link to download ICQ software is sent to the friend. ICQ claims to have signed up 32 million users without spending anything on marketing support.

Do be cautious, however. On the one hand, your message needs to be worth passing along. On the other, there's a fine line between spam and sending a link; keep your viral messages short and simple.

What's New With You?

In Chapter 5 we talked about the importance of changing content to draw return visitors to your site. You've developed a schedule for content updates and expansions. Every time you change your site, repeat the announcement and publicity processes described here.

A What's New icon on the menu is one of the most effective ways to make it easy for repeat viewers to find new information quickly. The icon should link to the new page or information, or to a submenu (maybe one that pops up or pulls down) of new material on a variety of pages.

By placing new information on a separate page, you may be able to generate another search engine submission with a new extension on your URL and keywords. (For more on search engines, see Chapter 8.)

What's New announcement sites accept changes in content on an existing page. Use any changes as an excuse to send a press release or notify news. You can certainly inform site e-mail registrants or use NetMind.

Pat Yourself on the Back

Is your site on a list of Hot Sites or Cool Links? Did it win an award from one of the many organizations that recognize good Web sites? Shout it from your cybertop! Besides putting out a press release in traditional and Web media, incorporate a notice on your page. Award postings not only keep a record of your site, they act as a testimonial to your talent and will help draw new and repeat visitors. See all the awards won by Ragu at *http://www.eat.com/trophy-room.html* (Figure 7.10). (This screen shows only a fraction of their awards.)

Think of awards as part of a press kit. A press kit would include a list of magazines, online and off, that have reviewed your site or mentioned your product or service. Preferably a kit would include copies of the actual reviews. (Ask the original publisher for permission to reproduce their reviews on your site; reviews and articles are usually copyrighted.)

There are dozens of awards for Web prowess. They range from serious (the Golden Tag Award for excellence in HTML design or the IPPA Award for Design Excellence for commercial sites), to sarcastic (The Dancing Finger O'Sarcasm Award), to silly (The Cow Pie Awards). Some awards are designed for specific enterprises (Golden Tin Award for law enforcement sites) or features (Red Eye Award for best use of plug-ins or Digital Media Awards for multimedia). Usually, sites must be nomi-

Figure 7.10. Internal calls to action on Ragu. The three oblong internal banners alternate in the lower left hand corner. (*http://www.eat.com/goodies/index.html*). Courtesy Lipton Investments, Inc. and Unilever USA, Inc.

nated for awards, with the submission sometimes requiring a brief description as well as the URL. Review previous winners before nominating your site to ensure that your site will fit well with the nature of the award. The creators of the SpunkyMunky Awards probably have very different criteria than the people who compile Lycos's Top 5%.

Try one of the sites listed in Figure 7.11 or use a search engine for a more complete list of award URLs and links. Several sites (e.g., Award-It) offer the opportunity to submit to multiple award sites, usually a few at a time. Spacing award submissions makes sense: Every new award or listing gives you a reason for a Web announcement and an addition to your What's New feature. You should maintain a spreadsheet or table in your notebook for award submissions, showing the name of the award,

```
http://www.award-it.com
http://www.bizbotweekly.com/awards.html
http://www.coolgraphics.com/award.html
http://www.happymall.com/awards.htm (on-line shopping sites)
http://www.netprobe.net/body_submit.html
http://www.register-it.com/O-register/plus/index.html
http://www.smartbiz.org.submissi.htm
http://www.webflier.com/addsite.html
http://www.yahoo.com/picks
```

Figure 7.11. Award submission sites, *http://www.bizbotweekly.com/ awards.html*. Courtesy BizBot Weekly.

URL, date submitted, date of response, date notice appeared on the award site, and date you posted the award icon on your site.

The Webby, from the International Academy of Digital Arts and Sciences (IADAS), is one of the premier awards for Web designers and advertisers. Webbies, judged by professionals in the field, are given annually in 22 categories, along with a People's Voice Award for a site chosen by the online community. For more information on nomination criteria, go to *http://www.iadas.net*. Check out *http://www. webbyawards.com* to seek inspiration during your Web research forays. Besides the 110 best sites of the year, the Webby site keeps archives of past winners. A great site to bookmark!

Promotional Giveaways, Contests, and Games

Promoting your site with giveaways, contests, and games is no different from offline promotions that keep your name or brand in front of your audience. These activities give viewers a reason to return. You can further entice repeat visits by highlighting future promotions.

Use your mailing list to tell people when a new game has been placed online or remind them to visit your Web site to see if they have won in a drawing. Give away one of your products, a related item, or something with your name on it. Make it attractive enough that people will talk about your promotion online and off.

For example, a travel agency could enter people who leave their e-mail addresses in a drawing for a free trip to Hawaii. It could pick a winner every time it reached some preset number of registrations, say 50,000. It could offer a free piece of carry-on luggage for every 10,000 names and a luggage tag for every 100th e-mail registration. Figure 7.12 (*http://www.krxo.com/2000/games/midi*) shows a site that pulls repeat visitors by posting four new contests every week. For a list of contest sites, see *http://www.korax.net/~quest/shtml*. The site *http://www.sweepsadvantage.com* offers a list of online sweepstakes.

Chat Lines, Forums/Boards, and Events

Consider scheduling a moderated live chat with a professional or well-known figure, or offering opportunities for viewers to consult with business experts through a forum or **message board** (nonsimultaneous chats in which messages are posted for others to read). Free software for both these features is listed in Chapter 5. Forums are an ongoing feature available at any time, while chats are booked and promoted on the site (and sometimes off) well in advance. For example, Figure 7.13 shows

Figure 7.12. Online contest draws repeat visitors, *http://www.krxofm.com/2000/games/midi*. KRXO-FM Courtesy Bryan Kerr, Oklahoma Internet Consulting, Inc.

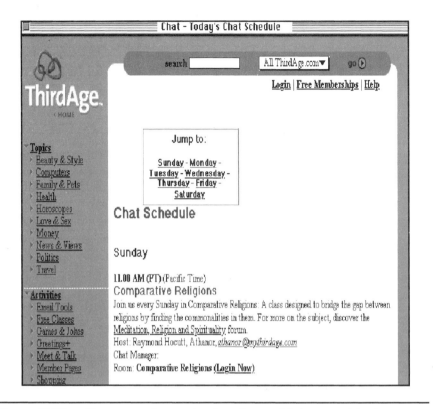

Figure 7.13. Chat promotion onsite, *http://www.thirdage.com/chat/schedule.html*.

how Third Age handles on-site promotion for its chats at *http://www.thirdage.com/chat/schedule.html*.

You could also host a special online event, as simple as a chat or as elaborate as a **sitecast** with live audio or video. Collaborate with some complementary businesses to share the cost, help with publicity, and bring in participants through their own sites. For example, a company that makes monogrammed athletic uniforms could team with a manufacturer of soccer balls and the local soccer association for a real-time event that includes a coach or player from a professional or local team. Use the event to discuss contemporary soccer issues, from its popularity as an intramural sport to rules changes or the need for more sponsors for local teams.

Each company's site promotion can be subtle—a logo link at the bottom of the sitecast page. Drawing the right visitors is ample reward. Once again, promote the event both online and off, especially on your own site. (See *http://www.bluenote.net* shown in Figure 7.14.) It's no different from what you would do if you had a star athlete come to your store to autograph sports caps.

More Ideas

For a unique way to drive traffic to your site, distribute a browser preset to have your home page appear whenever a user boots it up. You could collaborate on this promotion with a local ISP or online service that offers a free trial period. An excellent Web site announcement, this CD-ROM-based promotion can be mailed out to current customers with an invitation to visit your new site or given away free at your physical location. Of course, you know your customers well enough to assess whether they have a computer, whether or not they are already online, and whether they are likely to buy online if they buy from you in person. You can distribute a customized Netscape browser for free, in ex-

Figure 7.14. Live event promotion onsite, *http://www.bluenote.net/live.html.* Designed and hosted by InterJazz.

change for filing a quarterly report on distribution, by going to *http://
www.home.netscape.com/partners/distribution/index.html?cp=
leb21hig4*.

Many portals, ISPs, and other sites offer free, small (2–5 MB) Web
sites to viewers and clients, usually without a domain name. These sites,
which often aren't indexed by search engines, may not work as a full-
fledged business site, but they can become an effective place for a splash
page or subset of your site with a link to your URL. If your target audience uses the host service, they might well stumble on your site through
the host's directory.

An expanded listing in a directory is another variation on this theme.
For instance, Women's Work offers free, multiple directory listings to
businesses in their marketplace at *http://wwork.com/servicecenter/
bizdir.htm*. This is somewhat akin to a business card ad in a mini–telephone directory of local businesses, but it draws focused traffic instead
of a general audience.

Promoting Your Site on the Web

The opportunities for on-the-Web promotion are many, whether free or
paid. You'll run out of time—or money—long before you run out of
ideas. Let's look at some.

What's New Listings

These free announcement sites, easily found by browsers, are an excellent place to pick up new "eyeballs." What's New listings, which remain up for about a week, announce a new site, a new page or simply
new content. Expect a brief flurry of 5,000 to 10,000 additional visitors
(mostly looky-loos) to your Web site as a direct result of these announcements. Be sure that your ISP knows that you plan to make such postings
and that it will be able to handle the traffic generated without overloading your site. As mentioned earlier, a What's New posting is an occasion
for a NetMind notice to past visitors.

What's New facilitators are overwhelmed with announcements. Each
list posts anywhere from 200 to 1700 new sites per day! In general, you
submit by clicking on each site's "submit" page. As with directory and

search engine registrations, you may need to customize your submission. A typical listing appears on the What's New Too site, *http://www.nu2.com/index.html*, in Figure 7.15. As with search engines, check the postings every several days to see if you've been listed. Resubmit if you haven't appeared after a week.

Hits from What's New announcements follow a pattern: a rapid, straight-up peak right after publication; a less rapid, but still steep decline; and finally a plateau slightly higher than the base level of hits. To keep the hit rate high and more balanced, make announcements on each What's New list as often as possible. Instead of making submissions to all the What's New sites at once, space them out to a different one every day or so. Add to your content regularly so that every several weeks you have something new to announce.

The table in Figure 7.16 provides a list of some popular What's New pages. You can find a directory of more What's New pages at *http://www.stpt.com*, at *http://www.yahoo.com*, or on most of the other search engines. As with awards, make a spreadsheet or table to keep a record of the What's New URLs, submission date, and appearance. See if you can correlate appearance with traffic statistics for your site.

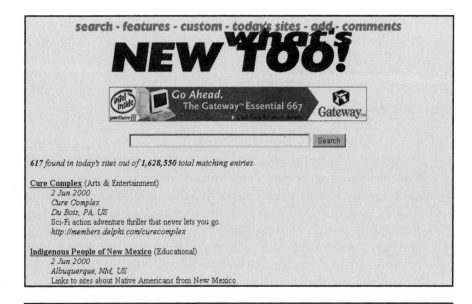

Figure 7.15. Sample What's New listing, *http://www.nu2.com/index.html*. Courtesy Manifest Information Services.

```
http://dir.yahoo.com/new/
http://home.netscape.com/netcenter/new.html
http://www.stpt.com/
http://www.newtoo.com/
http://www.yahooligans.com/new/
```

Figure 7.16.   Some popular What's New sites.

Hot Sites and Cool Links

Unlike What's New pages, which publish all the announcements they receive, Hot Sites or Cool Links lists are discretionary. The compilers of these lists use their own intensely personal criteria to sift through sites, just as film critics and restaurant reviewers do. Cool Links lists range from a site of the day maintained by an individual, to rankings from USA Today, the San Jose Mercury News, Netscape, and Yahoo! A number of sites are shown in Figure 7.17. For a list of more sites that post their own Hot Sites and Cool Links, check *http://www.bizbotweekly.com/awards.html.*

If criteria for a list are unpublished or too vague to determine if your site is qualified, evaluate the sites recommended on the list. Nominate your site only for lists that endorse sites similar to yours. As before, record your submissions and appearance on a table so you can determine if there is a correlation with traffic to your site. Sites like NetGuide at *http://www.netguide.com* review useful sites organized by category, much like an annotated bibliography, for their members. You'll need to search out such opportunities individually based on your business needs and target audiences.

Because appearing on one of these recommended lists can result in thousands of additional hits, competition for placement has become intense. An appearance on a Hot Site or Cool Link list, which lasts between a day and a week, generates a brief but predictable flurry of hits. At the same time, the number of such sites has multiplied like bunny rabbits, saturating the Hot Site/Cool Link field itself.

Create your own list with a unique, topical twist and accept nominations or allow viewers to vote. It's another way to generate repeat visits. Or exchange nominations with a complementary business that also maintains a Hot Site list.

```
http://usatoday.comlife/cyber/ch.htm
http://www.coolcentral.com/picks/
http://www.coolsiteoftheday.com
http://www.mediacom.it/siti2/hotsite.htm
http://home.netscape.com/netcenter/cool.html
http://www.ten_tenths.com.links/index.html
www.yahooligans.com/docs/cool/index.html
```

Figure 7.17.   Some hot sites and cool links.

Some agencies and service providers specialize in getting your site listed as a Hot Site or Cool Link, just as some PR firms specialize in getting articles placed in the Wall Street Journal or local business magazines. The application process for most sites involves sending an e-mail with your URL and a short description (with style and verve) of your site, its features, and its value to the user. You must decide whether appearing on this list, or on any other award list, will draw the audience you are looking for.

Links with Other Sites

Links can be a reciprocal exchange with another site, one-way outbound, or one-way inbound. **Reciprocal** linking with other sites is one of the most effective and least expensive ways to attain greater visibility for your own. Be sure to visit the other site to confirm that it attracts the same people you want to attract. Figures 7.18 and 7.19 show two sites with reciprocal links.

To establish an individual reciprocal link, e-mail a request to the other business, as seen in the sample request in Figure 7.20. Attach a digital logo, in case the other site will let you have something more elaborate than straight text for your link. You might generate some goodwill by creating a link to the other site's home page first. Try to find sites with more traffic than yours. Generally, a link from their home page is preferable to one from a page further down, but that will vary according to your needs, the structure of the other site, and the willingness of the site owner. You might want to direct the inbound half of the link to a page other than your home page, bringing visitors directly to relevant information based on the referring source.

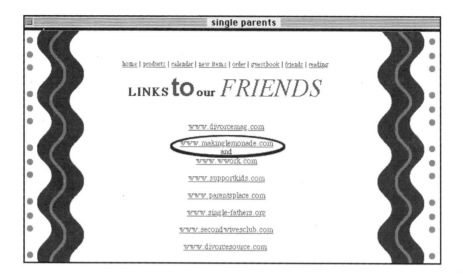

Figure 7.18.   Reciprocal link, *http://www.mytwohomes.com/friends.htm.* Courtesy Ladybug Press.

Free link matchmaking services (also called banner exchanges) are available at many places such as *http://www.exchange-it.com*, *http://linkmanager.linkmatrix.com*, or *http://adnetwork.bcentral.com* (shown in Figure 7.21). You can specify categories of sites that would be a good fit for your business, but you will usually be asked to provide more links than you receive.

Outbound links to complementary, informative sites add value for your user. Think of linking to your business customers, subsidiaries, suppliers, or reps, or to the manufacturers of products you carry. These links expand your virtual presence because the link title can be topical, using a keyword rather than the destination name. For instance, your veterinary hospital site might have a link reading "Learn more about hay and oats," instead of "Burley's Feedstore." One disadvantage of outbound links is that users must use the Back function on their browser to return to your site. Alternately, ask your Web developer to open outbound links in a new window on the screen so that your site remains visible.

Think strategically about how many links to include. You want to hold your visitors on your site as long as possible. If you provide too many links early in your site, viewers may jump away and never return.

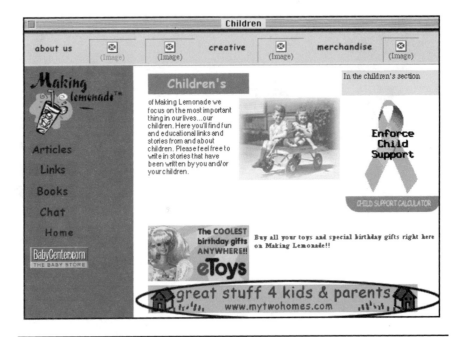

Figure 7.19. Reciprocal link, *http://www.makinglemonade.com* © Making Lemonade.com 1997. Making Lemonade: The Single Parent Network.

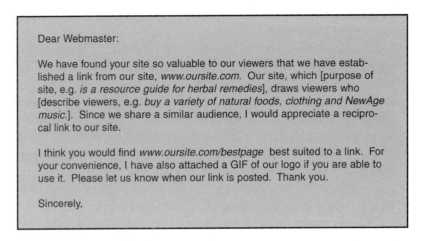

Figure 7.20. Sample request for a reciprocal link. © 2000 Watermelon Mountain Web Marketing.

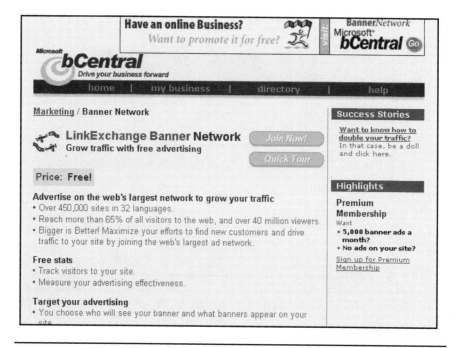

Figure 7.21.   Link exchange service, *http://adnetwork.bcentral.com.*
Screenshot reprinted by permission from Microsoft Corporation.

Instead of placing links in context throughout a site, some organizations collect links on a page fairly far down in the site structure.

Finding **inbound** links is a matter of good Web research. The trick is to identify places where your target audience is likely to be found online and encourage them to link to you from those sites. (The same process will work for banner ads.) Some sites, like Teletrade (shown in Figure 7.22), are so open to inbound links, they post code for banner ads on their site for anyone to pick up.

Certain types of sites are more likely to support an inbound or one-way link from their site to yours:

- Professional, business, and trade associations to which you, your company, or your target audience belong.

- Online sites for any magazine or other places where you advertise; often a link is included in advertising contracts for other media.

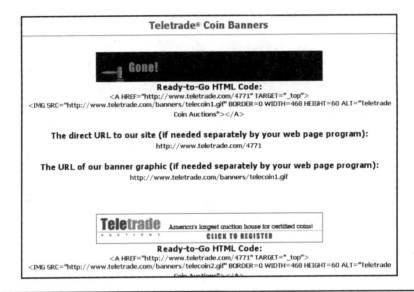

Figure 7.22. Code inserts for a banner ad, *http://www.coins.com/banners* c/o *www.teletrade.com.* Courtesy Greg Manning Auctions, Inc.

- Sites that offer directories of service providers or distributors.

- Web sites with search engines that provide Web company references and sources for their viewers (your audience), such as *http://www.abcparenting.com*, shown in Figure 7.23.

- Home pages owned by satisfied clients or customers for whom you've provided service (e.g., Web designers often put a link from their clients' sites back to their own home page).

- News group announcement sites.

Some of these sites may charge a modest amount for a link, some may have a routine submission form, and some may need an individual e-mail contact. To track the status of all three types of link requests, you'll need another table in your Web notebook. Columns could include name of the site, URL, contact person, e-mail address, contact date, response date, and nature of the link. Add columns for verifica-

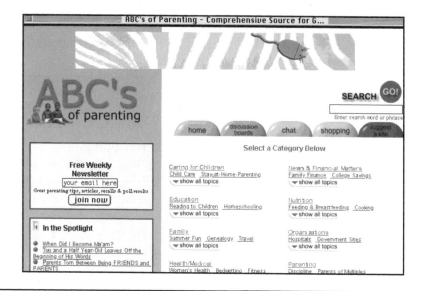

Figure 7.23. Links from a reference site, *http://www.abcparenting.com.* Courtesy Parenthood Web *(www.parenthoodweb.com).*

tion that the link has been established, and regularly scheduled confirmations that the link (and the referral site) still exist. It's well worth the effort to get inbound links.

Not only are links one of the most common ways for viewers to find new sites, they also increase your ranking on search engines. As you'll learn in the next chapter, each search engine has a unique, complex formula for ranking sites by importance. The number of domains and the number of pages that link to your site are part of this formula. Recently, search engines have started to rank the quality of your inbound links, which rank higher if they have related content, have been reviewed by a human editor, or have many inbound links themselves.

Web Rings

Web rings (also called alliances) are multisite, reciprocal links connecting a group of sites, usually with similar content. Viewers click on a next, previous, random, or selected link to go to another site on the ring, eventually returning to their starting point. For an example, try the Women's Health and Wellbeing Web ring shown in Figure 7.24 (*http://www.shpm.com/webrings/whwring.html*).

To join a ring, you copy HTML code provided by the ring onto your site. A **ringmaster**, who maintains the ring database, may review each application for inclusion. Some rings have specific criteria; others may consist solely of personal pages or might include a number of competitors. Check out all the sites on a ring before you join.

You can obtain a list of rings on the Web by going to a RingWorld directory at *http://www.owt.com/arts/webring/ringinfo.html* or Ring Managers at *http://www.webring.org/#ringworld* or *http://www.daytaless.com/webring/webring.shtml*. Of course, if the Star Wars, fashion, personal coaching, or any of the hundreds of other rings don't meet your needs, you can always start a ring of your own.

Links from Meta-Indexes

Meta-indexes supplement the search engines and directories described in the following chapter. These lists of Internet resources organized by

Figure 7.24. A Web ring, *http://www.shpm.com/webrings/whwring.html*. Courtesy Pioneer Development Resources, Inc.

topic consist of lists of URLs. The people who compile these indexes will often include your site for free, so it's worth requesting a link. Usually, a simple e-mail request is enough. Include the URL, a brief description, an explanation of why your site is appropriate for the index, and your contact information. Meta-indexes may also be potential sites for banner ads or for the purchase of a more prominent link with a logo. For a directory of meta-indexes, check

- *http://www.clearinghouse.net*

- *http://www.fys.ruu.nl/~kruis/h3.html*

- *http://www.infospace.com*

- *http://www.metaIQ.com*

- *http://www.referthem.com/pad/links.htm*

Promoting Your Site Elsewhere on the Internet

In Chapter 3, we talked about using non-Web services on the Internet to promote your business. Use these same tools to promote recognition and repeat visits for your Web site.

News Groups

News groups and mailing lists offer a unique opportunity to reach a highly targeted audience with information about your Web site. Although news group patronage is declining, it's still an exceedingly valuable means of reaching a prequalified audience. Remember to follow the rules of Netiquette whenever you operate in this section of the Internet.

As we discussed in Chapter 3, news groups or forums on online services provide an opportunity to leave your signature file and URL all over the place, but don't stop there. Some news groups and mailing lists now accept sponsors to defray the costs of maintenance and monitoring.

To find news groups that permit site announcements, check out the FAQ files of well-trafficked topical groups, such as

- comp.internet.net.happenings

- comp.infosys.www.announce

- misc.news.inet.announce

Most moderated groups (e.g., misc.news.inet.announce) state that postings to the group are for new and revised Web site addresses only. Check the FAQ files if you are not sure. There are many regional, event-oriented, or industry-, company-, and product-specific news groups that might be appropriate, depending on the nature of your business. Search through the news groups on Liszt (*http://www.liszt.com*) for names ending in .announce. Most of these sites allow you to post once for each unique URL.

Like What's New and Hot Site/Cool Link postings, news group announcements remain up for only a few days to a week. From a strategic point of view, spread out your announcements. Post to a different news group each week to increase traffic without overloading your server.

For this audience, your title, message, and form of announcement are all important. If you post a press release on one of these groups, try to include a photo, sound file, or video, unless the site accepts only text.

As mentioned in Chapter 4, news groups are a good place to recruit testers. Having tested your site, these viewers are likely to become repeat visitors because they have developed a "proprietary" interest in your site; they'll want to see if you've implemented their suggestions.

Mailing Lists

Like news groups, some mailing lists now accept sponsors and Web announcements. The Internet Marketing Discussion List and news group, which supports itself with sponsorships, is a good one to try. To join this list, which has over 10,000 subscribers, go to *http://www.o-a.com*. It's a great list for companies that sell marketing-related products and services.

Check FAQs and watch the types of mailings going out to determine whether a particular list is a good one to promote your site. As mentioned in Chapter 3, there are now dozens of companies like colonize.com (*http://www.colonize.com*, shown in Figure 7.25) that can supply names and/or manage opt-in mailings for you.

Promoting Your Site Offline

Take advantage of all existing offline promotional methods to tell people about your Web site. Use the opportunity not only to provide your URL, but also to describe the benefits of visiting your site. You might tell customers "to see the flavor of the month," or "receive instant price quotes," or "place custom orders."

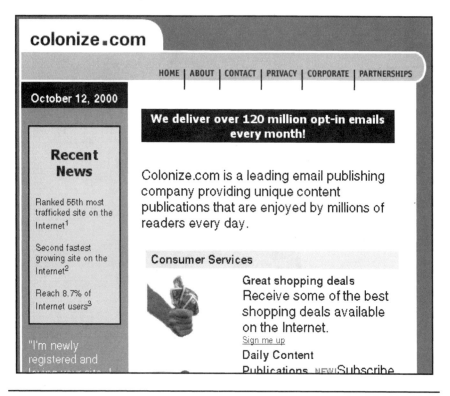

Figure 7.25. An opt-in e-mail company, *http://www.colonize.com*. Courtesy Colonize.com, Inc.

Coordinate Your Campaign

Advertise your new site in other media—print, radio, billboard, or TV—as your budget permits. One marketing analyst recently compared sales following the broadcast of an infomercial and found that the Web generated 20% of all orders.

In addition to passively including your URL in an ad, create ads specifically to increase awareness of your Web address. Etown (*http://www.etown.com*), an electronics distributor, comparison tested its Web site promotion in print, on billboards, and on radio. Their test ad, which ran prior to launch, appears in Figure 7.26; the destination Web site appears in Figure 7.27. Although the print ads worked well, their best response was actually from radio.

Figure 7.26. eTown print ad. Courtesy eTown.com: The Home Electronics Guide.

7.27. eTown Web site, *http://www.etown.com.* Courtesy eTown.com: The Home Electronics Guide.

Literature, Stationery, Packaging, and Promotional Items

Depending on your budget, you may want to update all your literature and stationery at once or replace the items as you run out. You may be able to add a designer-created label to existing brochures to draw attention to your Web site address. Order your next batch of giveaway pens imprinted with your URL as well as your company name, or send customers a desk magnet or calendar imprinted with it.

You know that URLs have come into their own when political candidates appear behind a podium or in front of a banner emblazoned with their Web address. Every campaign ad, yard sign, and placard now features politicians' Web sites as well as their names!

Several companies, such as *http://www.dotcomgear.com*, specialize in labeling products like shirts and mouse pads with URLs. Figure 7.28 shows a range of promotional options, from T-shirts and coffee mugs to magnets, screen cleaners, and ice cream sticks!

Don't forget to update your packaging. Labels on everything from Quaker Oatmeal at *http://www.quakeroatmeal.com* to Michelob Beer at *http://www.hopnotes.com* now carry a URL along with a toll-free number for customer service.

Figure 7.28. Promotional items can drive traffic to your Web site. Clockwise from top: T-shirt courtesy Pablo's Mechanical. Screen cleaner courtesy of IEI Marketing, Inc. Ice cream stick courtesy Blue Bunny. Magnet courtesy American Hospital Association/Health Forum.™ Mug courtesy Black Lab Advertising and Marketing.

Remember direct mail and other print promotion techniques. Web post-cards to announce your site are now available for a reasonable price (500 for $95) from such sources as *http://www.digitalwork.com* or *http://www.printing.com*. Avery inserts a paper with a call to visit their Web site into packages of labels, and eBay advertises on the back of ATM slips from Wells Fargo Bank! Some sample print promotions appear in Figure 7.29.

When it comes to brand awareness, packaging covers more than products. Southwest Airlines applies window clings with its URL to airport windows; Superfast Ferries in Athens, Greece, paints its URL on window awnings; HomeGrocer.com in San Diego identifies its trucks with its URL, and Canada's tourist bureau flies high with a hot air balloon.Perhaps one of the most famous Web site promotions is "The World's Largest E-mail" displayed on Joe Boxer's (*http://www.joeboxer.com*) 100 foot-long billboard at 42nd and Broadway in New York City. (E-mail, *timessquare@boxer.com* to put an e-mail into rotation for one week.). There are even services like DriveAd.com and FreeCar.com that create a traveling billboard: For $1,000 to $1,500 a month, they "wrap" someone's car with your URL printed on adhesive vinyl. See Figure 7.30 for examples of large scale promotions.

Word-of-Mouth, Word-of-Web

Community efforts require more time than money, but the investment can pay off in goodwill and credibility. It doesn't have to be as expensive as a postseason college football game like the Insight.com Bowl sponsored by the discount computer software/hardware house or an extensive as the event program sponsored by Jelly Belly shown in Figure 7.31 (*http://www.jellybelly.com/events.html*). You could sponsor several runners (or walkers) in a 10K race who agree to wear T-shirts with your company name and URL. The URL for your RV or powerboat Web site might work well on the back of shirts worn by a local bowling team.

If you deal in computer-related products, enlist in one of the many business-to-school partnerships. See if any of your employees, wearing that ubiquitous T-shirt with your URL, will volunteer for litter or graffiti cleanup campaigns. Doing good for others often does well for you.

We've now looked at many, many ways of drawing an audience to your site and bringing them back. In the next chapter, we'll look at two of the most popular promotional methods: search engines and online advertising.

Buy postage from E-Stamp® and get a
$25 *Super*Certificate™
from GiftCertificates.com.™
(Being naughty or nice is not a prerequisite).

Figure 7.29. Sample print promotions. Clockwise from top: Coupon courtesy E-Stamp Corp. Shopping bag courtesy Reitman's Canada Ltd. Postcard courtesy *www.PaintingsDIRECT.com*, painting by Marie-Louise McHugh. ATM slip courtesy eBay, Inc.

Figure 7.30. Sample large-scale promotions. Top, window clings courtesy Southwest Airlines. Bottom, window awning courtesy Superfast Ferries S.A.

Figure 7.31.   Promotions at special and community events, *http://www.jellybelly.com/events.html.*© 1998 Herman Goelitz, Inc. All rights reserved.

8

Marketing with Search Engines and Online Ads

We've already discussed dozens of ways to promote your site online and off. Now it's time to address the two 800-pound gorillas grappling in the promotional living room: search engines and banner ads. While nearly half of all Web surfers tout search engines, only 1% confess to watching banner ads. Yet you know advertisers wouldn't pour billions of dollars annually into online ads if they weren't getting something for their money.

Many Web site owners don't realize that their presence remains unknown to search engines unless they submit their sites. Others are surprised to learn that they can advertise online without driving their companies into bankruptcy. In this chapter you'll learn how to tame both gorillas with guerrilla marketing to garner the maximum visibility for your site. We'll cover

- How to submit your site to search engines and directories.

- Strategies to improve search engine ranking.

- Online advertising costs and methods.

- Banner ad effectiveness.

- Selling ads on your Web site.

Search Engines and Directories

Viewers find new sites in a variety of ways: Search engines, word of mouth, and random surfing (inbound links) are by far the most common, as seen in Figure 8.1, which ranks viewers' most often used strategies. Of course, many viewers use more than one strategy, and they may use different techniques to find a site a second time. In any case, with 46% of users pointing to search engines, it's critical to understand their advantages and limitations.

There are about 20 major search engines (Figure 8.2) and directories (Figure 8.3) on the Net, and hundreds of lesser-known ones. Don't dismiss the latter out of hand. If they are specific to your business area, smaller engines and directories may be the most likely to be searched by your target market. Among other sources, there's a list of search engines at *http://www.bizynet.com/web-srch.htm* and a list of business directories at *http://www.bizynet.com/web-dirs.htm*. Or look them up at *http://www.DirectoryGuide.com*. There are even search engines for search engines at

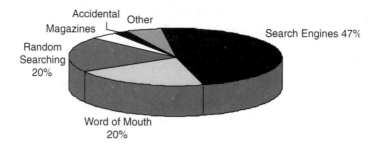

Figure 8.1. Traffic to new sites, *http://www.emarketer.com/estats/022100_imt.html*. Courtesy eMarketer, Inc.

Name	Submission URL	Time to Appearance
Alta Vista	*http://www.altavista.com/cgi-bin/ query?pg=addurl*	2 weeks
Google	*http://www.google.com/addurl.html*	
Excite	*http://www.excite.com/info/add_url*	2-3 weeks
Hotbot/Lycos	*http://hotbot.lycos.com/addurl.asp*	21– 60 days
Infoseek/Go	*http://www.go.com/addUrl?pg= SubmitUrl.html&svx=CTOC_Add_url*	up to 6 weeks
MSN Web Search	*http://search.msn.com/addurl.asp?q= &RS=CHECKED&co=15*	4-6 weeks
Northern Light	*http://www.northernlight.com/ docsgen_help_faq_webmaster. html#turnaround*	about 6 weeks
Web Crawler	*http://www.webcrawler.com/ info/add_url/*	2-3 weeks

Figure 8.2. Major search engines.

- *http://www.searchengine.com*

- *http://www.invisibleweb.com*

- *http://www.beaucoup.com*

The terms search engine and directory are often used interchangeably, but actually these sites are quite different. A **directory**, such as the Yellow Pages, is a hierarchically organized database arranged by categories and subcategories. A directory may index and link only to a site's home page. **Search engines**, on the other hand, use indexing agents called **spiders** (also known as robots, crawlers, or wanderers) that automatically explore the Web, visiting and revisiting URLs to collect links and pages of text that are eventually analyzed for **keywords**. Assuming there are internal links to every page on a site, search engines will ultimately review an entire site. Once the pages and URLs have been collected, search engines apply various logic **algorithms** (computer formulas)

Name	Submission URL	Notes	Time to Appearance
AT&T	*http://www.anywho.com/ addyp.html*		instant
Downtown Anywhere	*http://www.awa.com/ easyreg.html*	$10 for 6 months, emailed	
Galaxy	*http://www.galaxy.com /cgi-bin/annotate?/galaxy*	$25 US non-refundable fee	reviewed within 30 days
Open Directory	*http://dmoz.org/add.html*	emailed	
Yahoo	*http://add.yahoo.com/ fast/add?8590822*	Business special: 7 business days for a 1-time review; non-refundable fee of $199 does not guarantee submission	
Big Yellow	*https://customer.super pages.com:887/cgi-bin/ gx.cgi/AppLogic%2b Marketing.Start?B=1*		24 hours

Figure 8.3. Major directories.

to check the relevance of keywords. From these results, engines rank sites in response to a search request.

The growth of the Web makes search engines' tasks nearly impossible; their indexing success has fallen dramatically in the past few years. A 1999 study by the NEC Research Institute showed that 11 of the major search engines indexed no more than 16% of the estimated 1.5 billion Web pages. Northern Light led the pack (16%), followed by Snap and AltaVista (15.5%), HotBot (11.3%), and MSN Search (8.5%); the others, including Infoseek, Yahoo!, Excite, and Lycos, found 8% or less. Some engines no longer index sites without a registered domain name. In spite of the published time to appearance in Figure 8.2, the study found that it takes more than six months on average for a new listing to appear.

Even combined, the search engines cover perhaps one-third of the Web, or less if the July 2000 analysis by BrightPlanet is correct. This company, which sells a special search engine called LexiBot for $89.95, claims much of the information on the Web is stored in giant, dynamic databases ignored by surface-skimming search engines. They estimate the "deep Web" at 550 billion documents. A list of 20,000 of the content-rich databases they've found is located on *http://www.completeplanet.com.* InvisibleWeb offers a similar directory. If you provide searchable online databases, either free or for a fee, you might want to register at both these sites.

Submission

To promote your site on search engines and directories, you need to accomplish two things:

1. Your site must be found.

2. It must be ranked in the top 20 or 30 sites resulting from a search of likely keywords. Most Web surfers go only to the top few sites on a list.

Search Engines

Theoretically, search engines eventually visit URLs whether or not a formal submission has been received, as long as enough links exist for the site to be identified. However, given that fewer than one-third of all sites are usually found, submitting your URL to search engines will speed up the process. Most search engine sites require only your URL for submission.

Directories

Sites can't be found by directories unless you submit your URL, usually with proposed keywords and categories. Yahoo! and the Yellow Pages allow only a single URL per site, with a single description and title or keyword. Most other directories permit multiple pages from the same site, as long as each page has a different description, keyword list, and URL. (Change the extension name following your domain name, e.g., *http://www.yourdomain.com/extension.*)

Every directory has a slightly different registration form and process, so you may want to individualize submissions, at least to critical sites; look at online forms and existing listings to see what's appropriate. In most cases, you simply fill out the Web-based form with your site name, the URL, and a brief descriptive paragraph that will appear in a list of search results. A few locations require that you e-mail your entry instead of submitting on the Web.

Yahoo! is unique among the search engines and directories because it shares the characteristics of both. Like a directory, it is hierarchically organized; it uses 14 main categories, and requires the detailed submission form found at *http://add.yahoo.com/fast/add.* Yahoo! has a robot that searches announcement sites and other collection points on the Web, but human beings rate your site for relevance and category accuracy. Yahoo! incorporates Google's popularity engine, which is derived from inbound links, for ranking appearances on its "Web Page Matches" section, but will retain the more relevance-driven Inktomi engine for its proposed corporate Yahoo! service.

Yahoo! has recently added an express submission service for $199, guaranteeing to review your site, but not necessarily post it, within seven days. To make sure your Yahoo! submission is successful—with over 1,000 sites added daily, it may take several months to find out—note the following:

- Commercial sites for the directory or Yahoo! Site Matches must be placed in a Business and Economy subcategory.

- Locate up to two good subcategories by searching until you find businesses like yours, or use a likely keyword to see where responsive sites have been categorized.

- Since you can't suggest keywords for Yahoo!, the Title and Description fields are particularly important. The title can be a maximum of 60 characters; try to include keywords in that count. The description has a maximum of 25 words; try to create a complete sentence that includes keywords while providing a good description of your company's products or services.

- Yahoo! reviewers check your categorization for appropriateness and your description for accuracy. If they aren't correct, your site won't be listed.

To see how well your initial keyword selection works, submit to Infoseek (*http://www.go.com/AddURL?=submiturl& svc=CTOC_add_url*, shown in Figure 8.4) or another fast-posting search engine. When you're satisfied with the results, submit at least to Yahoo!, AltaVista, and HotBot. Directory-wise, list in the AT&T White Pages and at least one Yellow Pages Directory, such as WorldPages (*http:// www.worldpages.com/docs/forms/add_bus_listing/whtml*) shown in Figure 8.5. Other companies also maintain free Yellow Page listings.

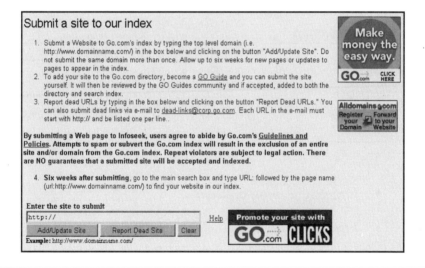

Figure 8.4. Infoseek submission, *http://www.go.comAddURL?=submitURL&svc =CTOC_add_url*. Reprinted by permission. Infoseek, Ultra-smart, Ultraseek, Ultraseek Server, Infoseek Desktop, Infoseek Ultra, iSeek, Quickseek, Imageseek, Ultrashop, the Infoseek logos, and the tagline, "Once you know, you know," are trademarks of Infoseek Corporation which may be registered in certain jurisdictions. Other trademarks shown are trademarks of their respective owners. Go Network is a trademark of the Walt Disney Company, Infoseek Corporation authorized licensee. © 1998-2000 Infoseek Corporation. All rights reserved.

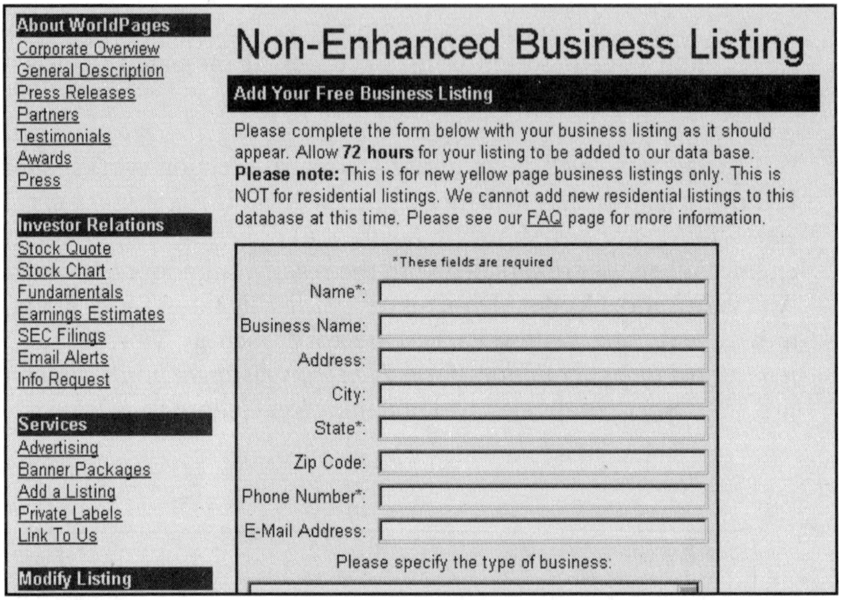

Figure 8.5. Yellow Pages submission, *http://www.worldpages.com/docs/forms addbuslisting/whtml*. Courtesy WorldPages.com.

Try

- *http://www.infospace.com*

- *https://customer.superpages.com:887/servlet*

- *http://www.switchboard.com*

- *http://www.four11.com*

Check the FAQs of each search engine or directory if you have specific questions. For example, from the FAQs for MSN Web Search seen in Figure 8.6 (*http://search.msn.com/help/FAQ.asp*) you learn that your entire site will be crawled from a one-page submission.

Depending on the engine or directory, it may take anywhere from two minutes to six months for your site to appear. Several days after its anticipated appearance (see Figures 8.2 and 8.3), start searching for

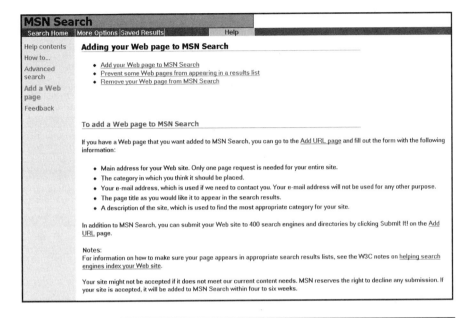

Figure 8.6. Search engine FAQs, *http://www.msn.com/helpS_FAQ.asp.* Screenshot reprinted by permission from Microsoft Corporation.

your entry until you confirm it has been listed. If you don't find your listing within a week after the anticipated time, resubmit your site.

As tempting as it may be to submit your URL to search engines as soon as you decide to have a Web site, wait until the site is up and running first. Many things can change or go wrong. You could easily turn off a future customer or directory researcher who reaches a page under construction or a page whose content has nothing to do with the keywords you anticipated using.

You can list your site in each engine and directory one by one, or point to a free, one-stop interface to the most popular engines. There are dozens of free submission sites, but Submit It! (*http://www.submit-it.com*, shown in Figure 8.7), and Register-It (*http://register-it.netscape.com*) are two of the largest. You might also want to try *http://www.top-pile.com*. After you enter your information at one of these sites, it automatically registers one URL with the top 10 to 25 search engines and directories on the Web.

For submission to over 400 engines and directories, Submit It! charges a fee of $59 for two URLs and up to $500 for 40 URLs. Other sites also

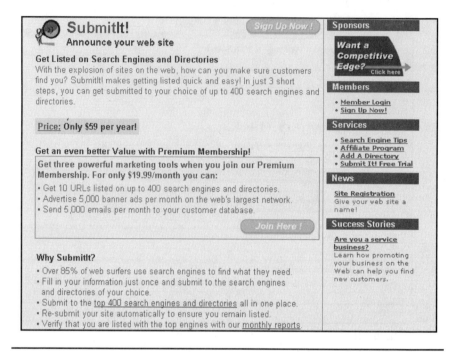

Figure 8.7. Multiple submission site, *http://www.submit-it.com*. Screenshot reprinted by permission from Microsoft Corporation.

charge for more extensive submissions. Bear in mind that these services consider each announced page to be a separate URL and that they don't customize their submission lists. All sites are submitted to the same engines and directories, regardless of where your target audience might be. Be careful: Some engines have started to refuse these multiple, simultaneous submissions, considering them to be spam.

Most search engine announcement services charge for regular monthly submissions of multiple URLs to multiple search engines, for example SearchTrends (*http://www.searchtrends.com*) or Position Agent (*http://positionagent.linkexchange.com*). Submit It!, bCentral (*http://www.bcentral.com*), Smart Age (*http://www.smartage.com*) and others offer a number of promotional services, from free mailbots (automated e-mail response) to banner exchanges.

Improving Search Engine Ranking

Frequently thousands, sometimes hundreds of thousands, of matches are found in response to a search on a particular topic. Most directories present results of a search in alphabetical order; most search engines rank by relevance or popularity.

Combined, these search engines and directories have literally millions of entries and receive tens of thousands of submissions a day. The search engine world has become so competitive that several engines including AltaVista now let advertisers pay to have their sites listed at the top of search results on 500 of the most commonly used keywords, such as "computer." Goto.com and Looksmart require payment for a listing. Although "paid" results are bracketed, it remains to be seen how users will react. If more engines adopt this policy, search engines will become less accessible to small businesses seeking to enhance their online presence.

Given the delay in appearance on many engines, it can be frustrating to realize that you need to optimize your submission, resubmit, and wait again to see what happens. To avoid this, you can purchase software, like WebPosition at *http://www.webposition.com*, to test your keywords on the major search engines before submitting. Some vendors allow you to download trial positioning software from their sites.

Web marketing consultants like those listed here use one of these packages or proprietary tools to improve their clients' placement and/ or provide an optimization service on a per page basis. Before you go with a consultant, read the fine print in the contract regarding guaranteed results—which may be a myth—and ask for references from other customers. Some of these sites say that you pay only for rankings achieved, but require a minimum purchase.

- *http://www.macor.com/faq.htm*

- *http://www.coastsites.com*

- *http://www.searchtrends.com*

- *http://www.searchenginegeeks.com/faq_geeks.htm*

Many sites offer search engine tips online, through e-mailed newsletters, or in newsgroups. Look at

- *http://www.submitit.linkexchange.com/subopt.htm*

- *http://www.webposition.com* (as seen in Figure 8.8)

- *http://www.searchenginewatch.com* or

- *http://www.searchsecrets.com*

These reports usually provide suggestions to improve ranking according to the approach used by each engine. The engines change their algorithms over time, partly to increase accuracy, partly to outwit people who are trying to outwit them, and partly to distribute visibility among indexed pages. If you want to get really fancy, you can optimize splash or **doorway** pages (special entry pages) based on different search engine

---

The BEST tips to improve your rankings:

1. **TITLE:** Include and repeat keywords that people might search for to find you in the TITLE of all your pages. This is very important. Keep common word groups or phrases that people might search on *together* if you can. The TITLE is EXTREMELY important to achieving good rankings.

2. **PROMINENCY:** Keywords that are more prominent will be weighted much higher with the search engines. Most engines rank you higher if the keyword or phrase is near the beginning of the title and as close to the beginning of the page as possible.

3. **LENGTH OF PAGE:** Keep your pages short while including and repeating keywords frequently, particularly in the first 3-5 lines of the pages. Some engines ignore or largely ignore wording beyond the first paragraph or two. Having a short page goes much farther to improve your rankings with many engines than you might think, even if the keywords are not repeated very many times.

4. **"DOORWAY" PAGES:** Unfortunately, what is appealing to the search engines is not always the best way to display the content for you Web site. Therefore, strongly consider creating a secondary page for each product or service you offer designed for the search engines. Describe the product/service clearly but make sure you make generous use of keywords in your sentences. At the bottom of this short paragraph, put a link to your primary page such as "For more information on XYZ click here".

The reason this works, and generally works better than most methods, is that engines often take the keywords being searched and divide it by the total number of words in the page or in the first portion of the page. Therefore, you may only have the keyword on the page a couple of times, but if there's not a lot of other words, those keywords appear to be much more "significant" to the page's overall content.

You don't have to have links to these secondary pages from your home page. They simply act as a "doorway" to the appropriate page on your Web site so are not seen by other visitors. If you don't link to them though from your home page or a close secondary page, you'll need to submit each of these pages manually for the search engines to find and index them. Be sure to review the warnings in Submitting Your Pages before doing this though.

5. **REPEATING KEYWORDS:** Experiment with repeating keywords up to six times and more on some engines. If this makes your page look bad, consider putting the keywords at the top of the page preferably in the same color as the background. That way nobody can see them but they should still get indexed. **Warning:** Some engines are now detecting wording in the same color as the background and either ignoring such text or leaving the page out of the index altogether! We'll try to update you on these kind of specifics in our MarketPosition Newsletter. Proper "netique" discourages blatant "spamming" of keywords. You should not try to go overboard repeating the same keyword or using keywords that don't apply to your site.

Figure 8.8.   Search engine tips, *http://www.webpostion.com/usersguide/how topreparyourpageforsubmission.htm.* Courtesy *www.Firstplacesoftware.com*, developers of WebPosition Gold.

techniques. In spite of differences, there are some general principles about the way most search engines determine ranking.

Keyword Weighting

This is a ratio between the occurrence of a keyword and the total number of words on a page. Try to keep your total word count per page to 350 to 450 words. Look at what percentage of the total words on the page are keywords, counting all occurrences of all keywords on that page. Keywords should represent somewhere between 3 and 10 percent of total words. Instead of trying to get the maximum number of different keywords on a page, try to focus your pages so that different keywords pop out as the most relevant on different pages.

Popularity of Your Site

Many engines judge your value to the world by the number of inbound links to your site. This increases the importance of reciprocal and inbound links (described in the previous chapter). Not only do inbound links boost your rankings, they also represent your most likely target audience. Several sites have ways let you know who's "voted" your site "most popular" with links. The free link checkers here yield lists of inbound links, or you can go directly to AltaVista, Infoseek, or HotBot:

- *http://siteowner.becentral.com/sitecheck.cfm*

- *http://websearch.about.com/internet/websearch/library/searchwiz/bl_linkpopularity.htm*

- *http://deadlock.com/promote/search- engines/tools.html#link*

- *http://linkstoyou.com/CheckLinks.htm*

- *http://www.linkpopularity.com*

At AltaVista and Infoseek, you simply type your URL on the screen without www. to obtain the number and identity of sites that link to yours. HotBot requires the full URL, but you change the default setting to "search." It's worth running more than one of these spiders: They rarely produce identical lists!

Keyword Emphasis

Think newspaper article, not essay. Write in the inverted pyramid style of classic journalism. The lead—the first sentence or paragraph—answers all the essential questions (who, what, why, where, when, and how) in case a reader doesn't have time to complete the story. Don't save the best till last: Make your title and the first 25 words of your page keyword-rich. Most search algorithms expect keywords specific to a page to be located near the top, relatively close to each other (as in an abstract), and then scattered in various places around the page. Each search engine has a unique, proprietary set of criteria to determine keyword emphasis.

Keyword Density

Sophisticated algorithms not only count how often a keyword is used on a page, they watch where keywords appear with high frequency. Some engines will bounce sites that try to boost their ratings by repeating keywords over and over behind a graphic or hidden in one section of the background. Draw a delicate balance between good repetition of a keyword (6 to 10 times each per page) and overuse.

Search engines are not static. To increase the likelihood of getting your Web site ranked highly, submit multiple pages with different URLs whenever possible, optimizing them for different keywords. If you use multiple doorway pages, be sure to change the META tags (see "Optimizing Your Pages" later in this chapter) for each one. Besides your home page, submit major topic pages, unique content or pages describing a special product or service. Your Web designer should follow the principles outlined here, such as using keyword-laden TITLE tags, on these subpages as well.

Finally, submit new pages as they are created and resubmit pages if their content changes significantly. Although these changes should eventually be caught on a revisit by a spider, submission will speed up the process. Schedule a resubmission of your entire site every 2 or 3 months to account for changing algorithms and random drop-offs from the search databases. Keep track of all your submissions and rankings in your Web notebook.

In the case of directories, consider carefully the categories to which your site belongs. Directories may define the same category names differently and divide up broad categories into subcategories on a unique basis, so this submission process can become quite cumbersome. Search each target directory until you find other companies like yours. If you can't find a subcategory that fits, suggest a new one. There is no point in going into a less appropriate category—your audience won't find you. Resubmit to directories if your URL, category classification, or description changes.

Schedule a monthly maintenance visit to all your directory and search engine listings to confirm your presence, check your rankings, and see whether there have been any changes to the engine.

A Few Words about Keywords

For search engines that operate by using keywords to rank relevance, an accurate and extensive list of keywords is crucial to improve your ranking. An online florist who stops with the obvious keywords flowers, bouquets, and florist will lose anyone who searches for gifts, weddings, houseplants, funerals, or floral arrangements.

Brainstorm as many keywords as you can—at least 50. Since some engines restrict the number of keyword entries, you might not be able to use them all. However, spreading keywords around to different engines and assigning them to different pages will improve the likelihood of attaining a reasonable ranking somewhere.

Think like the audience you are trying to reach. What words or phrases might they type in? People looking for a small, intimate hotel in San Antonio might not type the word hotels. Instead, they might try bed-and-breakfast San Antonio. The more narrowly focused the phrase or keywords used, the smaller the list of search results, and the higher in the rankings you are likely to be. For instance, instead of the word gifts, try women birthday presents, fresh flowers $30, or office-warming plants. Try electronic funds transfer software, not just software program.

Most of all, test your keywords. Create a spreadsheet or table with a proposed list of keywords and the list of search engines and directories in Figures 8.2 and 8.3. See how many sites and which ones result from a search on those words. Are the results similar to your company? If so, you're on the right track. You can improve your keywords by working backward as well. Go to the sites like yours that consistently rank well in search engines. Look at their source code (under "View" on a browser menu bar) to see their keywords.

If you find a phrase that returns a reasonable number of results (say less than a thousand instead of several hundred thousand), optimize your page for that phrase: You're more likely to end up at the top of the list. Of course, you can't choose words just because they return a good result—it's a meaningless victory to rank first if no one in your target audience would type that keyword or phrase.

If you are already listed in the search engines, be honest with yourself: Type in your existing keywords and see where you rank. If you are not in the top 30 sites for at least one page in each engine, start revising your keywords. Ask potential viewers, either now or in your testing cycle, what keywords they would use to find your site. Everybody's brain works differently—you might be surprised.

The following list of tips may come in handy:

- Your company name should be one of your keywords, especially if it is not obvious in your domain name or if it could be spelled or abbreviated several ways. If your company name isn't obvious, you may want to arrange for it or your brand name(s), trademark, or slogan to map to your Web site. "Keyword subscriptions" are also available for small businesses with low Internet traffic. The charge is $100 annually per keyword for 1,000 keyword-driven visits. For more information go to *http://customer.realnames.com/Virtual.asp?page=Eng_Subscribe_GetY ourKeyword.*

- Use only keywords that apply to your site. In the end, any other choice of words will be self-defeating for a business presence.

- In general, use two- to three-word phrases instead of individual keywords.

- Make sure your keywords are spelled correctly.

- You might want to target commonly misspelled words deliberately, perhaps creating a doorway page with a keyword slightly misspelled (e.g., Caribean for Caribbean).

- Don't use stop words, common words that search engines skip (e.g., a, an, the, and, but, or, of, that, Web). Try to avoid "the" as the first word in a title, since it might reduce the prominence of keywords in the TITLE tag. If you must use a stop word, put it in quotes.

- If you have purchased banner ads (discussed later), coordinate keywords with words in the ad.

- Don't be afraid to include regional words or phrases to target your audience, (e.g., Appalachian).

- Use long versions of words, such as photographer instead of photo. The short "root word" will usually be derived by the engine.

As described earlier, some sites try to increase keyword frequency by hiding the words behind graphics or in a text color that matches the background. This technique, called **keyword stuffing**, may increase the ranking if it is based on absolute numbers or on the ratio of keywords to text, but not for long. Most search engines now set a limit on the number of occurrences per word per page they will accept. "Web watchers" like CNet also review the Web for stuffing techniques and the use of keywords inappropriate to a site.

If you try to stuff the ballot box or "spam" an index by submitting too many pages or too many keywords (more than 6 to 10 uses per word per page), or by using keywords unrelated to the content of the site, you may find your submission rejected. If you persist, many engines will permanently ban all your pages.

Optimizing Your Pages

By adjusting your Web pages slightly, you can increase the likelihood of a high ranking on a search engine for one or more of your pages. Here are some tips to share with your Web designer.

1. Include one or more descriptive keywords in the TITLE tag of the document. This TITLE tag is what a browser displays in the title bar of a page. See Figure 8.9 from *http://www.finecoffee.com* for an excellent example of title bars for different keywords to distinguish pages on a site. A good title helps your viewers find your site again in their bookmark list as well.

2. Use a page description in META tags to define what will appear as the summary of your site in an index listing instead of a sen-

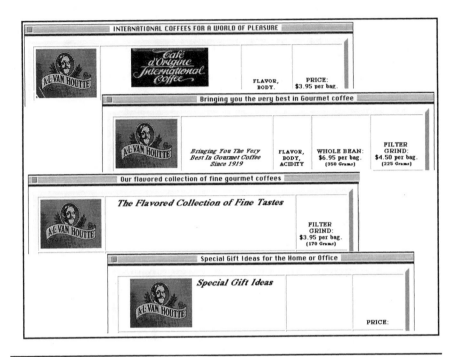

Figure 8.9. Good title bars with different keywords, *http://www.fine coffee.com.* Courtesy Fruba, Inc. dba College Hill Coffee Shop.

tence fragment from your first paragraph of text. META tags are especially important when a site uses Netscape frames or Java script at the top of the page. Your Web designer will know the syntax and location of META tags (see the comprehensive example in Figure 8.10 from *http://www.phs.org*), but you need to provide the content, preferably from a marketing perspective. META tags can encompass keywords that appear on other pages and incorporate singular, plural and other forms of keywords (e.g., clothes, clothing, shop, shopping). Not all search engines score on META tags, so be sure to utilize keywords within page content as well. Repeating the same word too many times in a META tag can get a site bounced from an index.

3. Provide keywords in a comment tag in the first few lines of HTML code, as well as in a header tag.

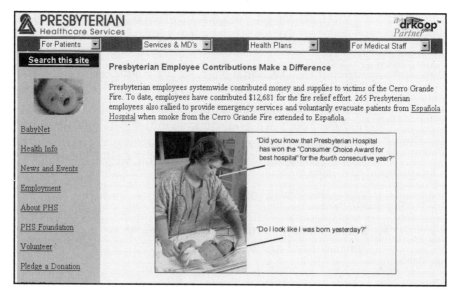

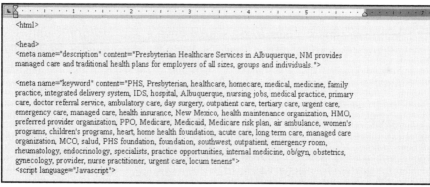

Figure 8.10. META tags for a site, *http://www.phs.org*. Courtesy Presbyterian Healthcare Services, New Mexico.

4. Since the top of a page is assigned greater relevance, a graphic near the top should have text immediately beneath or next to it.

5. If the site uses multiple photos or graphics, use text within ALT tags to give search engines a basis for determining keywords. The 20 to 40% of viewers who download pages with graphics

turned off also find this helpful in deciding whether they want to see a specific image.

6. After indexing a home page, search engines return at a later time to index internal links. In a frame-based site, frames are treated as internal links, delaying a correct analysis of the home page. Since this may result in a poor ranking initially, include descriptive text between the <noframes> and </noframes> tags of the sourc code. This gives the search engine something to work with.

7. Use keywords in internal links.

8. Substitute keywords in URL extensions for a page instead of a generic word like index.

Optimizing Your Submission Process

With the time it takes to do search engine and directory submissions, it makes sense to prioritize them. Select first those engines and directories where your target audience is most likely to be found, not just the ones with the most traffic (seen in Figure 8.11) or the ones on which users spend the most time (seen in Figure 8.12). If you survey your target market, ask viewers for the engines they most often use or think about the characteristics of the various engines and decide which ones your audience would like.

Yahoo! is the grandma of all the directories, as well as the easiest to use, with more than 145 million viewers per month. Since information is arranged in a category tree and reviewed by real people for consistency, search results may be more accurate than on other engines. HotBot, by contrast, uses an automated spider to search the Web by keywords. It yields broad, sometimes irrelevant, search results. The widest net is cast by engines like MetaCrawler, SavvySearch, and CNet's Search.com, which search other search engines.

In contrast, Google ranks pages based on the number of inbound links, while Direct Hit ranks by popularity as determined by user clicks on prior search engine results. If you have to choose, optimize your pages for the search engine algorithm that best meets your audience's needs.

Many business users avoid all-purpose search engines in favor of smaller, faster, less-likely-to-be-bogged-down specialized ones. These business sites, located through one of the search engine directories listed

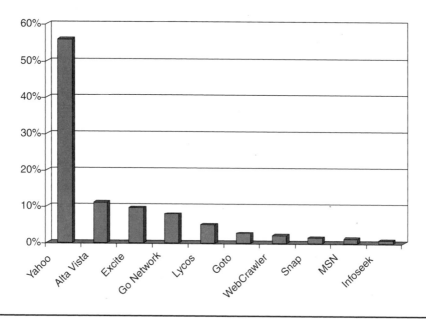

Figure 8.11. Top 10 referring search engines, *WebSideStory* on *http://www. emarketer.com/estats/122899_search.html*. Courtesy eMarketer, Inc.

at the beginning of the chapter, may be excellent places to submit. Don't forget business directories such as Dun & Bradstreet's Companies Online (*http://www.companiesonline.com*) or Hoovers database of companies and their competitors (*http://www.hoovers.com*). For the former site, you need to get a D&B number (*https://www.dnb.com/product/c-online/ register.htm*, the latter has a membership fee. Both are worth it depending on the size of your company, the purpose of your site, and the audience you are trying to attract.

All-purpose search engines are also less than stellar when it comes to shopping sites: Most indexed material is not product information. The largest engines have already created subdirectories like shopping.yahoo.com or shopping.excite.com. Buyers often seek out specialized search engines, such as Shopfind, Price Watch, PriceSearch, or bottomdollar.com, as well as well-known price comparison sites like DealPilot or MySimon.com. You can find a list of shopping search agents at BotSpot and SmartBots.com. If you're a B2C site, list on shopping search engines, which generally require product descriptions and current prices. Some sites require a fee per listing, per referral, or per sale.

Site	Hrs:Mins:Sec
yahoo.com	1:04:33
msn.com	0:38:52
excite.com	0:29:53
netscape.com	0:22:00
go.com	0:20:18
snap.com	0:11:40
askjeeves.com	0:10:25
altavista.com	0:08:47
lycos.com	0:08:16
google.com	0:08:00
northernlight.com	0:07:40
looksmart.com	0:06:51
webcrawler.com	0:06:46
hotbot.com	0:05:04
goto.com	0:03:29
dmoz.org	0:02:35
directhit.com	0:02:06

Figure 8.12. Time on search engines, *http://www.searchenginewatch.com/net ratings.html*. Reprinted with permission. © 2000 Internet.com, LCC. All rights reserved.

Advertising Online

It's amazing how quickly the advertising industry has found ways to sell the Web audience as product. Both space and time have been carved up in multiple ways, creating the online equivalent of every form of advertising and promotion that exists offline: classifieds, display ads, event sponsorships, product placement in movies, and logos, logos everywhere. We'll look at both paid advertising and free banner ads, which are generally handled through an exchange service. Ads are really hyperlinks dressed up with graphics and other media to draw attention to the advertiser's message. Different ads may rotate in the same position on different content pages or rotate after a fixed time.

Paid display advertisements on the Web, like the ones on the ShopNow mall at *http://stores.shopnow.com*, shown in Figure 8.13, generally take one of the forms shown in Figure 8.14. Sizes for ads have begun to standardize, but they may vary from site to site. Most ads are supplied in GIF or JPEG format. Check both the size and format before you submit an ad. Particular sites may have special advertising opportunities, such as a headline ad placed near the lead story on a newspaper site.

Figure 8.13. Variety of display ad sizes, *http://stores.shopnow.com/index.pl/568679673597.html*. Courtesy ShopNow.com, a division of Network Commerce, Inc.

Major advertising sites will have either a contact name and number or an online **media kit**, which usually includes online advertising rates, site demographics, ad dimensions, and graphics requirements. Most media kits spell out the submission process (ads can be placed on the site's server or called from yours), purchasing method, and special opportunities for media buyers.

If you carry brand items, see if the manufacturers will let you apply **co-op marketing dollars** (ad costs shared between the manufacturer and retailer) to online advertising. Manufacturers may require that their logos appear in your ad. You might also get them to place a link from their site to yours or pay you to place a link from your site to theirs.

Trends in Web Advertising

Surveys that track ad dollars show that advertisers are switching from print to online advertising, a category that didn't exist five years ago. Even some unlikely activities like political campaigns are shifting some

Type	Description	Size in Pixels (if applicable)
Banner	most popular size; short, wide ad with link to advertiser's site	468 × 60, 460 × 55, 460 × 60, 480 × 60
Box	a nearly square ad, with a link to the advertiser's site	125 × 125, 120 × 90
Display	usually quarter-, half-, or full-screen size, with a link to the advertiser's site; some full-screen ads appear between destination screens (interstitials)	
Ear	short banner, with a link to the advertiser's site, usually appears in a fixed corner position	120 × 60
Floating strip	medium size banner near bottom or middle of a page	392 × 72
Logo	paid sponsorship with a link to the advertiser's site usually smaller and less expensive than a banner	
Mini Nonlink	small, narrow banner, often just a boxed name ad or sponsorship of any size without a link; less expensive than linked ads; often used for name recognition or brand imaging	88 × 31

Figure 8.14. Typical online advertising sizes.

of their ad spending from expensive television buys to much more reasonable banner ads on the Web. Online ad expenditures are not distributed evenly across all product categories, as Figure 8.15 shows.

Web advertising revenues exceeded $3 billion in 1999. As seen in Figure 8.16, that's a 50% increase from the prior year. Web ad revenues are expected to grow to $4.8 billion in 2000, $13.3 billion by 2003 and $22 billion by 2004. Even then, the dollars spent online will represent less than 8% of total advertising expenditures. In 1998, Web advertising approached annual expenditures on billboards; by 2004 it should surpass magazines and the Yellow Pages and rival radio as the third largest ad medium, behind only television and newspapers, as seen in Figure 8.17.

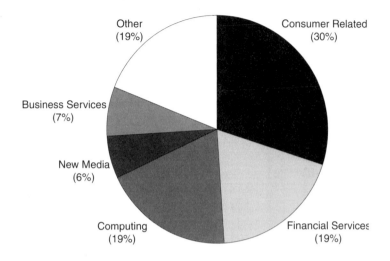

Figure 8.15. Online ad spending by categories, *http://www.estats.com/estats/041900_iab.html*. Courtesy eMarketer, Inc.

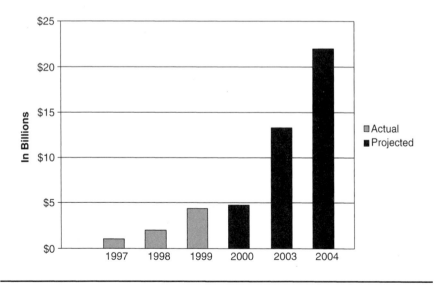

Figure 8.16. Estimated Web advertising revenue.

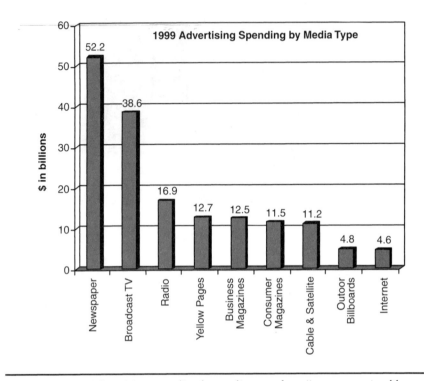

Figure 8.17. Advertising spending by media type, *http://www.veronissuhler.com/ articles/article_202.html*. Source: Veronis Suhler Communication Industry Forecast, 14th edition, July 2000.

By far, most online ad dollars are aimed at consumers; B2B companies account for only 5% of online advertising overall. Still, the corporate kahunas spent millions online in 1999: Microsoft, $36 million; IBM, $27 million; General Motors, $21 million. While those companies seek international brand identity, even local companies like pizza delivery services and dress shops have started to advertise online.

Predictions for online advertising growth remain robust despite evidence that some Web users are tiring of commercial saturation. Internet Mate claims to have developed the Web equivalent of cable zappers to block ad windows, and one recent survey claimed 22% of Web users would pay extra to subscribe to sites without advertising. How many people would actually make such payments or buy such products remains to be seen. The majority of Internet users seem to accept that advertising is needed to keep content and many other online services free.

The distribution of online advertising by type appears in Figure 8.18. Each of the past several years, banner ads have declined in share, with sponsorships increasing. If trend lines for the mix of ads continue on their present course, banner ads will decline to perhaps 40%, with much of the slack picked up by strategic sponsorships. Increasingly, major advertisers try to match ad presentation to behavioral patterns online, seeking to hawk products and services specific to the interests of an individual Web surfer. The use of identifiable user data from cookies and site registrations for this purpose is the source of one argument about privacy described in more detail in Chapter 9.

For more information on advertising, check out the following sites:

- Online Advertising Index at *http://www.netcreations.com/ipa/ adindex.htm* tracks the rates requested by major sites accepting ads.

- WebTrack Information Services at *http://www.webtrack.com* surveys how companies are placing their ads and what they pay.

- Ad Resource has an Ad Rate Guide at *http://www.adre source.com/html/new/rate.html* and offers an advertising primer at *http://www.adresource.com/html/new/advertising_ terminology.html*.

- The Online Advertising Report (OAR), issued quarterly by Adknowledge, provides useful information about advertising trends at *http://www.adknowledge.com/corporate/press*.

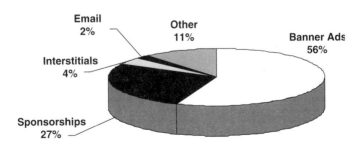

Figure 8.18. Online ad spending by type, *http://www.estats.com/estats/ 041900_iab.html*. Courtesy eMarketer, Inc.

- The Advertising section on Cyberatlas at *http://cyber atlas.internet.com/segments/advertising/ad_index.html* offers multiple reports on ad rates and trends.

Online Advertising Rates

Web advertising on major portals, which can cost far more per month than Web design and hosting combined, is best used to reach a mass audience, promote well-known brands, or build name recognition. For a small business, targeted niche marketing may have a much more positive impact on your bottom line.

Given the average online ad rates seen in Figure 8.19, it's clear that sites such as portals, search engines, news organizations, and financial services are now a promotional playground primarily for deep-pocket corporations. Many sites charge higher CPMs for premium page position (upper corners, **above the fold**—on the first half of the page so ads are visible before scrolling down) or offer different targeting options (e.g., appearance only when certain keywords are selected on a search engine). Others set a minimum on the number of impressions you must buy.

As you expect, the more targeted the online audience, the higher the CPM. Although a CPM rate may seem reasonable, the absolute cost on a major site is boggling. A portal site with 60 million visitors a week could easily guarantee 2 million impressions per month, costing over $44,000. E-mail newsletters are becoming a more attractive advertising venue given their relatively low cost for space and the reasonable production cost of text ads. For a more complete table, go to *http://www.adresource.com/html/new/rate.html*.

bCentral.com, LinkExchange, and other marketing support services buy ad space in bulk on portal sites to resell at a rate affordable to small businesses (as low as $100 per ad!). Occasionally other portals (e.g., Lycos), offer a nonpremium advertising package as low as $1,500. There is no substitute for research when it comes to spending your advertising dollars!

Ad agencies receive a 15% discount from ad prices but pass along the full charge to you. Are ads worth this much, with average click-through rates having fallen below 1% as seen in Figure 8.20? (For comparison, a good response to a mass mailing is half of one percent.) The sinking click-through rate has led to performance-based ad prices based on click-throughs or sales rather than impressions. Some forecasters

National Newspaper Site		E-Mail Newsletters*		Search Engine/Portal	
Placement	Rate	Impressions	One Month	Run of Site	One Month
Article-Top	$40/CPM	1,000,000+	$14/CPM	1–249,000	$29/CPM
Article-Bottom	$22/CPM	750k–999k	$18/CPM	250–499k	$28/CPM
Gateway-Bottom	$25/CPM	500k–749k	$22/CPM	500–999k	$27/CPM
Article-Button	$32/CPM	250k–499k	$26/CPM	1.0–1.9 mil	$24/CPM
Gateway-Button	$36/CPM	249k or less	$30/CPM	2–2.9 mil	$22/CPM
				3–4.9 mil	$20/CPM
				5 mil+	$18/CPM

* Rates for ads across all newsletters

Ad Network		Financial News Site Run of Site Prices		Technology Site	
Content * Category	Entire Category	up to 400K Impressions	$57/CPM Impressions	Monthly	One Month
Biz/Finance	$30/CPM	401–800K	$55/CPM	100k–250k	$70/CPM
Health	$30/CPM	801K–1.2 mil	$53/CPM	250k–499k	$61/CPM
News	$25/CPM	1.2–1.6mil	$51/CPM	500k–999k	$58/CPM
Sports	$20/CPM	1.6–2.0 mil.	$49/CPM	1 mil +	$56/CPM
Women/Family	$30/CPM				

*Selected categories only

Figure 8.19.   Sample online advertising rates, *http://adres.internet.com/ adrates/article/0,1401,00.html.* Reprinted with permission. © 2000 Internet.com, LCC. All rights reserved.

expect that the current 15% of ads sold on a performance basis will rise rapidly over the next few years.

At an ad auction in late 1998, clicks sold for 20¢ each in the computer and technology category, but 16.2¢ for women's interest. Overall, the average price for click-throughs at that auction was 10.6¢ per click. While the average price for click-throughs has been rising, the average online CPM (impression-based rates) has been dropping, down to $33.75 in 1999 from $35.13 in 1998. This is partially due to an increased supply in ad space as more sites seek advertisers.

If you decide to use paid advertising, set a dollar limit first, then decide how to distribute the funds. Keep your advertising expenses in line with the amount you spent on site development. It's not worth tens

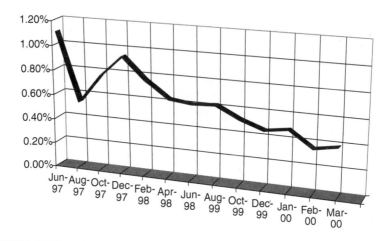

Figure 8.20. Click through rates, *http://www.emarketer.com/estats/sell_ead3.html*. Courtesy eMarketer, Inc.

of thousands of dollars to promote a minimal site that visitors click away from because it lacks interest.

Even if your business exists only in cyberspace, don't spend all your advertising dollars on the Web. The 1998 Webcensus survey on *http://www.iconocast.com*, shown in Figure 8.21, showed that Web users' time on the Internet exceeded time spent watching television, but still accounted for only one-third of their daily media exposure. Remember, the universe of Web users may not be identical to your universe of customers or other target audiences.

Always test a handful of different ad locations to see which ones work best before you lock up your budget in long-term contracts. Ask for a 30-day trial. Remember, it may be cheaper to advertise on several smaller sites than on one premium site. Ten sites with 100,000 weekly hits each may cost less than one site with a million weekly hits, but yield the same total exposure with an audience better targeted to your needs. Look around for options. For instance, Download32 (*http://www.download32.com/advertising/lessthanpackages.htm*) sells ads for business audiences in packages as low as $25 for 10,000 impressions spread across multiple sites. Or negotiate your own ad with a site you'd really like to be on.

Once you've determined which places work, stay there, whether online or offline: An advertising message repeated multiple times in one place is better than an ad that appears once in many places. You can

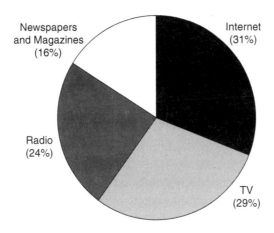

Figure 8.21. Web users' media time during the day, *http://www. iconocast.com/whatis/whatis.html*. Courtesy Iconocast, Inc.

change creative approach or content, but get viewers used to seeing your name in a particular location. Above all, don't overcommit your marketing resources to advertising; it isn't worth the anxiety. Do the best you can with what dollars you have available.

When making ad placement decisions, consider audience size, demographics and CPM, as well as absolute cost. This is tough, because Web advertising can be priced by impressions (number of contacts to a site or page), exposures (ad files actually seen on a user's computer, i.e., the user didn't click away before the ad downloaded), or click-throughs (executed links to the advertiser's site). The following factors may also affect the purchase price of an ad:

- Past history for the number of unique visitors to the site, page views for the page on which the ad appears, and/or number of click-throughs.

- Ad size, generally given in pixels.

- Placement on the screen.

- Frequency with which the ad runs. Most sites rotate ads in each screen location based on the relative number of impressions purchased. Ads are usually refreshed each time a page is requested, but some are now sold by fixed length of visible time. Confirm the length of time and the frequency with which your ad will appear.

- Specified time of appearance. You may want ads, such as those advertising a specific sitecast, to appear at a certain time or on a certain day. Late night placement might be available at a discount.

- The number of impressions, exposures, or click-throughs purchased.

- How many other advertisers share the same space.

- Demographics—usually the more targeted the audience, the higher the CPM.

In the end, sites charge what the market will bear. The ultimate proof of market pricing is an auction market for Internet advertising at sites like Askad (*http://www.askad.com.*) Some experts contend that banners are overpriced for what the advertiser receives. This may be true, given that many advertisers report negotiating significant reductions from published rate cards. It's worth a try. For assistance with advertising, you may need to try an online ad agency like Beyond Interactive shown in Figue 8.22.

How do you know whether you got what you paid for? You can subscribe to a service like WebSideStory's HitBox (*http://www.websidestory.com*) to track links generated by banners in real time. If you're willing to put a HitBox banner or button on each page of your site, the service is free; without the button, HitBox Pro runs $20 per month. Sites with over 250,000 page views per month are charged by total pages measured.

Large sites are routinely audited by an independent company like I/PRO (described in Chapter 6). I/PRO (*http://www.engage.com/ipro*), which claims a 70% market share of audits, includes session length, daily statistics, comparative reports, multimedia access, and site path analysis in its services. Nielsen NetRatings, PC Data, and Media Metrix track users' net time using techniques similar to Nielsen's TV rating system.

If you manage an extensive advertising campaign with multiple ads placed in multiple locations, you might want to purchase one of

Figure 8.22. An online advertising agency, *http://www.gobeyond.com.*
Courtesy Beyond Interactive.

the very expensive software packages that tracks ad performance in real time. Accrue Software (*http://www.accrue.com*) and Straight Up! (*http://www.straightup.com*) track ads from impression to sale, so you can determine the cost of sale or cost of inquiry for each ad.

At the very least, ask for a site's statistics to tease out the visitor profile. Try to avoid sites that offer only ad or page hit rates, since that rate inflates the number of impressions. The number of unique visitors is apt to be lower than the number of impressions implies, since visitors may repeatedly visit the same site and often ask for more than one page of information. Remember to delete hits from spiders or robots trolling the Web: They don't have eyeballs!

Alternately, try using an ad placement service like *http://www.goto.com/d/about/advertisers* that charges only on click-throughs. Less-expensive ways to reach an audience include classified ads (discussed in Chapter 3), a link from an electronic coupon site, such as *http://www.ecentives.com* (click "partner stores" on that site for information about participating), or banner ad exchanges.

Banner Ad Exchanges

Banner ad exchanges work like link exchanges. You register with the exchange, designating desired categories of sites, and provide your ad in the required format. Most banner exchange sites offer a 2:1 or 3:2 ad ratio. In the first instance, your ad is placed once for every two ads from others that you display. (The other ad is sold to a paying customer.)

You are usually required to place an ad near the top of a page, and some services demand exclusivity. Check the agreements posted on each exchange site listed in Figure 8.23 for details on ad size, credit ratio, placement control for your own ad, and other requirements. Credit ratios have become more competitive in the recent past. For instance, Macpromote, Banner Co-op, and Linksmart Clicks all offer 1:1 ratios.

Some of the banner programs are fee-based; bCentral's Banner Network, for instance, charges $20 per month for 5,000 impressions. Most others, including SmartAge, LinkExchange, and Hyperbanner, are free.

For a list of banner exchange services, go to *http://www.adresource.com* or *http://bannertips.com/exchangenetworks.shtml*, or search Yahoo! for banner exchanges. To operate your own banner exchange program, check out ClickTrade at *http://www.clicktrade.com*.

```
http://bannerco-op.com/
http://www.exchange-it.com
http://www.hyperbanner.net
http://www.impressionz.com
http://www.intelliclicks.com
http://www.exchange.com
http://www.linkhut.com/
http://www.linkshare.net
http://www.looksmartc.\licks.com
http://www.macseek.com/xchange.shtml
http://www.mactimes.com/macweb/exchanges
http://www.traficx.com
http://www.zenclicks.com
```

Figure 8.23. Banner ad exchanges, *http://www.adresource.com*. Reprinted with permission. © 2000 Internet.com, LCC. All rights reserved.

Banner Ad Effectiveness

With click-through rates on ads now averaging less than 1%, it takes some effort to make a banner ad work for you. Give viewers a reason to click through to your site by providing an incentive in your ad: a call to action, a teaser, or a free offer. Banner ads also lose their punch after seven to ten views by the same user, so you may need to create multiple banners that are swapped on a regular basis.

Advertisers have found that **interstitials** (full-page ads that appear between page clicks) and **superstitials** (pop-up ads that load into a browser's storage area and may display even after the viewer has left the original site) are more likely to generate click-throughs. The same is true for **rich media**—those ads containing some type of animation, audio, video, or interactive programming— and **javamercials** (ads done with Java script). At the high end of banner advertising, technology from companies like Narrative Communications (Enliven) or Thinking Media creates **live banners**, which allow viewers to complete a survey, play a game, or print a coupon without clicking through to the advertiser's site.

Besides being more expensive to develop, both rich media and live banner ads may download slowly on low-speed modems, require broadband connections, clog heavily trafficked sites, or crash servers and browsers. Not all places accept such ads, including AOL. Check first. However, studies showing that interstitials have a 5% click-through rate, while rich media and live banners show 10% to 30% click-throughs, have encouraged major advertisers to spend the extra dollars on development.

What can you do with a limited budget? Consider the responses to a recent iconocast survey shown in Figure 8.24. Let people viewing your banner ads know the benefits of clicking on your site. Tempt them with information, contests, awards, colorful graphics, and just plain fun.

If the purpose of your ad is brand imaging, the click-through rate is much less critical. Recent studies show that the immediate recall level for an online ad is about the same as that for a television ad. According to the research, 40% of those who view a static (non-click-through) online ad will remember it, compared to 41% who view a 30-second TV commercial. Since online advertising reaches an audience that is active and engaged, some might argue that online ads will ultimately prove even more effective at brand imaging than TV.

The implications for your own advertising are obvious. First, if your concern is name recognition, less-expensive, nonlinking ads may be just as

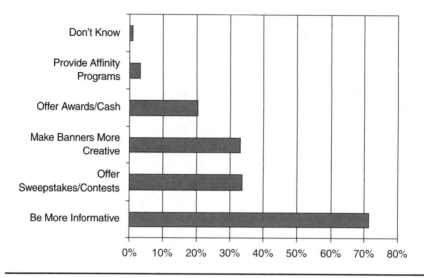

Figure 8.24. What makes users click more often? *http://www.iconocast.com/whatis/whatis.html.* Courtesy Iconocast, Inc.

cost-effective as linkable ones. Second, standard brand-imaging techniques, such as logo reinforcement or repeating themes across advertising venues, can be effective on static ads. Different techniques are required for a banner ad that generates a consumer click. Third, banner ads need strategic placement. For instance, image and message ads might be best on sites with huge audiences, with click-through ads on sites with more focused demographics. If you watch the ads being placed by major corporations on portal and search engine sites, you will see all these methods in action.

The top seven banner ads for one week, shown in Figure 8.25, represent a cross section of intriguing ads that encourage click-throughs or brand memory. Cyberatlas maintains archive files for each week's top banners at *http://209.249.142.16/nnpm/owa/NRpublicreports. topbannerweekly.* It also displays the top 50 banner ads for the prior month.

Online Sponsorships

Sponsorship of content sites is similar to advertising, but generally carries a lower price tag, a smaller link to your site and lower placement on

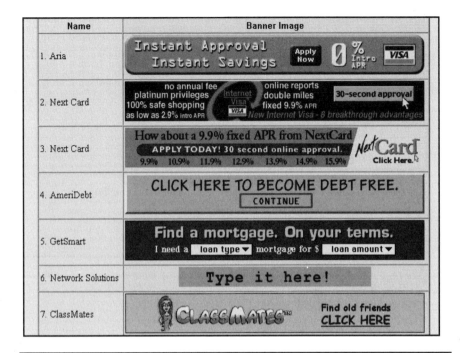

Figure 8.25. Top banner ads, *http://209.249.142.16/nnpm/owa/NRpublic reports.topbannerweekly.* Courtesy Net Ratings, Inc.

a page than a full advertisement. For an unusually large, explicit example, look at the sponsor button in Figure 8.26. Softer by nature than a banner ad, sponsorships are more comparable to the corporate ads on public radio or TV than to the 30-second spots on soap operas. As with links, be sure the content sites you sponsor relate to your field of business and that they draw your target audience.

An exclusive version of sponsorship, sometimes called **co-branding,** is a partnership with a content site. The link to your site is provided ostensibly as a source of additional data. Be cautious—there is some controversy about presenting advertising material as objective information.

Like ad rates, sponsorship rates are usually determined by a Web site's circulation and the number of impressions purchased. Sponsorships now account for about 27% of Web advertising purchases, compared to 56% for banner ads and 4% for interstitials as seen in Figure 8.18.

Figure 8.26.   Linkable sponsor logo, *http://www.teachertidbytes.com*. Courtesy Teach Tidbytes/Kid Info.

If you are creative with your selection of sites, you may find ways to locate your target market at a low cost or perhaps establish a barter arrangement. For instance, a CD store in a college town might sponsor student sites around the campus to reach its target market for world music.

Popular student-created sites might trade a sponsor ad in exchange for space on your server. (Student pages with heavy hit rates are often removed from university servers because they slow down the system.) You can find student sites by posting in news groups, advertising in college papers, or asking your part-time, student employees what sites are hot around campus. Students often put up highly creative sites, heavy in multimedia or pop culture. It's certainly easier to sponsor a student's site or e-zine than to create your own (unless it's your ordinary newsletter).

Consider sponsoring a not-for-profit site that's related to your business. For instance, a nursery specializing in native plants could sponsor some of the costs associated with a Web site for the local chapter of Tree People. A not-for-profit might agree to take a donation for every hit or registrant you receive from their site, instead of asking you to pay up front.

Figure 8.27 shows a program at GreaterGood.com (*http://www.greatergood.com*) that allows not-for-profits to benefit from doz-

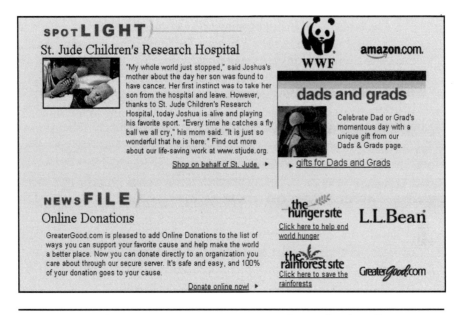

Figure 8.27.   An interesting way to sponsor not-for-profits, *http://www. greatergood.com/cgi.bin/WebObjects/greatergood*. Courtesy GreaterGood.com.

ens of shopping affiliate arrangements. GreaterGood splits the royalties it receives from merchants with its member not-for-profit organizations. You might want to seek out charity sites to become affiliates of yours. Similar sites include

- *http://www.givingboard.com*

- *http://www.iDonate.com*

- *http://www.iGive.com*

- *http://www.shopforchange.com*

- *http://www.thehungersite.com*

- *http://www.4charity.com*

The latest twist in advertising is "text sponsorship," the Web equivalent of buying a vowel on "Wheel of Fortune." Instead of a vowel, however, site owners sponsor a keyword. In this case, a text-based ad appears on the search results page across a network of destination sites and portals whenever a viewer enters a particular keyword in the search box. Pioneered by askJeeves, this auction-based approach opens bids at $5 per 1000 impressions.

Selling Advertising on Your Site

What if you want to reverse this process? You're not alone. The number of sites accepting ads increased by 38% during 1998, with the fastest growth in ads coming among shopping/transaction and classified sites. Advertising is only a modest source of revenue for most sites, as seen in a recent GVU survey (see Figure 8.28). If you're counting on major income, you'll need a site that generates a great deal of traffic or that delivers content reliably to a highly prized, selected demographic.

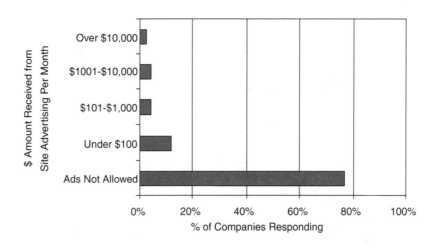

Figure 8.28. Advertising revenue received by sites, *http://www.gvu. gatech.edu/user_surveys/survey-1998-04/graphs/webmaster/q17.htm.* © 1994-1998, Georgia Tech Research Corporation. All rights reserved. Source: GVU's WWW User Survey at *www.gvu.gatech.edu/usersurvey.*

In preparation for selling ads, designate locations and sizes for ads in such a way that you can meet advertisers' demands for space above the fold without disturbing the look of your site. Confirm the amount of traffic your site currently draws. Make sure you can obtain meaningful statistics from your Web host. If its statistical package doesn't count unique users and requests for a specific file, supplement your host's statistics with HitBox, WebTrends, or some of the other tools described in Chapter 6. Any demographic information from user registration would help recruit advertisers.

Estimating charges for advertising on a small site is a bit tricky. Advertising prices are based on a combination of impressions from the desired audience and the frequency with which ads run. Start with a guess-timated CPM of $10 per month and adjust within a $5 to $70 range based on your traffic and the specificity of your demographics. If you're essentially a small local site, price yourself like one of the coupon advertisers, such as *http://www.nmcoupons.com.*

You can research ad pricing information by e-mailing a request to similar, but noncompeting, sites that accept ads. Or try to do a brief survey of potential advertisers you've identified to see what they pay to advertise on other sites and what they pay (CPM) for other media. Set up a trial rate card (media kit) with the types, sizes, and prices of ads you are willing to sell. Unless you expect to be a truly major advertising link, don't worry about ad rotation. (Major ad servers use special software to rotate ads, track impressions, and change creative content for each advertiser on a regular basis.)

Assume that you will need to discount rates for early advertisers and for those who sign up for longer terms. Once you have an experience base and an established viewer rate, selling online advertising will be more straightforward. If the process of finding buyers for your ad space seems too daunting, list your site for free on WebConnect's W.I.S.E. database of sites that accept advertising at *www.webconnect.com.* WebConnect is one of the few "open network" agencies that will sell space on sites not owned by its clients. An online media strategy and placement firm, WebConnect will place ads on sites with relatively light traffic as long as the sites deliver their clients' target audience. (The large agencies like DoubleClick look for sites drawing a minimum of 500,000 to one million impressions per month.)

Congo's Money Maker at *http://www.globalserve.net/~bloemink/ money/brokers.html* lists a number of other companies like Burst Media (*http://www.burstmedia.com*) or CyberLoft Hot Buttons (*http://*

www.cyberloft.com/buttons.html) that promise to sell your ad space. To be sure these companies can do this well, check with other clients before signing a long-term exclusive agreement. You could always try your own little ad auction on eBay. Finally, work with your Web developer and host to iron out any technical details.

Now that online and offline promotion has drawn viewers to your site, let's deal with the nitty-gritty issues that ensure your site will be private, secure, legal, and profitable. In the next chapter we'll address such concerns as maintaining user privacy, securing transactions, protecting intellectual property fromrip-offs, and doing business internationally.

9

Business Sense

It's time to move from the glittering promotion of Web sites to the nitty-gritty: privacy, security, legal issues, and doing business internationally. As you've already found, there is much more to marketing your business online than having a Web site. The functions discussed in this chapter not only protect your own business, they also enhance customer loyalty. By the end of this chapter, you'll know about

- Privacy issues.

- Digital signatures.

- Security for financial and personal data.

- Legal concerns, such as intellectual property, liability, and fraud.

- Marketing electronically worldwide.

The Privacy Zone

For good reason, Web visitors are concerned about protecting their personal information as well as their financial data and credit card numbers. In the past several years, there have been many stories in the press of companies selling personal profiles over the Internet. For instance, DoubleClick, the largest online advertising agency, collected data from millions of cookies placed by its clients' Web sites. It then bought an offline database company that profiles catalog shoppers and shared the data with them.

Several dot-coms that went out of business in early 2000 found themselves scrounging for assets to pay off creditors. Toysmart.com advertised the sale of its mailing lists and customer purchase databases in the *Wall Street Journal*. This was considered particularly egregious because the site, which had promised never to sell its lists, had posted an endorsement from Trust-e *(http://www.truste.com)*. Trust-e verifies over 2,000 sites for safeguarding customers' privacy. The resulting uproar led Disney, the owner of a controlling number of Toysmart shares, to buy up the lists and databases to keep them private. Toysmart wasn't alone; failed companies Boo.com and CraftShop.com also tried to sell their databases.

Sites may sell information they collect about users' whereabouts on the Web, often without the users' explicit knowledge. They also market data that users enter in registration programs, such as their demographic profile, buying habits, hobbies, and housing. Online list brokers now combine this data with standard mailing lists and sell it to anyone who pays for a self-service search. Of the 100 top shopping sites, more than half permit sharing information with third parties but make it easy for viewers to block data sharing; 11% actually make it difficult to prevent the sharing of personal data. No wonder some 64% of consumers told Jupiter Communications they didn't trust Web sites because of privacy concerns!

The most basic way to reassure customers doesn't require technology: Just develop and maintain a privacy policy. Inform site visitors of your policy on any registration or order screen with a simple statement such as, "We sincerely honor your online privacy. We will not sell or share your e-mail address or other personal information with any third party." The Federal Trade Commission (*http://www.ftc.gov/privacy/index.html*) publishes a sample privacy policy on its site.

Your policy should apply not just to e-mail, street addresses, and credit card numbers, but also to demographic information and purchase records. Would you want someone to be able to obtain a list of all the books, videos, or prescriptions you buy?

Kids Are Special

Because of concerns about collecting data from young children, Congress passed the Children's Online Privacy Protection Act in 1998. The law, which went into effect in April 2000, prohibits Web sites from collecting personal information—including names, e-mail addresses, and zip codes—from children under 13 without verifiable parental permission. Companies in violation are subject to thousands of dollars in fines. A scan by the FTC in July 2000 found that of the 75% of children's sites that collect data, about half still had a substantial compliance problem.

As it turns out, Congress might have stopped at too young an age. A recent study by the University of Pennsylvania's Annenberg School for Communication found that teenagers 13 to 17 were more than twice as likely as younger children to "spill the family beans" in exchange for a free gift.

Privacy Options

Perhaps stronger privacy protection will ensue when companies perceive revenue risk or worry about public relations disasters; some larger corporations have already created a new job slot for a chief privacy officer to protect themselves. Or perhaps technology will save the day. Because of the nuisance to consumers of dealing with different sites, the World Wide Web Consortium Platform for Privacy Preferences established P3P, a standard for computer-readable privacy policies. Once consumers select their desired level of privacy, their browser automatically scans only for sites that meet or exceed that level. Several companies, including PrivacyBot.com (*http://www.privacybot.com*), provide a $30 tool to make Web sites compliant with the P3P standard.

The Federal Trade Commission voted in July 2000 to allow Internet companies to regulate themselves within certain limits, such as notifying customers of Web profiling and giving viewers a chance to opt out of information collection. A group of e-mail direct marketing companies has proposed a similar plan for self-regulation aimed at reducing or banning spam. One thing is certain: If industry self-regulation and technology don't work, more laws will follow.

For other resources on privacy, check out these Web sites:

- *http://www.privacy.org*

- *http://www.epic.org*

- *http://www.w3.org/p3p*

- *http://www.privacypolicy.com*

For a list of online privacy tools, from cookie-blockers to e-mail encryption, go to *http://www.epic.org/privacy/tools.htm.*

Security: Raising the Barricades

Although the bigger risk with data may be misuse after transmission and collection, dishonest people do roam the Internet to obtain credit card information and make illegal charges. As a merchant, you face more risk than an individual does, since your files may contain the numbers of many cards. One **hacker** (someone with deep computer knowledge who accesses computers illegally) actually stole 300,000 card numbers from an online music retailer and demanded $100,000 in ransom not to post them!

How does a hacker intercept card numbers over the Internet? Messages are routed from one point to another, passing through many different servers, potentially all around the world. Because there is no control over the security of these different systems, a message may be subject to snooping or modification. A variety of technologies have been developed to make it difficult for hackers to intercept or understand some messages, particularly financial ones.

Digital Signatures

When it comes to transacting business, it's important that the person who receives the message be the person for whom it was intended and that the sender be the person who was supposed to send it (**authentication**).

You can authenticate (guarantee) orders with a digital signature, which is not a picture of a signature, but rather a mathematical formula that produces an individual answer. Thanks to legislation signed in 2000, a digital signature can now be used legally to sign a contract, as well as to verify personal identity and age, sign secure e-mail, or confirm credit card charges. Under the new legislation, businesses must confirm that their customers have the necessary technology and customers must opt in to use digitally signed agreements. Of course, the documents must be capable of being reproduced for later reference and all existing consumer protection laws apply.

To obtain a digital signature, a user supplies proof of identity offline to a digital ID company and receives a coded ID number in return. Depending on the company, it costs $5 to $15 annually for an individual ID. A server license runs $395 to $1295, depending on the level of security identification desired; under a host's server, the cost is $349 per licensee. VeriSign (*http://www.verisign.com/server/index.html*, shown in Figure 9.1), and Rhyton (*http://www.rhyton.com/support/oug/out-7-2.htm*) are two of many third-party vendors of digital ID products.

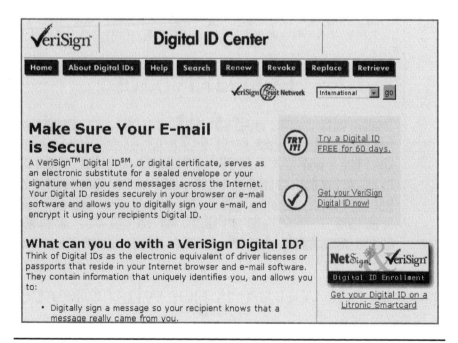

Figure 9.1. Digital ID vendor, *http://www.verisign.com/client/index.html*. Courtesy VeriSign, Inc.

Encryption and Firewalls

The next line of defense is data **encryption** (putting a message into hidden code). Public key cryptography, which is often used with digital signatures, pairs a public and private key, both of which are needed to encode and decode a message. (A **digital certificate** ties the signature and public key together.) The key holder encodes his or message with a private key; its matching public key is used to decode it and vice versa. Older encryption standards used only 50 characters; the newer standard, called strong encryption, uses a 128-bit key, making it almost impossible to unscramble the message. Even if an encrypted message is intercepted as it crosses the Internet, it cannot be read, as represented in Figure 9.2. The Digital Millennium Copyright Act of 1998 made it ille-

Figure 9.2. Encryption, *http://www.primefactors.com*. Courtesy Prime Factors, Inc.

gal to create or distribute devices that circumvent encryption codes or other means of security or copyright management for digital data.

A third defense is a **firewall**, a combination of hardware and software that separates a network into two or more parts to prevent unauthorized access. Your company may have firewalls on its internal computer network to make it difficult for people who access one part of shared information, such as a product database, to reach another, such as financial records. Your Web hosting service should have firewalls on its server. Good firewalls combined with regular checking for viruses can help ensure that your server stays up and running.

Hackers have succeeded in temporarily shutting down sites with coordinated "denial of service" attacks, which flood their targets with so many fake requests for information that sites can't respond. Such attacks hit ETrade, ZDnet, eBay, Amazon.com, CNN, Buy.com, and Yahoo! among other major sites in February 2000. If you run a large, attractive site, your best bet is to install protective software and to maintain an alert system that quickly identifies and bans requests issued from specific computers causing the "traffic jam."

Secure Socket Layers (SSLs)

Many browsers exchange secure transmissions across the Internet using a **Secure Socket Layer (SSL)**, a technology developed by Netscape to enable authenticated, encrypted communications. Users can tell that SSL is in use by looking for an icon on the page: Netscape 4.0 and higher shows a locked padlock; earlier versions showed an unbroken key; Internet Explorer shows a lock on the status bar. In addition, the URL on the secure page will generally change to one beginning with https://, with the "s" identifying a secure server.

Both the merchant's Web server and the customer's Web browser must use the same security system to exchange information. Because SSL can be used by all URLs that start with http, in most cases this is not a problem. SSL is included free on Netscape 2.0 or higher, Internet Explorer 3.0 or higher, and America Online 3.0 or higher. Users can set most browsers to provide notification when they connect between secure and nonsecure servers. If you intend to process transactions or secure data online, confirm that your Web hosting service offers SSL. One-time setup charges to use a secure server differ by host, ranging from free to $90, plus a VeriSign site license for $349.

SET: Secure Electronic Transactions

To resolve conflicts among different types of encryption and improve security beyond SSL, the major credit card companies (Visa, MasterCard, and American Express) worked with a number of technology partners (including GTE, IBM, Microsoft, Netscape, RSA, SAIC, Terisa Systems, and VeriSign) to establish a single standard for secure credit card transactions on the Internet.

Combining encryption, digital certificates, specific content parameters, and secure transmission technology, the **SET** (**Secure Electronic Transactions**) protocol protects consumers' bank card information worldwide when they shop on the Web. The protocol not only increases transaction security, it authenticates the identity of the card user. This is particularly valuable if your products might tempt children to use a parent's card without permission.

Many software developers and electronic security providers are now implementing the SET 2.0 release. Products that conform to this protocol will display a SET-compliant icon. If you're curious, check out the SET specification at

- *http://www.setco.org/faq_usr.html*

- *http://www.visa.com/*

- *http://www.mastercard.com/shoponline/set/*

Customers need two things to use SET: first, a digital ID (described earlier) for identification on electronic payment slips. Customers may request a digital ID from a card-issuing bank, from a digital ID company, or by filling out a form on a Web site. Rates start at $4.95 per year depending on the level of security desired.

Second, customers use the digital wallet described in Chapter 4 to make electronic purchases without the hassle of retyping their credit card information. Because multiple card numbers and addresses can be stored in a wallet, consumers can select both their payment method (confirmed by a password) and the shipping address with a simple click.

The MasterCard site (*http://www.mastercard.com/set/demo.html*) shown in Figure 9.3 illustrates the process of making a purchase under SET. At the virtual checkstand, customers select their digital wallet (click on the "Pay Using SET" icon). They are asked for confirmation on their digital payment slip. As in the tangible world, copies of the transaction are sent to the consumer, to the merchant, and to the bank card issuer.

Legalese

In its early days the Internet was an electronic Wild West. People grew fairly cavalier about **intellectual property** (any idea protected by copyright, trademark, or patent) and business practices. However, now that the Web has become such a popular commercial trading route, the chances of intellectual property infringement and incidences of fraud have skyrocketed. Everyone, from Web designers to merchants to ordinary users, must be far more cautious.

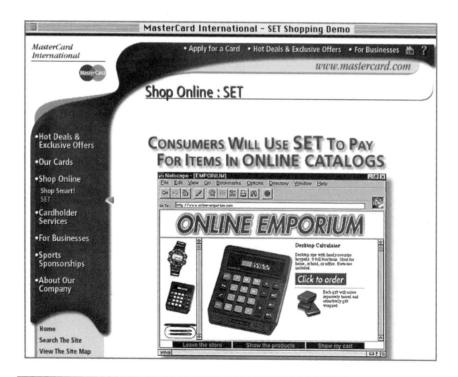

Figure 9.3. SET demo, *http://www.mastercard.com/shoponline/set/screen1. html*. Reprinted with permission of MasterCard International.

You need to protect your own online material as well as ensure that you do not misuse the property of others. Be sure that any agreement with a Web developer specifies that you own the copyright; otherwise, the developer will own the material that you've paid for. Some legal issues are still murky, given the ease of moving information on the Internet from one place to another and of downloading it to an individual's computer. In most—but not all—cases, downloading by an individual is considered fair use. But republishing copyrighted material on a commercial site without permission is a giant no-no. So is using someone else's copyrighted high-design buttons for navigation or incorporating another company's trademark in a domain name.

Trademarks

A trademark or service mark confers the exclusive right of use of a particular name or logotype within one or more specific classes of commercial activity. Recent court decisions have held that trademark rights apply to domain names. Legislation introduced in 1999 would make **cybersquatting** (i.e., registering someone else's trademark or a celebrity's personal name as a domain name with the intent to resell it at a profit) illegal. This applies internationally as well: The UN World Intellectual Property Organization recently finalized its rules against cybersquatting. You might also infringe a trademark if you use someone else's marks in your list of keywords, depending on the circumstances. A dealer carrying a trademarked product would have a legitimate use, whereas a competitor or unrelated business would not.

A name may be available in the InterNIC database but still be trademarked and therefore not acceptable for use in a particular category of goods or services. To determine trademark status and ownership, go to the free online search engine for the U.S. Office of Patents and Trademarks (PTO) (*http://tess.uspto.gov*) shown in Figure 9.4.

To trademark your own company or product name, you must file with the PTO at a cost of $325 per name per class of use. More information on what qualifies as a trademark and how to file is available from the PTO home page. Some states also maintain a trademark database for registration only within that state.

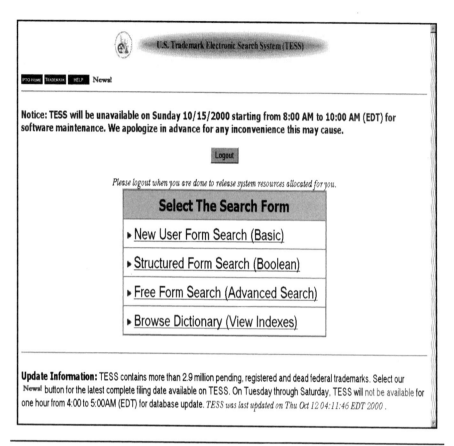

Figure 9.4. Patent and trademark search, *http://tess.uspto.gov.*

Many companies refer to their own trademarked names or the trademarks of other companies within their pages. Put the ® symbol after a registered trademark the first time it appears, and provide a notice of trademark ownership somewhere on your site. (The symbol ™ is used when a trademark application is pending.) Use a statement such as "Quaker is a registered trademark of the Quaker Oats Company." For multiple trademarks, use a blanket statement such as "All trademarks are the property of their registered owners" as ThirdAge does at *http://www.thirdage.com* (see Figure 9.5). Or have fun with the legalisms as Ragu does at *http://www.eat.com/site-credits.htm* (see Figure 9.6).

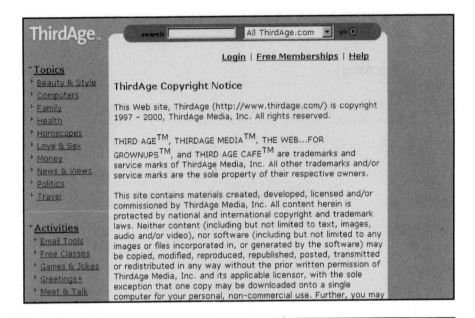

Figure 9.5. Sample trademark and copyright notice, *http://www.thirdagecom/copyright.html.* © 1997-2000 Third Age Media, Inc. All rights reserved.

Patents

A patent covers an underlying concept or idea that has been "reduced to practice." The Patent Office is under fire for its generous granting of "business method" patents. Some businesses contend the USPTO has awarded rights to broad claims that are "obvious" to practitioners in the field. For instance, the PTO has granted patents to Priceline for the concept of "reverse auctions" online and to Amazon.com for its "one-click" checkout process and its affiliate program software. While Amazon seems to be enforcing its patent selectively against its major competitors, it pays to be careful about using technology that isn't clearly marked as "freeware." Obtaining patents is an expensive and complex process; if you think you have a patentable invention, it's best to consult an intellectual property attorney.

Figure 9.6. Fun copyright notice, *http://www.eat.com/site-credits.htm*
Courtesy Lipton Investments, Inc. and Unilever USA, Inc.

Copyright

Copyright is a form of intellectual property protection that applies to
the design (look and feel) and content of audiovisual and print media. It
ensures that you own your particular expression of an idea. Copyright
covers text, data, icons, graphics, audio, video, music, and software
programs. Infringement is rampant on the Internet, which makes it easy

for anyone in the world to copy digital data. While copying MP3 music files and pirating online game software receive the greatest publicity, copyright infringement is also a potential issue with databases and other compiled information that is linked to or copied on other sites. The Web raises issues about intellectual property that lawyers worldwide will be arguing about for decades!

When a copyright notice appears on others' material, you cannot use it on your Web site without permission. (Certain forms of personal "fair use" are permitted; government material is not copyrighted.) If you wish to republish or mirror the contents of a site, obtain permission in writing first. Start by sending a letter with a permission form, such as the one in Figure 9.7. It is very possible that the owner will give you permission for free or that you can negotiate a reasonable fee. If you are unable to negotiate permission, consider linking to the owner's clearly identified site, allowing your Web viewers to jump to related information.

It's easy to copyright your own site. A simple notice consisting of the symbol © or the word Copyright or Copr., followed by the year of first publication and the name of the copyright owner (usually your company name), confers common law copyright protection. At a minimum, this notice should appear on your site; you can supplement it

---

The undersigned authorizes Maximum Press, 605 Silverthorn Road, Gulf Breeze, FL 32561 to print electronically, publish on its Web site at *http://www.maxpress.com*, and otherwise distribute throughout the world in all languages and versions, the following (information) (article) (screenshot) (art).

Material covered by this permission: (attached)

Please specify the credit line you would like to have appear:

Please sign this permission and enter your desired credit line. You may return it in the enclosed SASE or fax it back to:
Thank you.

Signature: Date:
Printed Name: Title:
Company
Address:
City: State: Zip:
T: F: E:

Figure 9.7. Copyright permission letter.

with a statement of rights and permissible uses as ThirdAge (*http://www.thirdage.com/copyright.htm*) did in Figure 9.5.

For a nominal fee of $30, you can obtain more complete copyright protection by registering your copyright with the Library of Congress (*http://lcweb.loc.gov/copyright*), shown in Figure 9.8). Registration gives you greater rights in court and allows you to collect additional damages and legal expenses if you prove that someone else has infringed your copyright.

To file for protection on the design of your site, print out Form VA (Visual Arts) from the Library of Congress Web site. As directed, attach printouts of relevant pages of your Web site to the application. To protect original information or an original compilation of information offered on your Web site, file Form TX (nondramatic literary works) as well. Read the information on the Library of Congress Web site carefully to determine whether other forms of copyright, such as for sound or audiovisual works, would be appropriate. Mail the completed forms and your check to the Library of Congress at the address shown. Within several months, you will receive official notice that your copyright has

Figure 9.8.   Library of Congress copyright page, *http://lcweb.loc.gov/copyright*.

been registered. Place copyright notices with other important legal documents in your safe deposit box or vault.

If you hire an outside Web designer or any other Web subcontractors, be sure their contracts give your organization the right to use any material they incorporate on your Web site. Make the contractors responsible for clearing ownership of whatever elements they obtain from another source; if your in-house staff acquires elements (e.g., photographs), then the responsibility is yours.

The contracts should also give your company all intellectual property rights to the contractors' work, which should be designated as "work for hire." If your page is designed in-house, your employment contracts should include a notice that your company owns the intellectual property of all work performed by employees.

Hyperlinks

Federal judges have ruled that linking without permission is acceptable as long as consumers understand whose page they are on, even if the link goes deep within a rival's site. Although it is not required, notifying another site when you are planning a link is good business practice. Because you offer visibility to them, you may be able to obtain an agreement for that site to link to you in exchange. Be careful, however, that you don't eliminate someone's identifying information, implying that you have created their work. Also, avoid manipulating a link to make it seem that others have endorsed your site or company, unless, of course, they have.

Nasty Beasties: Liability, Disclaimers, Fraud, and Other No-Nos

The Internet is still so new that no one is quite sure what liability vendors will face. You should simply assume that any liability you have off the Web, you also have on it. You can be just as liable for unsafe products, false advertising, or financial fraud as you are offline. Many Web sites post an online disclaimer and/or consumer license, similar to the one that appears on their packaging. ThirdAge uses a standard disclaimer, as shown in Figure 9.9.

Activities that are illegal off the Internet are illegal on it. For instance, you can't operate a pyramid scheme or other scams. The Federal

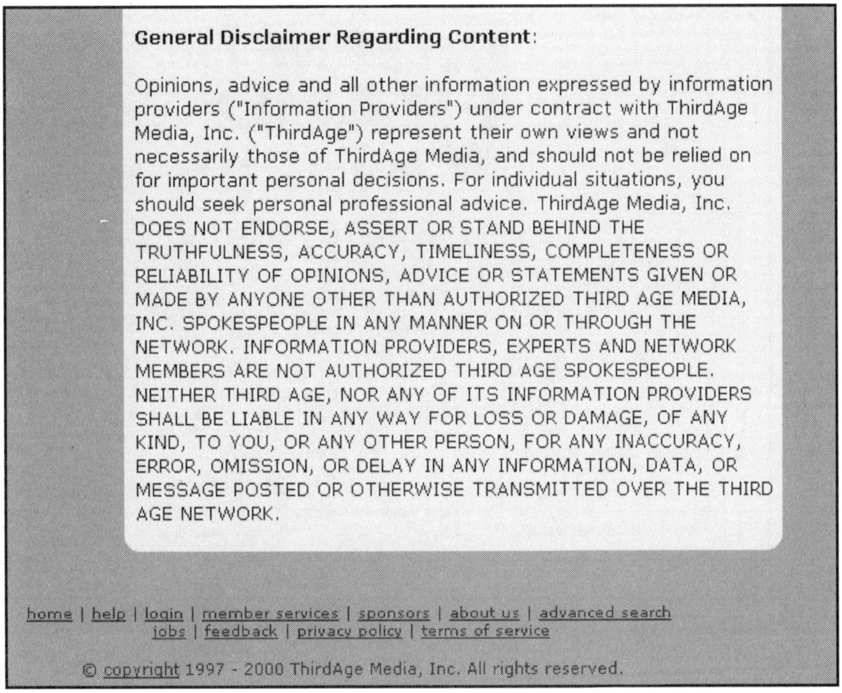

General Disclaimer Regarding Content:

Opinions, advice and all other information expressed by information providers ("Information Providers") under contract with ThirdAge Media, Inc. ("ThirdAge") represent their own views and not necessarily those of ThirdAge Media, and should not be relied on for important personal decisions. For individual situations, you should seek personal professional advice. ThirdAge Media, Inc. DOES NOT ENDORSE, ASSERT OR STAND BEHIND THE TRUTHFULNESS, ACCURACY, TIMELINESS, COMPLETENESS OR RELIABILITY OF OPINIONS, ADVICE OR STATEMENTS GIVEN OR MADE BY ANYONE OTHER THAN AUTHORIZED THIRD AGE MEDIA, INC. SPOKESPEOPLE IN ANY MANNER ON OR THROUGH THE NETWORK. INFORMATION PROVIDERS, EXPERTS AND NETWORK MEMBERS ARE NOT AUTHORIZED THIRD AGE SPOKESPEOPLE. NEITHER THIRD AGE, NOR ANY OF ITS INFORMATION PROVIDERS SHALL BE LIABLE IN ANY WAY FOR LOSS OR DAMAGE, OF ANY KIND, TO YOU, OR ANY OTHER PERSON, FOR ANY INACCURACY, ERROR, OMISSION, OR DELAY IN ANY INFORMATION, DATA, OR MESSAGE POSTED OR OTHERWISE TRANSMITTED OVER THE THIRD AGE NETWORK.

home | help | login | member services | sponsors | about us | advanced search
jobs | feedback | privacy policy | terms of service

© copyright 1997 - 2000 ThirdAge Media, Inc. All rights reserved.

Figure 9.9. Sample disclaimer notice, *http://www.thirdage.com/copy right.html.* © 1997-2000 Third Age Media, Inc. All rights reserved.

Trade Commission (*http://www.ftc.gov*), which received more than 19,000 consumer complaints about Internet fraud in 1999, has already warned more than 500 Web sites and filed lawsuits against 33 companies alleging online scams, such as illegal multilevel marketing schemes that focus on recruiting members, not selling products. The Commodity Futures Trading Commission took similar warning action against 1600 sites promoting get-rich-quick schemes.

Complaints of online fraud have escalated with the increase in online sales. According to the Internet Fraud Watch, a system maintained by the National Consumer's League (*http://www.fraud.org*, shown in Figure 9.10), complaints more than tripled between 1998 and 1999. Online auctions account for more than half the complaints (see Figure 9.11). Issues include whether an auction site can be held accountable for sell-

Internet Fraud Watch

1-800-876-7060

Internet Fraud Watch

Online services and access to the Internet provide consumers with a wide world of information, and sellers with a new way to promote their products or services. "Cybershopping," "banking online," and other conveniences will spur an increasing number of consumers to do business by computer. But crooks also recognize the potential of cyberspace. The same scams that have been conducted by mail or phone can now be found on the Internet, and new technologies are resulting in new ways to commit crimes against consumers.

That's why the Internet Fraud Watch was launched in March of 1996 enabling the NFIC to expand its services to help consumers distinguish between legitimate and fraudulent promotions in cyberspace and route reports of suspected fraud to the appropriate law enforcement agencies. Our thanks go to the organizations who have helped to support the Internet Fraud Watch.

Figure 9.10. Internet Fraud Watch, *http://www.fraud.org/internet/ intinfo.htm.* Courtesy Internet Fraud Watch, a program of the nonprofit National Consumers League.

ers who misrepresent their goods, or whether there are rings of people who bid up prices on each other's items.

If your Internet business falls into one of the categories in Figure 9.11, you might consider boosting consumer confidence by joining the Better Business Bureau Online (*http://www.bbbonline.org*). The Bureau allows members, who agree to certain methods of resolving customer disputes, to display the BBB logo on their sites. Customers can then check out your business history for customer complaints and see how they were resolved. Or offer to use a third-party online escrow service, such as *http:// www.safebuyer.com* or *www.iescrow.com*.

Merchants can be victims of online fraud as well as perpetrators. Businesses can be held liable for all or part of the cost of goods or services delivered even when customers are released from paying by credit card policies. To protect yourself, request address verification from your online credit card service and flag orders with different billing and shipping addresses. Be careful with orders from customers using free

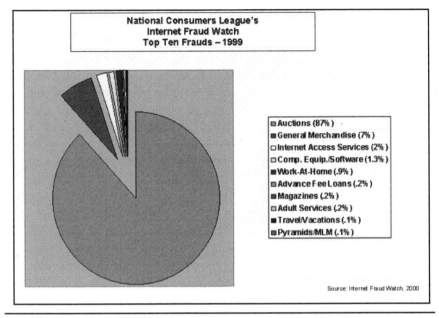

**National Consumers League's
Internet Fraud Watch
Top Ten Frauds – 1999**

▣ Auctions (87%)
▣ General Merchandise (7%)
▢ Internet Access Services (2%)
▢ Comp. Equip./Software (1.3%)
▣ Work-At-Home (.9%)
▣ Advance Fee Loans (.2%)
▣ Magazines (.2%)
▢ Adult Services (.2%)
▣ Travel/Vacations (.1%)
▣ Pyramids/MLM (.1%)

Source: Internet Fraud Watch, 2000

Figure 9.11. Top 10 online frauds in 1999, *http://www.fraud.org/graphics/
1999graphs/top10pie.gif*. Courtesy Internet Fraud Watch, a program of the
nonprofit National Consumer League.

e-mail accounts—they have a greater history of fraud. Fraud alerts for
merchants can be found in the newsletter Internet Scambusters, *http://
www.scambusters.org*.

On the Internet dissatisfied customers can fight back with bad publicity. Prior to the Internet, a happy customer was likely to tell three
other people; an unhappy customer would tell twenty. Now, an unhappy customer can tell millions by posting an anticompany Web site
or starting a negative discussion group. One company, Third Voice in
Redwood City, California, created a way for surfers—including dis-
gruntled customers—to paste a comment on any Web page; the comments can be viewed by others running the same software. The notes,
which can't be removed by the site owner, could easily become a matter
of embarrassment at the point of sale. There is even a National Consumer Complaint Center at *http://www.alexanderlaw.com/nccc*. If you
sell products, you might want to check their ratings on one of many
consumer review sites like *http://www.deja.com*.

Content and the First Amendment

The content of the Internet is covered by the First Amendment. However, in some recent cases, courts have considered online and Web hosting companies to assume the responsibility of publishers for what appears on pages they host. You can't sell alcohol, gambling chances, or pornographic material to minors online, but so far these laws have proved difficult to enforce. Pornography, in fact, is one of the most lucrative businesses on the Web, with online earnings for the adult entertainment industry topping $1 billion annually.

The Supreme Court has upheld a federal law aimed at limiting obscene material in e-mail as well as on Web sites. Many interest groups now demand that Web sites carry warnings if they contain material that might be objectionable, although not legally obscene, if seen by children. Some organizations provide their own lists of "indecent," violent, or hate-filled sites; others recommend the use of blocking and filtering software. In the wake of episodes of school violence in 1999, ISPs will provide a link to a new site that offers technology for restricting children's access to sites, monitoring sites visited, and limiting the time children are able to spend online.

There is bound to be a great deal of continuing litigation about these issues. If you're not sure what you want to do is legal, consult an attorney. Background information on computer law and current cases is available at such sites as The Computer Law Association (*http://www.cla.org*) or the American Bar Association Committee on the Law of Cyberspace at *http://www.abanet.org/buslaw/cyber/home.html*. Or contact the Electronic Freedom Foundation at *http://www.eff.org*, which seeks to protect the open exchange of ideas and expression on the Internet.

Insurance

One way to reduce your exposure to all these issues is to obtain insurance for your Web operations. Under the heading "Internet insurance," insurance companies have started to offer policies that address the various legal risks of doing business online. They may cover expenses or lost business due to hacker attacks, product liability claims for an item sold on your site, or your liability for infringing on another firm's trademark. Check your current business owner policy for coverage—most do not cover intellectual property issues, which generally appear only in professional liability policies.

Doing Business Internationally

Online services and the Internet are not restricted to the United States and Canada; it is the World Wide Web, after all. U.S. dominance is expected to fade quickly. Experts believe that 66% of Web users (up from 49%) and 40% of e-commerce revenue (up from 10%) will be outside the United States by 2005. There will be lots of opportunity to sell to the global market.

The immediate growth of online commerce is likely to be greatest in Europe, where Internet access is expanding quickly, the new Euro simplifies electronic currency exchange, and the European Union has lowered barriers to commerce. Don't make the mistake of treating Europe as a monolith, however. The Scandinavian countries are fully and enthusiastically wired, with Britain, Switzerland, the Netherlands, and Germany close behind. However, France, which has had Minitel, its own non-Web online service, since 1981, is just now reaching the 10% mark in Internet use. Southern and Eastern European countries lag the others.

Asian countries are recovering from their economic downturn in the late 1990s, but massive Internet presence is several years downstream. Internet use and electronic commerce in Latin America is just starting to pick up, but is growing faster than any other area of the world. Once again, there is great variation with Brazil, Mexico, and Argentina having the largest online populations. The developing world is still on the far shore of the digital divide, although the G-8 summit in July 2000 pledged to create a "dot force" to expand Internet access and reduce its cost in developing nations. After the United States, Japan and Germany have the greatest number of online users, as seen in Figure 9.12.

The Global Marketplace

Let's consider what the world market looks like in more detail. Barely 50% of all those accessing the Internet speak English as their first language, about 24.4% speak one of the European languages, and the remaining 25.3% speak an Asian or other language (Figure 9.13). The

Rank	Nation	Internet Users (millions)	Share %
1.	United States	135.7	36.2
2.	Japan	26.9	7.18
3.	Germany	19.1	5.10
4.	UK	17.9	4.77
5.	China	15.8	4.20
6.	Canada	15.2	4.05
7.	South Korea	14.8	3.95
8.	Italy	11.6	3.08
9.	Brazil	10.6	2.84
10.	France	9.0	2.39
11.	Australia	8.1	2.16
12.	Russia	6.6	1.77
13.	Taiwan	6.5	1.73
14.	Netherlands	5.4	1.45
15.	Spain	5.2	1.39
	Worldwide Total	**374.9**	**100**

Figure 9.12. Forecast top 15 nations in in Internet use by year-end 2000, *http://cyberatlas.internet.com/big_picture/geographics/article/0,1323,59911_151151,00.html.* Reprinted with permission. © 2000 Internet.com, LLC. All rights reserved.

	Internet access (in M)	% of world's online pop.	Internet access 2003 (est. in M)	Total pop in 2003 (est. in M)
English	172.3	50.3%	230	322
Non-English	163.7	49.7%	696	5,630
Total World	336.0	100%	926	5,952
European Languages (non-English)	100.6	24.4%	223	1,089
Asian & All Other Languages	63.7	25.3%	473	4,541

Figure 9.13. Percent of world population with Internet access by major language groups, *http://www.glreach.com/globstats.* Courtesy Global Reach.

distribution of languages appears in Figure 9.14. By 2001, non-English speakers will predominate.

Although many people in Europe and Asia speak English as a second language, they prefer to access the Web in their native language.

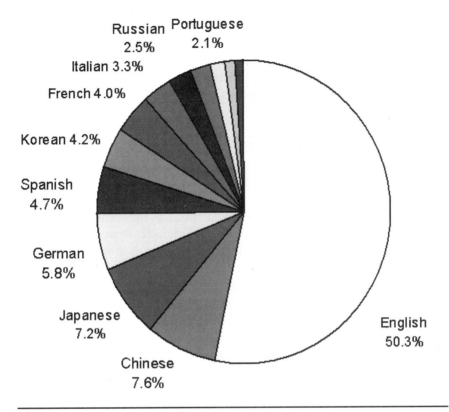

Figure 9.14. Online language populations August 2000, *http://www.glreach. com/globstats.* Courtesy Global Reach.

According to the marketing company Global Reach, only 32% of European Web surfers consult the Web in English at all. How are you going to sell to them? As former German chancellor Willy Brandt put it, "If I'm selling to you, I speak your language. If I'm buying, dann müssen Sie Deutsch sprechen" [then you must speak German].

Try to translate several key pages of your Web site into the target language(s), and promote language-specific gateways to your site in each country. Companies like Global Reach (*http://www.glreach.com*) assert that this way you can raise the number of non-native English speakers visiting your site from 15% to 50% or more.

Although North America currently dominates direct online sales, that too is changing, with total revenues from European e-commerce estimated to jump from $16.8 billion in 1999 to $425 billion by 2003. Jupiter Communications anticipates explosive growth this year in European B2C spending in the areas of travel, computers and electronics, groceries, books, apparel, music, and other categories. By comparison, Latin American online spending is projected at less than $10 billion by 2005, with an emphasis on personal computers, travel, groceries, and books.

Global How-To

If your product or service has international appeal, you will need to think about **localizing** your products and info-tools as well as creating multilingual versions of your Web site. Localization addresses cultural issues, offers local contact points, and includes items of country-specific relevance, such as a local singing star on a site that sells CD-ROMs. It also recognizes that different countries may require different marketing, pricing, and payment strategies.

Even encryption standards, consumer protection, and privacy policies differ from country to country. The European Union's Data Protection Directive, for instance, is far more restrictive than U.S. policy. It limits collection of personal information to specific purposes and prohibits data disclosure without explicit permission. Residents of the Mediterranean countries in particular are reluctant to share private information online, regardless of any policy protections. At least a dozen organizations are trying to deal with international distinctions on everything from the length of time for buyers to change their minds about online purchases to the publicizing of an unconditional refund policy, from the use of comparative advertising to the enforceability of digitally signed contracts.

Multilingual Sites

If you're not certain where to start, target just a few countries at a time. Begin perhaps with Japan and Germany, the countries outside the United States with the greatest number of Internet users. Add Spanish and French versions when you can afford them. Major computer dealers, such as Apple, Dell, Cyberian Outpost, and Cisco have taken the lead in international marketing. Dell Computer, for instance, has unique Web sites for 82 countries in 21 different languages, and 34 of those sites conduct e-commerce. If you have a global presence, let people know quickly, as DoubleClick does in Figure 9.15 (*http://www.doubleclick.net*). Major multinationals are not the only ones out there. Look at Spyzone (*http://*

Figure 9.15. Displaying international options, *http://www.doubleclick.net.* Courtesy DoubleClick.

www.spyzone.com) or Eagle Machinery Ltd. (*http://www.eagle machinery.co.uk*).

Many European companies routinely use multilingual Web sites to build sales; see Swiss Army Knives (*http://www.victorinox.ch*), Floritel (*http://www.floripro.com*), or Damart (*http://www.damart.com*). The screen shots in Figures 9.16 a-d and 9.17 a-d show SpyZone's splash screens and Floritel's fully translated sites in four languages.

A number of companies offer site translation and localization services. You can expect to pay $50 to $80 per Web page for translation, though many companies offer special packages for multiple languages or multiple pages. Take a look, for instance, at Global Reach (*http:// www.glreach.com/GR/trans.html*) or Intertrans at *http:// www.wetranslate.com.*

Localization Services

Localization might include anything from maintaining a virtual overseas office with a local voice-mail/fax contact point (an international version of MailBoxes Etc.) to advising on culturally relevant content. Should your product be positioned differently since your competition differs? What about pragmatic issues? Do you need to register your URL with your target country's domain name? What about trademark registration elsewhere? Is your product known by another name in other places? You may have to accept a 56-bit encryption instead of 128-bit "strong encryption." Is this acceptable? Do you need to speak with a company like Baltimore Products (*http://www.zergo.com*) that specializes in global security?

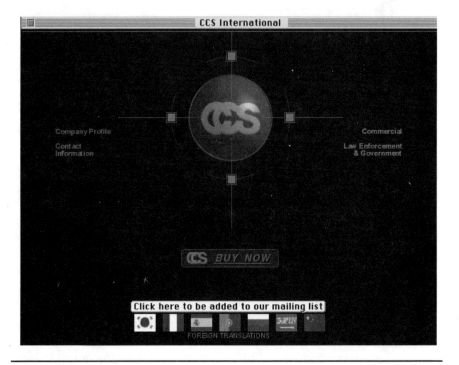

Figure 9.16.(a)   Spyzone English splash screen, *http://www.spyzone.com*. Courtesy C.C.S. International, Ltd. and the Counterspy Shops of Mayfair, London.

Figure 9.16.(b-d)   Spyzone splash screens in three other languages (Chinese, Arabic, and Korean), *http://www.spyzone.com/foreign/index.html*. All three images courtesy C.C.S. International, Ltd. and the Counterspy Shops of Mayfair, London.

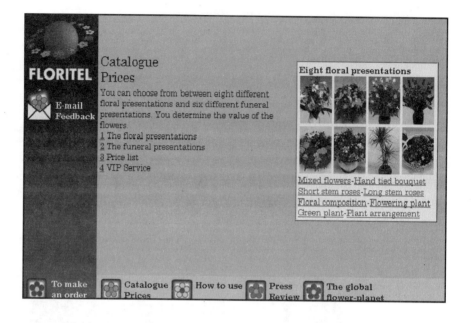

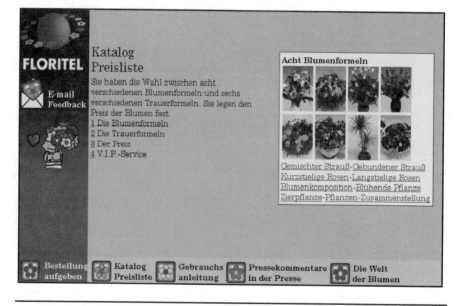

Figure 9.17. (a-b) Floritel, English and German versions, *http://www.floritel.com/En/index.html?* and *http://www.floritel.com/De/index.html?* Courtesy Floritel.com.

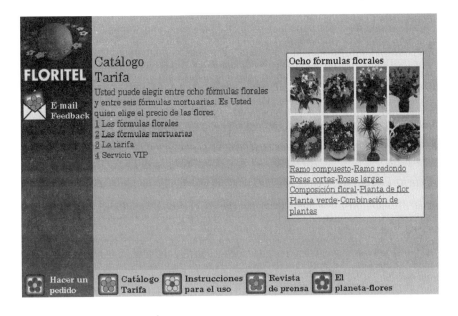

Figure 9.17. (c-d) Floritel, Spanish and French versions, *http://www.floritel. com/Es/index.html?* and *http://www.floritel.com/Fr1/index.html?* All images courtesy of Floritel.com.

Payment and Shipping

From a practical point of view, you must also consider how you will handle payment and delivery. Can you consolidate pricing to a single price per item and then add shipping, tariffs, and local taxes by country? That will make it easier to handle pricing through an electronic checkstand. What about currency exchange instead of insisting on dollars? For amounts over $10, the simplest solution is to accept credit cards. However, not all countries are credit card oriented. Europeans, especially Scandinavians and Germans, prefer debit cards like the Eurocard, COD, or billing for check payment. You might want to explore other options in international currency exchange, such as the Virtual Trading Desk and other payment options offered by Thomas Cook (*http://www.fx4business.com*).

Delivering goods in a timely manner at a reasonable price is a difficult problem overseas. Your options will vary by shipping location, size, weight, and type of product.

International Search Engines and Indexes

Major search engines like Yahoo offer country-specific engines for Canada, Europe (Denmark, France, Germany, Italy, Norway, Spain, Sweden, the United Kingdom, and Ireland), the Pacific Rim (Australia and New Zealand, Hong Kong, Japan, Korea, Singapore, and Taiwan), Asia (in English and Chinese), and Latin America (in Spanish). Some of the many other international search engines are shown in Figure 9.18. More can be found at *http://www.glreach.com/eng/GR/regis.html*, along with other resources organized by country.

International Promotion Services

Many companies offer to promote your site in your target market in other languages and countries. They will submit your Web page to international indexes and search engines in your target language. To be listed on many of those sites, you must translate at least a localized page, a home page, or a one-page summary of your site, along with keywords, categories, and page descriptions.

Most offer Web promotion services besides index listings: local domain name registration if desired, monitoring search engine rankings, optimizing pages in the target language to improve placement, strategic linking, and banner advertising. These services will also handle a variety of Internet marketing tasks off the Web, such as posting to

Name	Region/Language	URL
Alta Vista Canada	Canada/English	*http://ww.altavistacanada.com*
Alta Vista France	France/French	*http://www.i3d.qc.ca/*
Alta Vista Germany	Germany/German	*http://altavista.de/*
Ananzi	South Africa	*http://www.ananzi.co.za*
AusIndex	Australia	*http://www.ausindex.com*
El Faro (the lighthouse)	Spain/Spanish	*http://www.apali.com*
EuroFerret	Europe	*http://www.euroferret.com*
Euroseek	Europe	*http://www.euroseek.net*
Globe Page	Asia/Eng. Chinese	*http://www.globepage.com*
Heuréka	Hungary/ Hungarian	*http://heureka.hungary.com/*
In2 Ireland	Ireland	*http://www.iol.ie/~kasst/ in2ireland/*
India Search Engine	India	*http://www.indiaseek.com/*
Italian Spider	Italy	*http://rango.plugit.net*
Lokace	France/French	*http://195.242.78.15/ or http://www.lokace.com*
Matilda	Australia	*http://www.aaa.com.au/*
MOSHIx2	Japan/ Japanese, English	*http://www.moshix2.net/*
Nordic Web Index	Scandinavia, Iceland	*http://nwi.dtv.dk/index_e.html*
Radar	International/ English, Spanish	*http://www.radar.com.mx/*
Search NZ	New Zealand	*http://www.searchnz.co.nz*
Search NL	The Netherlands	*http://www.Search.NL/*
Sesna	Ukraine	*http://www.uazone.net/sesna/*
Simmany	Korea/Korean	*http://simmany.chollian.net/*
Swiss Search	Switzerland/ English, German	*http://www.search.ch/*
TechnoFind	Singapore	*http://www.technofind.com.sg/ index.html*
Ugabula	Latin America, Spain/Spanish	*http://ugabula.com/*
UKMax	United Kingdom	*http://www.ukmax.com/*
WebIndex	Greece	*http://www.webindex.gr/*
Zebra	South Africa	*http://beta.zebra.co.za/zebra-cgi/webdriver*

Figure 9.18. Some international search engines, *http://www.glreach.com/eng/ GR/regis.html.* Courtesy Global Reach.

newsgroups and forums in the target language. They will prepare autoresponders, handle mailing list submissions, participate in chat rooms, and answer your e-mail.

You can try to do some of this yourself using automatic translator software, including free packages at *http://www.dictionary.com/translate/* and *http://www.tranexp.com:2000/InterTran,* or multilingual proofing software like Microsoft's checker for 30 languages (*http://www.microsoft.com/office/multilingual/proofing.htm*), but beware. Such solutions, while inexpensive, can lead to some hilarious errors—and also to some offensive ones. (For a funny example, check out *http://babelfish.altavista.com.*) You might be better off with an e-mail translation service at $2 a pop.

International Advertising

Both international ad agencies like ClickExperts (*http://www.clickexperts.com*) and audit firms like I/PRO (*http://www.engage.com/ipro*) are now actively serving the Latin American and European communities. For additional international support, try some of these sites:

- *http://www.internationalworkz.com*

- *http://www.glreach.com*

- *http://www.asia-links.com*

- *http://www.blueskyinc.com*

International Resources

You must be able to answer some essential questions before you can do business internationally. Are you set up for export? Do you know how to find distributors in other countries? Handle letters of credit? Process items for customs and international shipping?

Take advantage of free or low-cost government programs to put your tax dollars to work. For information, check out the Office of International Trade at the Small Business Administration site, shown in Figure 9.19 (*http://www.sba.gov/oit.* Try a local international trade council, visit the International Trade Administration Web site shown in Figure 9.20 (*http://www.ita.doc.gov*) attend a Department of Commerce ex-

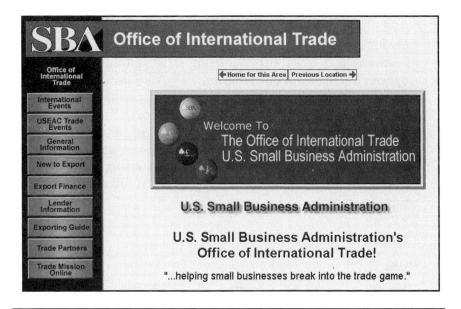

Figure 9.19. Resource site for international trade, *http://www.sba.gov/oit.*

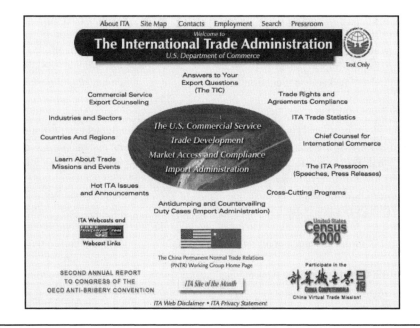

Figure 9.20. Resource site for international trade, *http://www.ita.doc.gov.*

port training session, or check out some of the other sites listed in Figure 9.21. Most of these sites offer extensive information, including publications, links to export counseling services, trade statistics, financing options and educational programs. The Department of Commerce offers a low-cost "virtual booth" at its cybermall, E-Expo USA, for as little as $100 per year. For more information, go to *http://e-expousa.doc.gov/ExpoWeb2.nsf/pages/Registration.*

We have now covered both the glamorous and the gritty parts of creating, maintaining, promoting, and protecting your Web site. Let's have some fun in the next chapter looking at successful sites you might want to emulate.

Name	URL
Dept. of Commerce (DOC) homepage	*http://www.doc.gov*
DOC, Bureau of Export Administration	*http://www.bxa.doc.gov*
DOC, E-Expo (electronic trade show)	*http://www.e-expousa.doc.gov/ ExpoWeb2.nsf/pages/ UsefulLinks*
DOC, International Trade Administration	*http://www1.usatrade.gov/ website/website.nsf*
DOC, Trade Compliance Center	*http://www.mac.doc.gov*
DOC, Trade Information Center	*http://www.ita.doc.gov/td/*
*tic*Export-Import Bank	*http://www.exim.gov*
Global Marketing Discussion List	*email: globalmarketing-request@listserve.net* with word Subscribe in body and subject of message.
National Trade Data Bank	*http://tradeport.org*
Small Business Administration, Office of International Trade	*http://www.sba.gov/oit*
Stat-USA/Internet	*http://www.stat-usa.gov*
Trade Fairs International	*http://www1.usatrade.gov/ Website/epc.nsf*
U.S Census Bureau, Foreign Trade Statistics	*http://www.census.gov/foreign trade/www*
U.S. Customs Service, Automated Export System	*http://www.customs.ustreas.gov*

Figure 9.21. Government trade resources.

10

Model Web Sites for Internet Marketing

Repeat this mantra: "Before adding a new feature or page to my site, I will see what others have done on the Web." You might want to bring the model Web sites in this chapter as examples when you meet with your Web developer. Remember, the more information you provide about sites you like and dislike, the more you will be satisfied with the way your site turns out. Make sure that every feature you include benefits both your customers and your company.

Each successful business site illustrates a different aspect of marketing on the Internet. We've already looked at multimedia sites, so the ones in this chapter focus on presentation style, content, and marketing techniques appropriate for the goals and target audiences of each business. All the sites in this chapter have something to sell, but not all of them sell on the Internet.

View these sites online to see how well their design matches their overall business concept. Flow through their Web pages as if you were a customer. Then look at the sites from the standpoint of your own product or service. How could you adapt their ideas? Can you borrow their marketing wisdom? When you check these sites, the pages may have changed from the ones presented here. Study the changes to see whether you can determine the reason they were made.

Most business people are generous with advice and experience. If you find a noncompeting site that uses a marketing technique, such as a registry, that interests you, e-mail the owner to ask how well it works. You'll be surprised at the useful information a noncompeting owner will provide and the mistakes you can avoid as a result.

We'll follow the sequence of the business process as we look at sites that

- Draw customers to a cyber-storefront on the basis of information, service, or original artistry.

- Hold people on the site and bring them back through online communities, continually changing trade opportunities, or real-time, interactive teaching.

- Exemplify good marketing by offering giveaways, providing product detail, or making purchases easy with a good catalog.

- Maintain a strong customer focus that adds value through customized product or personal contact.

- Create an innovative marriage of traditional service businesses with cyberspace.

Getting Customers in the Door

This is basic. Even in cyberspace you can't sell something to a customer who doesn't know your business exists. As you've learned, you need to have a payoff for viewers who find your site by creating a desirable destination, one that offers the information, product, or service a customer seeks.

Turning Offline Insecurity into Online Service: Wine.com at *http://www.wine.com*

Wine.com is one of the most venerable sites on the Web. It evolved from VirtualVin.com, the site of an early Web pioneer, Master Sommelier Peter Granoff. Originally an information-based site that answered the age-old question that befuddles every nervous host ("Do I serve red or white?"), Wine.com has become a premier e-tailing site that does everything right.

With a reputation for demystifying wine and making it more accessible through simple and helpful information, the site draws both new and repeat visitors. The most popular feature remains Peter's Tasting Chart, seen in Figure 10.1, which analyzes wines by seven key taste attributes. The chart, which makes it easy to select a wine that fits the menu, is also used by the team at Wine.com to profile each of thousands of wines selected for the site.

Other value-added information ranges from wine trivia to serious discussions of oenology. This site also earns high marks for easy navigation, a well-structured transactional component, and its ability to notify customers of sale items, related gourmet foods, or other fine wines based on their purchases. Most important, Wine.com focuses on maintaining customer loyalty through a positive online experience. Given the high expense of acquiring new visitors to a Web site, every Web owner could learn from their emphasis.

Finding a Need and Filling It: Theatre.com

Another Internet pioneer, Theatre.com (see Figure 10.2), formerly known as BuyBroadway, was the first Broadway souvenir merchandiser on the Web. Dubbed "The Macy's of theater," BuyBroadway started selling online in March 1997. Theatre.com is now a one-stop site for information, schedules and ticket purchases to hundreds of shows around the country, as well as on the Great White Way.

Founder Toby Simkin writes that the site's focus is consumer marketing: "driving consumers to the theatre and putting people in seats." The Web site boasts "an extensive consumer news service focused on major theatre markets, writing stories that motivate users towards ticket purchase." The stories include links for both ticketing and merchandising. The site also has a search engine that scans over 125 Web sites, stores, news groups, and other listings.

To further commitment to the site and drive repeat users, Theatre.com has a special membership community (the Circle Club) that offers ticket and souvenir discounts, e-mail newsletters, and access to "members-only" portions of the Web site. The online store supplements standard theater memorabilia with exclusive items available only on the site. Promotion includes active partnerships with CompuServe, AOL, and Avantgo.

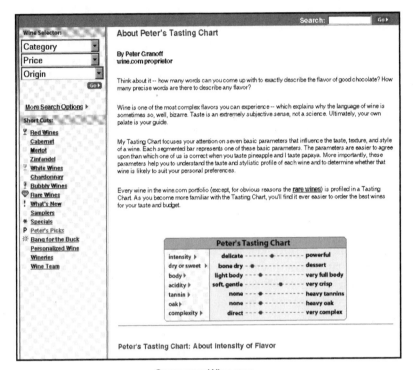

Company: Wine.com

Year Founded: 1994

Web Site First Established: 1995

Gross Annual Revenues: NA

Annual Revenues from Web Site: NA

Percentage of Revenues from Sales on Web: NA

Site Start-Up Cost: NA

Site Maintenance Cost (monthly): NA

Most Successful Feature of Site: Peter's Tasting Chart, which profiles thousands of wines by seven taste attributes.

Lesson Learned: It's expensive to drive new customers to the site, so it's absolutely critical that every customer experience with Wine.com be outstanding—we will succeed only by creating delighted life-long customers.

Advice about Marketing on the Web: "Be specific about what sustainable value you are providing in the marketplace versus every other potential competitor."

Laura Grams, Public Relations Manager

Figure 10.1. Turning offline insecurity into online service, *http://www. wine.com.* Courtesy Wine.com, Inc.

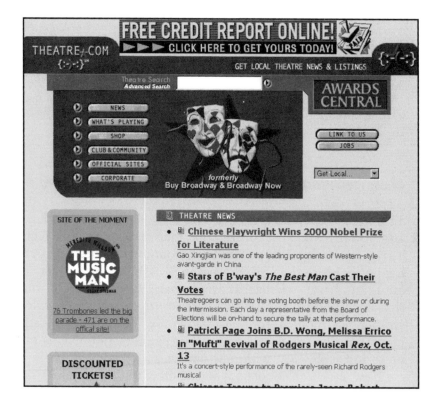

Company: BroadwayOnline.com, Inc.

Year Founded: 1995

Web Site First Established: 1996

Gross Annual Revenues: $1M–$5M

Annual Revenues from Web Site: $2M

Percentage of Revenues from Sales on Web: 100%

Site Start-Up Cost: $45,000

Site Maintenance Cost: NA

Most Successful Feature of Site: Official and exclusive Broadway show content and news.

Advice about Marketing on the Web: "It's not about ecommerce—it's about content, community and commerce."

Toby Simkin, Founder

Figure 10.2. Finding a need and filling it, *http://www.theatre.com*. Courtesy Broadway Online.com, Inc.

Simkin has a long-standing fascination with technology. He previously created a theater bulletin board called ShowCall in 1989, a theatrical link exchange in 1994, and the first Broadway show Web site in 1995 (for Victor/Victoria).

In addition to its own Web site, Theatre.com hosts, manages, markets, and maintains over 130 Broadway show and official organization sites using its own server farm and Internet connectivity.

Too Cool: New York Cabbie at *http://www.nycabbie.com/*

This site is a keeper! Trip once over New York Cabbie in Figure 10.3 and you'll bookmark forever this marriage of art and technology. The eye-catching, cab-yellow background with checkerboard trim is hypnotic. More than 97 photographs of New York streets by artist (and taxi driver) Michael L. Krygier are viewable in glorious intensity. Each photo is well worth the 20- to 45-second download time (with a 56K modem) for a 90K JPEG file. To keep downloading to a minimum, the site wisely offers four pages of thumbnails that blow up to full screen art, with new photos added constantly.

New York Cabbie contains several other features that keep people returning to the site: a Dear Cabby advice column, a series of true taxi stories from around the world, and a set of Taxi Tips for both battle-scarred New Yorkers and harried tourists. Photographic prints are sold online in three sizes at prices ranging from $60 to $160. To complete an online purchase by credit card, the order page links to *http://www.ccnow.com*.

Krygier has recently added several new features: NYCabbie Billboards, which feature a limited number of ads that "don't" take away from the artistic integrity of the site" the way standard banners would; links to several books about New York as an Amazon.com affiliate; several links to purchase taxi toys; and plans for a bulletin board called "Hail Cabbie."

Apart from the pleasure it provides viewers, the site provides recognition for Krygier as an artist. In essence, Krygier's site has become a multimedia performance piece. As he describes it, "I was thinking of making a coffee table book when I woke up one night thinking 'Internet.' I had never even seen the Internet, just heard about it. The whole site [was] intuition. It [came] very fast."

It had to be intuition: Before the site went up, Krygier didn't own a computer. He now uses WebTV to answer e-mail, which has become so voluminous that he plans to combine the story of his Web site with

Company: New York Cabbie

Year Founded: 1998

Web Site First Established: 1998

Gross Annual Revenues: Less than $1M

Annual Revenues from Web Site: NA

Percentage of Revenues from Sales on Web: NA

Site Start-Up Cost: $25,000

Site Maintenance Cost (monthly): $900

Most Successful Feature of Site: Its all-around visual impact.

Lesson Learned: Information is worth dollars. Don't give ideas away for free.

Advice about Marketing on the Web: "Be creative, simple, and focused with a strong visual appeal; always strive to improve your Web site."

Michael Krygier, Artist and President

Figure 10.3. Too cool, *http://www.nycabbie.com.* © 1999 MLK (tps); Web master, Paul Wallace.

his photos in the still-dreamed-of book. His friend and Webmaster, Paul Wallace, handles layout and programming, while Krygier provides the images and content. To establish the site, Krygier obtained financial backing from a patron, Thomas Savitsky. He has now created a sister site, TheSavyCabby.com, which he built using WebTV's PageBuilder feature.

New York Cabbie is an ideal example of the power of offline promotion. Following the site's announcement on Yahoo! and other search engines, the BBC in Scotland called for a radio interview; BBC TV also featured the site on their morning show. Other awards followed quickly, capped by a feature story in the Sunday City section of the New York Times on February 14, 1999. As the story cascaded through the media, HotLink lists, and word-of-mouth, traffic to the site zoomed from a few hundred to over 117,000 hits. More than 200 reviews of the site have appeared around the world.

Krygier's only paid advertising consisted of several hundred 5" × 8" reproductions of the Broadway photograph (#8) on the site that he occasionally mails out. He also printed 300 wallet-sized, laminated veredsions of the photo with the New York Cabbie logo to hand out to his passengers. This site is proof positive that you don't have to spend a fortune on advertising as long as you offer something unique that people want to see.

Hold onto Them Once You Have Them

Okay, you've caught your audience's attention. Now you want to reinforce their interest. Give them a reason to stay on the site and to return often. The techniques are limited only by your imagination, especially when you take advantage of the Internet's unique features: real-time communication, interactivity, and the ability to match fluid pools of buyers and sellers.

A Community of Cars: Wrenchead.com at *http://www.wrenchead.com*

A venture-financed, dot-com startup, Wrenchead's multipurpose site, shown in Figure 10.4, combines automotive interest with entertainment. The unusual combination builds a loyal (there's that word again) community of users who participate in online chats and forums about cars, racing, parts, and repairs. Simultaneously, the site delivers a dedicated niche audience to advertisers and distributors of products, services and events.

The Wrenchead community pairs the "do-it-yourself" crowd with professional mechanics to get advice interactively. It's "Click & Clack: The Tap-it Brothers" online, with a world of brothers and lots more

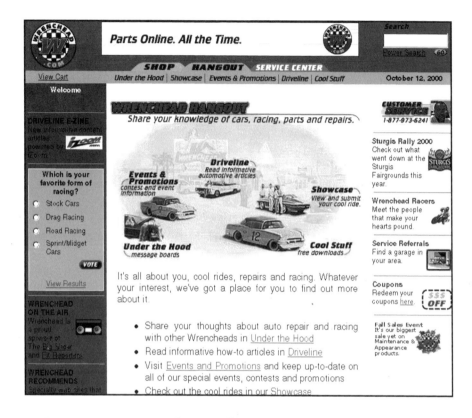

Company: Wrenchead.com

Year Founded: February 1999

Web Site First Established: June 1999

Gross Annual Revenues: $5M–$20M

Annual Revenues from Web Site: $5M–$20M

Percentage of Revenues from Sales on Web: 100%

Site Start-Up Cost: NA

Site Maintenance Cost (monthly): NA

Most Successful Feature of Site: Extremely strong community with a mix of professional mechanics and do-it-yourselfers who communicate interactively.

Lesson Learned: Make sure you understand the solution that your customers desire and then develop the technology to deliver that solution.

Advice about Marketing on the Web: "Pick up the phone and call the CEO of companies that you want to have as strategic partners. Don't be afraid."

Bryan Murphy, CFO and Cofounder

Figure 10.4. A community of cars, *http://www.wrenchead.com.* Courtesy Wrenchead, Inc.

opportunity for questions than exists on the radio. The site also includes auto news, online shopping, parts catalogs, coupons, and access to other resources.

Wrenchead made a shrewd move in seeking strategic partnerships critical to its success. They have partnered with CBS.com, a site with close to one million hits per month, and with Sam Frank, a $3B entertainment corporation, to cosponsor motor sports events and concerts. These strategic relationships, for which Wrenchead traded equity, provide essential financial support, marketing reach and advertising that broadens the audience base for the site.

Connecting the Rural World: Farms.com at *http://www.farms.com*

Farms.com, seen in Figure 10.5, is another mega-site that takes advantage of the Internet for real-time interactivity. Not lions and tigers and bears, but pigs and sheep and steers are sold on live video auctions at scheduled times, along with the forage to feed them and the combs to clean them. In addition, the site offers an amazing range of specific agricultural marketplaces, crop information, commodity futures, news, decision tools, and general information resources for anyone engaged in farming or ranching.

Additional services like classified ads, links, show and event calendars, weather forecasts, career opportunities, and chat provide even more reasons for visitors to return. The site has made itself so invaluable to its audience that advertisers know exactly whose eyeballs will be on this site.

Farms.com is just one of many B2B "middleman" sites that serve a well-defined industry in which most companies do not have the skills, volume, or desire to create competitive sites themselves. Instead, these go-between sites, like ChemConnect for chemicals, EcFood for food ingredients, or PowerOnline for energy, take a few percentage points of all transactions on their sites. Farms.com, with its patent-pending bid-ask software, merged with eHARVEST.com, a farm content site to create this agricultural portal.

Like the other sites in this section, Farms.com focuses on a particular niche market that considers this site its primary destination on the Web. Nationwide, about 29% of farms had Internet access in 1999. Surprised? Whether you're seeking wine lovers, theatergoers, piano players, car jocks, or committed hat-wearers, a narrow audience can make a huge contribution to your bottom line.

Company: Farms.com

Year Founded: August 1994

Web Site First Established: January 1995

Gross Annual Revenues: More than $50M

Annual Revenues from Web Site: NA

Percentage of Revenues from Sales on Web: 100%

Site Start-Up Cost: NA

Site Maintenance Cost (monthly): NA

Most Successful Feature of Site: Decision tools, e-commerce features, and search engine.

Advice about Marketing on the Web: "Formulate your plans with proper funding and alliances. Then go for it, remaining flexible and responsive to client needs."

Warren E. Clark, Communications Consultant

Figure 10.5. Connecting the rural world, *http://www.farms.com*. Courtesy Farms.com.

Making Music Interactively: OnlineConservatory.com (Full Tilt Music) at *http://www.onlineconservatory.com*

Ever dream of playing torch songs in a piano bar? Entertaining friends with a little boogie-woogie? Or just playing "Happy Birthday" at your kid's party? Now you can learn how to play the piano in the privacy and convenience of your own home, with online lessons from music teachers all over the world. The site allows students and teachers with OnlineConservatory software to connect over the Internet with live, streaming, two-way music and voice.

Positioning itself as "the world's premier source for online piano and keyboard education," OnlineConservatory.com (Figure 10.6) is developing partnerships to become "a full-service destination site for anyone interested in music instruction or performance." Their vision is all-encompassing: music students, teachers, music schools, industry associations, publications, curriculum and sheet music publishers, and equipment manufacturers. The company sees itself playing a unique role by aggregating the music lesson market, which is notoriously individualized, and providing the infrastructure to bring music schools without their own Web sites onto the Internet.

OnlineConservatory developed proprietary software technology that turns **MIDI** (Musical Instrument Digital Format) keyboard data into standard **IP** (interface protocol) format. Any piano or keyboard teacher with access to a Web server can utilize this proprietary technology to teach live, online music lessons. By offering a free sample lesson and a choice of styles and teachers, the site reduces the risk for participants. The site identifies its audience as buyers of electronic keyboards; non-traditional, older students who need flexible scheduling; and international students who prefer U.S.-based teachers.

Without a doubt, this is one of the most creative applications of Web interactivity that you're likely to find.

Marketing Magic

We saw in Chapter 8 that the advertising industry has quickly adapted its techniques to the Web, finding ways to carve up space, time, and audience for dollars. Advertisers have created the equivalent of classifieds,

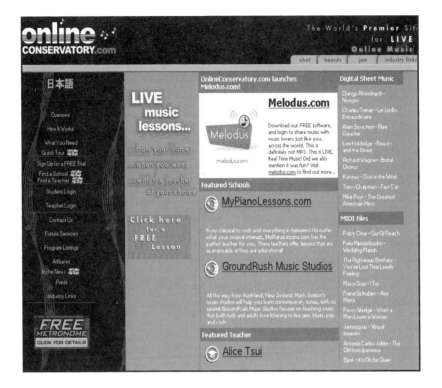

Company: OnlineConservatory.com

Year Founded: December 1999

Web Site First Established: January 2000

Gross Annual Revenues: Less than $1M

Annual Revenues from Web Site: NA

Percentage of Revenues from Sales on Web: 100%

Site Start-Up Cost: $5,000

Site Maintenance Cost (monthly): $1,000

Most Successful Feature of Site: Introduction of service via demo page, free trial offer, and complete listing of teachers (worldwide) offering Web-based keyboard/piano lessons.

Lesson Learned: As a 100% Web initiative, we would have liked to coincide our Web launch with search engine listings.

Advice about Marketing on the Web: "Be true, avoid the hype, and most importantly speak to your consumers without any Web jargon. Make it real and compelling for them to visit, do business and enjoy your site."

Ed Clarke, Director of Marketing

Figure 10.6. Making music interactively, *http://www.onlineconservatory.com.* ©2000 FullTiltMusic.com.

display ads, event sponsorships, product placement in movies, and logos, logos everywhere.

If your business carries a variety of products, it's worth asking manufacturers to let you use co-op advertising dollars for Web promotion as long as their logo appears on the page. Check out manufacturers' home pages, too. You might get them to link to your site, or pay you to place a link from your site to theirs. (Be careful, though, that they don't pull a sale from you.)

Marketing specialists have created Web equivalents for many forms of promotion and customer interaction besides advertising. These range from product demos to catalog displays, from giveaways to product tie-ins. Let's take a look at some companies that have applied these marketing techniques to increase their cybersales.

Free Is a Four-Letter Word: Underneath.com at *http://www.underneath.com*

Many four-letter words are used in marketing, but by far the most common one is free. Underneath.com uses a chance to win one of several prizes as an incentive to sign up for its e-mail newsletter. This effort and 100 other tricks, from a modeling search to fun contests and a boxer-of-the-month club, attract buyers to its site. Underneath.com, seen in Figure 10.7, is a small business site programmed and hosted by its owner, Jeff Johnson. This unprepossessing site demonstrates what a committed individual can do.

Navigation is exceptionally easy and clear, with one click from home page to product. Johnson uses company logos as product buttons, and offers sale items, a chance to win a free shopping spree, and a fashion show online. In his own mind, these ideas fall under the umbrella of "creative advertising," while keeping his site sticky and worth multiple visits.

Finding print and radio advertising expensive and nonproductive, Johnson takes advantage of low-cost PR and partnerships with manufacturers to drive traffic to his site. The site hosts its own affiliate program, with 11,000 associates who receive commissions on sales resulting from referrals. This modest enterprise now has six employees and sells to the United Kingdom, Japan, the Netherlands, Canada, Brazil, and South America.

Company: Underneath.com

Year Founded: July 1997

Web Site First Established: December 1997

Gross Annual Revenues: NA

Annual Revenues from Web Site: NA

Percentage of Revenues from Sales on Web: 100%

Site Start-Up Cost: In-house

Site Maintenance Cost (monthly): In-house

Most Successful Feature of Site: Ease of use; one click away from product, good design of Web site with easy navigation.

Lesson Learned: Need to use PR, partnerships, and creative ways to advertise.

Advice about Marketing on the Web: "If you have money, you can get brand awareness through off-line ads, but not necessarily make money. Need to use a gimmick to differentiate yourself from other sites."

Jeff Johnson, CEO

Figure 10.7. Free is a four-letter-word, *http://www.underneath.com*. Courtesy Underneath.com.

Finding a Niche and Capping It: Noggintops.com, Ltd. at *http://www.noggintops.com*

Doug Young and his wife are Internet entrepreneurs whose modest site reaches the world, in spite of its base in their rural Illinois home. Good writers write what they know; good business owners sell what they know. In his case, Noggintops.com (Figure 10.8) grew out of Young's own love of hats. His site now draws 3,000 people a week and sells about 100 hats. The hats themselves—contemporary, traditional, unusual, or hard-to-find—come from the United States, Australia, Ireland, England, and Austria, with buyers stretching from Europe to Japan.

To provide customers with a good purchasing experience, the site offers detailed instructions on how to measure hat size and three carefully photographed images of each hat ranging from thumbnail to blow-up (Figure 10.8). Like Underneath.com, this site actively uses manufacturers' logos and gift certificates as a draw. Calls to action include one to bookmark the site.

High search engine rankings have proved elusive, so Noggintops.com relies on other methods to drive traffic. Young spends his limited advertising budget on traditional marketing tools like sales brochures and magazine ads to draw customer attention.

The Right Catalog Is the Right Stuff: Social Studies School Service at *http://www.socialstudies.com*

Many Web sites demonstrate their commitment to customer service by making the ordering process easy, convenient, and secure. Most of all, they make product information easy to find. Social Studies School Service, a well-established offline business, discovered the value of this when it launched its Web site, socialstudies.com, seen in Figure 10.9. Its flexible on-site search engine, which is critical for a site with as many products as this one, allows viewers to search by grade level, topic, or type of product.

Originally designed simply to promote educational materials and increase visibility, the site has multiplied sales many times over. A print catalog, mailed to teachers and educational institutions nationwide, remains the primary vehicle for driving visitors to the site.

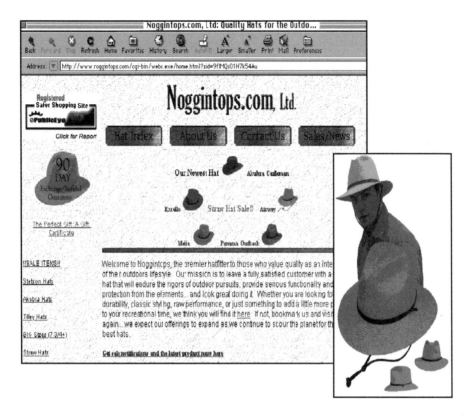

Company: Noggintops.com, Ltd.

Year Founded: September 1999

Web Site First Established: December 1999

Gross Annual Revenues: Less than $1M

Annual Revenues from Web Site: Less than $1M

Percentage of Revenues from Sales on Web: 100%

Site start-up Cost: Less than $3,000

Site Maintenance Cost (monthly): Less than $200 for hosting, rest in-house

Most Successful Feature of Site: Pictures of hats constantly receive good comments from customers.

Lesson Learned: Having a Web site by itself doesn't mean anything.

Advice about Marketing on the Web: "You need to use traditional marketing tools like sales brochures and magazine ads to draw customer attention."

Douglas H. Young, Owner

Figure 10.8.   Finding a niche and capping it, *http://www.noggintops.com.*
Courtesy Noggintops.com.

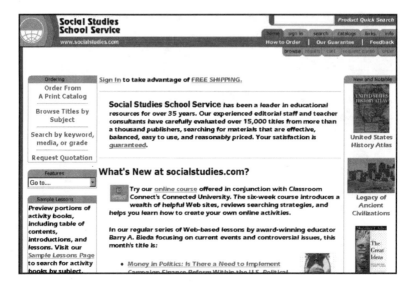

Company: Social Studies School Service

Year Founded: 1965

Web Site First Established: 1995

Gross Annual Revenues: NA

Annual Revenues from Web Site: NA

Percentage of Revenues from Sales on Web: NA

Site Start-Up Cost: NA

Site Maintenance Cost (monthly): NA

Most Successful Feature of Site: Allowing a customer an easy way to order online by entering the code from a print catalog sent via direct mail.

Lesson Learned: The print catalog was the best idea to drive sales.

Advice about Marketing on the Web: "Maintain a newsletter online and use print media to drive Web traffic."

Dr. Aaron Willis, Director of Online Development

Figure 10.9. The right catalog is the right stuff, *http://www.social studies.com.* Courtesy Social Studies School Service.

Putting Customers First

Let's look at two sites that focus on their customers through a combination of personalized product, tailored support, and customer contact. Both companies illustrate the importance of service in spite of their difference in size.

Customization Is for the Birds: Exotic Wood
Dreams at *http://www.exoticwooddreams.com*

Exotic Wood Dreams builds and sells a product most people never heard of: custom-made play gyms for parrots (see Figure 10.10) designed to fit a bird's foot size, personality, and favorite playthings. Talk about a niche market! For its first few years, this small, family-owned business built not only the individualized play gyms but also toys, which they sold through specialty ads and bird shows. Now, with a three-week backlog of custom orders flowing from the Web, they have decided to market bird toys from two different suppliers and concentrate on the gyms.

This classic small business story starts with a couple working on the side in a hobby business. Now Donna Prescott has quit her job to concentrate on Web marketing and her soon-to-retire husband will build parrot play gyms full-time. When she first put a handmade wooden bird on eBay, Prescott was astonished by the bidding frenzy. After customers from eBay and trade shows pressed for a catalog or Web site, the couple hired a local Web developer. Prescott takes the digital photos and uploads them herself, manages the catalog, and updates features on the site through an easy-to-use store-building program. She has hired a contractor to manage the popular chat room.

Like NYcabbie.com, Exotic Wood Dreams benefited from a cascade of publicity derived from a single source. A local newspaper in Riverside, California, featured the company in a story about unusual businesses in the area. Shortly after publication on June 24, 2000, the story was picked up by papers in South Carolina, New York, and dozens of other states. The cyber-floodgates opened!

Learning from her eBay experience, Prescott continually posts new items on an auction section on her own site. Not only does this draw repeat customers, but the auction section allows Prescott to benchmark prices on items too unique to price any other way. The gyms themselves are individually priced based on size, materials, favorite toys, and other customer requests. Prescott will quote a price and e-mail plans for the gym to the customer for preapproval. Prior to shipping the delicate, preassembled gyms via UPS or RSP ground, Prescott e-mails pictures and a detailed description to the bird owner for final okay. The net result is that even without asking for a credit card guarantee, Exotic Wood Dreams has never had a bad order. It's hard for customers to stiff a company with which they have developed a personal relationship.

Parrot Forum & Pictures
Parrot Talk Chat
Catalog
Parrot Hanging Gyms
Portable Playpens, Gyms, Stands
Durable Toys
Cage Feeders & Accessories
Bird and Small Parrot Toys, Little Tikes
Acrylic, Plastic Toys
Chewy Toys, Foot Toys and Sticks
Exotic Woods for Exotic Pets and Design
Parrot Gyms, Wood, Trees Available Now
Parrot Swings and Gym Accessories
Wholesale Wood

About Us

Contact Us

Links

Exotic
Wood Dreams

Pet-Safe Wood Products, Vet-Approved, Bird Tested
Home for: Sandblasted & Natural Grapevine-Ribbon Wood-Manzanita-Cholla
Unique, Quality, Handcrafted Creations for Exotic Birds, Large and Small

Company: Exotic Wood Dreams

Year Founded: 1994

Web Site First Established: 1999

Gross Annual Revenues: Less than $1M

Annual Revenues from Web Site: Less than $1M

Percentage of Revenues from Sales on Web: 100%

Site Start-Up Cost: $1,200

Site Maintenance Cost (monthly): $70–$125/month

Most Successful Feature of Site: Customized play gyms specially designed to suit their customers' birds.

Lesson Learned: Wish we had started sooner to get more toys from suppliers so we could concentrate on the play gyms.

Advice about Marketing on the Web: "Get your feet wet! Online auctions work. Customer relationships are very important; spend the time to take care of them."

Donna Prescott, Owner

Figure 10.10. Customization is for the birds, *http://www.exoticwooddreams. com/index.html.* © 2000 Exotic Wood Dreams and CitiVU. Hot-links welcome. Wingin it Marketing Online Marketing & Promotions: sturner6@mediaone.net. All rights reserved.

Bubbling over with advice to other Web-preneurs, Prescott recommends constantly updating sites with new information, and building links to related sites (in her case sites connected to the bird market, such as parrot associations, publications, and events).

Prescott's developer taught her how to select keywords and submit to search engines, which she prefers to banner ads. Already a speaker at the local Chamber of Commerce about her Web marketing success, Prescott talks like a business school instructor, emphasizing the importance of customer relationships and responding quickly to e-mail and phone. She's acutely aware of costs, urging other small companies to interview Web developers to find someone they can work with someone who will deliver what's needed within a budget. "Don't go overboard," she warns.

With three parrots in their family, the Prescotts are flying high themselves. "We love what we're doing."

A Shipping Solution to a Shopping Problem: Tema Contemporary Furniture at *http://www.tema-usa.com*

No one was more surprised than Graham McInnes, Vice President of Tema Contemporary Furniture, when their Web site (shown in Figure 10.11) became a business engine of its own. When they launched the site in 1996 as an information source for local shoppers in Albuquerque, New Mexico, Tema expected customers to research items online and come into the retail store to purchase. The site didn't drive any noticeable traffic to the store, but quickly accumulated sales, all from out of state. Now Tema's Web site has become a premier furniture site on the Web, outlasting competitors who had millions in venture-capital funding, such as everythingdecor.com, furniture.com, and living.com. "I just ignore them and keep plugging away," says McInnes.

The company began as a specialty store for Danish modern furniture in 1980. Since then, it has expanded to a general contemporary furniture retailer with a 60,000-square-foot building (half warehouse), 65 employees, and sales of $7.5 million.

The Web site, however, has redefined Tema as a national retailer. The store now buys inventory specific for the Web, such as Italian dining room sets, that doesn't sell well in New Mexico, and price points differ: Some things that won't move at sale prices in the store sell quickly online at list. From a merchandising perspective, McInnes avoids putting anything either promotional or clearance-priced online.

Company: Tema Contemporary Furniture

Year Founded: 1980

Web Site First Established: 1996

Gross Annual Revenues: $5M–$20M

Annual Revenues from Web Site: $750K–$1.3M

Percentage of Revenues from Sales on Web: 10%

Site Start-Up Cost: $150,000 per year (includes in-house labor)

Site Maintenance Cost (monthly): $6,000

Most Successful Feature of Site: Its simplicity; the catalog is HTML, not database driven.

Lesson Learned: Should have tried to solve shipping and logistic problems earlier; we didn't put enough emphasis on it.

Advice about Marketing on the Web: "Do it! Take small steps, but start somewhere."

Graham McInnes, Vice President

Figure 10.11. A shipping solution to a shopping problem, *http://www.tema-usa.com.* Courtesy Tema Contemporary Furniture.

Tema's online sales are expected to zoom from $125,000 in 1999 to $1.5 million in 2000, more than 1,000% growth! McInnes projects Internet-derived revenue to surpass in-store sales within 18 months and then continue growing until Tema.com becomes one of the top five Internet furniture sites in the country.

What's even more amazing is that McInnes and four self-taught staff program the site in-house. They have financed the $750,000 in site development, maintenance, and expansion costs solely through revenues, without either debt or equity financing.

Tema's site is straightforward: an HTML catalog (not database driven) that includes store inventory, prices, and a full-color photo. To make finding products in the 1,500-page catalog easy, the three-tier structure is simple: home page, furniture category, and items. Viewers can go laterally, forward, and back on the site, but are never more than three clicks away from a desired product.

Currently, users call an 800 number to place orders. The store dedicated three phone lines and hired more staff to handle all the Internet inquiries by phone and e-mail. "We're swamped," McInnes acknowledges cheerfully.

McInnes believes one reason Tema succeeds is that they have figured out how to ship bulky pieces of furniture and still guarantee quality. Think about it. Furniture manufacturers are not equipped to drop-ship a single bed or chair directly to a residence; they ship pallets of furniture as commercial freight only to a "bill to" address (i.e., a store). International shipments often remain containerized cargo all the way from manufacturer to retail outlet.

Freight-forwarding companies are a problem, too. Local delivery vans are owned by a store and staffed by drivers who expect to help a buyer move the old couch and put the new one "a little more to the left, please." Commercial trucking companies make a delivery and leave, and the items are too large for delivery by a service like UPS. "We had to educate customers to a different level of expectation," McInnes says. "They have to place the furniture themselves, sometimes even bring it in the house, and discard old pieces."

Tema does not have stores or warehouses all over the country, an exorbitantly expensive proposition. Right now, manufacturers ship to the Tema warehouse in New Mexico, where the order, which may include items from several different vendors, is repacked, reshrinkwrapped, and reshipped. It's slow and expensive to double ship, but it does give Tema the opportunity to check items for damage before sending them to the customer. Since there can still be problems on the last leg of shipment, McInnes has started to track performance by carrier. It's a problem he wishes he'd recognized earlier; it took about a year to select reliable combinations of shippers and suppliers.

As an added challenge, some manufacturers limit what can be sold online in an attempt to shield other retailers from online competition, not to mention resentment from retailers themselves. With the power of Tema's Web presence now behind him, McInnes has dropped several manufacturers from the store who wouldn't let him show, price, or even indicate online that Tema was a dealer. Other manufacturers, however, have asked to be included on the site.

Future site expansion will require new dedicated UNIX servers, new applications development packages, new telecommunications capability end-to-end, more office space, more staff including an MIS person, and a new warehouse devoted solely to Web sales. Tema plans to add more products and vendors to its site, incorporate an on-site search engine, and establish online 24/7 ordering.

"It really makes my mouth water," McInnes says, referring to the possibility of tying the site into back-end systems for inventory control. Since staff must currently check stock daily and upload inventory changes, the site lacks online ordering based on real-time availability. He would also like to follow the Land's End model of tracking inventory and orders online from start to finish, including shipping data that freight companies already have online. Tema recognizes that the next step is orders of magnitude beyond their current site; it's an upgrade they couldn't afford three or four years ago.

All this traffic growth was driven by a disciplined program of search engine submission, adds McInnes. They enter very specific phrases for individual pages so whenever someone types in "Maple Sleighbed Headboard," for instance, a Tema page is likely to rank in the top ten. (Since the site is not a dynamic database, no active server pages (**ASP**) are produced; active server pages are ignored by most of the search engines.) Tema uses the search engine Metacrawler to monitor which other search engines return the most hits to his site, MySpy.com to see which keywords people type in, and Web Trends to monitor site traffic. Tema-usa.com now receives over 125,000 unique visitors per month, with some people visiting as many as 10 times.

McInnes advises others to follow in Tema's footsteps: Grow one step at a time. By growing slowly, Tema identified and solved small problems before they became huge ones. Future growth holds great potential, but also some risk. Right now, the staff engages customers in conversation, so people feel a connection to the company, and there's a lot of personal service as staff recommend fabrics and colors, reinforce customer's decisions, and close sales; they don't just take orders. "It will be hard to hold onto that small business service as the site grows," McInnes realizes, "but that's our goal."

Service in Cyberspace

Some businesses take your breath away with the originality of their vision and the risks they take. Any small business that reengineers its entire concept of service delivery to adapt to the electronic world deserves tremendous credit. Such is the case with our last two model sites.

Merging the Real and Virtual Worlds: The Shoe Guy at *http://www.shoeguy.com*

With imagination, personal services can indeed adapt to the Internet. Witness the Shoe Guy, a small business that transforms the face-to-face transaction between customer and cobbler into a hassle-free, convenient online service for busy professionals. By combining the Internet with modern shipping technology, the Shoe Guy intends "to be the best shoe repair and shoe care product business in the universe." They've made a great start with their Web site, shown in Figure 10.12.

As the animated home page shows, The Shoe Guy offers one-of-a-kind express shoe repair service directly from home or office. Fill out the online form to order service, receive a UPS box to ship your shabby shoes to The Shoe Guy, and welcome them back, repaired and polished, within a week.

The icons borrowed from the 1920s and 1930s are a thematic element of the site, which includes "shoe news," a catalog of shoe care products and accessories, and a shoe photo/story contest. The shopping cart and checkstand software by ActivCart, which keeps a virtual order form on-screen, is one of the friendliest cart interfaces available.

Company: ShoeGuy.com

Year Founded: 1985

Web Site First Established: November 1997

Gross Annual Revenues: NA

Annual Revenues from Web Site: NA

Percentage of Revenues from Sales on Web: NA

Site Start-Up Cost: $50,000

Site Maintenance Cost (monthly): NA

Most Successful Feature of Site: The quick shoe service section.

Lesson Learned: It takes longer to get things going and more capital resources than originally thought. Wish I had put up the site sooner.

Advice about Marketing on the Web: "Work with a company…that has been successful marketing on the Web and has been in business for a long time and is forward thinking. They must understand the ins and outs of Web business and how it works. Take everything you know about traditional marketing and advertising and throw it out the window."

Jim Rice, President

Figure 10.12. Merging the real and virtual worlds, *http://www.shoeguy.com.*
Courtesy Shoeguy.com.

This was an expensive site. "It [took] longer to get things going and it [took] more capital resources than I originally thought," explains Shoe Guy President Jim Rice. The investment of working with a talented Web designer paid off, though, in the elegant details of the art deco design and the transparency of navigation. Unfortunately, Rice learned the hard way about copyright when the original developer sold out to a new company that isn't providing good service. "In the absence of a work-for-hire clause in the contract," he says ruefully, "you don't own the site."

In spite of current challenges, The Shoe Guy so successfully achieves its claim to have "merged old world craft with modern hi-tech abilities and management" that the government asked Rice to participate in a program to train small business owners in Ireland on using ecommerce to overcome distance barriers. Jim Rice has only one regret, "I wish I had put the site up sooner."

Plumbing the Virtual World: Pablo's Mechanical Heating & Plumbing at *http://www.pablosmechanical.com*

If you don't think a Web site makes sense for a local plumbing company, think again. Pablo's Mechanical Heating & Plumbing, whose site is shown in Figure 10.13, has carved an amazing niche in northeastern New Mexico. Combining a simple, inexpensive Web site with basic business tools—a cell phone, a fax machine, and e-mail—owner Paul May has differentiated his company from all his competitors. When you realize this region is predominantly rural, with a few well-entrenched heating and plumbing companies, May's rapid achievement of market share is even more remarkable.

Although he certainly provides service to many locally owned residences and small businesses (there are few large ones!), May has generated particular interest from long-distance builder/owners of summer and retirement homes. To them, he represents security and convenience, offering easy communication regardless of time zone. Customers, who may have met May only once if at all, e-mail requests for service; May returns his bid by e-mail or fax. As one Oregon customer told him, "I really don't care if you can set my toilet, but you have e-mail and know about this technology revolution, so you get this job."

His site leverages the power of other, larger sites with links that simplify product choice, reducing the stress of long-distance construction and maintenance. Customers can select new plumbing fixtures, for in-

Pablo's Mechanical
Heating and Plumbing

Mora Office
PO Box 29
Buena Vista, NM
87712
(505) 387-2080

Angel Fire Office
The Inn Business
Center
Hwy 434, Angel
Fire
(505) 377-0681

mobile (505) 760-8608
pablo@pablosmechanical.com

NM Lic#061148 MM98

Residential - Commercial - Industrial

*"Specializing in Steam and Hot Water Heating Systems, Custom Plumbing
and Water Treatment Equipment"*

Radiant, Hydronic and Steam
Boilers, Pumps and All Related Controls

Company: Pablo's Mechanical Heating & Plumbing

Year Founded: January 1998

Web Site First Established: July 1999

Gross Annual Revenues: Less than $1M

Annual Revenues from Web Site: NA—doesn't sell on site

Percentage of Revenues from Sales on Web: Has improved business 30%–40%

Site Start-Up Cost: $270

Site Maintenance Cost (monthly): $19.50/month

Most Successful Feature of Site: E-mail and links to vendors.

Lesson Learned: Wish I had done this much sooner.

Advice about Marketing on the Web: "Not as hard as you might think, and not as expensive either. But you have to deliver the goods."

Paul May, Owner

Figure 10.13. Plumbing the virtual world, *http://www.pablosmechanical.com.* Courtesy Pablo's Mechanical. Web Design: Jack A. Rains, Webmaster@arco-iris.com.

stance, by reviewing items in suppliers' online catalogs and e-mailing back the catalog numbers of their choices. Since clients may be in the region only briefly to hire contractors, they like making decisions about fixtures, colors, and finishes at their leisure instead of making a snap decision.

Customers can also save money by doing the legwork to identify necessary replacement parts, while May saves time traveling to a customer's home just to see what part is needed. Vendor links also save his time waiting for distributors to locate a part; instead, May searches online supplier catalogs himself and calls in the part number.

May e-mails regular updates on major jobs to inform home builders as far away as Missouri, Ohio, Kansas, Tennessee, or California about the progress on their houses. He includes digital photos to document work underway (even signed permits and inspectors' reports!) and to showcase the finished job. In turn, customers e-mail the photos to their families worldwide.

Given the difficulty we've all experienced trying to contact contractors, it's hard to put a price on the peace of mind May offers. The value he adds to his service means he doesn't have to compete on the basis of price alone.

It's also hard to put a price on the time and money May has saved by putting technology in his toolbox. May uses technology in other ways. With long distances between job sites in northern New Mexico, May's decision to use cell phones for himself and his employees means that customers and contractors can always reach the company. He uses e-mail at off-hours or on weekends to handle correspondence, make appointments, place orders, or respond to questions.

Like Donna Prescott, Paul May has kept his Web costs within reason for the audience he reaches. Like her, he watches his costs and recommends comparing rates for Web services. Although U.S. West put up his first site as part of a Yellow Pages deal, it charged much more than he pays now and people had trouble finding the site until it had its own domain name.

In a business that depends on word-of mouth, May plans to include his URL on the items delivered by his promotion-of-the-month service, *http://www.promoofthemonth.com*, which sends him a set of 100 promotional giveaways, such as keychains, flyswatters, magnets, or pencils for $90 a month. (In a business like plumbing, you want something people will keep around; you can't predict when a faucet will leak or a hot water heater fail!) Pablosmechanical.com now appears on his trucks and is embroidered or silk-screened on shirts his employees wear. He includes his URL in direct mail pieces and local radio ads.

Although May doesn't get co-op ad dollars from linked suppliers yet, they'll often send him a new sample product or discount his costs. Right now, many suppliers contribute to the cost of a Yellow Pages ad or a sign on a truck that incorporates their logo, but they haven't quite caught up to the Web.

May is like a kid in a toy store when it comes to the Internet and new technology. He's already shifted money from Yellow Pages advertising (a standard in service businesses) to the Web site because it offers greater value. "I get calls saying they're looking at my site and want me to bid," he exclaims. May is not afraid to take a reasonable risk trying something new. "Look, the worst that happens is I'm out a couple hundred bucks."

May, of course, is staying more than one step ahead of his competitors: "I really need a laptop for the truck," he muses, "and I'm looking at PCS digital phone service with the Internet on it." He has plans for improving his site and gets input from his customers, many of whom are telecommuting executives.

With ambition and unerring instinct—he had minimal computer knowledge until he taught himself to use his first computer in January 1999—May has quickly built on his 15 years of trade experience as a steamfitter and two years of independent contracting work. His business has more than tripled since he opened in 1998; the company now counts one part-time and three full-time employees. As Paul May puts it, "Oh, wow! I've taken this little one-man, bucket-of-handtools company nationwide. Oh, wow!"

Moving On

We've now looked at a variety of sites that utilize Web marketing techniques to achieve their business objectives. Although the larger companies spent a small fortune researching their customers' needs and developing their sites for maximum impact, some of the small businesses achieved their Web success with relatively tiny budgets. If they can do it, why can't you? Regardless of cost, successful sites have several things in common: They make the Web experience a pleasant one for their customers, follow through with support, offer quality products, and provide good service.

In the concluding chapter, we'll look at the potential impact of government activity and long-term business trends on Internet marketing, as well as review the integration of Web activities with the rest of your business.

11

Conclusion

Clearly, the Internet is redrawing the map of the business world. With business life online running at "Internet speed," there is as much change in one year as there used to be in seven. The horizon for strategic planning has shrunk from three years to 18 months. And it's often impossible to foresee new technologies and applications beyond six months. How many foresaw taxicabs equipped with Palm Pilots for wireless Internet access? Internet kiosks spreading from Internet cafes to laundromats and amusement parks? Besides checking your tarot cards online, what can you do? For one, take comfort in the knowledge that the more things change, the more they stay the same: If you forget the basics of business, all the fancy Web sites in the world won't make you rich.

At the core of your business, you must have a solid product or service and the commitment to put your customers first. If your online activities reflect a desire to build a long-term relationship with customers—the most basic of business rules—the rest is window dressing. This concept applies whether you're creating a signature file, participating in a news group, adding streaming video to your Web site, or running a print ad to draw attention to your new URL.

In this chapter, we will

- Look at long-term trends in legislation, regulation, and taxation that may affect Internet marketing in the future.

- Review current trends in B2C and B2B that may impact your business landscape tomorrow.

- Check out what the dot-com jitterbug, the Wall Street waltz and the *pas de deux* of corporate mergers might mean for you.

- Consider the impact of rich media on your Web plans.

- Review the importance of planning and of integrating online marketing with other business activities.

Trends to Watch: Government

You might be able to ignore a ferret in your living room, but you can't ignore a gazelle. When the Internet was primarily an academic research tool, when only ten thousand Web sites had established residence in cyberspace, not many people in Congress, state legislatures, or single-interest groups paid attention. No one can ignore the Internet now.

The fastest growing communications technology in history, the Internet reached 50 million people in less than 5 years. It took radio 38 years, television 13 years, and cable 10 years to reach the same audience. With that kind of impact, it's no surprise that the Internet has drawn vastly different interest groups into action. State governments worry about losing sales tax revenue, not-for-profit organizations battle over censorship (pro and con), citizens complain to Congress about junk e-mail, and investors sue over profits lost when online stock brokerages shut down by heavy traffic.

If you market your business online, you need to keep your antenna up for trends that will affect your ability to survive and thrive on the Internet. Here are a few things to watch in the next several years.

Legislation and Regulation

When it comes to the Internet, many people are saying, "there oughta' be a law." Pretty soon there will be—probably many of them! Legislation has been proposed at the federal and state levels to deal with such issues as data privacy, encryption, online fraud, spamming, access by minors to salacious information, and online gambling. With the exception of the last, some form of regulation or legislation has already been enacted for all of these.

Spamming

Spam mail costs ISPs an estimated $1 billion annually to cope with the added traffic; the costs for larger servers and greater telecommunication capacity are underwritten by legitimate users, while the burden of a clogged Internet affects everyone.

In 1998 the state of Washington became the first in the nation to pass an antispamming law, requiring e-mailers to use real addresses and making it a crime to put false or misleading information in e-mail solicitations. A dozen more states and the U.S. Congress have considered similar laws. Legislation passed the House in July 2000 that would give both the Federal Trade Commission and ISPs the ability to sue spammers. *You* don't spam, of course. *You* always obtain approval to send out newsletters and e- mail updates, don't you? *You* always make it easy for recipients to remove their names from your e-mail lists, right?

Encryption

Even the cool topic of encryption, which many consider key to electronic commerce, is a matter of hot debate, positioning U.S. competitiveness versus national security concerns. Current federal regulations prohibit exporting the strong encryption technologies described in Chapter 9. The CIA, FBI, and Department of Defense argue that this technology could make the United States vulnerable to terrorists and criminals, and want access to the key to monitor encrypted transmissions.

On the other side, businesses argue that the United States will lose its competitive edge and that encryption technology is needed to ensure the growth of global online trade. Recent Commerce Department regulations define Internet postings as exports, so even publishing encryption algorithms on private Web sites makes them subject to regulation.

In September 1998 the Clinton administration relaxed export controls on strong encryption technology to 45 countries by industry sector, starting with banking, insurance, and health care. Some online merchants in these countries now have access to the same technology used in the United States to protect electronic transactions, an important step if you wish to sell internationally. For more information on encryption, try the Center for Democracy and Technology at *http:// www.cdt.org/crypto/admin*.

Privacy

We spoke previously about the possibility of federal privacy legislation if industry self-regulation doesn't work. A free-for-all policy on personal data ownership is unique to the United States. In Europe, individuals own their data by default and must agree to its release; in the United States data default to the collector, with individuals needing to request that their names be removed from mailing lists or that demographic and purchasing data not be sold. As of October 1998, all firms conducting business within the European Union must certify that their data practices meet EU standards. This requirement, too, may affect your international online marketing. Look for U.S. law eventually to correspond in the interest of global trade.

As described in Chapter 9 your best defense is to establish and maintain a policy that honors the privacy of your customers. For an overview and updates on the privacy issue, see *http://www.cdt.or*g to learn about the efforts of the Internet Privacy Working Group.

Access to Sites

So far, the U.S. Supreme Court has found that attempts to restrict access to the Internet in public settings like libraries run afoul of the First Amendment. Various courts have ruled against federal legislation requiring Web hosts and online services to restrict access to certain sites for those under 17, against mandating the use of software filters, and against attempts by libraries to install filter software on publicly accessed computers.

Software filters are often used by parents at home and are offered as an option on online services. Filtering software may deny access to information on topics such as breast cancer or AIDS in an attempt to limit access to sexually explicit sites. Other filters prohibit access to information on subjects like homosexuality or Wiccan religions. If your Web site contains such content, monitor commercial filtering software, object to the manufacturer, and use publicity to counteract the filter if its search algorithms block your legitimate site.

Regulation

Some issues are more likely to be addressed through regulation than legislation. For instance, the Federal Trade Commission (FTC) is attacking online fraud, while the Securities and Exchange Commission is strengthening oversight of day trading on online brokerages. Consumer affairs departments in several states are actively pursuing complaints about online auction houses.

The FTC fined seven Internet retailers to settle charges they didn't meet legal requirements to notify consumers of shipping delays during the 1999 holiday season. Macys.com, CDnow.com, KBkids.com, Minidiscnow.com, The Original Honey Baked Ham Company of Georgia, Patriot Computer, and ToysRus.com were all hit for their violation of the Mail and Telephone Order Rule, which requires retailers to ship within the date promised or within 30 days of receipt of order.

Other laws crop up where least expected. For example, all but 17 states restrict the ability of wineries and breweries to ship some inbound products. The issue is less one of legal drinking age than a battle with the wholesale liquor industry to control what products are sold where. The distributors have financed initiatives to prohibit the direct sale of alcoholic beverages to consumers, although some support *http://www.wineshopper.com*, which allows online orders to be picked up at a local retailer.

To monitor the status of federal legislation on these and other Internet-related topics, go to one of the sites that tracks the progress of bills through Congress, such as *http://thomas.loc.gov/*, or briefing papers by Internet organizations, such as *http://www.internetpolicy.org*. Similar efforts on state levels can be monitored state by state at such sites as *http://gse.ucla.edu/iclp/gen.resources.html*.

Democratization and Governance

Public advocacy organizations have expressed growing concern about undue corporate influence over the activities of the ICANN (Internet Corporation for Assigned Names and Numbers), the quasi-governmental organization that oversees the Internet. The Internet Democracy Project, a coalition of Computer Professionals for Social Responsibility, The Electronic Privacy Information Center, and the American Civil Liberties Union, encourages participation by nongovernmental organizations, while other nations seek to dilute U.S. dominance with a greater worldwide presence on the ICANN board.

The Internet has begun to influence the delivery of government services from paying taxes to obtaining a small business loan or competing for a government contract. The Federal government has consolidated its 20,000 Web sites under an umbrella, *http://www.firstgov.gov*. President Clinton conducted the first online "fireside chat" in November 1999.

Furthermore, the Internet has profound implications for the exercise of democratic principles, from elections online to candidates' Web sites. Political Web sites are used for everything from personality profiles to position papers, from volunteer coordination to fundraising. With access to information becoming the defining lever of power, the Web represents not only economic opportunity, but electoral empowerment. Some 25 percent of voters now get at least some election information from the Internet at a time when political coverage by broadcast networks is declining.

Finally, whether the digital divide—access to computers—is within the United States or between the industrial and less- developed nations of the world, the disparity in information access is crucial. As the Internet increasingly supplants geographic communities with electronic communities of interest, society becomes more fragmented and decentralized. The decoupling of political power from residence will need to be addressed. As a citizen, as well as a businessperson, issues related to governance, social responsibility, and ethics online concern you.

Taxation

You have to believe that projections of $40 billion in B2C online revenues and close to $200 billion in B2B sales will get the attention of state and local governments wondering how to collect taxes. State governments worry about the eventual loss of sales tax revenue, as well as the loss of Main Street businesses. Most governors are searching for ways to tax Internet commerce, citing a recent study by the University of Tennessee that by 2003 states will have lost an estimated $20 billion in sales taxes on Internet commerce. Compare that to $4 billion in sales taxes lost to mail order per year and the aggregate sales taxes of $147 billion collected in 1998.

Without sales taxes, argue states and municipalities, there will be a shortfall in services. Alternately, other taxes will need to be raised to make up for the loss, or low-income consumers purchasing on Main Street will end up bearing the brunt of local taxation. The U.S. Department of Commerce just began monitoring Internet sales independent of catalog sales to get a handle on the amounts involved. Figure 11.1 shows state dependence on sales taxes.

The challenge is to figure out an equitable way to deal with the complexity and cost of collecting and distributing taxes across more than 6000 taxing jurisdictions around the country. To some, the Internet should always remain a tax-free zone, but brick-and-mortar businesses on Main Street argue that not taxing the Internet gives their online competitors a cost advantage. For others, the patchwork of multiple state and local taxes provides even greater impetus for a national sales or value-added tax. This will be a national issue; the Supreme Court previ-

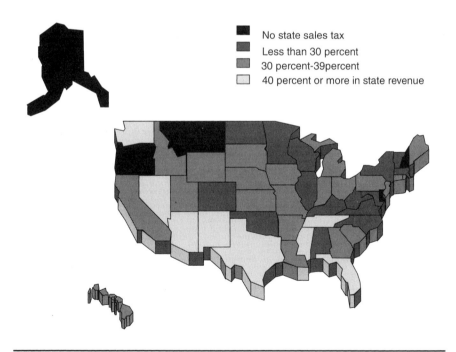

Figure 11.1. States' dependence on sales taxes, Source: U.S. Census Bureau.

ously ruled that Congress must authorize the imposition of state taxes on interstate mail order sales.

In 1998, Congress, heeding cries that taxation would impede the growth of online commerce and stifle small businesses, passed the Internet Tax Freedom Act. The Act initiated a three-year moratorium on state and local Internet taxes and established an advisory commission to study the issue. In March 2000, the majority of the deadlocked commission recommended extending the moratorium for five years until October 2006 to provide time for state and local governments to simplify their sales tax systems. They also asked Congress to clarify the concept of business "presence" in a state and hoped that new technology would emerge to assess sales taxes on remote purchases. A minority of the panel wants Congress to allow states to develop their own interstate compact for sales taxes on e-commerce by December 2003. The panel did agree that states should not collect taxes on ISPs.

Stay tuned to events in the tax arena. They could affect your bottom line or, at the very least, the checkstand software you use. You might want to review current information at *http://www.vertexinc.com/ etax_central/etax_central_home.asp.*

Trends to Watch: B2B and B2C

We've already learned that B2B online revenues, projected at $1.3 trillion by 2004, will exceed B2C by a factor of 9:1. What's amazing is the degree to which the large, lumbering giants of industry have finally boarded the cyber-train and are using it to remake how they do business, not only how they sell to customers, but also how they manage their own supply chain.

The B2B Explosion

Since analysts estimate that online purchasing can save companies 10% to 20%, this process is critical to companies whose products are under constant price pressure and tight profit margins. Consider the following:

- Hyatt Corporation and Marriott International have formed a joint Internet venture to supply the hotel industry with everything from shower caps to ice machines. Starting with their own $5 billion in annual purchases, the two companies will open their site to other North American hotel chains.

- The founding members of e2open.com—IBM, Nortel, Toshiba, Motorola, Nokia, Ericsson, Philips Electronics, Matsushita, Hitachi, Seagate, Solectron, and LG Electronics—promote the site as the world's largest B2B electronics marketplace. They plan to manage their billions of dollars in annual purchasing from this site.

- Hewlett-Packard, Compaq, Gateway, NEC, Advanced Micro Devices, Samsung, and six other high-tech companies plan another online marketplace for electronics and computer parts. Seen as a way to speed up supply chains while reducing costs and lowering inventories, the mega-site will use catalogs and auctions for chips, hard drives, and other components.

- Ford, General Motors, and Daimler Chrysler plan to mirror the hotel supply chain for the automotive industry with their Newco marketplace for $250 to $300 billion a year in purchasing parts and office supplies. Boeing and three other aerospace giants plan a similar network for that industry.

- Farms.com and Cattlesale.com already act as agricultural marketplaces, while Ventro matches buyers and sellers of medical equipment, chemicals, and other goods. GoCargo.com matches shippers with available cargo space, and Freemarket.com hosts B2B online auctions.

- There are some cooperative buying networks for small businesses, too. Chevron connects its 8,000 stations for ordering everything from motor oil to cases of soda and prepaid calling cards. At the same time, it manages Petrocosm Marketplace, an online energy market. Chevron estimates savings from the first venture at $10 million a year in field sales costs, but expects ten times that amount from Petrocosm as more of its 35,000 suppliers sign up.

Such purchasing alliances erode any concept of national borders as global companies agree to price hikes or cut costs by pressuring their suppliers. Watch for the impact on the small supplier, whose own ability to respond quickly while maintaining a profit will come under attack. Gartner Group estimates that some 600 online marketplaces already exist and predicts six times as many marketplaces by 2004. Companies like Ariba, Broadvision, and CommerceOne specialize in software packages for creating these online marketplaces. For a ranking of some of the biggest and best of these marketplaces, go to *http://www.netb2b.com*. The current highest rated B2B sites are seen in Figure 11.2. Figure 11.3 provides a breakdown of the B2B sector by industry and size. More information on what to expect in the B2B sector is available at the Business 2.0 site, *http://www.business2.com*.

In addition to changing the nature of purchasing, the Internet is having a profound effect on parcel and document delivery. The impact on UPS, Federal Express, and the U.S. Postal Service (used by Amazon.com) is well known. Forrester Research estimates over 2 billion packages shipped to residential addresses by 2003, more than double the number in 1999. The problems of at-home delivery have fostered creative thinking to enable buyers to get their packages safely even when they aren't at home: everything from a password-protected outdoor shopping bin from Mental Physics in Arlington, Virginia, to a drop-off system for package delivery at a local merchant (PaxZone) or to a Mail Boxes Etc. store.

The merger of secure electronic document transmission and hard copy document delivery is something new. Companies like NowDocs

Company	Industry Sector
IBM	manufacturing-high tech
Cisco	manufacturing-high tech
Real Networks	software
Office Max	wholesale/retail/distributor
Federal Express	transportation/shipping
Merrill Lynch	financial services/insurance
Burlington	transportation/shipping
W.W. Grainger	wholesale/retail/distributor
Compaq	manufacturing-high tech
Dell	manufacturing-high tech
Hewlett-Packard	manufacturing-high tech
Sun	manufacturing-high tech

Figure 11.2. Highest rated B2B sites, *http://www.netb2b.com*. Reprinted with permission, B2B, a publication of Crain Communications, Inc.

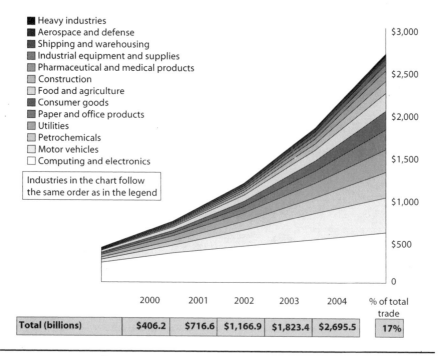

■ Heavy industries
■ Aerospace and defense
■ Shipping and warehousing
■ Industrial equipment and supplies
■ Pharmaceutical and medical products
□ Construction
□ Food and agriculture
■ Consumer goods
■ Paper and office products
□ Utilities
□ Petrochemicals
□ Motor vehicles
□ Computing and electronics

Industries in the chart follow
the same order as in the legend

| Total (billions) | $406.2 | $716.6 | $1,166.9 | $1,823.4 | $2,695.5 | 17% |

| | 2000 | 2001 | 2002 | 2003 | 2004 | % of total trade |

Figure 11.3. Online B2B growth by industry, Source: February 2000 "eMarket Places Boost B2B Trade," Forrester Research, Inc.

(*http://www.nowdocs.com*, seen in Figure 11.4), Net Documents (*http://www.netdocuments.com*), and the U.S. Postal Service (*http://www.framed.usps.com* seen in Figure 11.5) already offer this combined service. Other "last-mile" delivery services like Kozmo (*http://www.kozmo.com*) and UrbanFetch (*http://www.urbanfetch.com*) flourish in metropolitan areas, marrying Web buyers to direct-to-the-door messenger services. Lunch anyone?

Businesses are also forming partnerships to package new technologies. For instance, General Motors will partner with Sun Microsystems in e-GM to computerize vehicles and connect them to the Web. GM's Web cars will incorporate existing OnStar emergency communications, voice activation of Internet services, and integrate automotive services (like scheduling an oil change) with providers. Boeing will partner with CNN, CNBC, and two Japanese electronics companies to install special Internet phone jacks in airplane armrests. The venture, called Connexion, would allow travelers to hook their laptops to the Web, watch TV, and check e-mail.

Figure 11.4.   Changes in document delivery, *http://www.nowdocs.com*. © NowDocs, Inc. *www.nowdocs.com* was recently awarded Forbes "Best of Web 2000" and CIO Magazine's 2000 Web Business 50/50 Award.

A B2C Implosion?

While the catalog companies took to the Internet like hummingbirds to nectar, it's only in the past year that major retailers decided they have an online future as well. Their advantages are

- Brand name.

- Customer base.

- Infrastructure.

Figure 11.5.   Even the U.S. Postal Service is attuned to changes in document delivery, *http://www.framed.usps.com/postecs*.

- Supplier relationships.

- Ability to supplement online shopping with in-store returns and service.

- Warehousing capacity.

- Inventory control.

- Distribution and shipping.

What is their incentive? Although the Internet still represents only 4% of U.S. retail sales except cars, it is the fastest-growing segment of retailing. Since Internet sales growth could affect the profitability of chain stores and their investment in real estate, going online for many is a matter of "if you can't beat 'em, join 'em." Their existing customer base makes many of these "clicks-and-mortar" operations immediately more profitable than their clicks-only competitors. A traditional retailer generally budgets $20 each for customer acquisition, while established **e-tailers,** who sell only online, spend $40 to $50; some new virtual businesses are spending over $100. It's pretty hard to make money at those rates!

Among the successes is WalMart, whose relaunched site takes direct aim at e-tailers like Amazon.com and eToys. ToysRus.com, which had deep pockets to rebound from a damaging initial launch, as well as serious holiday server and shipping problems, now runs head to head with eToys for the most visitors to an online toy store. REI, the outdoor and sporting goods chain, brings its virtual store into its physical locations to showcase more items than a store can display.

Major retailers, while proceeding cautiously onto the Web, do not seem concerned that they will lose customers, who prefer to touch goods and interact with knowledgeable sales staff. Many chain store owners agree with Jerry Storch, president of Dayton-Hudson Corp. (owner of Federated, Marshall Fields, and Target Stores), who believes that the myth of lower overhead for online sales is just that: "Moving small quantities of products all around the country is vastly more expensive than store-based retailing. When they invent the transporter on `Star Trek,' then the Internet will be a real threat," he says.

Whether or not you agree with Storch about selling online (obviously, many people dispute his assessment of relative costs), you can focus on the ability of the Internet to reduce your costs for communication and inventory. Think how the Internet can create cheaper channels to reach your distributors or suppliers.

You might be surprised at some of the industries finding a niche in cyberspace. For instance, the funeral industry sells everything from monuments and memorials to caskets and obituaries online (check *http://www.heavenlydoor.com* for a list of sites). Other retail segments are engaged in a brutal fight on two fronts: market share and investor dollars. Both travel sites and pet companies (petsmart, pets.com, petopia, and allpets.com) are ready for a shakeout.

Today's hot areas in e-tailing are health and beauty, watches and jewelry, groceries, sporting goods, and yes, the woof-woof, meow-meow market. The cold areas are guns, shoes, and heavy things, like major appliances. Of course, those lists don't mean there's no room for the small business with brains to carve out its unique niche and do extremely well.

Online launches by heavyweight retailers may cause rough seas for small businesses trying to stay afloat. Forrester Research warns that the Web will reduce local commerce in favor of national brand stores. In 1999 the top 10 e-commerce companies already accounted for 32% of e-commerce revenue, up from 27% the year before.

In spite of the potential of the Web to level the playing field, Forrester claims that several barriers will limit the ability of small sites to attract a national audience online. In their forecast, the share of online sales by local retailers will decline from 9% in 1999 to only 6% in 2003. This compares to the 50% share of retail dollars garnered offline by small and medium-sized business. National retailers enjoy inherent advantages in technology, brand, scale, and financial resources that permit the WalMarts of America to build expensive, full-featured online stores and advertise heavily to drive traffic to them. Small businesses can't compete on resources or price; they simply can't reduce their costs enough to match prices and make a profit.

However, as you saw from some of the stories in the last chapter, nimble, creative businesses can overcome these barriers. In particular, Forrester notes, local services are better off. Since only a portion of the transaction is online (generally order placement), location remains an advantage for service delivery. As a group, both the local and national businesses expect online sales to double from 8% to 17% as a percent of their business by 2002. Similarly, both groups expect to increase local Web advertising from 28% of their online budgets to 33%, shifting their dollars from radio, print, and Yellow Pages.

The Forrester study can be found at *http://www.forrester.com/ER/ Press/ForrFind/0,1768,0,FF.html*. More information on B2C changes by product category is available at the Business 2.0 site, *http://www. business2.com*.

Trends to Watch: Dot-Coms and Corporate Mergers

The dot-com world is a crazy dance, with **IPO** (initial public offering) valuations soaring higher than Baryshnikov and then crashing to the floor when they lose favor with investors. The past year has seen contradictory moves, with investors dumping nonproductive dot-com start-ups, yet pouring millions more into new Internet venture funds.

In fact, over $17 billion—about 75% of venture investments—poured into Internet companies in the first quarter of 2000 and $20 billion in the second quarter. However, much of the funding shifted from e-commerce and content sites to companies developing Internet infra-structure. For these investors, www. still has the potential to translate into World Wide Windfall.

All this capital was collected even as many Internet start-ups folded up their tutus and went home. One reason is that increasing revenues couldn't make up for the enormous amounts— sometimes up to 70% of their budget—that e-tailers were spending on marketing and advertising to acquire new customers. The net result was red ink and disenchanted investors.

Forrester Research has predicted that 75% of venture-financed e-tailers will go out of business by the end of 2001. Slim profit margins for books and music are driving the first shakeout; Forrester predicts that garden supplies and cooking will follow, with apparel and furniture next to thin out. As many companies have discovered to their chagrin, e-tailing involves a lot more than a Web site, leading to a shift from the supposed "first mover" advantage to a recognition that "best mover" may be the secret. In the early days of the Internet, being the first company to offer a product or service online was considered enough to guarantee success. Now, with increased competition from traditional retailers, more cautious investors are betting on the best company to win market share.

The Dot-Com Jitterbug and the Wall Street Waltz

In 1999 dollars flooded into Internet stocks, drawing unprecedented attention in the press. iVillage went public. Autobytel and AutoWeb went public. PC Flowers & Gifts.com went public. Priceline.com went public. These darlings of the investor community drove the bull market of 1999 with stock prices that rocketed to the moon, although only eBay and Yahoo! turned a profit. According to one IPO firm, Renaissance Capital Corp., Internet stock gained more than 200% over initial asking price in 1999 while non-Internet IPOs gained only 2%. That's a far cry from March 2000, when half of publicly traded dot-coms sold stock below their first day close and one quarter sold below their IPO valuations.

In spite of the Spring 2000 tumble, more than 200 companies await their chance to spin the IPO wheel of fortune, including such well-advertised sites as autotrader.com, BrandsForLess.com, Freeinetworks, liquor.com, lowestfare.com, Playboy.com, and Staples.com.

Among the wounded seeking to staunch the flow of financial blood:

- Garden.com, a venture-funded enterprise, is frantically seeking a new round of financing, while losing millions and watching its stock sink to less than 25% of its initial offer price. This has occurred in spite of increasing revenues, a membership base of more than a million buyers, a passionate online community, 42% of orders from repeat customers, and a drop-shipping program that allows the site to support 20,000 products.

- Go.com, the Internet unit of Walt Disney, which includes the Go.com directory, ABCNews.com, and ESPN.com, is bleeding dollars as it tries to redesign and reposition its portal from general interest to leisure and entertainment.

- Amazon.com and eToys, neither of which have any plans for profitability in the near term, as well as AltaVista, are among 70 dotcoms cutting jobs as their stock value drops and analysts issue gloomy reports citing negative cash flow, poor working capital management, and/or high debt loads. Although Amazon.com's original books, music, and video division is finally turning a profit, its increasing revenues have not kept up with losses on new merchandise areas. Even profitable sites like eBay have lost stock value.

- Nickelodeon sold the inventory of its online shop, RedRocket, to Toys R Us, which will create a Nickelodeon boutique with reciprocal links between ToysRus.com and Nick.com. Toys R Us has also announced an alliance with Amazon.com for a co-branded toy store site. Toysmart.com and ToyTime.com have also shut the lid on their toyboxes.

- The roll call of other cash-strapped sites, some mortally wounded, is sobering: Autoweb.com, Beyond.com, Buy.com, Car Order.com, CDnow, Cookexpress, Cybershop, Drugstore.com, Egghead.com, Fogdog.com, Furniture.com, HomeGrocer.com, KBKids.com, Peapod, Petplace, Petstore.com, PlanetRx, Quepasa, Salon.com, Streamline.com, and TurboLinux. Notably, content sites as well as e-tailers and even one B2B (Egghead.com) are on that list. The British e-tailer Boo.com, online news services APB-News.com and newswatch.com, the furniture site living.com, Value America, and Hollywood Entertainment's Reel.com are among the well-advertised dotcoms that are already history.

The lessons to be learned sound like Business 101. Just throwing money at marketing doesn't work; you have to build brand. Tying staff loyalty solely to stock valuation is a disaster. Back office infrastructure for order fulfillment (inventory, warehousing, distribution, order tracking, return policies) is essential. Customer service and support are critical. The numbers have to work: There must be a plan to improve margins and increase profitability. Duh?

If you're intent on seeking equity financing for your online enterprise from venture capitalists or angel investors, have a credible plan that realistically offsets expenses with revenue and shows when and how profitability will be reached. Be sure you will have enough cash to last until then. The same holds true whether you're seeking debt financing (a microloan, bank loan, a small business loan) or financing your business from your own savings.

When the money is there, spend it on (market) share; when the money is not, keep it in the pot (reduce costs to raise profit margins). Many states now run programs for local "angel" investors and microlenders. For a venture capital directory, try *http:// www.nextwavestocks.com/vcindex.html*. Angel investors can be found at *http://www.vfinance.com/angelsearch/as_searchtest.asp*, *http://ace-net.sr.unh.edu/pub* or *http://www.biz-angels.com*. Find your local Small Business Development Center at *http://www.sba.gov/INV*. The SBA site also has a list of microlenders at *http://www.sba.gov/ microparticipants.html* and a list of certified participants in the Small Business Loan program at *http://www.sba.gov/gopher/local-information/certified-preferred-lenders*.

The Corporate Pas de Deux

It makes you dizzy just to read the headlines in the business press. CNet buys the integrated online service network ZDnet for $1.6 billion in stock; this merger of two of the largest providers of news online yields a combined audience of 16.6 million users per month. Cisco, the top manufacturer of networking components, announces its acquisition of Netiverse for $210 million, its 13th of 20 to 25 planned acquisitions for the year. The digital ID company VeriSign parts with $17 billion to merge with Network Solutions, the prime registrar of domain names. Meanwhile Web ratings service Media Metrix merges with the consulting and analysis firm Jupiter Communications for $350 million. AOL and Time Warner have proposed the world's largest merger ever, valued between $163 and $180 billion. This highly contested proposal is seen as changing the Internet landscape forever by marrying broadband cable, Internet, and content providers.

On the retail side, Amazon.com diversifies, purchasing drugstore. com, pets.com, and accept.com (an e-commerce company). Some brick-and-mortar stores, like the pharmacy chain CVS Corporation, buy a cyber-equivalent (Soma.com) while eBay does the reverse, buying the long-established real-world auction firm, Butterfield & Butterfield. The conglomerates of Internet content companies mirror the conglomerates of distribution technology companies discussed in Chapter 1. Now that AT&T is the largest cable operator in the country, Microsoft invests in AT&T in exchange for AT&T's agreement to use Microsoft technology in cable set-top boxes! A lot of money is changing hands.

CMGI acquires AltaVista and DoubleClick as building blocks in an all-Web strategy. Yahoo! buys the online audio and video giant Broadcast.com for $5.6 billion, enabling Yahoo! to deliver broadband multimedia to more than 30 million monthly viewers. Yahoo! buys rival portal GeoCities for $5 billion. Yahoo!, which has several hundred acquisition deals underway at any one time, buys everybody.

What does all this hype and hyperactivity mean to small businesses seeking a mere hyperlink in cyberspace to call their own? The concentration of corporate interests on the Internet is not without precedent in the history of communications, only the speed with which it has occurred. The 12 major telecommunications companies in 1996 are now down to six; some two dozen companies now control almost all the U.S. media culture. Is this the "free media" that the Internet portended?

Watch for media giants, such as CBS, Disney, AT&T, and Hearst, to acquire more and more Internet companies as adjuncts to their computer, cable, phone, news, and entertainment empires. Of the 20 most popular Web sites, none remained independent of large corporate ownership by August 2000. As displayed by Cyberatlas (*http://cyberatlas. internet.com/big_picture/traffic_patterns/article/0,5931_466411,00.html*), these sites, arranged by millions of unique visitors per month, are shown in Figure 11.6.

Watch for the increased importance of portals, those gateway screens people use as their entree to a multitude of Web services, from stock quotes to news and e-mail. Portals are seen as adding not only advertising value, but informational worth: They are expected to make the Web a more organized place to exchange both data and dollars. What they organize, however, is corporate depth, not Web breadth: Portals are now the entry point to the network of multiple sites owned by a single

Rank	Sites	Unique Visitors (in 000's)
1	AOL Network	62,659
2	Yahoo!	52,012
3	Microsoft Sites	51,963
4	Lycos	32,907
5	Excite Network	28,167
6	Go Network	23,126
7	About.com Sites	19,783
8	AltaVista	17,795
9	Time Warner Online	15,825
10	Amazon	15,688
11	Real.com Network	14,940
12	NBC Internet	14,688
13	Viacom Online	14,290
14	LookSmart	13,403
15	eUniverse Network	12,713
16	eBay	12,675
17	Go2Net Network	12,576
18	CNET Networks	12,159
19	Ask Jeeves	10,889
20	ZDnet Sites	10,122

Figure 11.6. Most popular sites on the Web, August 2000, *http://cyberatlas. internet.com/big_picture/traffic_patterns/article/0,5931_466411,00.html.* Reprinted with permission. © 2000 Internet.com, LLC. All rights reserved.

corporate entity. (Specialized portals may draw an audience too low to be profitable from advertising; several Hispanic and African-American portals are already in trouble.)

Thus, AOL bought Netscape not only for its browser software, but also for NetCenter, another of the largest portals on the Web. The NetCenter site at *http://home.netscape.com* (seen in Figure 11.7) complements AOL's own portal and gives AOL ownership of two of the most popular Internet destinations. Their combined viewership, along with viewers on AOL's other acquisitions like MapQuest, gave AOL the number one ranking, with over 62 million visitors in August 2000.

Need more evidence? Blockbuster struck a 20-year deal with Enron to deliver video-on-demand over Enron's high-speed fiber optic lines nationwide. This will complement Blockbuster's arrangement with DSL providers like Verizon, SBC, and Covad to provide "last-mile" trans-

Figure 11.7. Portal site, *http://home.netscape.com*. The Netscape Communicator interface is © 1999 Netscape Communications Corporation. All rights reserved. Netscape, Netscape Navigator, and the Netscape N logo are registered trademarks and Netscape Communicator is a trademark of Netscape in the United States and other countries.

mission into customers' homes. And in an unusually overt marriage of commerce and information, search engine portal Lycos merged with USA Networks, a consumer goods company that already owns Ticketmaster, CitySearch, and the Home Shopping Network. Together, USA/Lycos Interactive Networks will be a $20 billion Internet/television conglomerate.

To continue to draw audiences, portal sites may increasingly become a medium for multimedia entertainment rather than information. (Does this sound like the history of broadcasting yet?) Should you care? Yes, because the cost of creating those sites is part of the upward pressure on Web site creation prices overall, as you learned in Chapter 4. Yes, because entertainment on those sites crowds out the very thing you may be using to draw people to your site: information. This may bounce either way: forcing people to look at smaller sites to find what they are looking for or forcing them off the Web altogether in frustration.

It also means that the Web will segment into monster sites, increasingly, albeit invisibly, linked to one another to reinforce marketing messages and to keep buyers within a cyber-conglomerate for purchasing. Several strategies exist if you are trying to reach the consuming public: You can affiliate with one of the mega-monsters, participate in a segment at a lower tier (equivalent to cable television), or stick it out as an independent. The answer, as always, depends on your business goals.

Portals are the mass marketing sites of the Web, like first- tier broadcast networks. To make the numbers work for their investors, these sites have to deliver one thing: eyeballs. They sell an audience to advertisers, particularly to huge corporations concerned with brand name imaging. As for your eyeballs, keep one eye on trends influencing activity on the Internet, but keep the other on your bottom line.

The Promise and Peril of Rich Media

On the Web, a "sticky" site attracts visitors, keeps them there, and brings them back. To achieve "stickiness," more and more Web sites incorporate **rich media**, the Web term for **multimedia** incorporated on a site. Rich media refers to the presentation of animation, video, sound, real-time information feeds, 3-D, virtual reality simulations, games, interactive programs, and even aromas! See Figures 11.8 and 11.9 for examples of rich media sites using animation and virtual reality.

You may want rich media to create a unique Internet-based form of entertainment. Or perhaps your site is designed to promote your corporate identity as an innovative Web designer. Some reports show that rich media pages generate 20% to 60% more traffic than static pages and that rich media ads have 8% to 18% click-through rates, compared to 1% for regular banners. But many companies add rich media to their site simply because everyone else is doing it, or because they think it's "in."

As tantalizing as it may be to incorporate rich media, you must always ask yourself whether it will enhance the communication goals for your site and whether it's appropriate for your target audience. Just because something *can* be done, doesn't mean it *should* be done.

Some rich media options—simple animation and audio files—now run automatically on browser software. In other cases, files are downloaded to a user's machine to be played later. Most new computers come with the built-in capability to play back downloaded video, audio, and

Figure 11.8. A site loaded with animation and other rich media, *http://www .mamamedia.com.* Courtesy *MaMa Media.*

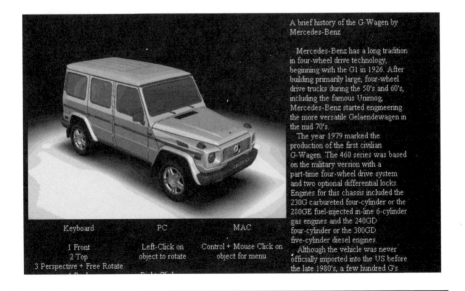

Figure 11.9. A site that uses 3D virtual reality for product demonstration, *http://www.gwagen.com/ext_hi.htm.* Courtesy G. Wagen USA and Flying Rhino Productions.

3-D graphics. By definition, however, users can't interact in real time with a downloaded file except to start, stop, fast-forward, or reverse it. Since it can take a while, viewers may be reluctant to download a long video clip they watch once and discard. Worse yet, they could end up resenting a business that requires this method to obtain information.

Streaming media files, whether video (seen in Figure 11.10) or audio, play out as they are transmitted over the Internet to the user's computer. This is particularly valuable when files would be too big to fit into memory, when they would take an unacceptably long time to download, or when you want interactivity. However, to play streaming media or virtual reality files, users may need to reconfigure their machines and install **plug-ins** (special pieces of playback software downloaded into a browser). The newest versions of browsers incorporate many plug-ins, but not all users have the latest version. You may want to offer viewers choices as done in Figure 11.11.

Figure 11.10. A site that uses streaming video, *http://www.atomfilms.com*. Courtesy Atom Films.

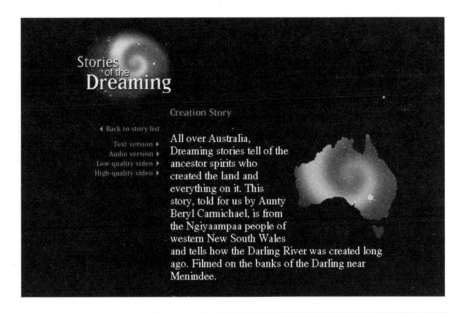

Figure 11.11. Allowing multimedia options, *http:www.dreamtime.net.au/ creation*. © 1999 Australian Museum.

Usually, it is straightforward to download and install plug-ins, but the time-consuming process may deter harried, casual, or inexperienced users. As new versions of browser and plug-in software are released, users may have to repeat this process. At the very least, users need RealPlayer from RealNetworks *(http://www.real.com)*, Microsoft's Windows Media Player, and Apple's Quicktime player to obtain good coverage of the various media formats on the Internet.

Most plug-ins can be downloaded free from the developer's site. Before you decide to implement rich media, go through the installation process yourself to decide whether your users are likely to do it. Be sure to offer directions about the plug-ins and incorporate hyperlinks to their source. If possible, mirror the plug-ins so users can download them without leaving your site.

Several other factors may affect your rich media decision. Most streaming media require high speed, wide bandwidth connections to play well. Agonizingly slow delivery results from low-speed modems, the number of people online at any one time, bandwidth limitations, and the capacity of the server. Remember, fewer than 10% of the 33 million homes currently on the Internet have high-speed connections.

Compared to static pages, rich media sites also require that your users have more memory, faster processors, more recent system software, and better skills. Consider the importance of providing an alternative for users who lack adequate hardware and software for rich media displays. Finally, make sure you can assemble the technical and financial resources to produce multimedia. Rich media compounds the complexity and expense of Web site development.

Back to Basics

Let's reconsider the basic issues of doing business, wherever your location, wherever your customers are found online.

The Customer Is the Measure of All Things

Regardless of the online task in front of you, put yourself in your customer's place. Is the message clear? Will the customer know how to take the next step toward a purchase? Does the message impart a sense of trust?

A site that indulges multimedia fantasies but frustrates users who lack the necessary software or hardware does not put its customers first. A site that takes hours to download sends a message that the user's time is not important. A site that forever hangs out a sign "Under Construction" loses viewers as fast as a retail store that never flips over its "Closed" sign.

Customers, clients, future employees, even suppliers like to be stroked and made to feel important. Successful online marketing makes it easy for customers to do business with you. They can find you easily; they can communicate with you easily; they can navigate through your Web site easily. When you offer useful information or entertainment, you offer value that tells customers they are worth the effort.

We have talked about tracking many forms of hits and winning awards for site design. In the end, the most meaningful measures of success are the return of existing customers and the arrival of new ones.

Sell More Than Air

A solid Internet marketing effort starts with something of value—a product, a service, technical support, or additional information. A washing machine maker can offer a list of hints for removing stains. A car manufacturer can provide a maintenance checklist. The Federal Express site enables customers to track their packages' locations instantly. Not only does that feature meet its customers' needs, it reduces costs for Federal Express.

Customers who hear of others' bad experiences often shy away from purchasing online. They worry about guarantees, quality, service, and misuse of credit cards. Although you are not responsible for online problems created by others, you must overcome misgivings about using the Internet. Offer alternate ordering methods, warranties, solid return policies, and secure forms of electronic payment.

Plan Before You Program

Throughout this book, we've talked about the importance of planning your activities and following that plan during the implementation phase of Internet marketing. Figure 11.12 is a checklist of the various planning tools, surveys, questionnaires, and record logs you've learned about in previous chapters. By now you have long since created the Web notebook described in Chapter 2, so you have an organized place to store the results from all these tools and questionnaires.

Whew! So much for the paperless office! To be sure, you can keep many of these documents electronically as databases, spreadsheets, or word processing tables. However, you may as well set aside shelf space for your Internet marketing notebooks now. You will need some way to remember the hundreds of details required to implement your ideas successfully.

Apply Existing Marketing Know-How to Online Efforts

The more you know about the results of your marketing activities, the better off you will be. Closely monitor new and repeat visitors to your site and the rate of response to other forms of online marketing. Just as you monitor the results of any other promotional or sales activities, you

- Business plan: basic strategic guide showing where your business is going over the coming 1-5 years.
- Marketing plan: subset of business plan that lays out overall marketing goals and quantifiable objectives for all marketing activities combined.
- Internet marketing plan: subset of marketing plan that lays out the goals and objectives for all types of online marketing, including e-mail, mailbots, mailing lists, news group announcements, classified advertising, and Web site.
- Customer/user survey: if appropriate, a survey (online or off-line) of current and/or prospective members of target audience to understand their online activities, computer resources, and interest in electronic information, purchasing or service..
- Info-log: a schedule for regular maintenance, updating, and creation of non-Web electronic marketing tools, including news group postings, electronic press releases, and blurbs; log shows when activities were performed and by whom.
- Telecommunications survey: analysis of in-house computer and communications resources and needs.
- Web designer questionnaire: tool for selecting the best Web designer for you.
- WHISP questionaire: tool for selecting the best Web Hosting Service Provider for you.
- ISP questionnaire: tool for selecting the best Internet Service Provider for you.
- Team list: shows all participants in Internet marketing efforts, including Web creation, promotion, maintenance, and monitoring activities both in-house and outside.
- Budget: costs, cash flow, and/or revenue streams for Web and other Internet marketing activities.
- Schedule: timeline of activities for implementation and maintenance of Web site and other electronic marketing activities.
- Web site planning worksheet (treatment): goals, objectives, and outline of elements for a Web site.
- Scripts and storyboard for Web site (may be produced by contractor): depiction of narrative content, navigation pathways, links, and proposed design (look-and-feel) for Web site and/or its individual elements, especially multimedia.
- Web site maintenance plan: schedule of activities for repairing, updating, linking, and adding to your site.
- Web site monitoring schedule: list of which Web statistics will be collected and how often; results kept individually and with a historical log for comparison.
- Web promotion log: list of methods, cost, and frequency for promoting a Web site, with a record showing when activities were performed and by whom.
- Web site advertising plan: plan for paid advertising and sponsorships, including costs, CPM, frequency, and results.
- Copyright and trademark forms for filing if needed.
- Merchant card application if needed.
- Other electronic banking application forms if needed.

Figure 11.12. Checklist of Internet planning tools.

should monitor your electronic results for individual Web pages, for visitors arriving from different links, for changed wording in ads, or for response to different giveaways.

Whenever possible, use source code numbers or modify entry pathways so that you know the effectiveness of each kind of advertising or promotion that you do. Don't be afraid to experiment with several approaches until you find the ones that work best. Then repeat the successful ideas and drop the losers. Online marketing takes work, but it is not rocket science.

If you have an online catalog, apply known techniques to make it alive with animation, photos, and careful use of color. Your Web site is like an ad that needs constant freshening. Update it frequently with new products, special offers, announcements, customer service tips, games, or new information.

Remember that an online site still needs offline marketing. Every time you send a message, write a letter, put up a sign, print your business cards, go to a conference, join a news group, or create a mailing list, you should funnel attention to your Web site, listserver, and e-mail address. As you already know, constant promotion is another key to business success.

Above all, don't be afraid to talk to your online customers to see what they like or don't like about your site, your service, or your products. Ask how they found you and what else you can do for them. Your customers know you better than anyone else.

Integrate Online Marketing with Other Business Activities

Even if you sell only in the virtual world, the rest of your business functions in the real world. From marketing to finance, order processing to supplier relations, banking to warehousing, a business deals with human beings in physical space and real time. Ignoring these elements of your business can lead to a downfall, no matter how brilliantly you execute your online marketing strategy. Think before you act electronically. Make sure you've estimated viewer response and have plans to handle it.

For most companies, online activities are only a portion of their overall marketing and promotion efforts, only one sector of their sales, and only one element in their customer service or employee recruitment tool kit. Staff buy-in and involvement will help you integrate online business techniques successfully.

Have Fun

Extrapolating from its growth, the Web—with its sizzle, graphics, entertainment, and information—will eventually draw almost everyone with serious intentions to market online.

Try to approach the Internet in a spirit of discovery and delight. You're going to spend a lot of time online researching, monitoring your site and looking at what others are doing. If you experience sheer horror at dealing with computers, delegate Internet marketing tasks to someone who enjoys it.

Like anything else worthwhile in business, marketing online takes time. But you can make it fun for your employees, your customers, and yourself with realistic goals and the right attitude. Log on!

Appendix A

Resources

Category/Company Name URL		Descriptive Phrase
Advertising		
Ad Auction	*http://www.adauction.com*	Online ad auction
Ad Knowledge	*http://www.adknowledge.com*	Rates on major sites
Ad Resource	*http://www.adresource.com*	Web advertising and promotion resources
Ads Guide	*http://www.ad-guide.com*	Internet advertising guide
Banner Tips	*http://bannertips.com/index.shtml*	Banner exchange and tips
Click Experts	*http://www.clickexperts.com*	Latino online advertising
Congo's Money Maker	*http://www.globalserve.net/~ bloemink/money/brokers.html*	Lists of companies that will sell your ad space
Cyberatlas	*http://www.cyberatlas.internet. com/segments/advertising*	General advertising information
	http://209.249.142.16/nnpm owaNRpublicreports.top bannerweekly	Archive of top banner ads
Digitrends	*http://www.digitrends.net*	News about advertising trends
Internet Advertising	*http://www.internetadvertising.org*	Current advertising information
Media Metrix	*http://www.mediametrix.com*	Advertising statistics
NetCreations	*http://www.netcreations. com/ipa/adindex*	Report on advertising rates

Online Advertising	*http://www.o-a.com*	Online marketing discussion list
Web Track	*http://www.webtrack.com*	Where companies are advertising

General Business

Better Business Bureau Online	*http://www.bbbonline.org*	Business information, certification, links to local BBB
Business 2.0	*http://www.business2.com*	Online business magazine
Business Wire	*http://www.businesswire.com*	News on the net
CommerceNet	*http://www.commercenet.com*	E-commerce resources
Department of Commerce	*http://www.ecommerce.gov*	Government report/ projections on digital economy
Inc.Online	*http://www.inc.com/virtual consultant*	Inc. magazine forum
Internet.com	*http://www.internet.com*	E-commerce trends
Openmarket	*http://www.openmarket.com*	Internet commerce statistics
PC World	*http://www.pcworld.com*	News about the PC industry
Small Business	*http://www.smallbizplanet.com*	Small business resources
The Standard	*http://www.thestandard.com*	Business news and statistics
Truste.com	*http://www.truste.com*	Privacy certification
U.S. Department Commerce	*http://www.doc.gov*	Export and statistical of commerce information
U.S. Small Business Administration	*http://www.sbaonline.sba.gov*	Multiple resources for small businesses
Venture Finance	*http://www.vfinance.com/angel.asp*	List of angel investors
WilsonWeb	*http://www.wilsonweb.com*	Marketing/e-commerce services and resource information
ZDNet	*http://www.zdnet.com*	Internet business information and multiple Web resources

Internet Resources

CyberAtlas	*http://cyberatlas.internet.com*	All-purpose information site
Domain Statistics	*http://www.domainstats.com*	Web statistics
Emarketer	*http://www.emarketer.com*	News and statistics
Iconocast	*http://www.iconocast.com/ whatis/whatis.html*	Internet statistics
Internet Indicators	*http://www.internetindicators.com*	Internet economy report
Internet Society	*http://info.isoc.org/internet/history*	History of the Internet

Internet.com	*http://www.internet.com/sections/ news.html*	Internet news
Internet Stats	*http://www.internetstats.com*	Internet statistic site links
PBS	*http://www.pbs.org/Internet*	Internet history
Web Com	*http://www.webcom.com/*	Tables of e-commerce growth

Legal and Privacy

American Bar Association	*http://www.abanet.org/busl aw/cyber/home.html*	Background information on many Internet legal issues
First Gov	*http://www.firstgov.gov*	Master site for federal government information
National Consumers League	*http://www.fraud.org*	Fraud watch
U.S. Federal Trade Commission	*http://www.ftc.gov/privacy/ index.html*	Privacy information
U.S. Library of Congress	*http://lcweb.loc.gov/copyright*	Copyright information
U.S. Library of Congress	*http://thomas.loc.gov*	Information about Internet and other legislation
U.S. Patent and Trademark Office	*http://www.uspto.gov*	Patent and trademark information

Marketing

Bannerworks	*http://www.bannerworks.com*	Sample banner exchange site
Bcentral	*http://siteowner.bcentral. com/sitecheck.cfm*	Multiple marketing site-checking, and development resources
Everything Email	*http://www.everythingemail.net*	E-mail resource site
Global Reach	*http://www.glreach.com*	Global marketing company and statistics
Hyperbanner	*http://www.hyperbanner.com*	International banner exchange
Interactive Traffic	*http://www.i-traffic.com*	Site traffic analysis
International Workz	*http://www.internationalworkz .com*	International advertising company
Internet Wire	*http://www.internetwire.com*	Online press release outlet
Linkexchange	*http://www.linkexchange.com*	Sample banner exchange site
Links:2000	*http://www.2000.ogsm.vanderbilt. edu/links.cgi*	Marketing analysis
Liszt	*http://www.liszt.com*	Source for news groups and listservers

New South Network Services	*http://www.nsns.com/ mouseTracks/tloml.html*	Links to marketing resources
PR Newswire	*http://www.profnet.com*	Online press release outlet
Promo of the Month	*http://www.promoof the month.com*	Promotional items
Tile.net	*http://www.tile.net*	Source for news groups and listservers
Virtual Remote	*http://www.virtualpromote.com*	Site promo info

Model Sites

A.L. Van Houtte	*http://www.finecoffee.com*	Good title bars and store-front
Exotic Wood Dreams	*http://www.exoticwood dreams.com*	Small business site with customer service and personalization
Farms.com	*http://www.farms.com*	Agribusiness marketplace, auctions
Jelly Belly	*http://www.jellybelly.com/ events.html*	Special events
Noggintops.com	*http://www.noggintops.com*	Clear navigation and product photos
New York Cabbie	*http://www.nycabbie.com*	Concept site with word-of-mouth promotion
Online Conser-vatory.com	*http://www.onlinecon servatory.com*	Interactive online piano instruction
Pablo's Mechanical Heating & Plumbing	*http://www.pablosmechanical.com*	Low-budget site that does everything it promises and more
Presbyterian Health Service	*http://www.phs.org*	Good META tags
Ragu	*http://www.eat.com*	Creative site with excellent marketing and calls to action
Social Studies School Services	*http://www.socialstudies.com*	Excellent catalog site with offline promotion
Tema Contem-porary Furniture	*http://www.tema-usa.com*	Catalog with high search engine rankings; deals with shipping/logistic issues
The Shoe Guy	*http://www.shoeguy.com*	Web selling for personal services
Theatre.com	*http://www.theatre.com*	Excellent service site
Underneath.com	*http://www.underneath.com*	Well-implemented budget site with creative promotion

Wine.com	*http://www.wine.com*	Well-structured, mature site
Wrenchead.com	*http://www.wrenchead.com*	Active community, commerce site

Multimedia

Atomfilms	*http://www.atomfilms.com*	Short films and animation
Broadcast.com	*http://www.broadcast.com*	Real-time broadcasting
iPix	*http://www.ipix.com*	Virtual reality reality and travel
Macromedia	*http://www.macromedia.com*	Shockwave and Flash plug-ins and more
Microsoft	*http://www.microsoft.com*	Downloads, products, support
MP3.com	*http://www.mp3.com*	Music player downloads
Netscape	*http://software-depot.netscape. com/plugins*	Software depot for plug-ins
Plug-ins.com	*http://www.plugins.com*	Multimedia plug- ins
Quicktime	*http://quicktime.apple.com*	Movie player
Real Networks	*http://www.realnetworks.com*	Streaming audio and video plug-in
Shareware	*http://www.shareware.com*	AVI applet
Sun Computer	*http://www.java.com*	Java applet

Site Monitoring & Tools

1-2-3 Webtools	*http://freeguestbooks.com*	Free guestbooks and link pages
Bcentral	*http://siteowner.bcentral.com/ sitecheck.cfm*	Multiple marketing, site-checking, and development resources
Cast.org	*http://www.cast.org/bobby*	Speed and ease of use emulation
HoTmetaL	*ftp://ftp.ncsa.uiuc.edu/ Web/html/hotmetal/*	HTML editor
Internet Profiles Corporation	*http://www.engage.com/ipro*	Web and server statistical software
MOMSpider	*http://www.ics.uci.edu/ pub/websoft*	Multi-Owner Maintenance spider and link checker
Netstore	*http://www.netstore.de/ Supply/index.html*	Analysis software
Toolzone	*http://www.toolzone.com*	Free guestboook
VBStats 3.1	*http://www.tech.west.ora. com/win_httpd/*	VBStat software

Watson-Addy	*http://watson.addy.com*	Web page analyzer
Web Trends	*http://www.webtrends.com*	Statistical analysis software package
WWWstat	*http://www.ics.uci.edu/pub/ websoft/wwwstat*	Basic log analysis
Yahoo!	*http://www.yahoo.com/ Computers_and_Internet/ software/Internet/World_Wide_ Web/Servers/Log_Analysis_Tools*	Log analysis tools

---

Transaction and Store-Building Sites

Catalog.com	*http://www.catalog.com*	Web transaction host
CCNow	*http://www.ccnow.com*	Credit card services
CyberCash	*http://www.cybercash.com*	Internet banking
E-commerce	*http://www.electronicfunds. com/index.html*	Electronic funds transfer and bill paying
EDI Information Center	*http://www.edi-info-center.com*	EDI links
Checkfree	*http://www.checkfree.com/*	Electronic funds transfer
GTA Net Order Form	*http://www.gta-tech.com*	Free shopping cart
Mall Surfer	*http://www.mallsurfer.com*	Mall- building software
MasterCard	*http://www.mastercard.com/ shoponline/set*	SET demonstration
Small Business Administration	*http://www.sba.gov/micro participants.html*	List of microloan lender
Verisign	*http://www.verisign.com*	Digital IDs
Visa	*http://www.visa.com*	Merchant card information
Wilson Internet Services	*http://www.wilsonweb.com/ articles/merch-cc.htm/*	Card rates

---

Web Site Creation

CNet	*http://www.cnetbuilder.com*	Site-building tips and vendor rankings
ICANN	*http;//www.icann.org*	List of companies doing domain registration
InterNIC	*http://whois.internic.net/*	WhoIs domain name database
Jakob Nielsen on Writing	*http://www.useit.com/papers/ webwriting*	Web writing resources
Network Solutions	*http://www.networksolutions.com*	One of many domain name registration sites
Top Hosts	*http://www.tophosts.com*	Ranks Web hosting companies

| Web Builder | *http://www.builder.com* | Web site-building resources |
| Web Pages That Suck | *http://www.webpagesthatsuck.com* | Learn from bad pages |

Web Site Promotion

Cool Central	*http://www.coolcentral.com*	Cool links
Clearinghouse.net	*http://www.clearinghouse.net*	Directory of meta-indexes
Directory Guide	*http://www.directoryguide.com*	Search engine for directories
FAQs	*http://ep.com/faq/web announce.html*	How to announce a site
Links To You	*http://www.linkstoyou.com/ checklinks.htm*	Checks inbound links
NetCreations	*http://www.netcreations.com/ postmaster/i ndex.html/*	Web promotion
Netscape	*http://www.netscape.com/ cenetcenter/cool.html*	Cool Links and announment service
Newtoo	*http://www.newtoo.com/ submit.html*	Announcement service
Searchengine.com	*http://www.searchengine.com*	Search engine for search engines
Submit It	*http://www.submit-it.com*	Web registration site
USA Today	*http:/tech.usatoday.com/lead page/usanew.html*	Cool links
WebPosition	*http://www.webposition.com*	Search engine placement software
What's New	*http://www.whatsnew.com/whatsnew*	Announcement service
Yahoo!	*http://www.yahoo.com/new/ Computers/World_Wide _Web_ Announcement_Service*	Announcement service and more

Appendix B

Glossary

Above the fold   Ad placement on the top half of a page before a viewer would need to scroll·down.

Agent log   A server record that shows which programs (e.g., spider, search engine, link verifier) have contacted a server.

Algorithm   A formula or model executed by a computer program.

Alias   An alternate e-mail address to which mail is forwarded.

Applets   Small application programs that can be embedded within a Web page. Applets cannot be directly activated from the operating system.

Archive   A compressed or backed up data file.

ASP   Active Server Page. A Web page created dynamically in response to a user request that uses ActiveX scripting.

AVI   Microsoft's format for packaging and playing video under the Windows operating system.

B2B   Business to Business. Refers to target market for a transactional Web site.

B2C   Business to Consumer. Refers to target market (retail) for a transactional Web site.

Backbone   Very-high-speed, wide-bandwidth transmission line forming a major pathway in a network.

Bandwidth   The information capacity, usually measured in megahertz or bits per second, that can be transmitted by a particular line or cable, or managed by a piece of hardware or software.

Banner ad   Standard, rectangular Web ad that links to another site.

Baud   Bits per second, also known as the baud rate. Measures the rate of data transfer within a specific time. (Also see *bps*.)

BBS   Bulletin Board System. Special-purpose electronic communications system in which messages can be entered or retrieved either privately or publicly.

Bit   Single item of information set to one or zero. It takes eight bits to specify one byte, or one alphanumeric character.

Blurb   Short message about a business, product, service, or related topic.

Bookmark   Online reminder that flags a URL for future reference.

Box ad   A square or almost square banner ad on a Web page.

BPS   Bits Per Second. Rate of information transfer. Modem speed is measured in K (kilo--thousand) bps. (See *baud*.)

Broadband   Telecommunications bandwidth large enough to carry several channels at once; often used to handle real-time video, e.g., cable TV.

Browser   Software that accesses the Web and other Internet resources.

Cable modem   Modem that uses coaxial cable to achieve greater bandwidth and thus faster information transfer.

Cache   Download information and store in memory for future use.

Call to action   A marketing and sales device that tells the customer how to take the next step toward a purchase or execute an activity; often uses an imperative verb.

Centerless network   Network architecture that uses a redundant design so that multiple nodes remain running even if one becomes inoperative.

CGI   Common Gateway Interface. Web programming method that turns non-Web information into a Web document on the fly and vice versa. Used for interactive online elements such as registration forms.

Chat room   Online communication in which typed messages can be exchanged in real time; some chat rooms on Webs run continuously; others are scheduled for a certain time for a certain topic. See *conference*.

Checkstand   A Web software program that reviews and totals prices for items in a shopping cart, adds shipping and taxes, and arranges for customer payment. Also called a *register*.

Classifieds   Short text advertisements organized by category.

Clicks and mortar   A business that sells both online and through a physical storefront. Compare to *e-tailer*.

Co-brand   Include two or more brand names in extended promotional activities to encourage viewers to associate the two.

Comps   Preliminary designs for a graphic or Web presentation.

Computer network   Two or more computers connected together to share resources.

Concatenate   Chain together in a sequence.

Conference   On the Web, a form of real-time chat, often moderated, with a guest speaker or speakers. Generally a specially scheduled event; can also be convened for only invited participants.

Cookie   Software downloaded to a viewer's machine that enables a Web site to identify return machines, reuse information the viewer has entered on the site, and/or track the path through the site the viewer has taken.

Co-op dollars   Advertising subsidy in which a manufacturer underwrites some of the promotional costs incurred by its retailers or distributors. Also called co-op marketing.

CPM   Cost Per Thousand. Advertising rate to reach one thousand possible viewers or listeners (M is the Roman numeral for 1,000).

Cyberspace   Term coined by William Gibson in his book *Necromancer* to describe an area that exists only online.

Cybersquatting   The illegal practice of registering someone else's trademarked, service-marked, or personal URL with the intention of resale.

Data compression   Method of reducing the amount of bandwidth required to transmit information, thus increasing the speed of transmission.

Data mining   The collection and mathematical analysis of vast amounts of computerized data to discover previously hidden patterns or unknown relationships.

Dedicated server   A Web hosting server used by a single client company; more broadly, a single computer in a network reserved for network needs. Compare to shared server.

Digital cash   Electronic money purchased in advance of expenditures, as with a debit card. May be stored as encrypted data in a digital wallet or in a cookie.

Digital certificate   Confirmation of identity in an online environment, often stored in a digital wallet.

Digital wallet   Secure encrypted envelope that seals personal information including bank accounts, credit card numbers, expiration dates, shipping and billing addresses, and digital identification.

Directory Hierarchical database arranged by categories and subcategories. Used to locate sites on the Web.

Display Large Web advertisement, generally varying in size from quarter-screen to full-screen, which links to another site.

Domain name Web site identification registered with InterNIC, ending in a "top-level" designation such as *.com*, *.edu*, *.gov*, *.mil*, *.net*, or *.org*. See *URL*.

Doorway page A page designated as an entry point for viewers arriving from another site or search engine. Can be an existing page on a site or a page independently created for that purpose. See *splash page*.

Dot-com A Web-based business (B2B or B2C); often refers to a venture-funded start-up that intends to make an IPO.

Download Send a file or program from online storage to a personal computer for later use.

DSL Digital Subscriber Line. High-speed transmission method used on standard phone lines to accommodate graphics, video, and sound. If speeds for downloading are faster than for uploading, it may be referred to as ADSL, Asymmetric Digital Subscriber Line.

E-mail Electronic mail. System that lets users exchange messages across a network.

E-tailer A business that sells only online. Compare to *clicks and mortar*.

E-zines Electronic magazines that are published and distributed solely online.

Ear ad A small banner ad usually found in the corner of a Web page.

EDI Electronic Data Interchange. The structured exchange of standard business information.

EFT Electronic Funds Transfer.

Electronic order form An online document filled in by customers to indicate the items they want to purchase. Less sophisticated than shopping cart and checkstand software, it may or may not calculate totals.

Encoder Software that converts "ripped" audio files into MP3 format.

Encryption Coding of confidential, personal, or financial information for secure transmission.

Extranet Wide area network with Weblike operations.

FAQ Frequently Asked Questions. Appear often on news groups, mailing lists, forums, and technical support sites.

Firewall Security procedure that sets up a barrier between an internal LAN (Local Area Network) and the Internet.

Flame   Send online communication involving personal attacks and/or derogatory remarks.

Flat file   A database contained in a single table; used for small applications.

Forum   Open, nonsimultaneous discussion on an online service or Web site. Operates like news groups on the Net.

FTP   File Transfer Protocol. Method used to upload and download files between a computer and Internet servers.

GIF   Graphics Interchange Format. A compressed, bit-mapped graphics format most often used to display nonphotographic designs on the Web. See *JPEG*.

Giga   Prefix for billion.

Gigabyte   One billion bytes.

Hacker   Individual who forces unauthorized entry into a computer system. Also slang for computer enthusiast or amateur.

HDML   Handheld Device Markup Language

Hits   Number of times any file of a Web site is downloaded.

Home page   Main page or welcome image for a Web site. Often shows a table of contents or refers to documents on other pages.

Host   Computer system (of any size) with a direct, high-speed transmission link to the Internet. Often used to describe servers on which Web sites are stored for Internet access. Most individual users connect to a host to reach the Internet.

HTML   HyperText Markup Language. Used to author Web documents containing links, graphics, and multimedia.

HTTP   HyperText Transport Protocol. Method used to transmit hypertext files.

Hyperlink   Same as *link*.

Hypertext   Any document with a link or links to other documents.

ICANN   Internet Corporation for Assigned Names and Numbers. The international organization that manages top-level domain assignments on the Internet.

Inbound link   Viewed from the target business site, a one-way link coming from another site.

Intellectual property   The protected ownership of rights in ideas or the expression of ideas, specifically trademarks, service marks, copyrights, and patents.

Intelligent agent   A software program that performs a human- style processing task, e.g., upselling customers by suggesting additional products.

Internal link   A link within a Web site between pages, files, images, or paragraphs.

InterNIC   Internet Network Information Center. Maintains the master database for domain name registration.

Interstitial   An online display ad that appears between two destination pages.

Intranet   Internal network with Weblike operations.

IP   Internet Protocol. Data format required to exchange packets of information over the Internet. See TCP/IP.

IPO   Initial Public Offering.   When a company first issues publicly traded stock on an exchange; offerings are regulated by the Securities and Exchange Commission.

ISDN   Integrated Services Digital Network. Older type of high- speed, wide-bandwidth, dial-up phone line for transmission of text, graphics, and sound.

ISP   Internet Service Provider. Company that sells the use of its powerful servers and high-speed transmission lines for access to the Internet.

Javammercial   An online ad containing Java script for animation or other rich media.

JPEG (or JPG)   Joint Photographic Experts Group. A compressed image format most often used to display photographs on the Web. Compare to *GIF.*

Kbps   Kilo (thousand) bits per second.

Keyword   Important concept word in Web site text. Entered in search engines to locate information in a database.

LAN   Local Area Network. Links computers in the same building or area, generally less than one mile.

Leased line   Telephone line set up between any two sites for dedicated, continuously active transmission.

Legacy site   A previous implementation of a Web site with which a new site must remain compatible.

Link   A technique in HTML that allows a user to jump from one location on the Web to another. Can occur within a site or between sites.

Listbot   Cross between *list* and *robot*. A type of mailbot that automatically processes requests, sending out information (e.g., a newsletter) or performing the specified task (e.g., entering a subscriber's name to a mailing list.) See *listserver.*

Listserver   Software that manages mailing lists on mailing list servers. Listserv and Majordomo are two of the primary mailing listservers.

Live banners   Ads that allow users to take an action without clicking through to another site.

Localization   The customization of a Web site for different countries and/or languages.

Logo Name-only, paid advertisement on the Web, usually smaller and less expensive than a banner. May not link to named site.

Lurk To participate in a news group or forum by monitoring traffic without contributing.

Mail bomb Useless e-mail that clogs an electronic mailbox.

Mailbot Cross between *mail* and *robot*. A program that responds automatically to routine e-mail.

Mailing list List of participants who exchange electronic mail messages regularly, usually focused on a particular topic or concern.

Mall Virtual area on a server or online service where people can sell or advertise their good or services.

Media kit Online or offline package of information for potential advertisers, including ad sizes, rates, demographics, submission information, and contact names.

Merchant account An arrangement with a commercial bank or card issuer that permits a business to accept credit card payments and deposit those payments, less charges, to its bank account.

Message board Allows users to post messages on part of a Web site for others to read, like a forum or electronic bulletin board.

META tag In HTML code, the lines that contain a list of keywords and the succinct page description of a site that will appear when the site is listed as a search result.

Meta-indexes Large category-based indexes of sites on the Web, usually arranged alphabetically within topics. Compare to search engine.

MIDI Musical Instrument Digital Interface.

Mirror Copy and display the material from one Web site on another.

Modem modulator–demodulator. Converts computer data to a form that can be transmitted over phone lines and vice versa.

Moderated News group or forum checked by an individual with the authority to censor messages.

Mouse-over In JavaScript, the element that changes an item (usually graphic) on a Web page when the cursor moves across or hovers over it; usually signifies a link.

MP3 A file compression technique that permits rapid downloading of audio information from the Web with CD-quality replay.

Multimedia Combination of virtual reality, graphics, video, animation, and/or sound in online or offline programs. See *rich media*.

Netiquette Guidelines for appropriate communication in news groups and mailing lists.

Network address   Electronic mail address or address of a host machine.

News group   One of thousands of open discussion groups on USEnet. Requires a full-service Internet account and news group reader software provided by an ISP or browser.

Node   (1) Any computer connected to a network. (2) In Quicktime Virtual Reality, one of 12 static images patched together to generate a panoramic view of a space.

Nonlink   Advertisement on the Web without a hypertext link. Usually less expensive than a linked ad.

Opt-in mailing list   An electronic mailing list to which a viewer must actively choose to subscribe before receiving it. If offered a choice, the default is not to subscribe. See *opt-out mailing list*.

Opt-out mailing list   An electronic mailing list to which a viewer must unsubscribe to stop receipt. If offered a choice, the default is subscription. Considered a violation of Netiquette. See *opt-in mailing list*.

Outbound link   Viewed from the target business site, a one-way link going to another site. Sometimes called an external link.

Packets   Means of dividing up and structuring information in a computer message for reliable Internet transmission to the correct address.

PDA   Personal Digital Assistant. One of many forms of hand- held computing devices; many now access the Internet.

Plug-in   Applet integrated with a browser that enables users to view text, images, sound, and/or video in special formats.

Pointcast   A push technology that delivers requested information to a specific site. Also the name of a proprietary news/advertising product.

POP   Post Office Protocol. Allows users to read e-mail from their operating system without logging onto a server.

Portal   A large, multipurpose Web site, often used as an entry point to the Web.

Post   Enter a message on a news group or mailing list.

POTS   Plain Old Telephone Service.

PPP   Point-to Point Protocol. Type of Internet account needed to access FTP servers.

Press kit   A collection of background and current information about a company for use by the media.

Protocol   Standard procedure for processing data.

Pull technology   Typical Internet interaction in which an individual must specifically request desired information. (Compare to *push technology*.)

Push technology   Internet interaction that sends data to an individual without a specific request. Also used for offline advertising. (Compare to *pull technology*.)

QTVR   Quicktime Virtual Reality. A method of virtual reality display that provides a 180- to 360-degree panoramic view from a fixed position or of a rotating object.

Quicktime   Apple Computer's format for packaging and playing video and animation.

Raw hit   Visit to a single file on a Web page.

Reciprocal link   Two sites place links to each other on their own sites.

Referrer log   Server record of which sources or URL addresses have launched a link to a file on that server.

Register   A Web software program that reviews and totals prices for items in a shopping cart, adds shipping and taxes, and arranges for customer payment. Also called a *checkstand*.

Relational database   Data stored in the form of related tables, each of which may have a different record format. It can be randomly accessed by a search of keywords or fields and reorganized on demand to provide maxium search flexibility.

Rendering-on-the-fly   The method used by VRML to create images of a three-dimensional environment as the user points a cursor. See *QTVR*.

RFP   Request For Proposal.

RFQ   Request For Quote.

Rich media   The inclusion of expansive graphics, animation, audio, and/or video on a Web site or in an online advertisement.

Ringmaster   Person who maintains the master database for a Web ring.

Ripper   Software that translates digital audio files from compact disk format to a computer.

ROS   Run of site. When a banner ad is allowed to run anywhere on a site, not just at specific position or on a specific page; usually a less expensive rate.

Roulette   Link on a page that sends visitors randomly to another page on the same site or to another site.

Search engine   Software designed for the rapid location of information in one or more databases on the basis of keyword identification;

usually results are ranked by relevance, as determined by engine-specific algorithms. Compare to *meta-index.*

Server   Computer used to control or manage a network.

Server report   Operational information for host computer.

SET   Secure Electronic Transactions. Standard for secure credit card transactions online that integrates SSL (Secure Socket Layer), digital signatures, digital wallets, and encryption technologies.

Shared server   A Web server that hosts the sites for multiple companies; commonly used for low-cost Web hosting since each site doesn't require a separate computer. Also called virtual server. Compare to dedicated server.

Shockwave   Macromedia's format for incorporating multimedia objects on Web pages.

Shopping cart   A Web software program that tracks items a customer selects from an online catalog.

Signature file   Three- to six-line, text-only, electronic file used as an online identity. Like an electronic business card.

Site index   An online map, outline, or plan of a Web site that enables viewers to access quickly any portion of the site.

Site launch   Public advertisement and notice that a site is available for use; usually takes place within a specific time period and/or is keyed to a specific event.

Sitecast   A Web-based, real-time event that incorporates streaming video, audio, graphics, and chat lines with prerecorded information. Sometimes called *Webcast.*

SLIP   Serial Line Internet Protocol. Type of Internet account needed to access Web servers.

Spam   Unwanted advertisements sent through e-mail or posted on inappropriate news groups.

Spider   A Web search program that automatically finds and stores pages and keyword information. Also known as a robot, crawler, or wanderer.

Splash screen   An introductory page or screen that users may see before they reach the home page for a Web site. Often created to identify a referring link, to maximize a site for keywords, or to allow software time to load.

Sponsor   Cost-effective type of advertising on the Web, usually featuring a small banner ad below the fold linked to another site.

Sprite   A small animated image in GIF format.

SSL   Secure Socket Layer. Netscape's protocol for sending confidential information, such as credit card numbers, over the Internet.

Stickiness   The qualities of a site that encourage viewers to remain on the site for an extended period of time.

Stop words   Words ignored by search engines, generally articles, conjunctions, and prepositions.

Store-building program   Web software that incorporates all the elements needed to display and sell products online, including catalog, shopping cart, checkstand, and transactional elements.

Streaming audio   Sound files audible as they are transmitted over the Internet. (Compare to *download*.)

Streaming video   Video images that can be viewed as they are transmitted over the Internet.

Subscribe   Add one's e-mail address onto a mailing list or news group.

Superstitial   An online advertisement that "pops up" after a viewer has left a site.

Syntax   The "grammar" and spelling of a programming language.

Syntax checker   Program that checks for "grammatical errors" in the structure of programming code.

Sysop   Systems Operator. Manager of a bulletin board system, news group, online service, or special interest group site.

Tag line   A brief phrase of three to five words that encapsulates a company's purpose or marketing message; often appears on business cards or in signature blocks.

TCP/IP   Transport Control Protocol/Internet Protocol. TCP is the communications protocol for connecting hosts to each other to exchange messages in IP format. See IP.

Thread   A topic of discussion in a news group or forum.

TITLE tag   In HTML code, the line that contains the words that appear in the title bar of a Web site.

Unsubscribe   Remove name from an e-mail list.

Upload   Send a file or program from a personal computer to online storage.

Upsell   To encourage a customer to purchase a more expensive item, an add-on, or a related product.

URL   Uniform Resource Locator. Address designating the location of resources on the Web; it includes the user's registered domain name.

Vacation mailbot   Mailbot notifying senders of e-mail that the recipient is away.

Viral marketing Using members of a target audience to distribute a marketing message to other potential customers, e.g., forwarding an e-mail newsletter.

Virtual reality Computer-mediated method for interacting with a three-dimensional environment.

VRML Virtual Reality Modeling Language. Programming language for displaying three-dimensional space as if the viewer were moving through it in any direction.

WAN Wide Area Network. Links distant computer systems.

Webcast Real-time audio and/or video event on the Web that occurs at a specified time, not on demand. Sometimes called *sitecast*.

Web ring A set of reciprocally linked sites, usually joined by a common interest. Also called a Web alliance.

White paper An in-depth policy or background statement on a subject or technology, usually several pages long.

Whois Computer database of domain names.

WML Wireless Markup Language

WWW World Wide Web. Portion of the Internet that contains data, graphics, sound, and video, and is accessed through a graphical interface.

WYSIWYG What You See Is What You Get. Word processing, graphic, layout, or Web programming software that displays on-screen exactly how results will appear in print.

XML Extensible Markup Language. A method of packaging data in a Web document in a manner that can be understood by EDI software.

Appendix C

URL Listings

The following is an index of the sites included in this book. For alphabetization purposes, the *http://* has been ommited, because most browsers add *http://* automatically if it is not typed in as part of the URL. Also, to avoid duplication, all listings include the home page URL, rather than the URL of specific pages.

Please remember that Web addresses change continually, therefore some sites listed may no longer exist by the time this book is printed.

Index

Reader Feedback Sheet

Your comments and suggestions are very important in shaping future publications. Please email us at *moreinfo@maxpress.com* or photocopy this page, jot down your thoughts, and fax it to (850) 934-9981 or mail it to:

Maximum Press
Attn: Jim Hoskins
605 Silverthorn Road
Gulf Breeze, FL 32561

_____
_____
_____
_____
_____
_____
_____
_____
_____
_____
_____
_____
_____
_____
_____
_____
_____
_____
_____

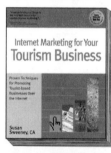